Linda P. Rouse, PhD

Marital and Sexual Lifestyles in the United States

Attitudes, Behaviors, and Relationships in Social Context

Pre-publication
REVIEWS,
COMMENTARIES,
EVALUATIONS . . .

"**F**or all the lip service given to the 'changing nature' of the American family, this text is the first that gives comprehensive, well-documented information on the current status of all dyadic relationships in our culture.

From the latest theoretical framework and research to the chemistry of attraction and rites of courtship through the legalities of cohabitation, Dr. Rouse has addressed all aspects of contemporary coupling. She has carefully incorporated current sociological and sexological research into her chapters on gender, sexual morality, and sexual orientation—all excellent and necessary additions to current academic materials for family studies.

For the professor looking for a new approach to an old topic, this text will offer a provocative and refreshing change that is sure to stimulate much class dialogue as well as personal thought for students of family studies. It is noteworthy too that Dr. Rouse has managed to present such a large amount of material without bias or politics."

Judith A. Seifer, PhD, RN
Past President,
American Association
of Sex Educators, Counselors,
and Therapists;
Professor, Institute
for the Advanced Study
of Human Sexuality,
San Francisco

The Haworth Clinical Practice Press
An Imprint of The Haworth Press, Inc.
New York • London • Oxford

Marital and Sexual Lifestyles in the United States

Attitudes, Behaviors, and Relationships in Social Context

HAWORTH Marriage and the Family
Terry S. Trepper, PhD
Executive Editor

Parents, Children, and Adolescents: Interactive Relationships and Development in Context by Anne-Marie Ambert

Women Survivors of Childhood Sexual Abuse: Healing Through Group Work: Beyond Survival by Judy Chew

Tales from Family Therapy: Life-Changing Clinical Experiences edited by Frank N. Thomas and Thorana S. Nelson

The Therapist's Notebook: Homework, Handouts, and Activities for Use in Psychotherapy edited by Lorna L. Hecker and Sharon A. Deacon

The Web of Poverty: Psychosocial Perspectives by Anne-Marie Ambert

Stepfamilies: A Multi-Dimensional Perspective by Roni Berger

Clinical Applications of Bowen Family Systems Theory by Peter Titelman

Treating Children in Out-of-Home Placements by Marvin Rosen

Your Family, Inc.: Practical Tips for Building a Healthy Family Business by Ellen Frankenberg

Therapeutic Intervention with Poor, Unorganized Families: From Distress to Hope by Shlomo A. Sharlin and Michal Shamai

The Residential Youth Care Worker in Action: A Collaborative, Competency-Based Approach by Robert Bertolino and Kevin Thompson

Chinese Americans and Their Immigrant Parents: Conflict, Identity, and Values by May Paomay Tung

Together Through Thick and Thin: A Multinational Picture of Long-Term Marriages by Shlomo A. Sharlin, Florence W. Kaslow, and Helga Hemmerschmidt

Developmental-Systemic Family Therapy with Adolescents by Ronald Jay Werner-Wilson

The Effect of Children on Parents, Second Edition by Anne-Marie Ambert

Clinical and Educational Interventions with Fathers edited by Jay Fagan and Alan Hawkins

Couples Therapy, Second Edition by Linda Berg-Cross

Family Therapy and Mental Health: Innovations in Theory and Practice by Malcolm M. MacFarlane

How to Work with Sex Offenders: A Handbook for Criminal Justice, Human Service, and Mental Health Professionals by Rudy Flora

Marital and Sexual Lifestyles in the United States: Attitudes, Behaviors, and Relationships in Social Context by Linda P. Rouse

Psychotherapy with People in the Arts: Nurturing Creativity by Gerald Schoenwolf

Critical Incidents in Marital and Family Therapy: A Practitioner's Guide by David A. Baptiste Jr.

Family Solutions for Substance Abuse: Clinical and Counseling Approaches by Eric E. McCollum and Terry S. Trepper

Critical Incident Narratives in the Development of Men's Lives: Between Fathers and Sons by Robert J. Pellegrini and Theodore R. Sarbin

Women's Stories of Divorce at Childbirth: When the Baby Rocks the Cradle by Hilary Hoge

Marital and Sexual Lifestyles in the United States
Attitudes, Behaviors, and Relationships in Social Context

Linda P. Rouse, PhD

The Haworth Clinical Practice Press
An Imprint of The Haworth Press, Inc.
New York • London • Oxford

Published by

The Haworth Clinical Practice Press, an imprint of The Haworth Press, Inc., 10 Alice Street, Binghamton, NY 13904-1580.

Excerpt from "Working Moms Face Backlash" © Tribune Media Services, Inc. All Rights Reserved. Reprinted with permission.

"Swinging in Dallas" reprinted with permission of Knight Ridder/Tribune Information Services.

"Letter on Bondage" reprinted from Ann Landers. Permission granted by Ann Landers and Creators Syndicate.

Excerpts from *There Must Be Fifty Ways to Tell Your Mother* by Lynn Sutcliffe. This material has been reproduced under license from the copyright holder. Continuum, London, England, reserve all rights in the material to them, including the right to make further copies. © 1995. Reprinted by permission of The Continuum International Publishing Group, Inc.

Excerpts from "No Wedding? No Ring? No Problem" copyright March 13, 2000, *U.S. News & World Report.*

Excerpts from *Sociology* by Ian Robertson © 1987 by Worth Publishers. Used with permission.

Cover of *Ms.* Magazine reprinted by permission of *Ms.* Magazine, © 1978.

Excerpts from *Understanding Sexual Attraction* by DeLora © 1982. Adapted by permission of Prentice-Hall.

"A Great Emptiness" from *Newsweek,* November 7, 1983, © 1983 Newsweek, Inc. All rights reserved. Reprinted by permission.

"Busy Parent Misses Joys of Fatherhood" reprinted with permission of Knight Ridder/Tribune Information Services.

Quotations from NBC News broadcast "Divorce Is Changing America" © National Broadcasting Company, Inc. 2001. All Rights Reserved.

Cover design by Marylouise E. Doyle.

Client identities and circumstances have been changed to protect confidentiality.

Library of Congress Cataloging-in-Publication Data

Rouse, Linda.
    Marital and sexual lifestyles in the United States : attitudes, behaviors, and relationships in social context / Linda Rouse.
        p. cm.
    Includes bibliographical references and index.
    ISBN 0-7890-1070-4 (alk. paper)—ISBN 0-7890-1071-2 (alk. paper)
    1. Marriage—United States. 2. Sex—United States. 3. Married couples—United States—Sexual behavior. 4. Single persons—United States—Sexual behavior. 5. Lifestyles—United States. I. Title.

HQ536 .R67 2001
306.7—dc21   2001024393

To my mother, Alice Britt, for making it all possible.

ABOUT THE AUTHOR

Linda P. Rouse, PhD, is a tenured Associate Professor of Sociology in the Department of Sociology and Anthropology at the University of Texas at Arlington. She received her doctoral degree from Florida State University and taught at Western Michigan University before coming to UTA.

Her current areas of research interest and program specialization are in social psychology, family, social statistics, and evaluation research. Her publications include articles in a variety of professional journals, as well as a book, *You Are Not Alone: A Guide for Battered Women.* Extensive review of social science literature and ten years of experience teaching a marital and sexual lifestyles course developed at UTA provided the background for this book.

CONTENTS

Preface   **xi**

    Needs Addressed by This Text   xii
    Content Covered   xiii

Acknowledgments   **xvii**

Introduction   **1**

    Marital Lifestyles in the United States   2
    Human Sexuality   8
    The Effects of Change   15
    Summary   16

Chapter 1. Research Methods   **19**

    Facts and Values   20
    Rules and Exceptions   22
    Validity and Generalizability   24
    Methods of Data Collection   29
    Research Methods Supplement   40

**Chapter 2. Marital Lifestyles: Single, Married,
and Cohabiting**   **45**

    Being Single   45
    Dating and Mate Selection   52
    Theories of Mate Selection   60
    Starting New Relationships   62

Chapter 3. Sex and Singles   **85**

    Premarital Sex: Attitudes and Behaviors   85
    Repercussions of Changing Sexual Standards   90

Sex and Communication   94
Contraception   104
Sexually Transmitted Diseases   105
Responding to STDs   110
The Individual and Social Change   114

Chapter 4. Marriage, Divorce, and Sex   **117**

Marriage and Overall Well-Being   117
Divorce As a Safety Valve   119
Sex and Divorce   122
Participation in Extramarital Sex   125
Open Marriage, Sexually Open Marriages, and Swinging   127
Marital Sex   133
Frequency of Intercourse   139
Talking to a Partner About Sex   141
Conclusion   142

Chapter 5. Sexual Morality and Sexual Hang-Ups   **145**

Sexual Morality   145
Institutional Perspectives   149
Personal Preferences in Social Context   164
Conclusion   169

Chapter 6. Homosexuality   **173**

The Nature of Homosexuality   173
Can Homosexuality Be "Cured"?   178
Public Attitudes   180
Prevalence of Homosexuality   182
Homosexuality and the Family   184
Conclusion   196

Chapter 7. Marital Relationships:
   Men, Women, and Children   **199**

Gender Roles   199
Working Wives   205

Egalitarian Relationships   210
Expectations of Parenthood   215
Work Versus Family: A Historical Overview   219
Effects of Divorce   220

Chapter 8. Growing Older and Improving Relationships   233

Growing Older   233
Improving Relationships   241
Theoretical Perspectives in Counseling   246
Myths About Relationships   251
Successful Relationships   255
Sex Therapy   259

Chapter 9. Looking Ahead   263

Marital Lifestyles: Divorce and Cohabitation Trends   263
Sexual Lifestyles: Continuing Concerns   268
Facts, Values, and Social Science Revisited   270
Diversity   272
Social Policy   273
Closing Comment   277

Appendix. Sample Survey Items   287

References   297

Index   319

Preface

The curriculum at the University of Texas at Arlington includes an upper-division elective sociology course about marital and sexual lifestyles that I have been teaching for many years. This book, *Marital and Sexual Lifestyles in the United States,* emerged from lecture notes developed in place of using an existing text. When the course was first offered, sociological marriage and family texts did not adequately address sexual issues, and human sexuality texts included too much material on biological aspects and too little on the social, cultural, and interpersonal context of sexual expression. The main course objective was to develop an integrated historical, statistical, and conceptual framework for analyzing diverse marital and sexual lifestyles in the United States, with the 1950s as a starting point that represented "traditional" family and sexual values. As a sociologist and social psychologist, I also wanted to help students understand ways in which social structure and social change influence individual experience. Thus the emphasis in this text is on attitudes, behaviors, and relationships in social context, using sociological concepts and research methods for understanding the connections between individual and society.

In early sections of the course, students were given the task of selecting topics they were most interested in studying; these formed the substantive units covered in the present text. A striking aspect of student participation in the marital and sexual lifestyles course has been the diversity of opinions held on the topics addressed. This is not to say that the full range of opinions is actually voiced in class. The impression of the prevailing value climate created by the most outspoken students often discounts a substantial minority of students in a class and can even be inconsistent with the actual majority opinion! Since group dynamics can result in misleading impressions of dominant values and individual opinions, a survey instrument is appended with this text. Administered at the beginning of a term, the questionnaire (or something like it) may be used to track student opinion and to provide a common framework for discussing survey research methods as a tool for studying marital and sexual lifestyles.

Survey research over the past several decades has provided an overwhelming wealth of facts and figures about changing marital and sexual lifestyles. This text does not attempt to be exhaustive in its coverage, nor to present only the most recent findings. Rather, it looks at a variety of selected studies over time for the purpose of encouraging students to consider reported findings more closely and to develop skills in interpreting statistics; e.g., to appreciate the import of lifestyle prevalence or distribution of particular attitudes, the gist of "explained variance," the relevance of "validity" and "generalizability," and how to better recall statistics as meaningful estimates rather than by rote memorization. Counseling professionals as well as researchers have contributed to knowledge of contemporary relationships, their stresses and strains, and how to improve their chances of success. Such work will also be considered in this text.

In marriage and family or human sexuality courses generally, the topics covered are uniquely interesting. Students are often reading for personal application and not as they might study other academic subjects. As a result, material about sex and family can appear superficially familiar ("I already know all this") or odd, if it is not what was expected ("not in my family; that can't be right"), or as bits and pieces of practical wisdom ("I can, or cannot, use that"). Too, mass media and popular culture in many ways lead us to expect entertaining and simplistic solutions to complex, difficult personal and social problems. This text challenges readers to look more closely at the details, to see connections among disparate facts, and to consider how they reflect larger themes about American society. Students are helped to examine their own values and assumptions, learning to distinguish values from facts, and to expand their knowledge of lifestyles other than their own. This text is not only about facts, but about *ideas* for making sense of life in contemporary society.

NEEDS ADDRESSED BY THIS TEXT

Upon a foundation of biological predispositions, drives, and capacities, culture fills in the particulars of human sexual behavior, attitudes, and feelings. Society always regulates sexual expression, and we tend to become the kind of sexual being we are raised to be in a particular culture. How this occurs is widely of interest. Further, standards of sexual morality in the United States have shifted away from conformity to absolute rules in the direction of individual choice; that is, informed, responsible choice. We confront many varied and often conflicting views of what is proper. With rising expectations for personal happiness and sexual fulfillment, and no one family form guaranteed to meet everyone's needs, individuals search for their own "right" marital and sexual lifestyles.

This text examines what people believe, expect, and do in various arenas of marital and sexual lifestyles to form a clearer picture of public opinion and private action. Predominant values in the United States today encourage more open questioning and lend greater legitimacy to lifestyle diversity. One of the consequences of change since the 1950s in family and society is that we face a larger and somewhat bewildering array of choices. Correspondingly, individuals have a greater need to look more closely and systematically at their options, at both the stresses and benefits posed by various marital and sexual lifestyles. Without an accurate picture of our overall social surroundings, we are basing important personal decisions on incomplete or faulty information.

Knowing something more about social systems and about how social forces shape our motivations, our actions, and their consequences gives us both greater insight into why other people do what they do and a better view of our own prospects. This means better preparation for the unexpected social roles or situations in which we so often find ourselves today—e.g., in a cohabiting relationship, divorced, premaritally pregnant, with a sexually transmitted disease, finding that a spouse has been "unfaithful," fighting over household chores, being a single parent, living in a stepfamily or finding out a family member is gay. Related questions such as "Why is it so hard for couples today to stay together?" are asked repeatedly. Sociology and social psychology provide not one but many uniquely thought-provoking answers. Study of the individual and society expands our understanding of what we experience, the kinds of people we are becoming, and why. The text also provides an informed, critical basis for making sense of media reporting on marital and sexual lifestyles.

Partly, perhaps largely, due to its title, the Marital and Sexual Lifestyles course at the University of Texas at Arlington has for many years been a popular choice among students, one that turns out to be more challenging than many initially expect. Teaching the course has given me an opportunity to reflect on what I have learned about sex, marriage, and family, and the general discipline of sociology in my own academic training and to engage students in many conversations about how such ideas provide insights about their personal marital and sexual experiences, about others, and about our society as a whole. Correspondingly, the main features of this text include the following. It is *informative* and detailed, based on social science research; *balanced* in considering both benefits and strains of various lifestyles; *effective* in connecting theory, facts, and figures with individual experience; and made *accessible* by its conversational writing style. Sociological concepts are clearly explained as they are introduced, so the book is suitable for the general reader and for students in any related field of study. Additionally, boxed inserts, figures, and tables provide textual variety, illustrate or amplify selected topics, and offer material for further discussion.

CONTENT COVERED

The introduction acquaints readers with the field of sociology, reviews important changes that have taken place in the United States in marriage and the family since the 1950s, and presents the basic assumptions about human sexuality that will guide presentation of material in later chapters. Chapter 1 examines how social scientists study marital and sexual lifestyles. It outlines the difference between facts and values, the meaning of rules and exceptions, and the measurement concerns of validity and generalizability. Various studies are then used to illustrate major methods of data collection. Chapter 2 looks at the decision to be single, married, or cohabiting; some of the pros and cons of each, the experience of loneliness, individual and societal-level concerns with dating and mate selection, the incidence, causes, and meaning of cohabitation; and the state's interest in marriage-like relationships. Chapter 3 examines various aspects of sex and singles; attitudes toward and actual participation in premarital sex, number of partners, age at first intercourse, sexually transmitted diseases, contraception and date rape as related to social scripting, sexual socialization, and communication between sexual partners. Chapter 4 turns to the benefits of marriage, divorce as a safety valve, infidelity as a factor contributing to divorce, and what infidelity suggests about a marriage. It looks at sexually open marriages, sexually distressed couples in counseling, gender differences in sexual preferences, rates of participation in intercourse, and advice on sex in marriage. Chapters 2, 3 and 4 include the greatest concentration of statistical information.

Chapter 5 discusses sexual morality and sexual hang-ups in terms of "freedom of individual choice within normative guidelines," ranging from the straitlaced to the libertine. It considers how the institutions of religion, law, and mental health contribute to definitions of what is right and wrong and examines paraphilias, sexual addiction, low sexual desire, and personal preferences in social context. Chapter 6 addresses homosexuality, first reviewing perspectives on the nature of homosexuality, estimates of its prevalence, and public attitudes toward sex with same-sex partners, then turning to more recent interests in gay, lesbian, and bisexual lifestyles, the social construction of identity, coming out, and family relationships. Chapter 7 explores consequences of gender, such as the influence on husband-wife interaction of culturally prescribed roles and socially defined identities for men and women, and raises issues concerning children. It looks at changes in work and family and at the effects on children of the divorce trend, which has resulted in growing numbers of single parent and stepfamily households with their own unique strengths and challenges.

Chapter 8 focuses on growing older and on improving relationships. It examines how aging influences sexual expression and relationships in later life, and looks into what social researchers and counseling professionals, using various therapeutic approaches, have learned about the myths that jeopardize relationships and the factors that promote their long-term success. Chapter 9 revisits trends in divorce and cohabitation with an eye to future prospects. It notes several continuing concerns about sexual lifestyles, reminds readers of the need to distinguish between facts and values, considers the challenges of diversity for social policies attempting to foster individual and family functioning, and offers some concluding comments about what lies ahead.

Marital and sexual lifestyles is an engaging area of study. I hope that the research findings and ideas presented in this text will spark among readers continuing thought, conversation, and debate within themselves and with friends, family, fellow students, and others. Readers are invited to communicate with the author at The University of Texas at Arlington via e-mail at lrouse@uta.edu. Instructors may also contact The Haworth Press for more information about the Instructor's Manual and other supporting materials prepared by the author.

Acknowledgments

I am especially grateful to Dr. Terry Trepper and to The Haworth Press for their support of this book. Thanks to Dana Dunn and Ron Durden for taking time to read and comment on early drafts of several chapters and to the University of Texas at Arlington for funding a one-semester faculty leave that facilitated development of the book. Thanks also to students in the many sections of my Marital and Sexual Lifestyles course whose reactions were often amusing, occasionally appalling, usually insightful, and always thought-provoking.

Introduction

This book explores the diversity of contemporary U.S. marital and sexual lifestyles. One underlying assumption is that contemporary beliefs and practices are best approached by developing an integrated historical, statistical, and conceptual framework. The objective is to help readers understand ways in which social structure and social change in the United States influence our individual marital and sexual lifestyle choices and experiences. Its emphasis is on attitudes, behaviors, and relationships in social context, as understood through sociological concepts and research methods.

Some initial clarification of what is meant by "sociological" concepts may be useful. **Sociology** is the study of human society and social behavior. Dave Barry, a humorist and nationally syndicated newspaper columnist, described his college sociology courses as restating the obvious in a complex and confusing way, memorable for sheer lack of intelligibility. British sociologist Anthony Giddens acknowledges that such a reputation is sometimes deserved but also argues that the field offers much more; sociology "deals with problems of pressing interest to us all, problems which are the object of major conflicts and controversies in society itself" (Giddens 1982: 1, 2). This is never more true than when the subject is marital and sexual lifestyles. When we think about personal matters such as this, we tend to think about our own immediate experience. Sociology and related social sciences broaden our field of vision and give us insights into larger social forces that shape our decisions even when we are not aware of them, in many ways that are not at all obvious.

C. Wright Mills, an early and influential American sociologist, used the term **sociological imagination** to refer to the ability to see connections between biography and history, private troubles and public issues, individual and society; to grasp how "the seemingly most remote and impersonal transformations" and "the most intimate features of the human self" connect. "The sociological imagination enables its possessor to understand the larger historical scene in terms of its meaning for the inner life and external career of a variety of individuals" (Mills 1959: 5). Mills referred to marriage as an example. Within a particular marriage, a man and a woman may experience private troubles that lead them to divorce as a personal solution. They thereby become, along with millions of other couples, a "divorce statistic." The overall divorce rate in a society, however, is more than a sum of personal, private troubles; it is a structural issue having to do with the institution of marriage and other features of society that are related to marriage. Individual decisions about marriage and divorce contribute to the divorce rate. In turn, the divorce rate becomes part of the social climate within which individuals interpret and evaluate their marital circumstances. The divorce rate also reflects societal values and policies about marriage and divorce; e.g., social and legal acceptance of irreconcilable differences as grounds for divorce. Thus, to understand our own lives, we need to look beyond them, to be more aware of the idea of social structure. By giving us a perspective that encompasses the recurring patterns of beliefs and behaviors connecting individuals to a larger social system, sociological concepts expand our view of what we experience, the kinds of people we are becoming, and why.

The next section of this chapter reviews some important changes in marriage and the family in the United States since the 1950s to give readers a background for evaluating contemporary marital lifestyles. The chapter then introduces the basic assumptions about human sexuality that will guide presentation of material in later chapters.

MARITAL LIFESTYLES IN THE UNITED STATES

According to dictionary definitions of "style," a lifestyle is a way in which living is done; a manner of being. Style refers to a kind or sort or type; the distinctive features of everyday performance. In addressing questions of marital and sexual lifestyles in the United States, notice that we are talking about lifestyles, plural; a number of different ways of being and doing.

For purposes of orientation, consider first the "traditional" family. We can describe its idealized (1) structure, (2) roles, and (3) values. Traditional family *structure* in this discussion refers to the "monogamous nuclear family"; that is, one husband and one wife, joined in a socially and legally recognized marriage that forms the center of family relationships, living together in a household with their dependent children under age eighteen. Family size might include three, four, or five children. Marriage is expected to last "until death do us part"; children will form their own independent households when they are grown. Traditional family *roles* popularized in the 1950s consist of an employed wage-earning male head of household and a wife who is a full-time homemaker and mother. Children are expected to respect the authority of parents. Marriage forms the keystone of women's identities and their economic livelihood; thus women are expected to defer to the wishes of their husbands and focus their attention on the domestic sphere. With respect to the *values* with which we will be most concerned, sex before marriage was traditionally disapproved of by the majority of adult Americans, but this public opinion existed alongside a double standard promoting virginity for women and premarital sexual experience for men, who "sowed their wild oats" before linking up with "the old ball and chain." Women were cautioned to save themselves for marriage and not risk falling on the wrong side of the good girl-bad girl dichotomy, which would ruin their chances for marriage. If they did not know what to do on the wedding night, they were advised to follow the husband's lead: "Just close your eyes and pretend you like it; it will be over quickly." Fidelity was expected in marriage, with women again held to a stricter standard than men.

This sketch of the traditional family is likely to be very familiar to most readers, who will also be aware that it represents a very limited, idealized view of family in the United States in the 1950s. It is the white middle-class suburban family as seen through the television sitcom window of *Leave It to Beaver* and *Happy Days*. In *The Way We Never Were,* a lively and detailed critique of this notion of the traditional family, social historian Stephanie Coontz (1992) cautions us that actual family life in the United States as a whole never quite corresponded to this picture. But this image of the traditional family lingers in assumptions, stereotypes, and myths shaping continuing debates about the relative strength or decline of the family in the United States and therefore provides a relevant starting point, a shared story of the past for purposes of comparison. To effectively address the dilemmas facing modern families, however, we should resist the temptation to simply try to return to a traditional family that "either never existed or existed in a different social context" (Coontz 1992:5). No one family form today seems able to meet everyone's needs. See Box 1 for a commentary on changes in marriage.

By the 1970s, texts in sociology of the family such as *Intimate Life Styles: Marriage and Its Alternatives* edited by Jack, and Joann DeLora (1972) came to speak of "alternate lifestyles," referring to any departures from the so-called traditional family structure, roles, or values. Thus examples included staying single, heterosexual unmarried cohabitation, sexually open marriages, gay couples, single parenting, voluntarily childless couples, and even dual-career couples. Alternate lifestyles are expected to arise when existing social institutions fail to meet individual needs. What was occurring during this historical period that induced so many individuals to experiment with a variety of alternate lifestyles? The social context included some major changes in society and family over three decades, the 1960s, 1970s, and 1980s. Consider the following transformations:

1. Liberalization in sexual behaviors and in attitudes toward sex
2. Birth control technology; the advent of the Pill
3. Increase in average age at first marriage
4. Increase in divorce rate
5. Rise in numbers of single-parent households and blended ("step") families
6. Increase in women in the paid labor force

7. Smaller average family size
8. New variety in household composition

Without getting bogged down in debates about which came first or which is the most important, we can view these trends as part of a changing whole. Briefly, the liberal trend of increased participation in premarital sex is not recent but has been going on since the late nineteenth century (Reiss 1988). Recent changes in attitudes have been well documented by survey research. For example, in samples of adult Americans in the 1960s, less than one-fourth approved of premarital sex, but by the 1980s nearly 60 percent approved (Robertson 1987: 233). Birth control technology separated sex from childbearing, but the Pill also separated birth control from the sex act. The Pill gave more control over reproduction to female partners, protecting them from unwanted pregnancy if they chose to be sexually active. Young adults were able to delay marriage in favor of education and work experience. Most did not feel socially pressured, as did young adults in the 1950s, to marry early for sex or for economic support or just because it was expected of them.

Box 1. The Changing Picture of Marriage in the United States

In 1968, David Mace, a family sociologist, addressed the already changing picture of marriage in the United States at an annual meeting of the Southeastern Council of Family Relations. Using anthropologist Edward Westermarck's classical definition, marriage was defined as "a relation of one or more men to one or more women which is recognized by custom or law and involves certain rights and duties both in the case of the parties entering the union and in the case of children born out of it." Worldwide, marriage is a universal human institution, but it has existed in many forms. For the most part, marriage was secondary to the family and controlled by the larger society or community to safeguard family life. In agrarian societies the family was the basic productive unit, with kinship groups cooperating as required for the common good. The Industrial Revolution brought a dramatic social transformation, "breaking up traditional institutions and forcing us to create new ones," generating concerns along the way about the demise of the family. Marriage and family relations are changing, not being destroyed, as they adapt to a new social environment, but marriage, in Mace's words, "is changing so much that it is literally being turned inside out." He explains:

> In the old days, the central goal in marriage was that it must fulfill certain social and familial obligations—the continuation of the family line, the family inheritance, the family tradition. . . . So long as familial obligations were met, nobody cared very much whether the couple were happy or unhappy in their interpersonal life.
>
> Today, however, the central goal in marriage is personal fulfillment in a creative relationship, and traditional familial and social obligations

(continued)

(continued)

have moved to the periphery. The mood of today is that if your marriage doesn't turn out to be happy, you quit, because finding happiness in marriage is the fulfillment of its fundamental objective.

Some people consider this change as a manifestation of selfishness and irresponsibility. But the change in goal actually corresponds with the change in environment. In the old rural-agrarian society, the major business of life was economic survival and physical safety, and marriage had to conform to these requirements. . . . In our urban-industrial society, many of the traditional functions of marriage and the family—[such as] education, economic production, recreation—have been taken over by the state.

Now our deepest need is for emotional security, for the survival of our sense of personal worth and individual significance. By shifting its focus, marriage has become the primary means by which this individual need for comfort, support, love and understanding can be met. Marriage is thereby displaying one of its dormant potentialities which was neglected in the past but is highly relevant today (pp. 5-10).

Family sociologist Ernest W. Burgess had earlier summarized the change in marriage as a fundamental shift to a focus on companionship (Burgess and Locke, 1945). The concept of husband and wife as equal partners, sharing life in openness and intimacy is, according to Mace, a radical break with tradition. Traditionally, husband-wife interaction was based on a dominant-subordinate relationship and segregation of their respective spheres of influence. Some marriages may have been close, affectionate partnerships, but now this criterion of success would be applied to all marriages. Correspondingly, marital relationships are driven in a more egalitarian direction, and the inevitable conflicts between two different persons living together will have to be managed in less rigidly institutionalized, more creative ways.

Mace concludes that marriages will no longer be held together by coercion from outside, but only by cohesion from within. When stability is not an end in itself, unhappy marriages are more likely to be terminated. This is not an abandonment of marriage as a social institution but rather reflects individual unwillingness to accept what is by today's standards a poor marriage. A good marriage, by contrast, provides suitable companionship, satisfactory resolution of the sexual needs of partners, and support for effective parenting when children are desired. As research more fully identifies the problems and prospects accompanying changing patterns of marriage in the United States, education will serve to enlighten more persons about the external forces shaping marriage and the skills necessary to make a good marriage. Counseling services can also help married persons negotiate the inevitable crises in their efforts to sustain a close, intimate "modern" relationship.

Source: The original unpublished address was printed with permission of David Mace (1985) as a chapter in *Marriage and the Family: Coping with Change*, edited by Leonard Cargan.

The proportion of marriages ending in divorce has increased dramatically since the 1950s, and there is now more acceptance of divorce as a response to marital dissatisfaction. Nevertheless, all but about 5 to 10 percent of the population is expected to marry at some time, and we still look to marriage and family for personal fulfillment, companionship, children, sex, good health, recreation, and economic assistance. Most persons who marry also have children; after divorce the custodial parent, usually the mother, and her children constitute a single-parent household. One-third of all U.S. families are now headed by a single parent, and over half of all children in our society will spend some time living in a single-parent household. However, the majority (two-thirds or more) of divorced persons remarry and, where children are involved, a stepfamily is thereby created.

The majority of women today, even married women, are in the paid labor force. They are not willing or able to devote themselves exclusively to keeping house. Many are also mothers who are not staying home full-time to raise children from infancy to adulthood, primarily due to economic pressures. When married women work outside the home, they are less economically dependent on the spouse, have more say in family decision making, and expect greater participation of the spouse in household chores; the balance of power in the marriage shifts. With so many other demands on parents' time, and as the cost of raising children increased significantly over several decades, average family size declined. Though social pressures still favor childbearing, more choice seems available to couples today regarding timing, spacing, and number of children, if any.

As individuals confronted changing social and economic opportunities and constraints since the 1950s, shifts and accommodations were made in our lifestyles. Traditional household structure, roles, and values increasingly did not fit all individual needs. Even where the traditional family remained the ideal, actual experience often proved less felicitous. Few couples marry with the idea that their own marriage will not last. A woman with her children leaving a violent, abusive spouse did not initially aspire to become a single parent. A husband's unexpected loss of employment may mean his wife must work outside the home for some period of time though both preferred she stay home. The real American family reflects the diversity of actual experience.

To picture trends in household composition, consider what the U.S. Census showed for 1977, as represented in Figure 1. Chronologically, this is midway between the 1950s and the 1990s. By this time, changes in U.S. marital and sexual lifestyles were already apparent, and public debate about the American family was well underway. Don't skip the numbers! Statistics such as these are relevant and personal; they reflect the living situations of millions of persons like yourself. The illustrations provide a reminder that the numbers are not completely remote and detached from actual human be-

FIGURE 1. Who Is The Real American Family? U.S. Household Composition in 1977

Source: Ms. Magazine, August 1978. Based on the 1977 U.S. Statistical Abstract.

ings. The statistics will help us evaluate how, how much, and when the impact of social change was felt by individual families. As you examine Figure 1, think about the following questions: What percentage of households in 1977 actually consisted of a thoroughly traditional family in structure and roles? How many households consisted simply of a single adult? What was the relative mix of women working outside the home versus full-time home-making among husband-wife households with children present? What percentage of households consisted of single parents and their children? Headed by women? Headed by men? What do you conclude about the "traditional" family in the United States toward the end of the 1970s? We will take a closer look at continuing and more recent changes in later chapters.

A final observation in this section concerns conflicting values in the United States. **Values** are the "oughts" and "shoulds" of a society or group, shared ideas about what is desirable.

In a marriage and family text organized around the theme of the contemporary quest for intimacy, Robert Lauer and Jeannette Lauer (1991: 22) make an interesting point: Americans value marriage and family, but are struggling between familistic "we" and individualistic "me" values. They refer to Robert Bellah's description of American culture in *Habits of the Heart* (Bellah et al. 1985) as one which strongly values **individualism,** including both personal achievement (instrumental individualism) and personal happiness (expressive individualism). Yet, judging by political debates, American society also appears to value family highly. Contrast familism as a value orientation with individualism. **Familism** emphasizes commitment, fidelity, and personal sacrifice; putting the family first and foremost above our own individual desires. Over time, and within different segments in U.S. society, value emphasis can shift between these two value orientations.

The conflict between individualism and familism in American society as a whole is reflected at the personal level in our own mixed or ambivalent feelings. We search for intimacy in family relations, but sustaining relationships always requires some degree of compromise. How much is too much? There is no unequivocal answer to this question. Some of our private anguish over marriage and family choices comes from the inherent difficulty persons in our society have in finding the right moving balance for themselves between individual and family. See the Sunday comic from 1996 reproduced in this chapter for an illustration of the impact of centrifugal social forces. Family members engaged in a variety of different outside activities may reside in the same household but are being pulled into their separate busy lives.

HUMAN SEXUALITY

Human sexuality is a subject that provokes much interest but also some discomfort and resistance. In Europe in the late nineteenth and early twentieth centuries, Sigmund Freud (1856-1939) shocked his contemporaries when he first claimed that sexual impulses are present in humans from birth and are a crucial factor in the formation of adult personality. The very suggestion that infants were sexual beings was an outrage to existing standards of morality. In our own society, human sexuality has only come to be regarded as a legitimate arena for scientific research and public discussion since the 1950s. In 1948, Alfred Kinsey, a zoologist, and associates, pub-

The Weekend Family Breakfast

THEN

NOW

LUANN by Greg Evans © UFS. Reprinted by Permission.

lished a book on the sexual behavior of American men (Kinsey, Pomery, and Martin, 1948) followed in 1953 by a companion volume on American women (Kinsey et al., 1953). These reports were based on survey research and were filled with masses of statistics, but quickly became best-sellers. Kinsey's work showed that it was possible to collect systematic empirical data on sexual values and behavior, and that the results were of widespread interest. Media attention was particularly captured by Kinsey's finding of many gaps between publicly expressed attitudes and actual reported behavior.

From the point of view of the individual, sexuality is an important aspect of our personal experience and our identities. From the point of view of society, sexuality is an important ingredient in the social institution of marriage and family. Though specific norms and values governing sexual activity vary cross-culturally, every human society regulates the sexual behavior of its members. Sociological perspectives on human sexuality may strike readers at first as somewhat odd. Most people initially regard the sex drive as essentially biological in character. It seems natural or instinctive to most Americans that they should mate in a particular way with a member of the opposite sex. Ian Robertson, author of a widely used introductory sociology text, says bluntly that this view of sex is in fact wrong. Robertson's (1987: 224) explanation is that human sexual behavior is learned through the socialization process and conforms to the prevailing norms in a given society (or deviates from them in predictable ways).

It is in our interactions with others that we learn sexual behavior and our feelings about sex. Unlike most other animals, our specific and complex patterns of adult sexual activity are *not* predetermined by our genes. Anthropologist Clifford Geertz (1968) noted that, for humans, what is innately given to us with our biological constitutions is extremely general response capacities which leave us much less precisely regulated and highly dependent on social learning. Consider a classic experiment by psychologist Harry Harlow (Harlow and Harlow, 1962). Harlow raised rhesus monkeys in the laboratory in isolation from other monkeys. He reasoned that if behaviors such as mating and mothering were purely instinctive and not learned in interaction with other monkeys, a monkey reared in isolation would exhibit the same behaviors as monkeys reared with others of their kind. Harlow found, however, that male monkeys reared in isolation did not know how to copulate effectively when presented with a female in heat. Females raised in isolation who later had offspring did not exhibit "normal" mothering behavior; they were more likely to reject the infant. Humans, of all animals, are the least regulated in their behavior by specific genetic programming. If even monkeys cannot mate or rear their young successfully without the opportunity to observe and learn, we have good grounds for skepticism about the idea that human sexuality is strictly biological in character.

We may still usefully speak of biological "predispositions" or "drives" or "capacities and limitations," but the particular practices we follow and the meanings attached to them are very much a reflection of the cultural definitions offered to us by our society. As Robertson (1987: 224) states the case, "ideas about what is sexually appropriate or inappropriate, moral or immoral, erotic or offensive, are purely social in origin. Anthropologists have provided us a wealth of cross-cultural information about sexual beliefs and practices in societies around the world which illustrates the amazing variety in how human sexuality has been expressed. Clellan Ford and Frank Beach in 1951 published a report on data from the United States and 190 pre-industrial societies which effectively demonstrated that the influence of biological factors on human sexuality is not simple and direct but is mediated by culture. With the brain having evolved as humans' most important sex organ, sexuality is patterned by learning. And what we learn depends on the societies and groups within which we are situated. See Box 2 for further details.

Arguments about what is "natural" or not should be carefully evaluated on their scientific merit. One of the problems we have in studying alternate lifestyles, particularly those involving sexuality, is that by definition they are considered "deviant." Sociologists use the term **deviant** in a simply descriptive way to refer to beliefs or practices that vary or deviate from prevailing **norms**—shared standards of acceptable conduct. In everyday usage, however, the label deviant often conveys that ideas or behaviors are regarded as sick, wrong, or bad. It is wise to remember that norms do change. Not only are there differences in standards of conduct across cultures, as illustrated in Box 2, but in our own society we see behaviors, attitudes, values, and laws changing over time. Examples range from changing standards

Box 2. Sexual Conduct Worldwide

In a chapter titled "Sexuality and Society" in his sociology text, author Ian Robertson considers what we know about sexual conduct around the world. In his words,

There is wide cross-cultural variation in the norms governing the particulars of sexual conduct. Even the position that the partners adopt in the sexual act differs from one society to another. The usual position in most Western societies is for the couple to lie face to face with the male on top; . . . Kinsey (1948) found that 70 percent of American couples had never tried any other position. In the South Sea Islands incredulous women laughingly called this approach the "missionary position," for it had been quite unknown to them until they had sex with visiting missionaries. In a survey of the evidence from 131 other societies, anthropologist Clyde Kluckhohn (1948) found that the "missionary position" was customary or preferred in only 17 cases. Other peoples conduct intercourse from the side, from the rear, with the female on top, with the male kneeling over the female, and in other positions.

The context and content of sexual intercourse is also highly variable. Some peoples regard full nakedness as desirable or obligatory; others, as quite improper or even dangerous. The Hopi Indians insist that sex take place indoors; the Witoto of South America insist it take place outside. The Masai of eastern Africa believe that sex in the daytime can be fatal; the Chenchu of India believe that intercourse at night can lead to the birth of a blind child. Some people insist on privacy; others are indifferent to the presence of observers. Some, such as the Trobriand Islanders, believe that women are sexually insatiable and expect them to take the initiative; others such as the Chiricahua Indians expect that a woman will remain completely passive. Kissing is unknown in some societies; the Siriono consider it a particularly disgusting act. Foreplay before intercourse is unknown among the Lepcha but may occupy several hours among the Ponapeans of the Pacific. Kinsey (1948) found that in the 1940s, the great majority of American males reached orgasm within two minutes of starting intercourse, but the Marquesan men of the Pacific habitually perform for several hours.

Even the frequency of intercourse is related to cultural norms. The Keraki of New Guinea are reported to average once a week; Americans, two or three times a week; the Aranda of Australia, three to five times a day; and the Chagga of eastern Africa are alleged to manage ten episodes in a single night. Some peoples have learned to experience violence during sex as erotically exciting. The Siriono find pleasure in poking their fingers into each other's eyes; Choroti women in South America spit in their partner's face; Ponapean men tug out tufts of their mate's hair; and Apinaye women in the Brazilian jungle are reported to bite off pieces of their lover's eyebrows, noisily spitting them out to enhance the erotic effect.

(continued)

(continued)

Robertson concludes that although comparing sexual behaviors across most industrial societies today may show less striking differences than these,

the value of the evidence from these preindustrial societies is that it shows how the interplay between biological potentials and cultural norms can produce extraordinarily diverse kinds of sexual conduct.

If you were raised in one of these other societies, you would probably follow its rules of sexual conduct. You would do these things with the full knowledge and approval of your community, and if your personal tastes ran counter to the prevailing norms, you might be considered distinctly odd—even wicked. [Y]ou would also regard American sexual attitudes and practices as most peculiar, to say the least.

Source: Ian Robertson, *Sociology,* Third Edition, pp. 227-229. New York: Worth Publishers, 1987.

of proper dress for public bathing to police procedures for handling domestic violence calls to mental health perspectives on homosexuality.

Sexual attitudes in Western societies are described by Robertson (1987) as historically favoring sexual activity with the purpose of reproduction and taking a negative attitude toward sex for pleasure, even within marriage. Doctrines of the church in the Middle Ages equated sex with sin. In the nineteenth-century Victorian period, sexual matters were not openly discussed in polite company, and modesty was prized for women, while prostitution also flourished. State laws in the United States continue to prohibit various sex acts, including oral-genital contact in private between consenting adults. On the whole, sexual attitudes in the United States traditionally were more restrictive than permissive.

The sexual revolution of the 1960s and 1970s encouraged more open discussion of sexuality, brought attitudes more in line with actual practice, challenged the double standard for men and women, and appears to have resulted in an important shift in the basis of sexual morality. Certainly there are differences by age, education, region, and religiosity, but in U.S. society as a whole we are less inclined to simply follow the absolute rules of the 1950s era and more likely today to follow a morality of individual choice. "Increasingly, judgments about right and wrong in sexual matters are based on the attitude that moral behavior is that which involves mutual affection and respect and does no physical or psychological harm to those involved" (Robertson 1987: 236). To say that the United States has become a sexually more permissive society since the 1950s is not to suggest that we have an "anything goes" policy. Some moral standards will always be applied and not all sex under any conditions will be considered good.

If we were to try to define "good sex" by contemporary standards, we might use the following criteria:

1. Does it enhance self-esteem and add to positive feelings about one-self?

Sexuality is one avenue of self-expression. Individuals have to decide whether to engage in sex at all and whether or not to engage in sex of a particular kind with this partner at this time. From a brief encounter to part of a long-term relationship, good sex increases one's self-respect. You know you will not "hate yourself in the morning."

2. Is it voluntary?

Being raped at gunpoint is not voluntary. What if I have sex with my boyfriend before I feel ready because he is pressuring me for sex and says if I don't he'll just do it with someone else, and I am afraid to lose him? Research and public discussion about date rape have raised awareness of a range of coercive pressures between full consent and violent assault. Good sex is openly, willingly chosen.

3. Is it enjoyable?

Some bad sex is simply not satisfying physically. In part this depends on the skills of the partners as lovers. Differences between men and women in preferred time and attention to foreplay, intercourse, and afterplay may lead to dissatisfaction. Poor communication is a contributing factor. The emotional and relational context can also make sex more or less satisfactory for participants. Good sex is enjoyable both physically and emotionally, as subjectively experienced by participants.

4. Will it lead to unwanted pregnancy?

Planned Parenthood estimates that routinely having sex unprotected, 90 out of 100 women would be pregnant within a year. Other than total abstinence, no method of birth control is completely without risk of pregnancy, and all methods require some effort. The personal troubles and social problems associated with unwanted pregnancy are already well known. Enjoying sex that is voluntary and adds to self-esteem is not enough; good sex is responsible about contraception.

5. Will it lead to getting or passing on sexually transmitted diseases?

Added to the "old fashioned" venereal diseases of syphilis and gonorrhea, sexually active persons are now widely exposed to viruses that cause herpes, genital warts, and AIDS. And these do not exhaust the list of sexually transmitted diseases (STDs). As televised public health promotions suggest, a moment of pleasure is not worth dying for. Good sex must be knowledgeable about STDs and take effective precautions to minimize exposure.

6. Does it include concern for the other person's well-being?

In all the previous points, our own personal needs and wishes were of foremost concern, yet most of our sexual pursuits involve other individuals. Sex that is good for oneself in all the ways above but exploits another person's vulnerabilities is bad sex overall. Making false promises, manipulating the situation, or deliberately misleading someone to get what we want sexually is inappropriate. Good sex is based on respect for the partner's needs as well as our own.

These are not scientific judgments but rather provide a reference point for discussion of contemporary sexual morality. It is worth thinking about what other items you might add to the list. Reflection on what defines good sex today is apt to raise other considerations. For example, outside parties may be indirectly involved in sex between particular persons. If one or both individuals participating in sex together are married to other persons at the time, their actions have potential consequences for the well-being of spouses and children. Focus on a morality of individual choice should not be mistaken for societal endorsement of unrestrained self-indulgence. Community and society clearly continue to have a vested interest in sexual expression, and the Golden Rule still applies to interpersonal conduct.

In a book with the provocative title *Sex Is Not a Natural Act*, psychologist Lenore Tiefer (1995) introduces another issue about proper sexual conduct. If sex is not about just doing what comes naturally and if we are no longer guided by absolute rules, how do we evaluate our sex lives, and why do we care? We are more open now about sexuality, sex is generally viewed as a central aspect of intimate relationships, and we have much higher expectations of sexual gratification than we did in the 1950s. Review some of the social changes in recent decades now with sexual intimacy specifically in mind. If the main purpose of marriage has shifted from economic survival to companionship, sexual intimacy becomes more important. Divorce and remarriage heighten people's concerns about finding and sustaining intimate relationships. Contraception allows more freedom of sexual expression. Personal relationships have taken the place of work and community as a source of a sense of personal worth and attachment in the face of modern mobility, technology, and bureaucracy. Sex has also gained in importance as we have shifted our measures of personal success to include "physical vitality and life enjoyment as well as material achievement" (Tiefer 1995: 11). Sex is more than a source of physical pleasure; psychological gratifications of closeness, competence, accomplishment, and a sense of well-being are also part of the package.

As sex becomes seemingly more significant, how do we know how well we are doing in this arena? Tiefer speculates that our current fascination with radio call-in and TV talk shows, magazine quizzes, newspaper advice columns, sex surveys, and sex books serves the purpose of **social comparison**—comparing ourselves to others. In addition to tips about how to improve our sex lives, we obtain feedback to reassure ourselves that we are okay, personal affirmation with less risk of shame (than if we reveal details of our sex lives to family or friends), and explanations for why we might be feeling unhappy or dissatisfied. Today the idea of knowing what is "in the ballpark" sexually seems highly salient, so we care what other people are doing.

THE EFFECTS OF CHANGE

One of the overall consequences of changes since the 1950s in family and society is a new set of choices facing us. It may have been limiting to be offered one basic, preset traditional way of conducting our marital and sexual relationships, but at least we knew what was expected, and it seemed as though there was some agreement on how to go about it. Different analysts come to different conclusions about whether the changes described in this chapter are "good" or "bad," but most agree that change does not come easy. Leaving behind what is accustomed, familiar, and predictable to face uncharted territory is often confusing and anxiety provoking. It also potentially creates conflicts among individuals promoting competing lifestyles, such as those for and against gay rights or abortion.

As society changes, we may individually suffer the effects. Emile Durkheim, an eminent eighteenth-century French sociologist, used the term **anomie** to denote a state of normlessness. Essentially, this is a social condition in which consensus about appropriate conduct is lacking. In the absence of clear normative guidelines, we have to work harder as individuals to negotiate an array of choices and make the right decisions for ourselves. Norms may be to varying degrees unclear or in contention; they are not entirely absent. We will investigate what people still believe, what they expect, and what they do in various arenas of marital and sexual lifestyles in order to form a better picture of public opinion and private practice. Predominant values in the United States today encourage more open questioning and give greater legitimacy to choice in marital and sexual lifestyles. Correspondingly, individuals have greater need to look more closely and systematically at the options, both the strains and possibilities offered by various marital and sexual lifestyles.

SUMMARY

Contemporary marital and sexual lifestyles are best understood using sociological imagination. The sociological imagination places individuals in social and historical context. It is useful in examining what social psychologists have called "how individual thought, feeling and behavior are shaped by the real, imagined or implied presence of others" (Allport 1968: 3). Sociologists bring into sharper focus the structure of society as a whole, its essential components, and how they are interrelated. They examine social organization and social change to form a picture of the features of a given society in a particular historical period that influence individual experience. As we come to see the connections between history and biography, we learn more about ourselves.

From the so-called traditional family of the United States in the 1950s to the diversity of households today, the family has proven to be a remarkably flexible and adaptable social institution. Alternate lifestyles—systematic departures from traditional structure, roles, or values—arise when existing social institutions fail to meet individual needs, often in response to larger social changes. Since the 1950s, we have seen a liberalization of sexual behaviors and attitudes, the adoption of the Pill, increase in age at first marriage, a higher rate of divorce, more single-parent households and blended families, more married women in the paid labor force, and smaller family size. By the 1970s, it was already clear from U.S. Census statistics that only a relatively small percentage (16 percent) of all U.S. households consisted of a husband and a wife who was a full-time homemaker and their dependent children. Contributing to changes in marriage and family in the decades since the 1950s was our strong cultural emphasis on individualism. We still struggle with some of the inherent contradictions between two favored value orientations: familism and individualism.

Human sexuality remains a controversial subject. Perhaps the most striking feature of human sexuality is its variability. We should not take for granted that what seems "natural" to us is in fact biologically determined or universal. Society always regulates sexual expression, and cross-cultural studies show remarkable diversity in sexual beliefs and practices worldwide. Against the background of biological predispositions, drives, capacities, and limitations, culture fills in the particulars of human sexual behavior, attitudes, and feelings. We tend to become the kind of sexual being that we are raised to be in a particular society. In the United States, past attitudes toward sex were largely restrictive, but Kinsey reported that actual practice did not necessarily correspond to avowed beliefs. As a result of changes in U.S. society, standards of sexual morality have shifted away from conformity to absolute rules in the direction of individual choice, understood as informed and responsible individual choice.

With rising expectations for sexual gratification and personal happiness, and no one family form guaranteed to meet everyone's needs, individuals search for the "right" marital and sexual lifestyle. A closer look at the diversity of marital and sexual lifestyles in the United States will help readers understand the overall possibilities and explore their own options. Studying the individual in society is like putting together a puzzle: "We gather small parts of the puzzle—for example, the way we select a mate, the high divorce rate, increasing numbers of women in the workforce, longer lives, greater commitment to individual choice—and the parts begin to make sense when we fit them together" (Charon 1995: 22).

In Chapter 1 we will first examine how social scientists study marital and sexual lifestyles. What research methods are used to gather information about people's beliefs and actions? How much confidence can we place in the findings of social research? What resources are available to learn more about marital and sexual lifestyles in the United States? If we do not have an accurate picture of ourselves in social context, our personal decisions are based on incomplete or faulty information. In the rest of the book, we turn attention to the following topics: being single versus married, sex and singles, heterosexual cohabitation, dating, marital sex, divorce, male and female roles, issues concerning children, sexual morality, homosexuality, aging, and successful relationships.

Chapter 1

Research Methods

When we make individual decisions about events in our personal lives, we would like to think that we are making well-informed choices; in other words, that we know something about the potential benefits and risks involved and about our own values and motivations. What do we generally know about marital and sexual lifestyles in the United States, and where does such information come from? Typically, our understandings are based on our own previous personal experience; what we have seen or heard about other people's lives from family, friends, and acquaintances; what we are taught in school, church, or other formal organizations; what we read in books; and images conveyed through mass media, such as television, radio, movies, newspapers, magazines, or computer networks. The resulting impressions we form are a unique blend of fact and fiction, objective description and prescriptive beliefs about how things "should" be, broad generalizations, specific convictions, unquestioned beliefs, and tentative conclusions. In order to get on with our lives, we have to do the best we can with the information we have available at any given time, but it might also be useful to stop periodically to look more critically at what we know, or think we know, about these matters. Essentially, this is what social scientists do.

To approach marital and sexual lifestyles scientifically is to be more objective, more systematic, and more thorough than we might be otherwise. As sociologist Joel Charon explains, given that social circumstances make an important difference for individual action, sociologists try to see the human being in society as clearly and carefully as they can. They do this through research, rather than by simple guesswork or wishful thinking. The *American Heritage Dictionary* defines research as "scholarly or scientific investigation." Scientific investigation requires that researchers "clearly describe in a step-by-step process how one arrives at one's conclusions" (Charon 1995: 11). Sociological research involves posing empirical questions, using established procedures to carefully gather information, interpreting the results against the background of previous findings, and maintaining a critical stance toward conclusions reached. Social science findings are reported in professional journals (see Box 1.1) and reviewed by other researchers so they are open to critical examination and can serve to guide future studies. Research literally means to search and search again.

Box 1.1. Professional Journals

University and public libraries provide access to research findings on marital and sexual lifestyles that appear in a variety of professional journals. Computer searches enable users to scan existing records of journal articles for selected authors, journal titles, or keywords. Abstracts of scholarly articles appearing in such journals are included in several computerized databases. The abstracts provide more detail than titles alone about the contents of each article. Look for Sociological Abstracts, Psychological Abstracts, and Social Work Abstracts. For compiling a bibliography on marriage and family topics, refer to the Family Resources Database, based on the Inventory of Marriage and Family Literature, and the Social Sciences Citation Index, an international, multidisciplinary index to the literature of the social, behavioral, and related sciences.

Readers may find the periodicals listed below particularly useful:

American Journal of Family Therapy
American Journal of Orthopsychiatry
Archives of Sexual Behavior
Family Law Quarterly
Family Law Reporter
Family Planning Perspectives
Family Process
Family Relations
Journal of Comparative Family Studies
Journal of Divorce
Journal of Family Issues
Journal of Family Violence
Journal of the History of Sexuality
Journal of Marital and Family Therapy
Journal of Marriage and the Family
Journal of Personal and Social Relationships
Journal of Sex and Marital Therapy
Journal of Sex Research
Marriage and Family Review
Mediation Quarterly: Journal of the Academy of Family Mediators
SAGE: Scholarly Journal of Black Women
Sex Roles: A Journal of Research
Signs: A Journal of Women in Culture and Society
Women and Society

FACTS AND VALUES

Many of the everyday discussions you will hear about society and social behavior can be characterized as "debates of competing intuitions." Consider the issue of sex education. One person is in favor of sex education in the schools because he or she believes parents do not discuss contraception with their adolescents and that learning about contraception will help re-

duce the likelihood of teen pregnancy. Another person is against sex education in the schools because he or she believes that learning about contraception encourages teens to be sexually active and therefore increases the rate
of teenage pregnancy. Who is correct? Arguments on both sides may be in-
tuitively appealing and appear plausible. Each person's claims "make sense,"
but how can we determine whether or not they are true?

Often embedded in such arguments are two kinds of questions: questions
of value and questions of fact. Values, as noted in the previous chapter, are
standards of desirability, assumptions about what is good or bad, right or
wrong. For example, "parents should talk to adolescents about sex" and
"teenagers should not be sexually active" are value statements. Questions of
value have to do with the basic standards individuals apply when judging
the desirability of particular situations. Matters of fact are fundamentally
different. They involve assertions about the actual occurrence of events. In
our sex education example, the assertion that parents do not talk to their
children about sex is an empirical statement, as is the claim that knowledge
of contraception causes greater participation in sexual intercourse among
teenagers. Social science research methods are designed to address these
kinds of factual, or empirical, questions; **empirical** means based on observation, not relying exclusively on logic or intuition.

To be objective and accurate about marital and sexual lifestyles, to see
what is really happening around us and not just what we want to see, we
have to be able to distinguish between matters of value and matters of fact.
Family sociologists Bryan Strong and Christine DeVault (1989) say that
family scholars and researchers seek to describe sexuality, marriage, and the
family

> as they are, not as they should be or as they themselves have person-
> ally experienced them. Scholars studying premarital intercourse, for
> example, seek to find its incidence, the characteristics of those who
> engage in it, and its relationship to marital stability. They do not ask
> whether it is right or wrong or whether people should or should not en-
> gage in it . . . [because] such questions are best answered within the
> domain of ethics and religion rather than social science. (p. 57)

As recent controversy over marriage and family texts illustrates, the distinction between facts and values is important and not always clear in practice, even among social scientists (Glenn 1997). Facts, after all, do not speak
for themselves. How they are presented and interpreted reflects the values of
the persons discussing them. Values, in turn, are sometimes based on or accepted because of untested empirical assertions that should be questioned
more closely. For scientific purposes, it is necessary to understand where in
the midst of various debates testable empirical questions arise.

The **Socratic method,** also, can be useful in everyday life to help us learn more about our own and others' values and motivations. Socrates, an early Greek philosopher, questioned people about their beliefs. He might have asked, for example, what is the good society, or the good family? As described in a sociology text by Joel Charon (1995: 23), Socrates then "met every answer with more questions, no matter what people answered. . . . To him, this is what education must be: a continual search for understanding through asking questions and exposing superficial answers, causing [us] to grasp an idea through careful examination rather than simply reciting what we [have been] taught." The Socratic method of questioning challenges the answers people have learned to give without much reflection and contests the beliefs we have come to take for granted. Our society and the groups to which we belong supply us with many ideas, values, and attitudes but, ultimately, we decide what we personally believe in. To do this, it helps to realize the extent to which the way we tend to see the world, our worldview, is shaped by socialization—how we are raised and our subsequent experience in a particular society. **Ethnocentrism** is the term most often used to describe the tendency to use one's own culture as the frame of reference for judging others. One of the reasons it is particularly valuable, though difficult, to be objective in studying marital and sexual lifestyles is that we all are so embedded in our own social experience that we have biases we are not even aware of. Issues concerning sexuality, marriage, and family, moreover, touch upon some of our most personally significant values and strongest convictions.

RULES AND EXCEPTIONS

Scientists believe that nature is lawful; in other words, that there are predictable regularities at work. Because events are not haphazard, we can identify causes of past events and, correspondingly, predict future outcomes resulting from the influence of those same causes. Sociologists likewise begin with an assumption that human behavior is not completely idiosyncratic; human society and social behavior will exhibit certain regularities or patterns. As we learn more about the processes shaping relationships among various social events, we better understand the underlying patterns of social life, including marital and sexual lifestyles. The natural laws governing society and human affairs, however, are probabilistic, meaning they follow the laws of probability. Probability refers to the likelihood of certain events occurring in the long run under particular conditions. For example, are persons more likely to divorce if they marry young? What if they live together before marrying; are they more or less likely to divorce? Social events cannot be predicted with certainty, but the likelihood of particular events, given specific circumstances, can be anticipated. Social scientists seek to describe, explain, predict, and understand observed tendencies and directions of influence in human affairs. They systematically investigate what is happening and why. Charon (1995:19) cautions that "sometimes we can discover patterns that apply to everyone [but] more often we uncover patterns that are true for large numbers of people." While cause is seldom easy to establish because multiple forces act together to produce given outcomes, usually we will be able to identify the most likely contributing factors and determine with increasing confidence over time their particular effects on designated outcomes. Outcomes of interest may include premarital sexual behaviors, courtship violence, division of household chores in marriage, child-rearing practices, blended families, or cohabitation. What we learn about rates of occurrence, causes, and effects become part of our culturally shared knowledge of marital and sexual lifestyles.

Confronted with a social research finding, people will sometimes reject it because they can think of an exception to the reported rule or pattern. This reaction seems to reflect an assumption that the pattern described must be true for all cases, but we have seen that the patterns observed in social life are understood to be probabilities, not certainties. Correspondingly, we will find exceptions to every rule. Have you ever heard the saying that "the exception proves the rule"? At least, exceptions do not necessarily *dis*prove the rule, because the rule applies to events in general, not to every single case. However, if we observe too many exceptions, we may have to be more careful in stating the rule to specify the conditions under which it is most likely to apply. This is in fact one of the ways that social research advances. Sociologist Joel Charon (1995: 15) gives an example: "People generally end up in the social class in which they are born—but not everyone does. We must ask why birth is so important to class placement and why there are exceptions. With each new conclusion there are new questions and new directions for investigation." In the marriage and family area, consider the finding that most couples who have children report a drop in marital satisfaction (though life satisfaction does not decline). Someone you know might be more satisfied with marriage after having children, but, if so, his or her experience is unlike that of most persons in our society. Another family pattern, discussed in a family text by Day and colleagues (1995), is that parental supervision influences adolescent participation in premarital sex. An earlier research study by Miller and colleagues (1986) had found that adolescents from the least strict homes had the highest levels of sexual activity, while adolescents who were most strictly supervised had higher levels of sexual activity than those raised in a moderately strict home. This does not mean that no sexually active teenagers will ever come from a moderately strict home, just that, overall, adolescents from moderately strict homes are less likely to be sexually active as teenagers.

In short, social scientists cannot tell precisely what will happen to any particular person: e.g., whom you will date; whether, or how many times, you will marry; how successful your relationships will be; or how many children you will have, if any. They can estimate the likelihood of such outcomes under certain circumstances by identifying what conditions promote occurrence of certain events, and why. How will this kind of information about marital and sexual lifestyles be useful to you? In his book *Life Choices: Applying Sociology*, Robert E. Kennedy Jr. (1986) emphasized that however much society constrains individuals, many important events in life are open to choice. Individuals will make decisions about education, living conditions, work arrangements, sexual activities, personal relationships, marriage, children, child care, and retirement. "Opportunities can be exploited or squandered; difficulties can be overcome or compounded. . . . Many problems and opportunities you face as an individual will be similar, though not identical, to those facing thousands, if not millions, of others. . . . You can anticipate some life situations by learning from others who have already been there" (Kennedy 1986: 4, 5).

Given their social context, personal actions have probable consequences. Knowing something more about social systems and about how social forces influence individual experience (1) gives us an educated view of our own life prospects, (2) provides greater insight into why other people do what they do, and (3) lessens the chances of finding ourselves unexpectedly in social situations or roles for which we are unprepared.

VALIDITY AND GENERALIZABILITY

To apply sociological knowledge to our own lives, we have to be able to evaluate the empirical "truths" presented by social scientists. How much confidence can we place in a particular finding? The techniques used to study marital and sexual lifestyles are varied, and the subject matter is complex. Social science research methods involve many details beyond the scope of this discussion, but several basic ideas will be very useful tools for the general reader. To judge the soundness of empirical claims, employ the concepts of validity and generalizability.

Validity of measurement means that the way information is gathered accurately captures what you intend to study. To be credible, studies of human affairs have to use valid measures of the outcomes and possible causes being investigated. Take the issue of marital happiness. The Declaration of Independence, one of the founding documents of our nation, guarantees us rights to "life, liberty and the pursuit of happiness." Not surprising, then, that one area of both popular and professional interest in marriage and the family is marital happiness: Who has it; who does not? What factors predict marital happiness? Can a marriage last without it? More basic yet, what *is* it? How can we tell whether particular couples are happily or unhappily married? In a decade review of research on contemporary families published by the National Council on Family Relations, family sociologist Felix Berardo (1991) noted that one of the most widely studied topics in the field was "marital quality." In the same volume, family sociologist Norval Glenn (1991: 29) added that "the literature on marital quality has for several decades been characterized by conceptual confusion and disagreement about measurement," though progress was being made. In other words, sociologists themselves were not in agreement on what constitutes marital quality. How much is marital happiness a part of marital quality? Is marital happiness the same as marital satisfaction or marital success? To measure marital happiness, should we simply ask married individuals to say how they feel about their marriages or maybe use a checklist of characteristics of the marital relationship that we think indicate quality?

Many confusions and debates arise in social research and in everyday discussion of marital and sexual lifestyles over how various terms are being defined and measured. Social scientists have the advantage of being more explicitly aware of validity concerns. What hope does the average person have of keeping up with it all? Fortunately, common sense provides some direction. When assessing social research findings, pay close attention to how the social events studied were defined and actually measured, and what the researcher has to say about why you should accept these measures as accurate indicators. Think about what is being included that maybe should not be, or what is being left out. **Content validity** refers to "the degree to which a measure covers the range of meanings included within a concept" (Babbi 1995: 128). For example, when reports talk about "sexually active" teenagers, does this term include adolescents who are kissing and petting or only those who have had sexual intercourse? When rates of "child abuse" are cited, are cases of incest and neglect as well as physical battering being counted as abuse? Are legally separated couples regarded as "singles"? One criterion of validity, face validity, is simply whether a measure appears appropriate "on the face of it," but take a second look. What do you think "marital happiness" means? When someone else uses this term, can you safely assume they mean the same thing? They may not. Thinking about definitions of concepts such as marital happiness and seeking clarification from others about the terms they use may clear up some misunderstandings in everyday discussions. In evaluating social research, always consider reported findings in connection with the definitions and measures used in a particular investigation.

Generalizability is another important concern about social research findings. Let's say that we are reasonably well satisfied with a researcher's definitions and measures. We believe his or her findings accurately describe the persons observed in a particular study. Now, can these findings be applied to anyone else? After all, "one of the chief goals of science is generalization. Social scientists study particular situations and events in order to learn about social life in general" (Babbi 1995: 302). The only instance in which information is gathered directly from the general population in our society is the U.S. Census, conducted every ten years by the federal government. This is the most complete enumeration available of the demographic characteristics of the entire U.S. population, some of which is indispensable for understanding marital and sexual lifestyles in our society (see Box 1.2 for a brief description of U.S. Census data and how to access this type of information). Information obtained directly from millions of Americans applies to social life in the United States in general, but the U.S. Census does

---

Box 1.2. Family Demography and the U.S. Census
Contributed by Robert Baker, MA, Sociology

Demography is the scientific study of population and is concerned with what influences and is influenced by the processes of fertility, mortality, and migration. Family demographers study topics such as age at marriage, divorce rates, family planning, female labor force participation, remarriage, and composition of households. *Demography* is a professional journal published quarterly by the Population Association of America. It contains research articles from various disciplines, including the social sciences, statistics, and public health. The August 1997 issue, for example, included articles such as "Cohabiting Partners' Economic Circumstances and Marriage," "Couple Childbearing Desires, Intentions and Births," and "Men's Career Development and Marriage Timing During a Period of Rising Inequality." *Studies in Family Planning, Family Planning Perspectives, American Demographics,* and *Population Studies* are examples of other periodicals addressing demographic issues.

Demographic data for the United States come primarily from the U.S. Department of Commerce, Bureau of the Census. The Bureau of the Census has conducted a **census,** an official population count, every ten years since 1790 as well as regularly reported surveys in the series *Current Population Reports.* To make demographic information about the U.S. population more widely available, statistical abstracts are published annually by the Census Bureau. The **Statistical Abstract of the United States** is an outstanding source for statistics on the social, political, and economic organization of the United States. Each year nearly 150 tables and charts are reviewed and evaluated, and tables and charts of current interest are added. The annual editions are divided into sections for easier access, including: Population (Marital Status, Households and Families), Vital Statistics (Marriages and Divorces), and Human Services (Child Support, Child Care). Answers can be found to questions such as: "What is the marital status of African Americans by sex?" "Which states have the highest and lowest divorce rates?" and "What were the child care arrangements used by working mothers for their children under five years of age?"

(continued)

(continued)

Demographic information about marital and sexual lifestyles can also be found in the *Information Please Almanac,* an easy to read, easy to access reference source published annually by the Houghton Mifflin Company. For example, the 1997 edition had a six-page section on "Family Trends" with information and statistics on the number of cohabiting couples in the United States, the current status of gay marriages, the numbers and types of interracial couples, and the number of unmarried couples with children, as well as other topics. The information comes largely from the U.S. Department of Commerce, Bureau of the Census.

The Population Reference Bureau is a nonprofit educational organization founded in 1929. The PRB produces a monthly newsletter *(Population Today),* a quarterly bulletin *(Population Bulletin),* and an annual "World Population Data Sheet." Available bulletins related to marriage and family issues include: "Gender, Power and Change," "Women, Work and Family in America," "New Realities of the American Family," and "Conveying Concerns: Women Write on Male Participation in the Family." These can be purchased directly from the PRB for five to seven dollars each.

Several Web sites provide population information as well:

The PRB produces a home page which can be found at http://www.prb.org/prb/. This site contains listings of PRB publications and ordering information. PRB also produces and maintains another Web site called POPNET, accessed at http://www.popnet.org, which is a resource for global population information with a comprehensive directory composed of hundreds of sources for population-related topics around the world. Searches can be executed by keyword, by organization, or simply by clicking on the site's world map. Topics include demographic statistics, gender, reproductive health, family planning, and changing family structure.

The home page of the U.S. Census Bureau, located at http:// www.census.gov/, is another comprehensive source for social, demographic, and economic information. Searches can be done by word, place, or a point-and-click map of the United States. A list of Census Bureau employees, with their phone numbers and e-mail addresses, is also included. The POPClock at this site gives up-to-the-second population estimates for the United States and the world. According to the U.S. Bureau of the Census, the resident population of the U.S. on June 16, 2001 at 12:40 p.m. EDT was: 284,444,398.

not address all questions of interest. When we need other kinds of information, practicality dictates that only a smaller portion of the general population, called a **sample,** can be studied. How do we know when sample results tell us about general patterns in our society?

If a sample is *representative* of people in the larger society, findings from the sample are more likely to apply to that population in general. If a sample is restricted, say, by gender, race, ethnicity, age, income, education, type of

Illustration by Tom Urquhart.

occupation, religion, or region of the country, the findings are not so generalizable. A commonsense rule of thumb is that sample findings apply more generally only to those other persons who are most similar. For example, a study of the dating experiences of white never-married college students in one public university in the Southwest should not be assumed to apply to all dating. Common patterns of dating may in fact exist across different segments of American society, but we cannot conclude that from one restricted study. Likewise, person-in-the-street interviews may have human interest but should not be confused with "public opinion."

   The key to representativeness and generalizability is in how a sample is chosen. Scientific samples use systematic methods for choosing participants in which every member of a population has an equal chance of selection; then we have a **random sample.** Even with random sampling, sample-based estimates of population characteristics vary. Social science research will therefore report "confidence levels" and "tests of statistical significance," which reflect attention to possible sampling errors. General readers should be wary of very small samples, which introduce a greater margin of error when trying to generalize results to larger groups, but may be surprised to learn that scientifically conducted random sample surveys of 1,500 adult Americans can accurately reflect the responses of all adult Americans. With this in mind, to evaluate social science findings ask yourself how many persons were included in a given research study, how they were selected, and who remained in the final analysis. If you closely consider the kind of people who participated, you can decide how widely you think the findings might apply.

METHODS OF DATA COLLECTION

Three major methods of collecting data in social science research are surveys, experiments, and naturalistic observation. Additionally, professionals in clinical practice, such as psychiatrists, counseling psychologists, and social workers, study the cases of individuals and families who are their clients. In this section, readers are briefly acquainted with each of these methods as they are used to study marital and sexual lifestyles.

Surveys

The survey is the most frequently used data-gathering method in studies of marriage and the family. Survey researchers gather information by asking a series of questions. They have to decide what to ask and exactly how to ask it; the questionnaire or interview schedule is their research instrument. Surveys asking people about their attitudes and behaviors can be conducted by mail, on the telephone, or in face-to-face interviews. Because the objective of a scientific survey is to describe the distribution of traits in a population and relationships among these traits based on a representative sample, survey researchers have to carefully determine who to question and how to select them. As discussed earlier, improper sampling undermines confidence in the generalizability of findings. Even random samples are subject to biases introduced by refusals since persons selected for the sample may choose not to participate. Those who refuse to answer may simply be uninterested or too busy, but they may also be different in more important ways from those who respond.

In the case of sex surveys, for example, if both the most conservative individuals, who feel their sex life is nobody else's business, and the individuals whose behavior most deviates from conventional practice, who may worry about disclosing illegal or "immoral" acts, systematically refuse to participate, the results will not accurately describe the full range of everyone's behaviors and opinions. After respondents complete the questions, survey researchers still have to summarize and analyze the answers. Typically, survey responses are numerically coded, entered into a computer, and evaluated statistically. In drawing conclusions about causal relationships from survey data, caution must be exercised. Surveys only allow us to detect correlations or associations among responses. These obtained correlations may be spurious, or misleading, with respect to causal inference, for reasons explained in detail elsewhere (e.g., see Babbi 1995).

Surveys can provide a large amount of information relatively quickly and are valuable in tracking social trends when the same questions are repeated in subsequent surveys. The General Social Survey, for example, which has been conducted regularly by the National Opinion Research Center (NORC) since 1972, allows us to document change or stability in public opinion about premarital, extramarital, and homosexual sexual relations. Survey responses can be anonymous or kept confidential to encourage honest answers. Still, surveys rely on people's willingness and ability to provide complete, accurate, and honest answers. How forthcoming will we be when asked about anal intercourse, extramarital affairs, or use of physical force in relationships? Will the specifics of a first date be remembered twenty years later? Do you know how many times you have kissed your partner this year or exactly how you feel about your teenage children? Can you say why you behave as you do in all instances? Some questions may be confusing; respondents are not quite sure what information is being requested. Other questions strike some respondents as too intrusive into private matters; maybe the true answer seems socially undesirable, or too odd and embarrassing to share. Sometimes we just do not know or remember events well enough to answer accurately.

Also, the response categories offered on a survey questionnaire, such as 1 to 5 from strongly disagree to strongly agree, may not permit the answer a person would really like to give. Surveys do not typically allow in-depth responses. In person, interviewers can probe and clarify responses but may unintentionally influence the answers given. In addition, surveys are usually completed by individual respondents, and thus do not show how people actually interact. Asking you how you and your parents or you and your children relate to one another, for example, is not the same as directly observing you together with other family members.

Despite these kinds of limitations, much that is of interest about marital and sexual lifestyles cannot be directly observed and must be approached through surveys, in which people tell us what they think or feel or do or expect and which are well suited to investigating the general incidence of self-reported behaviors and opinions. Two national surveys, for example, gave us representative samples of adult Americans in 1975 and 1985 which provided the best available basis for estimating rates of a variety of family conflict tactics, including use of physical force (Straus and Gelles 1990). Box 1.3 outlines the several stages of another survey, this one of human sexuality.

Box 1.3. Survey Research: The Janus Report on Sexual Behavior

The Janus Report on Sexual Behavior was written by Samuel S. Janus, PhD, an associate professor of psychiatry at New York Medical College, and Cynthia L. Janus, MD (1993), a physician and associate professor at the University of Virginia. Their book was the product of a nine-year investigation of sexuality in the United States intended to fill in gaps in knowledge about sexual behaviors and attitudes in the 1980s and 1990s. The project included a large-scale cross-sectional survey conducted between 1988 and 1992. The main stages of their study are outlined below:

I. Designing the Research Instrument
  • Determining the scope of the study (what topics to cover)
  • Reviewing existing research for previous findings and relevant ideas
  • Drafting two initial versions of a questionnaire
  • Running pilot studies, which lead to revising question wording and format so later respondents can give clearer answers.
  • Deciding to include in-depth interviews as well as questionnaires
II. Collecting the Primary Data
  • Their sample of persons eighteen years and older was not a truly random sample, but questionnaires were "distributed . . . at a wide variety of sites" to get geographic, age, and educational diversity and to include both males and females, married, divorced, widowed, and never married.
  • Systematic comparison of their final sample to the overall U.S. population based on census data was their basis for saying their findings are, "by and large, a valid reflection of the behaviors and attitudes of U.S. society as a whole, (p. 402)".
  • They distributed 4,550 questionnaires, of which 3,260 (72 percent) were returned, but another 495 were dropped because they were incomplete, leaving 61 percent of the original questionnaires available for analysis.
  • They also conducted in-depth interviews with 125 persons, a 4.5 percent randomly selected subset of the final 2,765 participants. They reported that they were careful to encourage candor in these interviews.
III. Data Analysis
  • Entering the responses into a computer
  • Generating statistical tables and percentages
  • Interpreting the statistical results and interview comments
  • Writing up a selection of their observations and conclusions

Janus and Janus included a copy of the final questionnaire in their book and encouraged readers to answer the questions themselves to compare with the sample's responses. A set of questions similar to those they asked are presented in the Appendix. Findings from their study are reported in later chapters.

Clinical Studies

Studies of marital and sexual lifestyles in therapeutic settings most often take the form of case studies. Clinical case studies are in-depth examinations of a person or small group of people who come to a mental health professional with individual or relational problems. Clinicians typically will see clients repeatedly over some length of time. They have an opportunity to learn about certain aspects of clients' lives in more detail than is possible in survey research. Clinicians are also in a position to observe nuances of family interactions and dynamic patterns of relationships. Clinicians can use standardized tests and questions as well as loosely structured, flexible interviews. Because this is an approach focused on the individual or small group, it is not directly concerned with the larger societal picture. Persons entering counseling settings are not a representative sample of the general population thus the generalizability of clinical findings is doubtful. Couples seeking marital therapy, for example, may be experiencing more serious conflicts than other couples or they may differ in certain characteristics that motivate them to seek help (e.g., they could be more highly educated or hold values making them more reluctant to divorce). Participants are "self-selected" or referred, not a random sample. What clinical studies uniquely provide is a closer look at family problems and troubled relationships. Along with other types of observational and case studies, clinical studies provide powerful insights into family processes, e.g., how rules and roles are created and maintained in the families of alcoholics or how incest perpetrators rationalize their conduct and how incest survivors cope with their family experiences.

A classic clinical study was reported in a book titled *Sanity, Madness and the Family* by psychiatrists R. D. Laing and Aaron Esterson (1970). Laing and Esterson described the cases of eleven families of origin of women diagnosed with schizophrenia: "We set out to illustrate by eleven examples that if we look at some [individual] behaviors without reference to family interactions they may appear comparatively socially senseless, but if we look at the same behaviors in their original family context they are liable to make sense" (p. 12). Suppose a patient says she thinks her parents are always keeping things from her and trying to trick her, and she generally believes that people are plotting against her. If the therapist finds in interviews with family members that they are indeed keeping secrets from her and deliberately confusing her about their intentions, her ideas and actions make sense. In their clinical practice, Laing and Esterson found this pattern of manifest contradictions in case after case when they looked at how a schizophrenic patient's parents and, sometimes, siblings interacted with one another and with the patient. Do these things go on in all sorts of families? Possibly. Laing and Esterson's data came largely from interviews conducted in the clinical setting, but their findings invite further consideration of the idea of the social intelligibility of individual behavior when observed against a particular family background.

Clinical studies occasionally may extend to natural settings. Behavioral scientist Jules Henry was able to spend time with five families of psychotic children in their own homes. In his preface and introduction to *Pathways to Madness,* Henry (1973) expressed the hope that other parents reading his findings and comments would become more aware of the consequences of their parenting behaviors and avoid some of the mistakes made by the families he interviewed and observed, since none of us is entirely free of defects or problems. These case studies are cautionary tales. They confirm our own experiences if we were ourselves raised in highly dysfunctional families and more generally provide insights into the less extreme but more prevalent transgressions we all make as parents. As compared to our own everyday observations of family life, Jules Henry was more disciplined in his study of these particular families and better anchored theoretically in his interpretations of the commonplaces he witnessed. He was able to identify and illustrate wider themes of family functioning, such as:

1. *Availability*—of family members to one another physically and emotionally.
2. *"Shamming"*—the extent to which we introduce false notes into our relationships.
3. *Poor judgment*—failures to learn culturally accepted frameworks of judgment and perception.

What distinguished the clinical cases Henry described was not the fundamental processes involved, which are widely applicable, but the extremes and frequency of the mistakes made in these families—too much, too often for children to grow up without severe harm.

Nonclinical Case Studies

In-depth study of particular cases can also be conducted with nonclinical subjects. Cases can be individuals, families, other groups, or larger communities. Researchers might study beliefs and practices in a teenage friendship group or in a utopian commune such as the Oneida community (Foster 1991; Kephart and Zellner 1994). We still have the problem in drawing conclusions from case studies of knowing whether any particular case is typical of others or highly distinctive. Bogdan's (1974) autobiography of "Jane Fry," for example, gives an account of the life history of a transsexual from early childhood through adult treatment. A transsexual is an individual who strongly desires to assume the physical characteristics and gender role of the opposite sex and who may undergo surgical and hormonal treatment for this purpose. If an autobiography is open, honest, and detailed, readers gain a more personal understanding of an aspect of human sexuality with which they might otherwise be unfamiliar. Based on this one case, however, there is simply no way of knowing the extent to which Jane Fry's experiences are representative of all transsexuals.

A series of case studies may be used to develop ideas about social life. To help students become more involved in discovering how families work, sociologist Ralph LaRossa (1984) published a collection of fourteen family case studies. Each was introduced with background material about why the case was selected and notations on key concepts and propositions illustrated by that case. The cases introduced various aspects of family life, such as the decision to marry (Dick and Gail), living with preschool children (the Bernard family), extended families (the Wards), single parenting (Lynn), and growing old (Gram). In *A New Look at Black Families,* Harvard sociologist Charles Vert Willie (1988: 1) used a series of eighteen case studies to analyze the way of life of black families in the United States: "The stories told to our interviewers provided a window through which we can see patterns of variation in the lifestyles of affluent or middle class, working class, and poor black households." Sociologist Lois Benjamin (1991) conducted interviews with 100 members of the black elite in the United States and used their cases to document the continued subjectively experienced influence of racism; the impact of the color line on social, religious, and family life.

These types of investigations, which do not present statistical information, combine narrative description from a relatively small number of cases based on interview data with the researcher's explanations of the thoughts, feelings, and behaviors recorded, framed by new or existing sociological theories. This is an important element in understanding when and in what ways case studies have scientific merit. They are most useful in advancing knowledge when they are connected to other research findings by a disciplined theoretical or conceptual framework shared with others in the field. Keep in mind that case studies are always selective in what they tell and what they leave out, and rely heavily on the judgment of the person telling the story. While they illustrate rather than "prove" patterns of social behavior, they are often interesting to read and generate new ideas for further research.

Experiments

The hallmark of experimental research is control over factors that are believed to influence the outcomes being studied. In the area of marital and sexual lifestyles, such control is typically not possible or practical; consequently little experimental research is conducted. When a relevant research question can be addressed by an experiment, however, we are most confident that we have actually isolated a cause of the events in which we are interested. Experimental researchers have to decide what factors to introduce and how to manipulate them. The participants, called subjects, in an experiment are self-selected volunteers, often college students in psychology, social psychology, or research methods courses. The researcher has to set up and run the experiment, using groups of subjects exposed to one "condition" (set of manipulated factors) or another, then compare results across different groups of subjects.

Experiments usually take place in a laboratory setting where conditions are easier to control, but not always. Paper and pencil measures can be experimentally manipulated if the researcher is able to randomly assign some subjects to complete one version and other subjects to complete a different version. Strong and DeVault's (1995) family text describes a simple experiment of this sort conducted earlier by Etaugh and Malstrom (1981), investigating social attitudes toward singlehood. Subjects were asked to evaluate twenty traits of a person described in a short paragraph. In different versions of the paragraph, the person described was identified as married, divorced, widowed, or never married. When the person was identified as married, the person was rated more favorably than when identified as single (whether widowed, divorced, or never married). Widowed persons were rated higher than the divorced or never married, and divorced persons were rated the lowest. This experiment indicated that the person's described marital status did directly influence the ratings given, so one might expect to find a bias in favor of married persons and against divorced persons in everyday life.

Caution would have to be exercised, though, in applying such findings, since experiments can be criticized as lacking generalizability both to other subjects and to other settings. Experiments are designed to test whether particular factors actually cause certain results, but in doing so deliberately simplify social circumstances. "Experiments are usually faint shadows of the complex and varied situations we experience outside the experiment. . . . We are likely to respond differently to real people in real life than in controlled settings or hypothetical examples" (Strong and DeVault 1989: 61). To know how people will act in real life, researchers have to observe social events in their natural setting. Still, one of the most interesting features of experiments as compared to survey research is that in experiments researchers have an opportunity to test what people actually do, rather than what people *say* they would do or have done!

Direct Observation

Direct observation in a natural setting, also called field research or participant observation, allows us to gather firsthand information about ongoing interaction and social processes in their natural social environment. To conduct field studies, the researcher must decide what to observe, how, and where. He or she will have to establish rapport with subjects, spend time in the field observing, record field notes, and finally, write up the findings. Since the presence of an observer may interfere with the natural flow of interaction, researchers try to remain as unobtrusive as possible. The more people are aware of being watched, the more likely they will censor themselves and try to avoid exhibiting socially disapproved behavior. Over time, however, people tend to reveal their attitudes and revert to their typical conduct.

Because field researchers can only be in one place at one time, observational studies are limited in setting. By now readers will appreciate the accompanying disadvantage of low generalizability; we cannot necessarily make inferences about the general population from direct observation of a few people in a specific setting. Observational research also depends greatly on the abilities and skills of the observer, and tends to be more subjective than some other research methods, thus vulnerable to observer biases. Different researchers studying the same group can (and have) come up with different findings (Kersten and Kersten 1988: 551). Confidence in findings is enhanced if similar results are reported from other settings. If observations of courting patterns in a singles bar, for example, are replicated in studies of church-based singles groups and of dating in workplace settings, and different researchers arrive at the same conclusions, a general courtship pattern is more evident.

The benefits of participant observation, again, include the accuracy of direct observation versus reports of behaviors, seeing social processes in action, and knowing the results apply to a real-life natural setting. Particularly if one wants to know how events unfold in face-to-face encounters, direct observation is useful. To keep track of events, "directly observed behavior can sometimes be recorded on tape or film and subsequently reanalyzed to check the accuracy of codifications of the behavior. . . . [However] if observation is used without accompanying interviews, much of the motivation and the meaning of the behavior may not be measured" (Kirby 1981: 584). Kirby notes the special difficulty researchers have in observing sexual activities. Few people are willing to have their sexual behavior directly observed by investigators and, even if permission is granted, the presence of the observer may affect the behavior being observed. Consider, Kirby suggests, how you the reader would behave sexually if people were observing you!

Several researchers have used participant observation to study swinging (Bartell 1970; Palson and Palson 1972). In these studies, researchers presented themselves as a couple interested in exchanging partners. In some cases they participated in sexual activities. Because the swinging couples were commonly unaware that they were being studied, they were more likely to be fairly open and direct in answering the researchers' questions about their lifestyle and to behave in the manner they characteristically would with a newly encountered couple considering a possible sexual exchange. How far researchers are willing to go, or should go, to establish rapport and gain access to observation of otherwise private activities is open to debate. One of the most widely known and controversial participant observation studies was conducted by sociologist Laud Humphreys (1975) and described in his book *Tearoom Trade: Impersonal Sex in Public Places.*

Humphreys studied homosexual encounters in men's public restrooms. His methods of data collection included two phases: observation of sexual interaction and follow-up interviews with participants.

> Playing the role of a "watchqueen" alert to the approach of police or minors to the restroom, Humphreys made detailed observations of the sexual activities, typically fellatio, of males in the rest rooms. . . . [He] recorded the car license-plate numbers of participants and traced their names and addresses. A year later, wearing a disguise, Humphreys interviewed them in their homes as if they were part of a routine survey; his respondents were unaware that he had observed them in tearoom encounters. He observed their social situation and asked them questions about their marital status, religion, attitudes toward homosexuality and sexual relations with their wives. (Kirby 1981: 588)

Since respondents were unaware of Humphreys' actual purposes, they could not give *informed consent* for participation in the study. Strong reservations have been expressed about the general ethics of covert observation in connection with Humphreys' research.

Other Research Methods

The research methods discussed above do not exhaust the possible scientific ways of gathering information about marital and sexual lifestyles. Examples of other methods include content analysis, secondary data analysis, and comparative studies (Kersten and Kersten 1988). **Content analysis** involves sampling from a universe of written, audio, or visual materials (such as magazines, books, songs, television programs, or commercials) and systematically classifying the content of the selected material based on particular themes or questions. Gender roles—socially shared expectations about men and women—can be studied using content analysis. A researcher might develop a classification scheme for recording different kinds of activities seen in children's book illustrations or magazine ads in which men and women are portrayed. How frequently are men pictured as active, women as passive? How often are women shown as housewives, men as being engaged in outside occupations? How many times do children appear with women and with men? Changes in popular culture may be explored in this way by analyzing materials selected from different time periods.

Secondary data analysis involves use of information already gathered by others. Studies using U.S. Census data, as discussed earlier, would be an example. Social historians interested in family matters have used existing documents, such as diaries or civic registries of dates of marriage and childbirth, to infer bridal pregnancy. Before national family violence surveys had been conducted, researchers used records from police and social service agencies to estimate rates of domestic assault. Secondary findings from such sources are, of course, limited by the quality of the initial data gathering and by availability of the particular kinds of information sought. **Comparative studies** look at more than one society or subgroup to highlight similarities and differences between them, for example in kinship systems, marriage customs, sexual practices, child-rearing patterns, or sex roles. Travel, language, and cultural barriers make comparative work difficult but no less important. See Box 1.4 for a description of a cross-cultural study of contemporary sexual behavior that also combined several methods of data collection.

Box 1.4. Comparative Research: Weinberg and Williams

Kirby (1981) discusses a comparative research study by Martin Weinberg and Colin Williams that narrowed the focus on sexual behavior by studying only male homosexuals but broadened it by studying adults in three countries: the United States, Denmark and the Netherlands. To form a more complete picture, Weinberg and Williams used both participant observation and survey methods of data collection. Their findings were reported in a book, *Male Homosexuals* (1974).

The Observations. Weinberg and Williams conducted observations of gay communities in four cities: New York, San Francisco, Copenhagen and Amsterdam. They described past and present homosexual organizations, the gay bars and private clubs, the relations between the police and the homosexual communities, and the general legal and social reactions of the heterosexual society. They visited many gay bars and clubs and observed firsthand interaction within them; they formally and informally interviewed customers of bars, leaders in homosexual organizations and the police; and they read and discussed the laws pertaining to homosexuality and previous accounts of past relations with the police.

The Questionnaires. Three different versions of the questionnaire had to be developed for distribution in the three countries studied. The English version was created and tested first. It was then independently translated into the two other languages by different translators, and the results compared and modified. An independent third party translated the Danish and Dutch questionnaires back into English for comparison with the original. Obtaining correct translations is important to accurately capture the meaning of various words. The questionnaire was short and clearly worded. Weinberg and Williams also made use of indexes combining items to improve validity and reliability. For example, six different questions were combined to create a single index of loneliness.

The Samples. The homosexual population at large could not be identified in advance so random sampling procedures were not possible. Instead a variety of non-random methods were used to obtain a diverse sample in each country. In the United States questionnaires were sent to some 2,700 men on the mailing list of New York's major homosexual organization, the Mattachine Society, of which about one third lived in New York. In San Francisco, similarly, 200 questionnaires were sent to men on a Mattachine Society mailing list. An addi-

(continued)

(continued)

tional 258 questionnaires were given to members of a second gay organization who attended any of the organization's social functions during a ten-day period. Finally, 234 and 225 questionnaires were given to a random sample of people in gay bars in San Francisco and New York respectively. Of the questionnaires distributed, 1,117 or 38.7 percent were returned.

In Europe sampling procedures resembled those used in the United States. Questionnaires were mailed to members of the major homosexual organizations of both Denmark and the Netherlands. In Amsterdam and Copenhagen, additional questionnaires were given to members of homosexual clubs and to people at gay bars. In Denmark, 303 or 24.3 percent of the distributed questionnaires were returned; in the Netherlands, 1,077 or 45.1 percent were returned. In addition, the authors took a random sample of 300 cases from the phone books of Amsterdam and Copenhagen in order to compare the homosexual populations with the heterosexual populations. Similarly, they compared their homosexual samples in the U.S. with a random sample of 3,101 adult Americans collected earlier by another researcher.

Although the total number of men in the samples is large, the haphazard sampling procedures used mar the representativeness of participants. Varying proportions of people were included from each of the different sources; e.g., all the people on some lists, only half the people in some bars. Some questionnaires were distributed and returned by mail, some were delivered and collected in person. On many important variables, however, such as self-acceptance and depression, Weinberg and Williams found that all their samples produced similar results, suggesting that sampling irregularities may not have affected all the findings. Overall, the samples include proportionately more open and organizationally active homosexuals than in the larger populations of all homosexual men in each country. Response rates were relatively low and may have been biased in favor of respondents who were better accepted and adjusted to their homosexuality than those who refused.

In conclusion, Weinberg and Williams combined a variety of research methods to gain understanding and insight into male homosexuals in several different contemporary Western societies. Thus, their analysis took into account societal level variation in the social context within which individuals experience their own sexuality. In the absence of random samples, researchers can only speculate about the possible differences between their sample findings and characteristics of the larger population of male homosexuals in the countries studied.

Comment

The discipline of sociology is a scientific attempt to understand human society and social behavior. Studies of marital and sexual lifestyles can be scientific when systematic, objective, and thorough research methods are deliberately employed with appropriate qualifications and reservations. The various research methods described in this chapter have different strengths and weaknesses that should be kept in mind when evaluating reported findings. Their common purpose is to draw conclusions about general patterns underlying social events *based on empirical observation.* Stepping into the role of a social scientist and becoming more familiar with research methods reminds us to be more disciplined in weighing evidence and more careful in drawing conclusions. Social research provides a larger window on U.S. society than does our limited individual experience and offers a preview of prospects, constraints, and opportunities we face in making choices about sex and family life.

RESEARCH METHODS SUPPLEMENT

This final section reviews several landmark studies of human sexual behavior, the Kinsey reports and the work of Masters and Johnson. Often mentioned in both the mass media and in reviews of social science research in the field of human sexuality, readers may be interested to learn in more detail about how these studies were conducted and to consider them in light of the previous discussion of research methods. The following descriptions and critical comments are excerpted from a review by Douglas Kirby (1981) that appeared in *Understanding Sexual Interaction* by DeLora, Warren, and Ellison.

The Kinsey Reports

Kinsey, Pomeroy, Martin, and Gebhard produced the two most widely quoted, most widely discussed, and for their time, definitive studies of human sexual behavior, *Sexual Behavior in the Human Male* and *Sexual Behavior in the Human Female,* using similar research methods in each.

The Samples

To prepare these two reports, Kinsey, Pomeroy, and Martin (1948) interviewed 5,300 white men for the first volume and, for the second, Kinsey, Pomeroy, Martin, and Gebhard (1953) interviewed 5,940 white women. Although these were large samples, they were not based on probability sampling.

> Kinsey and his colleagues made contacts in different communities and asked them to participate. They then asked these initial respondents to convince friends to participate. Many did so. Kinsey and his colleagues also asked entire groups, such as college classes, fraternities and sororities, professional groups, and residents of rooming houses, penal institutions, and mental institutions, to participate. Thus they developed community interest and used peer-group assurances and pressures to obtain full participation, so that 26 percent of the male

sample and 15 percent of the female sample came from such 100 percent participation groups. . . . Their explanation for not using random selection procedures is important. According to their experience, attempts to secure sex histories from lone individuals chosen by random sampling methods would have resulted in refusal rates sufficiently high to destroy the randomness of the final samples. Instead they used friendship patterns and group pressures to reduce errors from non-response (p. 569) by increasing the initial rapport and confidence of the participants.

This approach also served to improve validity and completeness of the interview reports they did obtain.

The final sample included respondents from ages two to ninety, from all occupational and educational levels, from several religions, and from both rural and urban backgrounds. Moreover, it included at least fifty respondents from each of the forty-eight contiguous states. Despite the heterogeneity of the samples, nonrandom sampling caused some groups to be either underrepresented or overrepresented. College students, young people, better-educated people, Protestants, urban residents, and residents of Indiana and the Northeast were overrepresented. Conversely, manual workers, less-educated people, older people, Roman Catholic and Jewish persons, rural dwellers, and people living west of the Mississippi were underrepresented. Consequently, when these samples were used to make inferences about the entire population of Americans, unknown errors were introduced. (p. 569)

In an effort to address this problem, for the male sample Kinsey, Pomeroy, and Martin used statistical procedures to give extra weight to responses from persons in underrepresented categories; which accordingly increased or decreased final estimates of various types of sexual activity.

The Interviews

Kinsey and his colleagues chose to interview respondents rather than administer written questionnaires. In contrast to their sampling procedures, their interview techniques have been highly praised. They appear to have been adept at using language appropriate to the respondent, at accepting descriptions of acts commonly considered deviant without condescension, and in general at establishing rapport and acceptance. They asked questions briskly to encourage honesty but did not produce a feeling of being hurried. They developed a sense of which types of respondents found which types of questions most sensitive and asked them at the optimal time. They learned when probes were likely to be successful in eliciting additional information and which probes were most successful. They also developed cross-checks for accuracy. (p. 570)

Reliability refers to a measurement concern with consistency. Kirby (1988) noted that Kinsey and his colleagues were careful to check the reliability of their data in several ways. (1) They considered whether the personalities of the three major interviewers could have affected the interviewing techniques and information elicited. Ideally, they might have randomly assigned respondents to each interviewer, but instead they compared the reports of hundreds of respondents for each interviewer and found the distribution of responses quite similar. Where differences occurred, they could be explained by the method of assigning participants; older and more sexually active respondents as when Kinsey was assigned to interview. (2) A subset of 319 respondents was interviewed a second time after eighteen months and their two reports were compared. Information about incidence (had the respondent ever participated in a certain behavior) and vital statistics (e.g., age at marriage, religion, education) were found to be very reliable; information about frequency of sexual activities, less so. (3) For 706 married couples, both partners were interviewed and their reports compared. Again, vital statistics and incidence reports were more reliable (consistent) than reports of frequency of sexual activities. (4) Stability of interviewing techniques over time was considered by comparing results obtained by Kinsey during the first four years of interviewing with results from the last four years. The two sets were very similar, and discrepancies could be explained by differences in the sample over time.

> In sum, Kinsey, Pomeroy, Martin, and Gebhard employed poor sampling methods and consequently inferences to the entire population of white men and white women should be made with caution. However, good interviewing techniques were used and consequently much of the data especially the vital statistics and incidences of [sexual] activity appear quite reliable, valid, and complete. (p. 571)

Masters and Johnson

William Masters and Virginia Johnson conducted the most unusual type of data collection in the area of sexual functioning: laboratory studies using direct observation. They were able to examine physiological changes occuring in men and women during sexual stimulation and to explore how and why these changes took place.

The Samples

Their book, *Human Sexual Response* (Masters and Johnson 1966), was based on eleven prostitutes from the St. Louis, Missouri, area and volunteers primarily from the academic community affiliated with a St. Louis university hospital. Masters and Johnson kept only those volunteers who had normal sexual organs, were sexually responsive, and could communicate minute details of their sexual reaction. Consequently, the final sample of 382 women and 312 men is not a probability sample of American adults; most were from one city, above average in intelligence and education, higher than average in socioeconomic background, and probably had somewhat unusual attitudes about sexuality. Nevertheless, the physiological responses that characterized most of these volunteers probably apply to most other Americans; there was no reason to believe their physiological responses would differ substantially. (pp. 584, 585)

Measurement Procedures

> Prior to observing volunteers in the laboratory, [the research team] carefully interviewed prospective participants, obtained psychosexual histories, and administered medical exams. In the laboratory, they observed episodes of masturbation, mutual masturbation, fellatio, cunnilingus, intercourse, and anal intercourse. They used direct observation and film to collect data on overt body reactions such as voluntary and involuntary muscle tension, sexual flush on the skin, perspiration, and respiratory rate. Changes in the primary and secondary sex organs of men and women were recorded in an imaginative way. Because all female sex organs are not visible during intercourse, the research team used an artificial coition machine created for the project. It was equipped with a clear plastic penis containing cold light illumination and photographic equipment capable of recording changes in the vagina and the lower portion of the uterus during sexual intercourse. Standard medical equipment was used to record covert body reactions such as blood pressure and cardiac rates. To aid in their interpretations of these physiological changes, the research team intensively interviewed participants after their sexual experience in the laboratory. (pp. 585, 586)

As Kirby comments,

> Masters and Johnson's laboratory analyses of sexual responses of men and women, both homosexual and heterosexual, are important because they [focused on] what actually happens during sexual stimulation rather than relying only on what respondents think or say happens; and they demonstrated similar physiological responses for both homosexual and heterosexual sexual activity. (p. 586)

To better understand sexual performance among adult Americans, Masters and Johnson also studied clinical samples consisting of patients who came to them for treatment of sexual problems. This work, discussed in *Human Sexual Inadequacy* (Masters and Johnson 1970), shaped the first systematic sex therapy developed in the United States.

Chapter 2

Marital Lifestyles:
Single, Married, and Cohabiting

This chapter begins with a look at singlehood as a lifestyle and some of the pros and cons of being single as compared to married. One boxed section looks more closely at loneliness, a problem people often associate with singles but which affects married persons as well. Individual and societal concerns with dating and mate selection are also addressed. The final section reviews the incidence, causes, and meaning of cohabitation. Given the state's interest in marriage-like relationships, consideration of written contracts for couples who are living together is included.

BEING SINGLE

Being single is the lifestyle that used to be termed "unmarried" and treated as a regrettable state of affairs. In the 1950s, never to marry was generally considered a failure resulting from an individual's shortcomings and inadequacies or misfortune. Later, singlehood emerged as a legitimate lifestyle choice. The women's movement in the 1960s stressed possible self-fulfillment for women by means other than exclusively being a good wife and mother. As women entered the workforce in greater numbers, they no longer had to marry for financial support. Changes in attitudes toward premarital sex in the 1960s and 1970s also meant that singles did not have to marry in order to have sex. Attitudes toward single life shifted, and social conditions changed in ways that supported being single (e.g., availability of apartments, jobs, fast-food restaurants, and entertainment). Sociologist Peter J. Stein (1977, 1981, 1985) has written extensively on single adults, recognizing that singles are an important and growing segment of the U.S. population. The distribution of U.S. households presented in Table 2.1 shows that single persons living alone constituted 25 percent of all households in 1991 as compared to 20.6 percent in 1977 (see Figure 1 in the introduction). Millions of other single adults reside with their children in single-parent households or as unmarried cohabiting couples.

TABLE 2.1. U.S. Household Composition in 1991 (Percent)

Married couples with children present	26
Married couples without children present	29
Other family with children	8
Other family	7
Men living alone	10
Women living alone	15
Other nonfamily	5
	100

Source: Ahlburg and DeVita (1992), p. 6, based on U.S. Census data.

We find single adults in varied circumstances. Many are young singles who will marry but have not yet done so. Another set are previously married, presently divorced. Older singles may be widowers or, more likely, widows, along with a number of lifelong singles. To understand the social context of single adults in the United States, it is useful to examine related trends in average age at first marriage, rates of divorce and remarriage, and the concept of an age cohort.

As Table 2.2 shows, the average age at which Americans enter marriage has been increasing over the past several decades. There seems to be a widespread desire not to let marriage interfere with education and to obtain some work experience before marriage (Thornton and Freedman 1982). By 1995, the median age at first marriage was 24.5 for women and nearly 27 for men. (The median is the middle value; half the persons were older at first marriage, half younger.) At any given time, then, there may be more single adults due to postponement of marriage. Additionally, demographers have noticed a decline in the first-marriage rate. Only a small percentage of adult Americans will never marry, but this minority is increasing (Kennedy 1986).

The likelihood of being single depends on sex, age, and birth cohort. A **birth cohort** is a set of persons who were born during the same period of time. This means that they will also reach later ages together. Birth cohorts are interesting because persons born in different periods of time are shaped by different historical events and population trends. They also differ from other birth cohorts in how they relate to the same historical events. For example, the social movements of the 1960s would have a different effect on persons two, twenty, or sixty years old at that time. Your own birth cohort connects you with millions of other persons born in the same years. You are likely to go through major life transitions such as graduation, first full-time job, marriage, having a child, home buying, and retirement at about the same time as other members of your birth cohort (Kennedy 1986). The choices

TABLE 2.2. Estimated Median Age at First Marriage by Sex from 1950* to 1995

Year	Men	Women
1995	26.9	24.5
1990	26.1	23.9
1985	25.5	23.3
1980	24.7	22.0
1975	23.5	21.1
1970	23.2	20.8
1965	22.8	20.6
1960	22.8	20.3
1955	22.6	20.2
1950	22.8	20.3

Source: U.S. Bureau of the Census, Current Population Reports, Series P20-484, "Marital Status and Living Arrangements: March 1994," and earlier.

*Prior to 1950, from 1890 to 1948, estimated median age at first marriage was declining, from 26.1 to 23.3.

they make provide an important part of the social context in which you will make your own decisions about marriage. Successive birth cohorts may share distinctive values and face unique opportunities or constraints that influence marital and sexual lifestyles.

Consider the 1946-1950 birth cohort. These persons are the first of the **baby boom** generation, born during an increase in the nation's birth rate following World War II. A person born in the late 1940s would reach age fifty in the 1990s. By 1995 the baby boomers were forty-five to forty-nine years of age, old enough to have married, divorced, and remarried. Projections made by the U.S. Social Security Administration, displayed in Table 2.3, indicate how the 1946-1950 birth cohort fared in marital outcomes.

TABLE 2.3. Marital Status in 1995 of 1946-1950 Cohort (Percent)

	Women	Men
Never Married	5	9
Divorced and not remarried	21	12
Widowed and not remarried	2	<1
Married	72	78

Source: Kennedy 1986: 73.

Notice the relatively small percentage of lifelong singles. As this cohort ages further, divorce and death of a partner will add new singles. Though many of these persons will remarry, "older women have less choice than older men about being married because the number of men declines more rapidly with age. After age thirty-five there are not enough never-married, divorced, and widowed men to marry all the unmarried women" (Kennedy 1986: 69), even if all these men wanted to marry. Among more recent cohorts, more than 90 percent still expect to marry, and there has been almost no decline in that proportion since 1960 (Thornton and Freedman 1982). When social surveys investigate issues related to family, a question about "marital status," not "single status," is typically asked. The standard response categories are never married, married, divorced, separated or widowed; all refer to one's situation relative to marriage. It remains true that the majority of individuals in our society choose to enter marriage at some time. As Table 2.1 shows, the combined percentage of all U.S. households in 1991 consisting of a married couple, with or without children present, was 55 percent. Demographers Dennis A. Ahlburg and Carol J. DeVita (1992: 5) compared this figure to 1960, when 75 percent of U.S. households included married couples. U.S. Bureau of the Census projections for the year 2000 suggested that the percentage of U.S. households with a married couple would remain at 55 percent.

Most young people plan to marry and expect their own marriages to be lasting, despite the widely publicized high U.S. divorce rate (Thornton and Freedman 1982). According to Kennedy (1986), the 1980 divorce rate was more than double that of 1965. Of those who divorced, fewer were remarrying. "With more divorces and fewer remarriages, the proportion of divorced and not remarried among all adults in the United States more than doubled between 1965 and 1981 (to seven percent)" (Kennedy 1986: 68). Still, approximately four out of five divorced persons do remarry. According to Stein (1981: 53), this was about five-sixths of the men and three-fourths of the women who divorced. Second marriages have higher rates of divorce than first marriages. Family sociologist Norval Glenn (1997: 5) notes that "about half of all marriages entered into in recent years in this country will end in divorce or separation if recent marital dissolution rates continue."

Demographers predict that between 40 and 65 percent of recent marriages will end in divorce or permanent separation based on analysis of marital outcomes over time for previous cohorts. For example, consider again the 1946-1950 cohort, our first-wave baby boomers. They would have reached the median age for first marriages by the 1970s. What became of these marriages? Of all first marriages entered into during the 1970s, we know from General Social Survey data that 39 percent had already ended in divorce or separation before a fifteenth anniversary (Glenn 1997: 5). While earlier cohorts had lower divorce rates, subsequent cohorts are expected to have divorce rates at least this high. For some of the reasons discussed earlier in the introduction, individuals in our society have become more willing and better able to end unsatisfying marriages. The acceptability of being single is connected with these changing patterns of marriage, divorce, and remarriage.

To summarize, demographic factors related to an increase in the actual proportion of U.S. adults who are single include the following: Most people eventually marry, but the small minority that does not is increasing, and those who marry are doing so at later ages. Men tend to marry later than women. The U.S. divorce rate is high, and while most divorced persons remarry, the minority that does not has increased. Subsequent marriages fail at a higher rate than first marriages, leaving more participants single again. As persons get older, death of a spouse is more common and remarriage is less likely, particularly for women. Along the way, successive birth cohorts display value differences and experience different social pressures.

- Most persons in the United States, at least nine in ten, will marry.
- The minority that does not has been increasing.
- Median age at first marriage has increased.
- Men and women differ in marital timing and opportunity.
- The U.S. divorce rate is high.
- Most persons, up to eight in ten, who divorce will remarry.
- The minority that does not has been increasing.
- Second marriages are less stable than first marriages.
- Age is related to marital status.
- Birth cohort can influence marriage chances.

U.S. society as a whole has moved toward greater acceptance of singles. Being married is still considered positive and desirable, but not necessarily the only valid lifestyle. Some persons are happier being married; some prefer remaining single. The choice can be made today with greater freedom than in the 1950s and early 1960s. It is now possible to examine more objectively the pros and cons, the payoffs and problems of being married and being single. Sociologist Peter Stein (1981) used the concepts of "pulls" and "pushes" for this purpose. **Pulls** (or benefits) are the positive features of a particular lifestyle that attract individuals to it. **Pushes** (or strains) are the negative features of a particular lifestyle that push individuals away toward an alternative. The benefits of being single are the pulls toward singlehood; the strains of being single are pushes toward marriage. The benefits of being married are the pulls toward marriage; the strains of marriage are pushes toward being single. For example, Stein (1981) suggests that security, social position, desire for children, an approved sexual outlet, and love are pulls to marriage. Pressure from family, desire to leave home, fear of independence, discrimination against singles, and loneliness are strains of being single that push people toward marriage. Box 2.1 takes a closer look at the problem of loneliness. Loneliness in marriage can be a push toward singlehood. Other

Box 2.1. Loneliness

Companionship is one of the benefits of marriage. When people discuss the drawbacks of being single, they often mention loneliness. Robert S. Weiss is a social scientist who has tried to better understand its nature and effects. This section reviews some of the ideas presented by Professor Weiss (1981) in "The Study of Loneliness," a chapter in Peter Stein's book *Single Life: Unmarried Adults in Social Context*.

Loneliness has been described as a sufficiently painful and frightening emotional experience that we distance ourselves from it, tending to forget our own past experiences with loneliness and expressing little empathy for others who are lonely. Stereotypes of the lonely can be disparaging, as when such persons are seen as "unattractive," "intentionally reclusive," or "self-pitying"; people who create distance between themselves and others, then feel bad because they are lonely; we feel justified in rejecting them. The assumed solution is to "be pleasant, outgoing, interested in others"; meet people and get involved in social activities. But, "loneliness is not simply a desire for company," (p. 154), Weiss notes; it is a need for emotional connectedness, for particular kinds of relationships. A person can participate in social activities and still feel disconnected. One can be surrounded by people and still feel lonely. Married persons can experience loneliness even in the company of the spouse! Conversely, one can also spend time alone and not feel lonely.

Loneliness can occur with reference to a variety of specific relational deficits: e.g., absence of a mate, meaningful friendships, satisfying ties to co-workers, linkage to a coherent community, or commitment to kin. "Different forms of loneliness respond to different remedies," according to Weiss (p. 158). A perceived need for an intense intimate relationship may not be satisfied by a friendship network, but a sense of social isolation also may not be solved by one exclusive partnership. A married person might be happy with his or her marriage but still feel socially isolated, "lonely." A single person can have satisfying friendships and community attachment but still be "lonely" for one-to-one emotional intimacy. Both types of loneliness are associated with restlessness and yearning; each has unique symptoms as well. Weiss suggests that *emotional isolation* creates distress that resembles childhood fears of being abandoned by one's parents; feelings of anxiety, apprehension, sense of threat, "nameless fear," inner emptiness, and "utter aloneness." A sense of *social isolation* is manifest in boredom, aimlessness, and feelings of marginality or being excluded—like a child who has no one to play with. Other loneliness syndromes may also exist.

How widespread is loneliness? In a national sample, respondents were asked in a telephone interview whether they had felt "very lonely or remote from other people during the last week," and 11 percent said they had.

(continued)

(continued)

Women more often than men reported loneliness (14 percent versus 9 percent), but women may be more willing than men to admit to feelings such as loneliness. Marital status was more important. Among those not married, 27 percent of the women and 23 percent of the men reported severe loneliness in the preceding week as compared to 10 percent of the women and 6 percent of the men who were married. Loneliness was even more prevalent among the widowed (half reported loneliness as a leading problem in their lives). Among the newly divorced, loneliness is also a common negative feeling—even when the divorce was desired.

How might we best deal with loneliness? Marrieds should give continuing attention to shared time and activities, confidences, showing appreciation, affection, etc., to maintain emotional intimacy. Also recognize that not all relational needs can be met by your partner, and this does not mean something is "wrong" with the marriage. Make room for other activities and attachments so neither partner feels socially isolated. Singles should develop and maintain ties with friends and family that provide a sense of emotional intimacy. Do things alone that you enjoy. Nurture yourself. Invest time and energy in work or in meaningful social activities that allow you to feel connected, give you a sense of belonging and making a contribution.

P.S. On friendship and gender roles, Stein (1981: 101) also mentions that "boys and men are taught the value of teamwork and surface good will toward many others. In contrast, women are encouraged to form close, confiding friendships with few others." This may have implications for how men and women typically respond to loneliness.

strains of marriage that push individuals to singlehood to avoid them include unhappiness, boredom, poor communication, and feeling trapped. Freedom, enjoyment, time to develop friendships, self-sufficiency, and economic independence are benefits of being single that serve as pulls toward singlehood. Readers are urged to consider what other items they might add to a list of pros and cons associated with being married and being single.

For single adults, a major source of intimacy is friendship networks, which can provide caring, continuity, and commitment. In his studies of single adults, Peter Stein observed that participating in validating groups helped singles discount remaining social pressures and negative social evaluations of single status. An article by Ralph Keyes (1975), "Singled Out," described some of the difficulties encountered by singles in meeting others with whom to socialize, whether marriage was or was not an objective. Some persons do remain or become single involuntarily; for example, when they cannot find a suitable marriage partner or when a husband or wife seeks a divorce. Whether being single is by choice or necessity influences individual satisfaction with the lifestyle. Since most audiences can readily generate a list of both strains and benefits for being single and for being married, the best advice is the most obvious: Successful adjustment to either lifestyle entails minimizing or compensating for the inevitable strains and taking good advantage of the inherent benefits. The personal appeal or "weight" assigned to the various pros and cons of being married and being single are also apt to shift with time and changing circumstances, so a periodic inventory is appropriate in making decisions related to the element of choice in being married or single.

DATING AND MATE SELECTION

If singles are to meet their needs for intimacy, and if those who wish to marry are to meet up with prospective partners, some social arrangements must exist by which this can be accomplished. As sociologist Ralph Keyes (1975) put it, America's contribution to the world's mating customs is "dating," an approach well suited to a nation of individualists. Singles are left pretty much on their own to seek one another out. Martin King Whyte (1990), sociologist and author of *Dating, Mating and Marriage,* observes that dating "is a curious custom." Because we are so immersed in our own culture, readers may not realize just how curious it is. First, dating is a relatively recent social invention, emerging in the twentieth century in the United States and well established by the 1950s. Second, in other, non-Western cultures, marriages are typically arranged by parents or other relatives, sometimes with assistance of hired matchmakers (Sprecher and Chandak 1992). Third, as Whyte points out, dating has become distinct from courtship, yet it is still expected to help individuals choose a marriage partner. In fact, dating is the primary basis for contemporary mate selection in the United States.

In a traditional non-Western society such as India, arranged marriage has been practiced for a long time, and to some extent the arranged marriage system continues today. In the process of matchmaking in India, the social characteristics of prospective spouses are prominent concerns for parents. They look for compatibility in religion, caste, social class, education, family, and region of the country and, secondarily, consider personal traits such as looks and personality. One is not simply an individual marrying another individual but a representative joining together of two families. In India the dowry system—money or property brought by a bride to her husband at marriage—is illegal today but operates informally in gifts from the bride's family to the bride for her future use in marriage (Sprecher and Chandak 1992). A couple is not required to be "in love"; love will develop as they come to know each other and share a life together over the years. Social researchers Susan Sprecher and Rachita Chandak (1992) surveyed a nonrandom sample of sixty-six young, educated, urban Indians to determine their attitudes toward both the arranged marriage system and Western-style dating. Few of these respondents, only 9 percent, believed that most arranged marriages are stressful and unhappy. Still, they thought that younger people in India now prefer dating and finding their own spouse rather than having arranged marriages.

A film on courtship in four different societies, produced by the National Film Board of Canada (1961), included the case of India as an example of arranged marriage. One of the film's hosts lamented the absence of romance and asked how a couple could possibly have a happy marriage if they were not sure they were compatible, in advance, by spending time together in private. The answer followed along these lines:

1. Individual happiness has not always been the focus of marriage and family life.
2. Historically and cross-culturally, family was not so private and separated from the rest of the community.
3. The idea that a lifelong commitment as important as marriage could be left to the vagaries of a possibly fleeting emotional state such as romantic love seemed ridiculous.
4. Traditional roles for husband and wife provided clear guidelines for how to conduct oneself in marriage.
5. Matching on social characteristics ensured that the couple would share many values in common.
6. They would have the support of parents and other relatives in times of crisis or difficulty.

Even within an arranged marriage system, a boy and girl might know each other fairly well and most parents would be reluctant to force marriage over strenuous objections. In the United States, although dating has gone very far in favor of couple autonomy, parents still attempt to influence their children's decisions.

The Structure and Functions of Dating

Structure-functionalism is a theoretical perspective in sociology that addresses *how society is organized* as a system of interrelated parts (e.g., family, school, church, government, and economy) and *what the various parts contribute* to the operation of this social system as a whole. Particular parts may be well or poorly adapted to the present needs of a society and its individual members. Recall that alternate lifestyles were said to arise when existing social institutions failed to meet individual needs, but individuals tend to maintain social patterns that they find useful. Social systems as a whole depend on participants being motivated to conduct the activities that ensure the continuation of the system—such as mating and child rearing. Individuals are viewed as having goals, but these goals are shaped by social experience and can be met by a variety of possible social arrangements. We act in social context. Societies present individuals with a set of ready-made patterns to follow, ideally meeting both individual and system needs. Dating would be an example of a widely recognized social ritual in our society. In "making a date," individuals have an existing cultural pattern to guide them.

The Structure of Dating

What kind of social arrangement is dating? What patterns of behavior are involved? A "date" occurs when two persons who are attracted to one another arrange to do something together and spend some time interacting, to get better acquainted. Dates have a beginning, a middle, and an end. A date is initiated when one person "asks someone out" and, if the other agrees, they plan where and when to meet. The middle of the date consists of the activities they engage in together; going to a movie, having a drink, talking, eating a meal, going for a walk. The date is over, typically after a few hours, when they part company. The goodnight kiss or handshake is a closing ceremony that is usually accompanied by a statement such as, "I had a good time" or "I'll call you." A date requires negotiation at the end over whether or not there will be future contact because a date, in itself, carries no extended commitment.

Functions of Dating

Functions are the purposes served by a specific social structure.

Considering the needs of society as a whole. First, dating has become the socially approved way in which mate selection occurs. Insofar as arranged marriages are no longer compatible with dominant American values, some alternative mechanism must be provided to allow prospective partners to meet, become better acquainted, assess their compatibility, and plan to marry. Dating, ideally, improves one's choice of a mate. Second, dating assists in the socialization of adolescents and young adults. It provides an opportunity to develop social skills and judgment in short segments of interaction, affording the possibility of making and learning from mistakes. Dating allows rehearsal of social roles that will later be important in marriage. Third, dating is big business. Singles provide a significant economic market for products and services—e.g., clothing, grooming, food and entertainment—that support dating activities. While this does not exhaust the possible societal-level functions of dating, it does convey some idea of what dating contributes to the needs of the larger society.

Considering individual needs. Dating serves quite a variety of goals and needs for individuals. If you ask people to list all the reasons they have ever gone out on a date, the reasons might include any or all of the following, and then some: companionship, affection, social status, ego enhancement, see and do new things, learn about life, entertainment, avoid boredom, revenge, make friends and family happy, expand general knowledge, practice social skills, meet a variety of people, learn more about oneself, find out what one likes or dislikes in other people, have fun, escape other pressures, stay active, sex, romantic experience, acceptance, understand the opposite sex better, get closer to another person, get a free meal, broaden one's outlook. The continuing appeal of dating as a social arrangement may be in part that it is able to accommodate such a wide range of individual goals.

Dysfunctions of Dating

Dysfunctions are negative consequences associated with a particular social arrangement. Even when a social structure is generally effective and contributes positively on balance to a social system, it may be associated with some undesirable consequences or system strains. One might argue, for example, that the high U.S. divorce rate signifies flaws in dating as a means of mate selection, since our choices often prove mistaken, or the failure of dating to socialize young people effectively to be good marriage partners, or both. Individuals involved in dating can also think of negative consequences at the personal level: initial awkwardness, exaggerated role playing, viewing a coarse or outrageous date as a bad reflection on oneself, social pressures to date, date rape, disillusionment, risk of rejection, one person being more interested than the other, partners having different motives for dating, misunderstandings, insecurity, feelings of guilt, distraction, and time and money "wasted."

Connections Between Structure and Function

Structure-functionalists are interested in how the particular ways social behavior is organized promote and/or detract from specific functions served. Dating can be analyzed more closely from this standpoint; how well does it serve its intended purposes, and why? For example, the perceived importance of making a favorable impression in social situations and the way dating essentially involves going *out* to do something contributes directly to dating as an opportunity for businesses to sell related products. The feature of a date that the couple spends time alone together permits the development of intimacy and communication skills. Family sociologists and media commentators have remarked, however, that the process of dating can be misleading, especially with respect to mate selection. Because dating encourages putting our best foot forward and requires only special, limited attentions, a "front" can be maintained. We may not know our partners as well as we think. Further, attributes of a good dating partner do not necessarily coincide with the qualities that will make an effective, long-lasting marriage partner.

Connections Between Dating and Other Aspects of the Social System

Structure-functionalists believe that parts of a social system are interrelated, so we expect dating to reflect in some ways the character and constraints of the society as a whole and of other system parts. What outside social influences affect dating? Several brief examples will give readers an introductory sense. For one, sexual values influence dating. If virginity is valued in a society, sex takes on a different meaning in dating than if sex before marriage is considered appropriate. Second, demographics play a part in determining opportunities and constraints with respect to dating and mate selection. The **sex ratio** refers to the number of males compared to the number of females and can be specified for particular age groups and geographic areas. The sex ratio influences how difficult or easy it is to meet eligible prospects. The scarcer sex is assumed to have more bargaining power. Third, social attitudes toward singles can encourage or inhibit dating. Stereotypes of divorced persons or never-married singles as lonely losers make coming together more uncomfortable. Dating may also be stereotyped as an age-inappropriate activity for elderly singles. Finally, **gender roles** are shared social expectations about men and women; how they think, feel, and should behave. In dating, our conduct reflects these general social understandings in many ways: who initiates the date, who drives, who opens doors, who pulls out the chair, who pays, who decides where to go. Traditionally, it is men. The women's movement in the 1960s challenged many assumptions about sex roles, but some ambiguity and mixed opinions remain about male-female interaction in dating situations. As a thought experiment, picture a dating encounter in which a woman calls a man up for a date, drives to his place to pick him up, brings him flowers, drives with her arm around him while he sits in the middle of the front seat next to her, and pulls his chair out for him at the restaurant, just to be polite. Resistance to these images is one measure of the residual authority of traditional sex roles in dating. For additional differences between men and women in dating, see Box 2.2 on the dating behavior of university students.

Box 2.2. Dating Behavior of University Students

David Knox and Kenneth Wilson (1981), family life educators, published an article in *Family Relations* motivated by their experiences teaching a marriage course at East Carolina University. Their study was designed to answer questions about how students meet dating partners, where they go on dates, what they talk about, how soon they expect sex in a dating relationship, and how much their parents influence their decisions about dating. This section will describe how they investigated these issues and what they found.

(continued)

(continued)

Students in twenty-nine randomly selected classes at East Carolina University were asked to complete a questionnaire (distributed in class) at home, then return it at a subsequent class meeting. The questionnaire included twenty-one closed-ended questions—questions with response categories provided by the researchers—about sex, dating, and parental behavior developed from a previous open-ended pilot study of 100 men and 100 women at the university, in which students could fill in their own responses to similar questions. The final sample consisted of 334 students (227 women and 104 men) who completed the questionnaires; a return rate of 60 percent of the 555 questionnaires initially distributed in class.

How the students in this sample met their current or most recent dating partner is shown below:

	Female	Male
Through a friend	33%	32%
At a party	22	13
At work	12	5
In a class	6	9
Other	27	41

For these students, through friends was a frequent way to meet a dating partner. The "other" category allowed students to fill in additional responses such as "I grew up with him" and "on the school newspaper."

Going out to eat, to a sports event, to a party, and back to his or her room were typical activities for an evening. Regardless of where they were, their relationship was the most frequent topic of conversation and, less often, school and friends. Sex was discussed less than 5 percent of the time.

Students were asked how many dates they felt they should have with a person before it was appropriate to engage in kissing, petting, or intercourse. Kissing on the first date was approved by half the women and 70 percent of the men; 14 percent of both women and men felt kissing could occur before dating. By the fourth date, all but 3 percent of the women considered kissing appropriate. Over three-fourths of the women and one-third of the men felt that petting should be delayed until after the fourth date, but another one-third of the men thought petting should occur on or before the first date. By the fifth date, about one fourth of the women and almost half the men thought intercourse was appropriate.

The respondents in this sample were aware of discrepancies in how much sexual behavior was desired, and how soon, by themselves and their dating partners. Less than 15 percent of both sexes said their dates always shared their understanding of how long people should wait before engaging in kissing, petting, and intercourse. The more emotionally involved a person was in a relationship—from "feeling no particular affection" and "feeling affection but not love" to "being in love" and "engaged"—the more likely increasing levels of sexual intimacy were considered appropriate, particularly by the female respondents. For example, intercourse with no affection was

(continued)

(continued)

seen as appropriate by only 1 percent of the women and 10 percent of the men.

Women in the sample (60 percent) were more likely than the men (40 percent) to report that their parents tried to influence who they dated. The women were also more likely than the men to say it was important to them that parents approve of the kinds of people they date; 20 percent of the men as compared to 10 percent of the women said they did *not* care what their parents thought.

In discussing their results, Knox and Wilson noted that in a large university setting students sometimes have difficulty finding dates. They recommended friendships with same-sex peers as the best way to meet opposite-sex dating partners. They observed that discrepancies continued in what men and women expect on dates, with men generally wanting to kiss, pet, and have intercourse sooner. Parents were seen as still playing a role in mate selection, more so for daughters, by exercising some limited involvement in their dating choices and by encouraging marrying "the right person." Only 25 percent of respondents in this student sample felt "negative" or "very negative" about parental involvement in their dating relationships.

Stages of Dating

Another view of the social structure of dating classifies dating into a set of stages, from casual dating to engagement (DeLora and DeLora 1975). Sociologists Jack R. and Joann S. DeLora identified five stages, presented in modified form in Box 2.3. These stages are not a new idea, but serve to provide a frame of reference acknowledging that not all dating is alike in a structural sense. The nature of the social interaction involved changes as

Box 2.3. Stages of Dating

	Casual	Steadily	Going Steady	Engaged to Be Engaged	Engaged
Goals:	Getting acquainted	Entertainment; enjoyment	Companionship	Trial engagement	Getting ready for marriage
Relationships:	Impersonal; uninvolved; self-interested	Liking; no commitment	Monogamous; emotionally involved; focused on relationship	Add oriented to future	Add making future plans

dating partners move along several underlying dimensions that are used to define the relationship by participants and in the eyes of others.

For example, focus on self versus relationship, exclusivity, present versus future orientation, and degree of emotional attachment are expected to change from stage to stage. Steadily dating means going out with a person on a regular basis while also seeing other persons during the same general period of time. Going steady becomes an exclusive attachment to one person, where the emphasis shifts to the relationship more than each individual, but remains focused on the present. The significance of the engaged-to-be-engaged stage is that the couple here begins to think ahead to possibilities of a longer term commitment and a future together. When couples become engaged, they are formally regarded as "betrothed" and begin making specific plans for their wedding and married life. Positive affect and emotional intimacy are expected to increase through progressive stages. As a model of the process of mate selection through dating, the stages imply that dating moves from initial encounters, if all goes well with a particular couple, to marriage. Although this orientation to dating can be challenged, the model does provoke some interesting questions applied to contemporary dating:

- Since love is accorded considerable significance in our culture, where does love enter into the social structure of dating?
- Where does sex fit? When is erotic intimacy appropriate in dating?
- Dating is sometimes described as initiated and dominated by the male in the first two stages (casual, steadily) and shifting to two-way initiation and equal authority in the later stages (beginning with going steady). To what extent does authority in the relationship change across stages?
- How do couples negotiate the move from one stage to another?
- What rituals, if any, exist to end the relationship at various stages?
- Has dating been modified more recently toward even greater informality? If so, with what effects? (E.g., dating around and going steady may become instead "seeing" and "being with" someone within a larger group of persons who regularly socialize—much as modern dating replaced having suitors and courting)
- Do different stages provide better or worse preparation for marriage than others?
- To what extent does engagement allow couples to rehearse marital roles?
- When is dating "courtship"? (that is, trying to win someone's affections with intention of proposing marriage.)

THEORIES OF MATE SELECTION

Dating can be regarded as evolving into mate selection at some time for most individuals in the United States. Due to the importance of mate selection, scientific study of the family has long given attention to the characteristics of individuals, relationships, social groups, and social forces that move couples toward marriage. Various theories of mate selection have been proposed. A **sociological theory** is a set of related concepts, definitions, and propositions presented to explain some aspect of human society and social behavior. *Concepts* are abstractions, captured in terms such as "gender roles," "functions," or "marital success." *Definitions* of such terms are an attempt to clearly express the intended meanings of the concept. *Propositions* link concepts together in statements of association and, when possible, cause and effect. In other words, propositions give us a theorist's view of how social processes and events are connected. Sociological theories represent explicit, systematic, organized efforts to identify and make sense of expected and observed patterns in social life.

Box 2.4 outlines a few of the ideas that have been studied about how prospective partners come to be attracted to one another. Early "filter models" organized such ideas into a sequence of events or stages that might predict which couples were most likely to marry. For example, Kerckhoff and Davis (1962) suggested that we prefer individuals with social backgrounds like our own *(social homogamy),* then are attracted to the ones whose values agree with ours *(value consensus),* and out of those persons are most likely to marry an individual whose personality "complements" our own *(complementary needs).* Murstein (1970) proposed that out of a relatively open field of eligibles, we are initially attracted to people based on physical appearance, observable abilities, and social status *(stimulus),* then look for shared values *(values),* and finally tend to marry those whose role expectations for dating and marriage are compatible with our own *(role compatibility).* Clayton (1979) described the process as beginning with *propinquity,* which allowed *physical and social attraction* to develop and, if we seized the opportunity for continued interaction, provided for the development of trust, disclosure, and commitment *(rapport),* leading to marriage.

More elaborate and complex theories of mate selection have also been developed. Interested readers are encouraged to refer to texts on theories of family, such as *Family Theories: An Introduction* (Klein and White 1996), *Frameworks for Studying Families* (Winton 1995), *Research and Theory in Family Science* (Day et al. 1995), and *Sourcebook of Family Theories and Methods* (Boss et al. 1993). Family sociologists continue to test, update, and debate the relative merits and limitations of progressive stage theories of mate selection. In the 1980s new "developmental" models also emerged. Catherine Surra (1991) reviewed trends in theorizing about developmental change in heterosexual romantic relationships and studies of how premarital relationships are established and maintained or dissolved. For example, she described how Cate, Huston and Nesselroade (1986) traced courtship pathways based on interviews with a sample of newlywed couples. Two common patterns that appeared were a slow "rocky" path with frequent obstacles and setbacks and a quick-start path with later loss of momentum. Different types of relationship development paths might be associated with different background characteristics of the couple, distinctive features of their relationship at various stages of dating, or other predictors. Research continues along such lines.

Box 2.4. Mate Selection in the United States

In a society where individuals are left largely on their own to find a suitable marriage partner, mate selection becomes an interesting problem. The divorce rate also urges closer examination of how individuals come to select a marriage partner. Family sociologists have proposed and tested various ideas about patterns underlying individual choices. Some examples are outlined below.

Ideal traits. Based on existing values in the society/subgroups to which you belong and your own personal experience, you form an image of the ideal spouse—one who will have the traits you desire.

Complementary needs. Persons with opposite personality traits are attracted to one another.

Social homogamy. Like tends to marry like with respect to social characteristics such as religion, race, education, social class, and age. (Women more often than men marry someone older and more highly educated than themselves and are more likely to "marry up" in socioeconomic status.)

Propinquity. Most people date and marry those they live near, or have other opportunities for repeated contact with. The greater the probability of interaction, the greater the probability of marriage. The greater the "intervening opportunities," the lower the probability of marriage.

Field of eligibles is defined by social norms. In the United States we have a relatively "open field," in keeping with the emphasis on individual choice, but some prospective dates or marriage partners may be viewed socially as more, or less, appropriate than others.

Value consensus. Couples with similar values progress faster toward marriage.

Role compatibility. From verbal and nonverbal cues in the course of dating, you determine whether your partner has role expectations that fit your own regarding male-female relationships in general and marital roles in particular.

(continued)

(continued)

Social exchange. We make rational decisions seeking to maximize our profit (rewards minus costs): Do I want to marry? Will the rewards of marriage outweigh the costs, including the foregone benefits of staying single? Do I want to marry this particular person? How good is he or she? Are other potential spouses available? Should I just risk staying single? In short, individuals will consider what they think they deserve and how appealing they find their various options.

Rationalization. The choice of spouse is essentially irrational; I select a mate for whatever reason, then later try to explain/defend my choice.

Love. Even children's rhymes identify love as a reason for marriage. "First comes love, then comes marriage."

Push and pull factors. Pushes are the pressures pushing us to marry (e.g., pregnancy); punishments for not marrying. Pulls are the positive attractions or anticipated rewards drawing us to marriage (e.g., sex, companionship).

STARTING NEW RELATIONSHIPS

For dating to accomplish its intended purposes, people first need to be able to make initial contact. Even before the turn of the twentieth century, young people in the United States took initiative in meeting eligible individuals, getting acquainted, determining their feelings, and deciding whether marriage was desirable and appropriate, subject to parental approval (e.g., asking a girl's father for her hand in marriage). They might meet at church, informally during everyday community activities, while on trips, or through introductions by friends and family members (Whyte 1992). Some ways singles meet today were not always so available. For example, in earlier eras fewer persons attained higher education, and schools were not coeducational after the elementary level. Leisure time was also more limited. Formal patterns of "calling" on people at home, going to dances, and "keeping company," which were at least partially supervised by family and community members, ultimately gave way to modern dating. Now youth can pair off, make dates via telephone, and go off in cars to spend evenings together. Dating activities are far less closely supervised by parents and peers determine the rules of dating (Whyte 1992). Adolescents have become highly dependent on the peer group for getting dates and tend to date within a peer group system, through personal contacts or friends' recommendations.

Traditional sex role patterns for obtaining dates were clearly defined in the 1950s. Finances and transportation were the boy's responsibility. With few exceptions, the girl was expected to wait until she was "asked out" by a boy. This placed different demands on the two sexes. The choice rested with the boy as to whether the initial step would be taken, making it difficult for some boys to ask for a date because of the possibility of being rejected. For a girl the problem was waiting passively or trying to let a boy know she was interested without seeming too "forward"; that is, chasing him until he caught her. In a "blind" date, arranged by others, both individuals started with an equal noncommitment. For girls, dating posed some unique strains. Given the increasing degree of privacy in dating and a sexual double standard, girls were assigned the role of moral guardian. They would be held responsible for setting limits on "how far" the couple would go sexually. As described by Alix Kates Shulman (1977), the stakes for women were high in "the war in the back seat." Nice girls did not lead on the dance floor, kiss on the first date, go to pool halls, or let boys go too far without risking loss of their good reputations ("respect") and diminishing their marriage chances. When young Americans start dating, though, they are primarily concerned with enjoyment rather than immediate selection of a spouse. "Playing the field" was an ideal for many, based on a developing belief that dating a variety of partners provides a valuable learning experience that would improve later mate selection (Whyte 1990). Extended schooling, growing affluence in the United States, growth of the leisure and entertainment industry, and access to automobiles all supported dating.

College generally provides students with extended opportunities for meeting a variety of different individuals for dating. However, this is not the case for the many individuals of the same age who are not in college. Since few approved agencies exist in the United States through which young people can meet, they are often left to their own devices, which may be ineffective. For some, so few dates may come along that any person who seems reasonably satisfactory will continue to be dated. Such limitations often have the effect of narrowing the market for mate selection. Some individuals may have to make a "forced" choice when marriage is their goal. This means that a particular partner might not have been chosen if more dating opportunities had been available. In short, while dating is a basic requirement for mate selection, social opportunities outside of college for meeting a variety of potential mates are often inadequate. This led to self-help books in the 1980s such as Joyce Jillson's (1984) *The Fine Art of Flirting*. The message was that you cannot meet people if you are sitting alone at home, so "put yourself where the action is": political groups, videocassette rental stores, computer stores, supermarkets, seminars, car washes, fitness centers, and so on.

The search for intimacy goes on in many places. One place is the singles bar. Sociologists Natalie Allon and Diane Fishel (1981) observed the New York City singles bar scene for their article, "Singles Bars As Examples of Urban Courting Patterns." Among their observations were the importance of physical appearance, the prevalence of touching, and the elaborate cues used to single out possible partners. Behavior in the singles bar often demonstrated an eagerness to form a relationship. Gazing with intense eyes, whispering, stroking hair, hugging, kissing, and displaying one's body were cues of readiness to be "coupled." One of the games played was staring; a woman might stare at a man she wanted to meet but would not actually approach. Mutual staring seemed to show that a man and woman were ready to begin their own party. Other games included touching each other—a pat on the shoulder, a hand placed on another's in order to light a cigarette, or an entire body touch. People in singles bars appeared to conform to traditional stereotyped sex roles. Men light women's cigarettes, buy them drinks, offer them bar stools, and so on; the women expect them to behave this way. Though singles bars developed a reputation as a place for "pickup sex," Allon and Fishel found a variety of motivations bringing patrons to the bars, primarily companionship. Reasons given by patrons for seeking out companionship at the singles bars included: intimacy, social integration, nurturing, reassurance, assistance, and guidance. Conversations with bar patrons might, for example, provide compliments, encouragement, shared stories, and useful general information.

Starting new relationships is not confined to singles bars. People meet at churches, colleges and schools, parks, lakes and beaches, sports events, work environments, parties and social gatherings, or ballet, theater, and museums. Social opportunities for singles to meet other singles expanded in the 1970s. With the advent of singles bars, hotels, resorts, country clubs, and apartment complexes, opportunities for singles to meet increased. Many churches have started singles groups. Special interest groups, college classes, and even laundromats provide other places for social interaction and possible coupling. While these settings offer companionship, intimacy, and nurturing for some singles, for many they prove unsuccessful. Barriers to starting relationships in singles bars, for example, include a sex ratio that tends to run 65 percent men, 35 percent women; persons whose physical and personality traits are viewed as undesirable may not attract favorable attention; and you may not encounter persons with whom you have much in common outside the bar (Allon and Fishel 1981).

One alternative is the more formal selection networks described by Davor Jedlicka (1985) and later by Aaron Ahuvia and Mara Adelman (1992):

- *Newspaper networks*—Personal ads sent in to a newspaper, which prints the ads without addresses. Responses are sent to the newspaper, then forwarded.
- *Copublishing networks*—Copublisher sells the magazine and solicits ads for the publisher. Not very discreet; personal information is widely distributed.
- *Go-between networks*—Pay a fee to join, and information is forwarded to a "membership coordinator" who calls and makes arrangements for people to meet. Can be international in scope.

- *Video mating*—Walk in and give an on-camera interview. Persons are then shown videos of others and choose the ones they like. The ones chosen are then shown the video of the person who selected them. If both agree, a meeting is set up.

Possible advantages of using formal networks are that the consequences of initial rejection are less than in face-to-face encounters; singles with children, or too busy to look around, can meet through correspondence networks; explicit expression of a desired type of relationship is facilitated; and the probability of finding a lasting relationship is no worse than in hit or miss face-to-face contacts.

Today, computers offer new possibilities, expanding individuals' range of contacts for dating and mate selection. Computers were originally used by mediating agencies as a sorting device to store records and match applicants' personal characteristics, location, and preferences, based on a relatively small set of predetermined categories. Modern technology provides far greater access to personal computers and new systems of electronic mail, virtual chat rooms, Web sites, and the like. Social research in this arena will be able to address many evolving questions about who is most likely to use such methods of "meeting" others, the benefits and drawbacks to users, the norms surrounding such contacts, how deviance is detected (e.g., exaggeration or misrepresentation of self), the extent to which computer-assisted communication complements or replaces going out as a means of getting acquainted, and how predictive of successful outcomes computer contacts are relative to more traditional procedures.

Comments on Dating

Although dating today may continue over a longer period of time than it did in the first half of the twentieth century, dating has not popularly been viewed as an endless social relationship or as a lifelong alternative to courtship (Whyte 1990). Taking singlehood seriously, though, raises the question whether dating, perhaps along with friendship networks and ties to one's kin, can adequately meet individual needs for intimacy among singles. Dating need not be ultimately "marriage minded." Commentators on dating often advise singles not to date exclusively with mate selection in mind, since this adds too much pressure, but rather emphasize the general benefits. Ralph Keyes' (1975) observations on being single underline the awkwardness and sense of desperation in the "step right up and meet your mate" approach to dating as compared to participation in events involving other singles but with some intrinsic appeal, the "but I'm here for a reason" approach. Catherine Surra (1991: 54), a human ecology professor at the University of Texas at Austin, noted in a 1980s decade review of research and theorizing about mate selection that "understanding heterosexual relationships in the future will require less attention to marital choice and more to the formation and development of romantic relationships generally." Research on "premarital" relationships will be joined with broader interest in nonmarital relationships of short or long duration. Even brief dating encounters can be pleasant and rewarding. They provide an opportunity to exercise one's social skills and validate one's style of relating to the opposite sex. As discussed earlier, dating experiences can expand knowledge, add insight, and maintain self-confidence in coping with sexual and love relationships. Being liked, appreciated, and admired is flattering and a boost to one's morale even when the encounter has no continuity. Dating is a distinctive social context within which to express one's personality and outlook on life outside of work or family relations.

Supposing we grant that dating can enhance single life, questions remain concerning what dating actually contributes to chances of marital success beyond the obvious point of introducing two people to one another. Family sociologist Martin King Whyte mentions in a 1992 article that after decades of research on dating and mate selection, it remains to be tested empirically and convincingly confirmed whether and, if so, in what ways dating promotes successful marriage. His own findings failed to show systematic effects of features of dating such as variety of dating partners, length of engagement, or premarital sexual intimacy. Marital success, defined by marital stability and happiness, was far more closely related to how couples structure their day-to-day marital relations—with respect to elements such as shared decisionmaking, enjoying leisure activities together, and having mutual friends and similar values—than to the partners' previous dating experience. To the extent dating continues to be regarded as a means of mate selection, closer investigation is warranted of the connections between dating experience and later marital adjustment.

Sociologist James Makepeace, widely known for his research on courtship violence, raises another type of concern about dating. Participation in peer-oriented, heterosexual social and recreational activities typically begins during junior high and continues through adolescence during the high school years. Seeking intimacy through dating is a source of stress as well as gratification. According to Makepeace (1997), courtship violence is partially attributable to the frustration experienced when expected rewards and fulfillment are not obtained in dating. Levels of individual maturity and available resources influence choice of coping strategies and effectiveness in managing the strains of dating. At the same time, U.S. society magnifies and publicizes the importance of romantic intimacy in dating and courtship. Jealousy, often implicated in courtship violence, can be construed as anxiety over perceived loss of intimacy and threatened self-esteem. In early dating through high school, adolescents are vulnerable due to insecure personal identities, lack of experience on which to base judgment, emotional immaturity, inadequate self-control, fewer resources, and increasingly permissive social norms regarding sexual expression. Pressure on adolescents can be gauged by the extent to which high school dating is "a car, sex and alcohol-party culture" with minimal adult supervision (Makepeace 1997: 33). With graduation from high school comes heightened social activity (e.g., proms, banquets, and other celebrations), emphasis on emancipation, and major educational and economic transitions that may all add to the social pressures accompanying dating.

Developmental Theories

Analysis of dating can be enhanced by considering the age of participants and their social location in terms of life transitions. Individuals move from infancy through childhood, adolescence, young adulthood, and middle age to old age. **Developmental theories** attempt to describe and account for processes of change through stages over time (Winton 1995; Klein and White 1996). Models of *family* development propose a series of stages in the family life course. One can picture a couple over time going through courtship, being newlyweds, childbearing, parenting (through preschool, elementary, middle school, and teenage years), launching their children, being alone together again, and growing older.* The nature of interactions within the family and between family members and other social institutions is likely to change across these stages. For example, having children influences the marital relationship, brings parents into contact with the school system, and may create conflicts with work. Priorities are altered, and focus shifts over time to new tasks and activities. Families encounter distinctive challenges in successive stages. Poor foundations in earlier stages may weaken the unit's ability to adjust to the demands of later stages. Movement from one stage to another involves important and often difficult *transitions*. Events such as marriage and childbirth, for example, are turning points in individual lives and in "family careers." Sociologist Alice Rossi (1977) discussed the transition to parenthood as compared with marital and work roles. She noted features facilitating or complicating transitions such as abruptness, irrevocability, social pressures and supports, preparation ("role rehearsal"), and adequacy of existing social guidelines. **Roles,** socially shared expectations associated with particular social positions such as "husband," "wife," and "parent," provide directions for individual conduct but are often incomplete, ambiguous, or contradictory. Individuals have to formulate their own sense of themselves as performers during a particular stage and adjust to changes in family structure and social roles over time. Social

---

* Larger social systems can also be examined with the idea of development in mind. Society itself develops over time (e.g., in stages from agricultural to industrial to postindustrial), with implications for the conduct of family life, and broad periods of social change in history both reflect and influence individual attitudes and behavior (e.g., the emergence of dating in the United States as a means of mate selection).

approval and personal happiness depend, in part, on successfully negotiating various stages and transitions.

Change is understood to be continual and ongoing but more conveniently studied in stages. Further, change is *socially recognized* in stages. Such a framework helps organize and make sense of everyday experience. For example, knowing that "all newlyweds go through adjustment problems" (because courtship and dating are not the same as married life) provides encouragement and reassurance; "it's just a stage." Klein and White (1996: 127) say that the "sociological meaning of development is in traversing normatively expected family events." In other words, development does not necessarily imply a universal invariant timetable, but members of a particular culture do typically share some beliefs about the proper timing and sequencing of major life events. Exceptions include events that are *out of sequence,* as in the case of premarital pregnancy, or *off time* with respect to chronological age, as when divorced persons take up dating again. Individual departures from expected sequencing or timing are sometimes idiosyncratic but are also sometimes influenced by changing structural conditions, as when job market conditions delay "launching" of young adults. When many individuals are affected by changing social pressures or opportunities, social scientists may detect patterned deviations. This is illustrated by an article in the journal *Family Relations* addressing a new type of family in which parents delay childbearing until after age thirty-five (Garrison et al. 1997).

Criticisms of early developmental models include the observation that the identified stages focus on the traditional U.S. nuclear family unit. Doing so neglects the impact of divorce and subsequent remarriage (Aldous 1990). Today, family theorists argue that multiple paths may be taken: "individual families are seen as taking different routes as they change over time" (Winton 1995: 9). Family development is not precisely parallel to the biological stages of individual life insofar as critical decisions are made along the way, and events occur that may change one's family career path in entering, continuing, or exiting family relationships. Persons can, for example, choose to stay single lifelong; unmarried persons can give birth; and married couples can decide, voluntarily, to be childless. Developmental perspectives applied to marital and sexual lifestyles remain useful in identifying systematic variations connected with different stages of development. They assume that social systems change over time in regular, somewhat predictable ways. Demarcation of periods in family life suggests that different families will experience similarities at shared stages and transitions, and the same family will undergo significant transformation over time. Following a life course perspective, we can look at "how varying events and their timing in the lives of individuals affect families in particular historical contexts" (Aldous 1990: 573). Without being wedded to a single track of family development, we can use models of stages and transitions to link the chronology of the family as a social group with individual biography and with history.

Winton (1995: 9) credits the Greek philosopher Heraclitis with the observation that "a person can never step into the same river twice." A family will be the same people but also not the same over time and, to return to singles' issues, dating is similar but not identical at different life stages. Single parents who date have unique difficulties that arise because dating is now out of sequence. In addition to practical problems of finding time and paying for child care, their children are confronted with the finality of the parental breakup, may become attached to temporary partners, can feel jealousy over sharing their already limited time with a working single parent, or have difficulty coping with a parent's sexuality newly expressed in dating. Older singles are off time for dating following death of a spouse. Physically, aging violates the youth-oriented U.S. standard of beauty and sexiness that shapes notions of attractiveness in dating. Elder women also have fewer available exclusive partners. Emotionally, widows and widowers can feel guilty or disloyal to the lost spouse if they enjoy dating. Greater awareness of mortality may encourage intimacy or, conversely, heighten a sense of risk in getting close (another loss). Clearly, the meanings and "stakes" involved in dating differ at different ages and stages in life.

Cohabitation

Increasing diversity in marital and sexual lifestyles in the United States is reflected in another pattern among singles that has received much attention from family researchers and demographers: namely, cohabitation. **Cohabitation** involves two unrelated, unmarried adults living together, sharing household responsibilities and having a sexual relationship. Essentially, a habitat is where an organism lives. *Co*habitation means shared living quarters. In the sense of sharing a household, married persons typically cohabit. Other households consist of unmarried persons living together who are not sexually intimate and may be related or not (e.g., roommates). When we talk about cohabitation as an alternate lifestyle, however, we are referring to something else. Since the U.S. Bureau of the Census (1996: 56) also defines unmarried couples as "two unrelated adults of the opposite sex sharing the same household," here we will be talking only about heterosexual relationships.

Like different types of singles, there are different types of cohabiting relationships. Many, especially among younger adults, involve two never-marrieds, but cohabitation can also involve the formerly married living with a never-married person or another formerly married person. Correspondingly, social researchers have looked at age and marital status of cohabitants. Among cohabitants who have never been married, the large majority will be under age thirty-five; previously married cohabitants are, roughly, as likely to be age thirty-five to fifty-four or over fifty-five as under age thirty-five (Stein 1981). Some of the reasons for cohabiting will be the same in these groups; some may be different. Previously married persons are more apt to have familial and financial complications that may make them hesitate to remarry. Based on data showing that 60 percent of people marrying recently for the second time reported cohabiting either with their spouse or someone else before their second marriage, Seff (1995: 145) suggests that "people who have been married before are opting for cohabitation prior to remarriage."

The total numbers of unmarried couples in the U.S. from 1970 to 1995, according to the U.S. Bureau of the Census (1996: 56), are presented in Table 2.4. Recent volumes of the Statistical Abstract of the United States also break down the total figures for unmarried couples by age of "householder" (adult listed first on the census questionnaire, in whose name the home is owned or rented). In 1995, 20 percent were under twenty-five, 60 percent were twenty-five to forty-four, 15 percent were forty-five to sixty-four, and 5 percent were sixty-five or older. One or more children under fifteen were present in 36 percent of the total 3,668,000 unmarried couple households.

These figures raise some interesting points about interpretation of statistics concerning marital and sexual lifestyles. Clearly, the total number of cohabiting couples has increased dramatically, from half a million in 1970 to over 3.5 million in 1995. (Today over 4 million couples are cohabiting.) During this time, the population of the United States has also grown. Increases in absolute numbers of participants in a particular lifestyle may not signify an increase in its popularity relative to other options if due simply to increasing numbers of persons in the United States. Looking at the number of cohabiting couples as a percentage of the overall U.S. resident population suggests that this alone does not explain the increase in cohabitation. However, the overall population figures refer to persons of all ages, but cohabiting couples consist of two unmarried *adults*. To determine the relative at-

TABLE 2.4. Estimated Total Number of Unmarried Couples and Percentage of Resident Population in the United States, 1970-1995

	Number of Couples	Percentage	Population
1970	523,000	2.5	(203,984,000)
1980	1,589,000	7	(227,225,000)
1985	1,983,000	8	(237,924,000)
1990	2,856,000	11.5	(249,403,000)
1995	3,668,000	14	(262,755,000)

Source: U.S. Bureau of the Census 1996: 56.

tractiveness of cohabitation as a lifestyle, what comparisons are most revealing? Should we think of it as a choice made by some single adults as compared to single adults living alone, or as a choice made by heterosexual couples who decide not to be married as compared to married couples?

For an idea of how statistics regarding cohabitation might look in several different comparisons, consider the following figures provided in a *Population Bulletin* prepared by Paul C. Glick and Arthur J. Norton (1979). In 1977, cohabitants were estimated to be:

- Less than 1 percent of total U.S. population (216 million population)
- 3.6 percent of unmarried adults (53 million unmarried adults)
- 1.3 percent of all households (74 million households)
- 2.0 percent of all couple households (48 million couple households)

Notice that the overall population is distributed across a smaller number of households, of which only a portion are couple households, and of all persons in the U.S. population only a portion consists of unmarried adults. In any one year examined, the same absolute number of cohabitants constitutes a different percentage depending on which comparison is being made.

Stein (1981: 191) reported that "some 2.3 percent of all couple households are unmarried men and women living together. In 1978 there were 1,137,000 (twice as many as in 1970). This was an 8x increase for couples under 25, 6x for couples under 45." The very striking increases in cohabitation in the 1970s and thereafter warrant another caution. Bear in mind how small a percentage of all couple households and of all unmarried adults cohabitants were to begin with. Small percentages have room for increases of large magnitude. By contrast, could the *percentage* of persons in the United States who ever marry double or triple in your lifetime? Considering that this figure is already about 90 percent, no! Percentages that are already large will not show the same kinds of dramatic increases seen for smaller figures. This simple principle is important for evaluating reports of changing lifestyles.

Another point is raised by an update on cohabitation presented at the 1995 annual meeting of the Population Association of America by demographers Larry Bumpass and James A. Sweet from the University of Wisconsin at Madison, based on data from the comprehensive longitudinal National Survey of Families and Households for 1992-1994. As reported by *Population Today* (1995), they found that 47 percent of people between twenty-five and forty-four cohabited *at some time,* up from the 1987-1988 figure of 37 percent, but the proportion of people cohabiting *at any one time* is smaller; closer to 10 percent for most age groups and one-fifth of twenty-five to thirty-nine-year-olds who are unmarried. These figures serve as a more general reminder that there are two ways to look at most marital and sexual lifestyles. One is based on numbers currently involved in a lifestyle; another reflects how many have ever tried the lifestyle or behavior. For example, individuals may try cohabitation and after a time move out or marry rather than remaining in this particular cohabiting relationship. More persons have tried cohabitation than are cohabiting at any given point in time.

To review several commonsense guidelines for interpreting descriptive statistics on marital and sexual lifestyles:

- Differences in reported percentages may reflect differences in the base used to compute a percentage. To clarify, determine percentage *of what.*
- Lifestyles that involve a small percentage of persons participating are more likely to show dramatic increases. To clarify, consider how large or small percentages are to begin with.
- Smaller percentages will be associated with the proportion of persons or households currently engaged in a particular behavior or lifestyle than percentages for having ever tried it. To clarify, confirm which applies to the percentage in question.

In studying marital and sexual lifestyles, one will be confronted with an imposing array of statistics. As discussed in Chapter 1, variability in figures reported may be due to how events such as cohabitation are defined by different researchers, the specific questions used to gather information about such events or lifestyles, and the types of samples being described. Persistence and educated questions can help clarify shifting and seemingly contradictory statistics in order to obtain a reasonably accurate working understanding of the dimensions of a given lifestyle. Private worries and public debates often rest on assumptions about how many people or what "kinds" of people participate in various lifestyles. Both in determining social policy and in making personal decisions, some basic knowledge of prevalence and trends is valuable. Whatever our quarrels may be with particular cohabitation statistics, it remains true that in absolute numbers and in a variety of different percentage comparisons, cohabitation has become more visible as a lifestyle. This has led to interest in the motivation of cohabitants, effects of cohabitation, and just how cohabitation fits into the larger framework of available choices.

In one early exploratory study of cohabitation, sociologist Eleanor Macklin looked at attitudes and involvement in cohabitation among college students, defining cohabitation as "sharing a bedroom at least four nights a week, at least three consecutive months, with a person of the opposite sex" (Macklin

1975: 292). Cohabitation was fairly well accepted in her sample of students from several classes at Cornell University. Of the eighty-six students (juniors and seniors) responding to her survey, twenty-nine (34 percent) had already cohabited, though 80 percent thought their parents would disapprove. What was the outcome of such relationships? In Macklin's sample, of the reported cohabiting relationships, one-third had already dissolved (lasting an average of four and one-half months), one-third of the couples were married or engaged, and another one-third were still in the process of defining their relationship. College students' experience of cohabitation mirrored the academic calendar and their unique social circumstances. How typical were Macklin's students of other cohabiting couples? Surveys of 355 students in eight sections of my own marital and sexual lifestyles classes from 1991 to 1997 showed that 36.9 percent had cohabited and 68.6 percent had either cohabited or "would cohabit," indicating their level of personal acceptance of this type of arrangement. For cohabiting couples in general, Stein (1981) indicated that they tend to stay together a relatively short time; about 63 percent for less than two years. Seff (1995: 147) noted that 59 percent of cohabiting couples continue to live together after one year, without marrying or breaking up; 33 percent remain after two years; and 9 percent last five or more years. About 25 percent of all first-time cohabiters will marry within the first year; half within three years.

Why the increase in cohabitation? Paul Glick and Graham Spanier (1980, 1981) suggested the following reasons for the increase in cohabitation they initially found in U.S. Census data, especially among young couples without children present.

Social Trends

- Greater tolerance of varied living arrangements and of premarital sex
- Changing sex roles, so women feel more independent and comfortable with cohabiting relationships (not "ruining their chances" for marriage)
- Postponement of marriage
- Financial considerations: increased cost of living ("two can live as cheaply as one")
- Larger cohort (of baby boomers) passing through their twenties and thirties
- More honest reporting

Personal Motivations

- For those who do not want children and do not see marriage as a prerequisite for sexual experience
- For those who experience loneliness as singles but do not feel ready for long-term commitment
- Provides companionship, emotional sharing, financial assistance, help with chores
- An opportunity for increased emotional maturity, self-understanding, relationship skills, and self-confidence
- Allows an affectionate monogamous live-in arrangement, more open than marriage

Early studies already began to raise questions about the meaning of cohabitation. Should we think of it as a trial marriage or as an alternative to marriage? Is cohabitation undermining marriage values, or is it simply a new stage in dating? The majority of cohabitation arrangements do not appear to be trial marriages in the sense of leading directly to marriage with a particular partner, but are experiments with marriage-like relationships, presumably providing greater understanding of self and relationships and a better basis for decisions about future partners. Not just about premarital sex, cohabitation is a lifestyle resembling marriage in many, though not all, ways. What do people want from cohabiting? What are the relative pros and cons, as compared to being single and living alone or to being married? Generally speaking, participants try to capture some of the benefits of a marital relationship without the commitment. This also distinguishes cohabitation from true trial marriage, because the goal is not necessarily marriage. Additionally, many couples describe the initiation of their living together more as a gradual drifting from dating into cohabitation out of convenience rather than a deliberate change in the relationship.

Ronald Rindfuss and Audrey VandenHeuvel (1990) examined data from a longitudinal national study of the high school class of 1972, which followed respondents through 1986, in order to address the question of whether cohabitation is an extension of courtship and precursor to marriage or an alternative to marriage for singles. They compared the behaviors and expectations of cohabitants with both single and married persons within a larger sample of 12,841 young adults (up to age thirty-two by 1986 follow-up) who had never married or were still in their first marriage. This sample did not have a sufficient number of African Americans to include in the analysis and was also limited in not including high school dropouts (who have higher rates of cohabitation). The operational definition for cohabitation was living in an intimate relationship with an unrelated adult of the opposite sex for at least a month. Rindfuss and VandenHeuvel (1990) looked at fertility expectations, marriage plans, work and school activities, and home ownership. Their findings included the following:

- Among those who had not yet had any children, cohabitants were closer to singles than to marrieds in the percentages intending to have a child within two years (5 percent of singles, 12 percent of cohabitants, and 15 percent of married persons).
- Among those who had never married or cohabited before, the probability of cohabitation in the next twelve months was unrelated to marriage plans.
- Among never marrieds, cohabitants were more likely than those not cohabiting to be planning marriage (26 to 44 percent versus 12 to 16 percent), but the majority in each group was not planning to marry in the next twelve months. "Typically, about 2/3 of the cohabiters do not have immediate marriage plans, arguing against the interpretation that cohabitation is equivalent to being engaged" (p. 711).
- An interesting note on marriage plans was that 3 to 5 percent of those who had no plans to marry within the next twelve months were actually married a year later, while around 42 percent of those who planned to marry within the next twelve months were still single a year later.
- From 1973 to 1985, percentage enrolled in school was typically highest for singles, lowest for marrieds, and intermediate for cohabitants, suggesting that the student role was more compatible with cohabitation than with marriage (p. 714).
- Cohabiting women were much less likely to be full-time homemakers than were married women.
- Cohabitants were much more likely to rent a house or apartment than to own their own home (80 percent of the married respondents versus about one-third of singles or cohabitants in 1985).

On the whole, Rindfuss and VandenHeuvel found cohabitants in their sample consistently intermediate between those who were single and those who were married, but more similar to the singles. Social researchers Robert Schoen and Robin Weinick (1993) also favored interpretation of cohabitation as a distinctive type of relationship rather than an informal marriage. No formal ceremony similar to a wedding marks the beginning of cohabitation, and it is still unusual to speak of "cohabitation plans" in contrast to "marriage plans." Cohabitants are also more likely to describe themselves as singles than as married (Rindfuss and VandenHeuvel 1990). Persons who cohabit have less traditional sex-role attitudes than noncohabitants, and are generally less likely to hold traditional family values (Bumpass 1990). As related to single life, cohabitation is more permissible now due to liberalization of values concerning premarital sex and, given both the amount of time some dating couples already spend with one another and the time, money, and emotional resources needed to sustain dating a variety of partners, it "may simplify their lives to share a dwelling unit" regardless of level of commitment to permanency (Rindfuss and VandenHeuvel 1990: 706, 707).

Sociological researchers continue to study and debate the meaning of cohabitation. One initially unexpected finding, now well documented, is that persons who cohabit before marriage have *higher* rates of divorce than those who did not. The extent to which this is due to cohabitation itself, the types of persons who are attracted to cohabitation ("selection"), or other factors is still contested (Brown and Booth 1996). In attitudes, cohabiting individuals are more likely to accept sex before marriage and to endorse nontraditional sex roles. If they marry, they tend to do so at later ages and are less willing to accept unsatisfactory marriages. They value individual freedom and independence. Such value orientations among persons attracted to cohabitation may well put their subsequent marriages at higher risk of dissolution. Married couples, and even long-term cohabitants, must be willing to compromise and able to effectively balance individual needs with relationship requirements. Marriage, moreover, is a distinctive social status with additional expectations beyond living together; cohabiting couples may underestimate the necessary adjustments. Among married couples who previously cohabited with one another will also be those who did so because of reservations about the partner or relationship in terms of personal, social, or economic circumstances that may ultimately be related to their marital breakup.

The changes in U.S. social structure and ideology that brought greater participation in premarital sex, delay in first marriage, shifts in women's roles, and higher rates of divorce are also connected to cohabitation. Despite the impression sometimes given that cohabitation itself is a cause of subsequent marital instability, it makes more sense that both are responses to similar social forces. Larry Bumpass, a past president of the Population Association of America, observed in 1990 that the historical shift in the United States toward *secular individualism* has influenced many aspects of marriage and family. As individual choice and romantic love gained ascendancy as a basis for marriage, and some of the practical considerations motivating earlier generations decreased in importance (Hendrick and Hendrick 1992), dissolution of unsatisfactory marriages became more accepted. Marriage delays, too, in part reflect pursuit of other individual (but socially approved) goals related to education and career that compete with attention to family and personal relationships. Young adults deferring marriage are more likely to be premaritally sexually active; acceptance of premarital sex permits delay of marriage. For previously married persons, the experience of a "bad" marriage, subsequent divorce, residual responsibilities, and changing demographics leave individuals less willing or able to marry but not without interest in intimate relationships. Accordingly, if living with someone of the opposite sex is more rewarding than living alone, single individuals should not be restricted from doing so, regardless of their marital intentions. By contrast, research generally finds more religious persons less likely to participate in premarital sex or nonmarital cohabitation and to have lower rates of divorce. Overall, religious persons tend to favor more traditional family values.

One concern prospective cohabitants should have is that, like dating, cohabitation attracts persons with a variety of motives and goals. Based on data from the National Survey of Families and Households, social demographers Larry Bumpass, James Sweet, and Andrew Cherlin (1991) reported that when both partners in a currently cohabiting couple were asked about marital expectations, nearly one-fifth of the couples disagreed on whether they would marry. The uncertainty and ambiguity of cohabiting relationships is potentially a source of conflict between partners, which is one of the explanations offered for the higher rate of violence observed among cohabiting couples than among those who are married or dating regularly (Makepeace 1997). Makepeace suggests that cohabiting couples share some of the same frustrations as dating or courting couples and in addition are susceptible to conflicts over housekeeping, meals, noise, furnishings, space, bills, and entertaining. Cohabitants also express more concerns than married couples over the stability and quality of their relationship (Bumpass, Sweet, and Cherlin 1991). While cohabitants generally report poorer relationship quality than their married counterparts, according to sociologists Susan Brown and Alan Booth (1996: 668), the relationship quality of cohabitants with plans to marry was not significantly different from that of married couples. Relationship quality will influence the emotional well-being of participants and the likelihood that a couple will break up. Cohabitants themselves may have difficulty assessing the quality of their union because shared social standards (*norms*) for what an ideal cohabitation relationship should be like are lacking.

Legal Aspects of Cohabitation

Individuals entering cohabiting relationships do not do so entirely by themselves, completely free of outside scrutiny. Because the family is a basic unit of society, society has a special interest in marriage and family relationships. In the United States, state-level governments establish rules, enacted in family codes, for the conduct of marriage and family within their separate jurisdictions. Marriage is a distinctive status, "with social and legal implications. . . . The active participants, the prospective husband and wife, do not always realize the state's concern with and control over their marriage" (Jentz 1992: 3). Society's interest extends to cohabitation, which is a marriage-like relationship. Cohabitation as a legitimate and desired non-marital arrangement is relatively new. Historically, cohabiting couples lacking only an official ceremony could be recognized as having a common-law marriage. **Common-law marriage** means that based on custom or court decision, a relationship is given legal standing as a marriage even where no official marriage ceremony has ever taken place. Given that some contemporary cohabitants may wish to be extended the legal benefits of marriage while others cohabit precisely to avoid the legal status of marriage, individual cohabitants are at risk of having their intentions contradicted by the state. Not every instance of a man and woman living together will be construed as a common-law marriage, but where states recognize common-law marriage, it is a lawful marriage with all the accompanying rights and obligations of both parties, and can only be dissolved by death or divorce (Speer 1961).

Texas is one of only thirteen states that recognize common-law marriage. (Duff and Truit [1991] list Alabama, Colorado, Georgia, Idaho, Iowa, Kansas, Montana, Ohio, Oklahoma, Pennsylvania, Rhode Island, South Carolina, Texas, and the District of Columbia.) The idea that six months together makes a common-law marriage is a myth! According to *Speer's Marital Rights in Texas* (Fourth Edition), Texas law provides three guidelines for determining common-law marriage:

- The couple agree to marry.
- They live together "as husband and wife."
- They represent to others that they are married.

An offer or promise to marry can be regarded as a contract, one that "need not be expressed in any formal language, either written or spoken, . . . if a preponderance of the evidence shows that the parties had mutually agreed to marry each other" (Speer 1961: 96). The fact that a couple lives together and represents themselves to others as married, in effect being married in both "habit and repute," may be used to infer an agreement to marry absent evidence to the contrary. Courts in Texas have also recognized that living together without matrimonial intention for reasons of "economy, convenience or lust" does not create a marriage (Speer 1961: 46, 47). Many other states officially view common-law marriage as "undermining the stability and sanctity of marriage," and some states have statutes criminalizing nonmarital cohabitation: Idaho, Florida, Illinois, Michigan, Mississippi, New Mexico, North Carolina, North Dakota, Virginia and West Virginia (Seff 1995).

Texas Family Code pertaining to "certain informal marriages" specifically provides that marriage of a man and a woman may be proved by evidence that "they agreed to be married, and after the agreement they lived together in this state as husband and wife and there represented to others that they were married" (*Texas Family Code* 1996: 8). Regarding termination of an informal marriage, it is rebuttably presumed that the parties did not enter into an agreement to marry if a proceeding to prove marriage is not commenced within two years after the parties separated and ceased living together (*Texas Family Code* 1996: 8). If couples live together, then separate without disagreement, the courts take no notice, but if either party takes legal action, the courts will be involved in defining their respective rights and obligations. This may come as an unwelcome and unexpected result for a cohabiting partner who sought to avoid the commitment of marriage. Complainants, in turn, cannot be certain the court will uphold their claims and may rightly feel exploited after investing many years in a cohabiting relationship. Some cohabiting situations will be deemed meretricious (illicit and unsanctioned); for example, if it involves a married person cohabiting with someone other than the spouse or is interpreted as an exchange of sex for economic benefit or when state law prohibits unmarried cohabitation. In hearing claims, the courts can nevertheless invoke other standards—e.g., of partnerships, trusts, and contracts—to reach equitable decisions on earnings and asset distribution. Both express and implied contractual relationships may be evaluated (Jentz 1992: 22) but outcomes vary.

"Palimony" suits, like the first, involving Lee Marvin and Michelle Triola in the late 1970s, also demonstrate the need for couples to give closer consideration to the possible legal implications of cohabitation. One trend is greater use of written contracts for living together. It is potentially an advantage to have a documented explicit agreement between the parties involved as to their mutual expectations and intentions. Apart from legal issues, discussing the terms of such a contract forces couples to think through their relationship more carefully and make plans together. Of course, a cohabiting contract may not seem "romantic," plans are subject to change and there is no guarantee that all the provisions would be upheld in court. Cohabitation is presently an area of changing norms and legal uncertainty. A sample nonmarital cohabitation agreement, concerned primarily with property rights, is provided in Box 2.5. The names used are fictitious. Every situation will be different, so there is no one example that would cover all possible circumstances. Read it to get a feeling for the perspective of the legal system, *not* as a how-to guide. Notice that it explicitly expresses the desire of the cohabiting partners that their relationship not be covered by family law and states their intention not to be married, either ceremonially or informally.

Formal contracts for living together are best drawn up with the help of an attorney experienced in family law, again, keeping in mind that this aspect of legal practice is relatively new and in flux. Fees, averaging from $150 to $750, vary with the amount of time it takes to produce the document,

Box 2.5. Sample Cohabitation Agreement

For educational purposes only, not to be duplicated.

NONMARITAL COHABITATION AGREEMENT

This agreement was made by and between JOHN DOE of [City, County, State] and JANE SMITH of [City, County, State], hereinafter collectively referred to as "the parties."

RECITALS

WHEREAS, the parties to this agreement are a man and a woman who desire to live together without the benefit of matrimony, to divide only their homemaking expenses and responsibilities, and to keep as their respective separately owned property, their individual earnings, income, and separately acquired property; and

WHEREAS, the parties do not intend to marry either ceremonially or informally in the foreseeable future, and they do not intend their nonmarital relationship to be governed by the [State] Family Code;

IT IS THEREFORE AGREED;

I.

The following described property and property acquired therewith shall remain the separately owned property of JOHN DOE, to wit: (list)

II.

The following described property and property acquired therewith shall remain the separately owned property of JANE SMITH, to wit: (list)

III.

All property acquired by gift, bequest, devise, descent, with the rents, issues, and profits thereof shall be the separately owned property of the party who acquires it.

IV.

All earnings, incomes, salaries, and commissions generated by each of the parties, and all property acquired therewith, shall remain the separately owned property of the party who generated it.

V.

This agreement shall terminate upon the earliest occurrence of either the ceremonial marriage of the parties performed pursuant to a valid marriage license issued by one of the fifty (50) United States, or upon thirty (30) days written notice personally delivered by one party to the other.

(continued)

(continued)

VI.

This agreement is made in consideration of the mutual promises of the parties to each other contained herein.

VII.

If any legal action is brought by either of the parties to enforce any provision of this agreement, the parties agree that the prevailing party shall be entitled to recover reasonable attorney fees and costs from the other party.

VIII.

Each party to this agreement warrants that he or she has made a full and complete disclosure to the other party of the nature, extent, and probable value of all his or her property, estate, and expectancy. However, each party to this agreement acknowledges that the mutual promises and covenants contained herein are not dependent upon such full disclosure, and that failure to disclose the nature, extent, and probable value of other property owned by either party shall not be the basis for this agreement nor make it unenforceable.

IX.

Each party to this agreement acknowledges that he or she has consulted an attorney of his or her choice, or has had an opportunity to consult an attorney of his or her choice. Moreover, each party to this agreement acknowledges that he or she has read the agreement, and is executing this agreement knowingly, voluntarily, and without reservation.

X.

This agreement supersedes any and all other agreements, either oral or written, between the parties relating to their rights and liabilities arising out of a nonmarital relationship. This agreement contains the entire agreement of the parties.

XI.

If any provision of this agreement is held by a court of competent jurisdiction to be invalid, void, unenforceable, the remaining portions shall, nevertheless, continue in full force and effect without being impaired or invalidated in any way.

XII.

This agreement may be amended or modified only by a written instrument signed by both parties.

(continued)

(continued)

XIII.

This agreement shall be governed by, and construed in accordance with the laws of the State of _____.

SIGNED on this _____ day of _____, year.

_____
JOHN DOE

_____
JANE SMITH

THE STATE OF:

COUNTY OF:

This agreement was acknowledged before me on the _____ day of _____, year, by JOHN DOE.

_____
NOTARY PUBLIC, STATE OF:

THE STATE OF:

COUNTY OF:

This agreement was acknowledged before me on the _____ day of _____, year, by Jane Smith.

_____
NOTARY PUBLIC, STATE OF:

SAMPLE, only for educational purposes – not to be duplicated.

depending on the complexity of the case; e.g., houses, investment portfolios, debts, careers, children. Attorney Terry Leedy of Arlington, Texas, suggests that, in general, the main issues are financial obligations, property rights, and children. Comingling of assets (e.g., joint purchases) without considering what happens if the couple breaks up often leads to problems later. This may be as simple a question as who gets the stereo, favorite albums, bookcase, dishes, or "custody" of a pet. Attorney Leedy observes that young never-marrieds, particularly, tend to "see the relationship going in but not coming out." Since most of these cohabitation arrangements will not last, it is appropriate to discuss potential problems early on, including how to handle an unplanned pregnancy. For more on cohabitation agreements, see a brief article by Barton E. Bernstein (1985), "So Put It in Writing."

Finally, cohabitation provides an interesting view of social change and the relationship between the social institutions of law and family. "One underlying theory of the common law tradition is that the principles of law are determined by the community's social needs and are adapted to new conditions as society changes" (Seff 1995: 142). How well have legal policy and practice kept up with the increase in nonmarital cohabitation? The law has lagged behind changes in social norms and actual practice in this area. "Since state laws have not established cohabitation as a legal relationship, the rights of cohabitors have been established through court decisions" (Seff 1995: 141). In Texas, Jentz (1992: 17) observed, the courts have dealt with nontraditional relationships on a case-by-case basis. Each state formulates its own family law, which is interpreted and applied in a particular court on a given day in response to the unique complex of facts presented in each case.

Cohabitation generally poses a dilemma for the courts insofar as it appears to undermine formal marriage. As family sociologist Monica Seff points out, if the state seeks to promote marriage and family and is concerned with social stability, long-term marriage-like relationships should perhaps be recognized as legitimate unions. At the same time, single individuals who do not wish to be married should be protected, but failure to uphold implied contracts may also lead to injustices for participants in cohabiting arrangements. Is the proper role of the law to continue to enforce traditional definitions of marriage, and can the courts effectively do so? The courts themselves (e.g., in the California Supreme Court's decision on the *Marvin v. Marvin* case) acknowledge difficulties in applying traditional moral standards that have been "so widely abandoned by so many" (Seff 1995: 154). So the statistics and debates about cohabitation as a stage of courtship, a "loosely bonded" informal marriage, or something new are certainly relevant. Neither social scientists, legislators, nor the public seem quite certain thus far what to make of cohabitation.

Chapter 3

Sex and Singles

PREMARITAL SEX: ATTITUDES AND BEHAVIORS

Sex and singles became an increasingly important concern as the average age at first marriage and the divorce rate in the United States increased, leaving more persons single for longer periods of time. During the first part of the twentieth century, there had been an increase in premarital sexual *behavior* but little change in expressed *attitudes*. Premarital sex was still considered sinful, wrong, unhealthy, and even abnormal, especially for women. It was generally disapproved of, still taboo and largely hidden. During the 1960s, social change was more pervasive and more visible as social movements such as the civil rights movement, the antiwar protest ("make love not war") and the women's liberation movement struggled to change social norms. Effects included changed perceptions of sex, marriage, and family relations, and of male and female social roles more broadly. Public attitudes toward premarital sex became more liberal. Abortion was legalized and a new birth control method, the Pill, was made widely available. This gave women greater choice in sexual behaviors and reproductive outcomes, and more direct control over their bodies and futures, heralded by publication and distribution of *Our Bodies, Ourselves* by the Boston Women's Health Book Collective (1971). By the mid-1970s, surveys were tracking an increase in women's sexual activity, particularly among college students. As a result, the sexual gap between men and women narrowed. Changing attitudes in the 1960s were translated into further changes in behavior as time went on. The longer term historical trend with respect to premarital sexual permissiveness is described in more detail by family sociologists Ira Reiss and Gary Lee (1988) in *Family Systems in America*. They noted that actual rates of premarital sexual experience had been rising since the late nineteenth century. Two periods of particularly rapid change were from 1915 to 1925 and 1965 to 1975, as indicated in Figure 3.1. Readers will appreciate, then, that the so-called sexual revolution of the 1960s was actually embedded in a much broader context of sociohistorical change.

By 1980, about three-fourths of females and nine-tenths of males entered marriage already sexually experienced, and Reiss and Lee's assessment was

FIGURE 3.1. Estimate of Change Over Time in Premarital Sexual Involvement in the United States

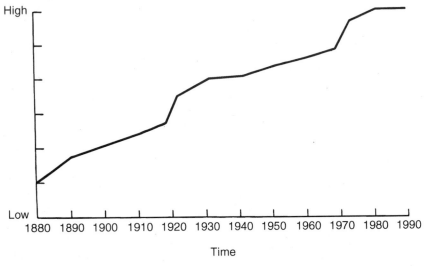

Source: Reiss and Lee 1988:134.

that by this time premarital sex was a stable and accepted behavior. A 1977 random sample survey of adult Americans by the National Opinion Research Center (NORC) had found the following percentages in response to a question about the permissibility of premarital sex: 31 percent of respondents said premarital sex is always wrong; 37 percent said it is always permissible; the remaining 32 percent said it is right or wrong depending on circumstances (Davis, Smith, and Stephenson, 1981). These reactions can be compared with more recent surveys. In 1986, a similar national survey of 1,425 adult Americans showed that 28 percent considered premarital sex always wrong, 9 percent almost always wrong, 23 percent only sometimes wrong, and 40 percent not wrong at all (Davis and Smith, 1986). Table 3.1 shows results from the General Social Survey conducted by NORC in 1994. In this table, respondents' premarital sex attitudes are examined relative to their attitudes toward two other types of sexual behavior. Since responses may be sensitive to question wording, readers might wish to check the original question wordings, reproduced in the Appendix.

Notice in Table 3.1 that acceptance of premarital sex does not extend equally to other types of sexual relations. Nearly 30 percent of the persons answering, even in 1994, indicated they believe premarital sex is "always wrong," though a greater number, just over 40 percent, said premarital sex is

TABLE 3.1. 1994 GSS Survey Results

	Type of Sexual Relations					
	Premarital		Extramarital		Homosexual	
Always wrong	361	29.1%	1067	80.2%	854	69.7%
Almost always wrong	144	11.6%	180	13.5%	53	4.3%
Wrong only sometimes	288	18.4%	58	4.4%	84	6.9%
Not wrong at all	509	40.9%	25	1.9%	234	19.1%
Subtotals*	1242	(100%)	1330	(100%)	1225	(100%)

Source: Davis and Smith, 1994.

*Not including "can't choose" or no answer. Results from the 1994 GSS are based on a representative sample of 1,545 adult Americans.

"not wrong at all." Some attention should also be given to the answers suggesting that the rightness or wrongness of premarital sex depends on the circumstances, which accounted for a substantial remaining 30 percent of respondents in these surveys. Case descriptions of different situations in which premarital sex occurs evoke different reactions. For example, family sociologist John Cuber (1975) administered a "moral evaluations" questionnaire that he administered to students in his marriage and family classes at a college in Ohio and, later, at Ohio State University. To avoid abstract statements, instead of simply asking "Do you approve of premarital sex?," he presented a brief case:

> Bob and Helen want to get married soon. They have been engaged for a year. As far as they can foresee, it will be impossible for the marriage to take place for another two years at least. Bob and Helen have already had complete sexual relations upon a number of occasions. Helen says she can see nothing wrong with this as long as people eventually marry and do not feel guilty. (Cuber 1975: 81)

Students were asked whether they considered this behavior right or wrong. Cuber's reported results, displayed in Table 3.2, differed for males and females.

The case of Bob and Helen, an engaged couple, was also presented to students at the University of Florida by the present author while teaching a course in marriage and the family there in 1978. By 1978, student sentiment about Bob and Helen's involvement in premarital sex was highly accepting.

TABLE 3.2. Student Reactions to Bob and Helen, Percentage Who Disapprove

	Males	Females
1939	About 33%	More than 2/3
1969	22%	Less than 1/3

Source: Cuber (1975).

The class was urged to develop another case description in which a couple would not be considering marriage but in other ways might meet students' criteria for acceptance. Collectively, the following case was outlined:

> Mike and Susan are dating regularly. Sometimes they go out with other people as well, but they do care about each other and are open and honest with one another. They both feel it is good to have sexual experiences before marriage and want sex to be a part of their relationship. They are not engaged and are not considering marriage because they know neither of them is ready for a lifetime commitment. They are, however, careful to practice effective birth control methods.

Again, males and females responded differently. Table 3.3 displays the results.

Considering these two tables together points to some interesting tentative conclusions about changes over time, male-female differences, and changes over time in male-female differences. Student reactions to the Bob and Helen case show the declining strength of disapproval toward engaged couples having sex before marriage. (Comparison of student samples with GSS random samples of Americans, however, shows that college students on the whole are a more liberal segment of American society.) In each year for which male and female respondents are compared, women are less permissive than men. Male college students were already more liberal than conservative even in 1939, thus had less room for change in a permissive direction. Not until Cuber's 1969 sample were his college student women more liberal than conservative (by then less than one-third disapproved of Bob and Helen). Women's attitudes were changing far more dramatically than men's,

TABLE 3.3. Student Reactions to Bob and Helen and Mike and Susan, Percentage Who Disapprove

		Males	Females
Bob and Helen (engaged)	1978	10%	14%
Mike and Susan (dating)	1978	31%	47%

resulting in a much narrower attitude gap in 1978 than in earlier years. It is also clear that both males and females in 1978 were more likely to disapprove of premarital sex for a dating couple than for an engaged couple, though women responded more strongly to the shift in circumstances. Aspects of the situation that may influence approval include whether the persons involved are "in love" or strongly affectionate, their commitment to continue the relationship, and its exclusivity (participants not involved with others).

Observed differences between men and women in sexual behavior and attitudes prompts mention of another related issue concerning sex and singles, the double standard. The **double standard** refers to the tendency to express different standards for members of one's own sex than for members of the opposite sex (Kaats and Davis 1975). Note that this is not the same as saying there is a difference between men and women in attitudes. Both men and women could *equally* endorse a double standard allowing men more latitude in sexual conduct; then they would have the *same* attitude. Historically, the sexual double standard in the United States has been more permissive toward men than women, but women themselves were in some ways stronger proponents of the double standard than men. For example, Robinson, King, and Balswick (1975) investigated attitudes toward premarital sex among college students using two small surveys at one large southern state-supported university in 1965 and 1970. Among the questions they asked were several concerning the morality of having intercourse with many partners. The results are reported in Table 3.4.

Robinson, King, and Balswick found differences in the direction we would expect between males and females in each year and over time, but this in itself does not provide evidence of a double standard. To tell whether or not there was a double standard and, if so, whether males or females most likely expressed it, one has to look carefully at the proper figures. Compare how males in one year, say 1970, answered the question on men's conduct with how the same respondents answered the question on women's conduct. Then look at how females in the same year answered the two questions. In 1970, Robinson, King, and Balswick's male college students were indeed more likely to strongly agree that a woman who had sex with many men is immoral (33 percent) than to agree that a man doing the same is immoral (15 percent). But the double standard was more pronounced among the female respondents (54 percent versus 22 percent).

By the 1980s, these types of items no longer elicited a double standard from students in the author's marriage and family classes, whether due entirely to altered convictions or in part to social desirability effects. Today, among college students, "everyone knows" you are not "supposed" to have different standards for men and women. In this respect, predictions made by family sociologists in the 1970s that American society was moving toward

TABLE 3.4. Attitudes Toward Having Premarital Sex with Many Partners

		% Strongly Agree	
		Males	Females
a. A man who has had sexual inter-course with a great many women is immoral:	1965	35% (127)	56% (114)
	1970	15% (137)	22% (157)
b. A woman who has had sexual inter-course with a great many men is im-moral:	1965	42% (118)	91% (114)
	1970	33% (137)	54% (157)

Source: Robinson, King, and Balswick (1975).

more egalitarian sexual standards came to pass. It may be most accurate to say that the double standard has clearly declined but has not yet fallen. Kaats and Davis (1975) had earlier cautioned that there are different aspects of the double standard, and item wordings on surveys may not tap the full range of personal feelings—for example, we may not feel the same about our own sons and daughters, brothers and sisters, prospective partners and ourselves as we do about men and women in general. Kaats and Davis (1975) found the double standard more apparent for both males and females when more detailed questions were asked. More recently, when Janus and Janus (1993) asked persons in their national sample of American adults whether they thought "there is still a double standard in sex regarding men and women," 75 to 85 percent of men and 91 percent or more of women in each age cate-gory over twenty-six agreed. Among the youngest respondents, age eigh-teen to twenty-six, who were least likely to agree, 75 percent of men and 87 percent of women still agreed. This means that whether or not Janus and Ja-nus's respondents actually supported a double standard themselves (they were not asked), they saw its effects still operating in American society.

REPERCUSSIONS OF CHANGING SEXUAL STANDARDS

All told, one change in American society amply documented by survey research is the overall shift toward greater permissiveness with respect to premarital sex, both in attitudes and behaviors. While still apt to be some-what more conservative than men in sexual matters, women have changed dramatically since the 1960s. Although not the focus of the discussion here, it is logical to assume that this permissibility also extends to divorced sin-gles (with complications raised by children in the household addressed later as an aspect of single parenting). Cohabitation, too, as noted in the previous chapter, is connected with declining disapproval of sex between unmarried adults. Having removed much of the shame and guilt associated earlier with premarital sex and having "liberated" women sexually, more options became available in choice of lifestyles.

The so-called sexual revolution was not, however, without accompanying personal and social problems. Its effects may thus be regarded as a mixed blessing. Raised expectations of sexual satisfaction led to disappointments as well as new opportunities. Standards of proficiency for sexual partners went up. "Keeping up with the Joneses" took on a sexual as well as economic meaning. Not only family, friends, and neighbors but advertising/soap opera/talk show/movie images of sexual prowess are held up for comparison. Acceptance of female sexuality required adjustments, described in part by psychologists Connell Cowan and Melvyn Kinder in their 1985 best-selling book, *Smart Women/Foolish Choices* (see Box 3.1). At one point, newspaper articles focused on an "alarming increase in male impotence" attributed to women's new sexual aggressiveness, but this concern faded rather quickly from public view. Public preoccupation with sexuality and increasing emphasis on sexual freedom seems to have had more enduring adverse effects in the areas of sexually transmitted diseases and teenage sex. The "new tyranny of sexual 'liberation' " discussed by Derek Wright (1975) entailed culturally heightened motivation to participate in sex and a corresponding shift in social pressures. Arguments in favor of sexual freedom, at extreme, portrayed societal efforts to regulate sexual conduct as misguided,

---

Box 3.1. On Men's Attitudes Toward Sex

"Often in therapy with couples we encounter a man who insists that he wants his partner to initiate sex more often, but when she does, trouble frequently ensues. Suddenly, he feels unprepared, taken off-guard. He may be tired or preoccupied with career concerns. He may not be able to achieve an erection. He often realizes that what he wanted was not that his partner be more aggressive, but rather more direct and expressive of her desire for him. Whatever men say, most of them still like to control the timing and frequency of lovemaking.

In sustained relationships, some men find they don't know how to tell a partner they are not in the mood for sex. They don't realize it is perfectly normal to feel this way at times, for many of them have been programmed to think the man should 'always be ready.' One maladaptive but all too common way men have learned to handle this feeling is to provoke fights to obscure their real desire to avoid sexual activity. Not only are men anxious about their ability to get erections, but they are also unnerved about the female orgasm. It wasn't all that long ago that the female orgasm was a mystery, poorly understood by either men or women. As the facts of the female orgasm were

(continued)

(continued)

revealed, men found they had a new fascination and, unfortunately, a new worry. Whereas in the past men didn't feel guilty when a woman failed to reach orgasm, now most men realize that any woman can climax, provided she and her lover have the requisite patience, interest, and skills. Women now expect more time and sensitivity from their lovers, and rightfully so. However, many men see the sensitivity and patience required of them in foreplay as work. And if a man feels it is an effort, the woman senses it.

To remove some of the pressure to perform, many men try to have the woman reach orgasm first. But in the process, men often lose some of their own arousal. When a man varies in the degree of his arousal, it is usually reflected in the quality of his erection. This is why many men are uncomfortable with the normal waxing and waning of arousal during lovemaking. Only through acceptance of these natural rhythms of arousal can men learn to relax, be less hurried, and participate in satisfying lovemaking. Fortunately, men seem to be learning this lesson."

Source: From *Smart Women—Foolish Choices* by Dr. Connell Cowan and Dr. Melvyn Kinder, copyright © 1985 by Connell O'Brien and Melvyn Kinder. Used by permission of Crown Publishers, a division of Random House, Inc.

and individuals who found sex relatively unappealing or unimportant now appeared distinctly odd. More, stronger, and more open support for sex translated into growing peer pressure for sexual activity, particularly problematic among adolescents. How early should involvement in premarital intercourse begin? The *Janus Report* (Janus and Janus 1993) included information on age at first intercourse by age and sex of respondent (see Table 3.5). Readers may be surprised to see that 21 percent of males and 15 percent of females who were between eighteen and twenty-six reported having had intercourse by the time they were fourteen years old.

Because the term "promiscuous" had been used, mainly against women, as a means of sexual control, it fell out of fashion after the 1960s, but related concerns linger. "Promiscuity" denoted having "too many" partners and being indiscriminate in choice of partners ("lacking standards of selection"). If sex is permitted for single persons, exactly what would constitute too many partners is unclear, but Janus and Janus (1993) asked their adult respondents how many persons they actually had sexual relations with (see Table 3.6). The results provide a basis for further discussion, which should include consideration of the age at which individuals are selecting their sexual partners. The most widely shared social concern remains the sexual conduct of teenagers; traditionally, as connected with unwed pregnancy (Voydanoff and Donnelly 1990). Developmentally, adolescents are less mature emotionally, more likely to embrace risky behavior, and more vulnerable to media and peer pressure. As compared to older groups, sexually active teenagers and

TABLE 3.5. Self-Identified Age at First Full Sexual Relations (Percent)

	18-26		27-38		39-50		51-64		65+	
	M	F	M	F	M	F	M	F	M	F
N =	254	266	357	378	284	300	228	231	214	218
By 10	3	2	2	1	2	0	3	1	1	0
11 to 14	18	13	17	10	16	7	16	2	16	1
15 to 18	70	68	54	61	51	43	58	47	43	40
19 to 25	9	16	24	26	25	48	21	49	38	55
26+	0	1	3	2	6	2	2	1	2	4
By age 14	21	15	19	11	18	7	19	3	17	1
After age 18	9	17	27	28	31	50	23	50	40	59

Source: The Janus Report on Sexual Behavior, Janus and Janus, Copyright © 1993 John Wiley & Sons. Reprinted by permission of John Wiley & Sons, Inc.

TABLE 3.6. Responses to the Question, "How Many Different Individuals (Including Spouses) Have You Had Sexual Relations With?" (Percent)

	Men N = 1,332	Women N = 1,391
None	1	3
1-10	28	42
11-30	32	39
31-60	21	9
61-100	8	3
101+	10	4

Source: The Janus Report on Sexual Behavior, Janus and Janus, Copyright © 1993 John Wiley & Sons. Reprinted by permission of John Wiley & Sons, Inc.

young adults are known to be less careful in contraceptive behavior and at high risk for sexually transmitted diseases. Nationwide, each year over 10 percent of teenage girls in the United States become pregnant, with attendant educational, economic, physical, and mental health problems for themselves, their children, and society at large. Decisions made by adolescents about sexual expression are not simply private and immediate but far reaching in their consequences.

SEX AND COMMUNICATION

Dating in our culture leaves individuals on their own, without direct supervision, to make decisions about the timing, extent, and kind of participation in sex they will have as single persons. Yet these decisions are not made in isolation. First, because most *sexual behavior involves interaction* with a partner, what happens depends on his or her values, beliefs, and actions as well as on our own. Having sex is not simply a personal act; it is a process of negotiating physical intimacy with other persons. How do we initiate sexual encounters? How do we discuss issues of contraception and sexually transmitted diseases with prospective partners in order to behave responsibly? How do we deal effectively with sexual pressure from partners? How do we make our preferences and wishes known with respect to sex? How do we interpret our partners' actions and know what they want? Effective communication is an important ingredient in "good sex." Second, *society provides us with sexual scripts* that shape our sexual experiences (Day et al., 1995). In this sense, too, we do not enter the bedroom alone; each individual is guided in his or her conduct by socially acquired ideas about sex. Francoeur (1991: 692) defined **social scripting:** "as the process whereby persons are subconsciously and consciously conditioned and gradually programmed to follow rules, values and behavioral patterns of a society, subculture, ethnic or socioeconomic group." Think of a script as the text of a play. It tells the performers how to act: what to say, where to stand, what props to use, when to enter and exit, and what they are supposed to be feeling. The groups to which we belong have shared **cultural scripts** that members generally recognize as the socially approved rules, values, and behavior patterns of the group. Individual actors also formulate their own particular understandings, or **personal scripts**, based on their past social experience. Because cultural scripts do not adequately cover in detail every situation the individual may encounter, performers in everyday life still have to improvise a lot. Individuals are also free to disagree with available cultural scripts and try to change them. In either case, internalized sexual scripts give us a starting framework of assumptions, definitions, and meanings, a sense of how to properly proceed, that we bring to our sexual encounters. Then we attempt to coordinate our actual ongoing performances with other persons.

Communication, in brief, means exchanging messages; making our ideas and intentions known to one another. To better understand how we communicate about sex, it is useful to take a closer look at: (1) how we typically initiate a sexual encounter; (2) the origin of these patterns in the kinds of socialization experiences we have had as men and women in the United States;

and (3) some implications of the ways we typically approach sex—problems and possible solutions. These types of questions have been used by counseling psychologist Mark Stevens, PhD, in a workshop titled "I Know You Said 'No,' But I Thought You Meant 'Maybe,'" which was designed to help students avoid sexually coercive situations in the context of dating. Sex refers here to physical involvement motivated by sexual interest or the sexual urge as it is manifest in behavior.

Initiating Behaviors

How do we let someone else know we want some kind of sexual contact? How do we "get something going" sexually? If readers had to make a list, what would be on it? College students included the following answers: just asking, touching the person a lot, flirting, tickling, verbal hints, sitting close, talking about sex in general, grabbing, heavy petting just gets heavier, drinking alcohol, dress a certain way, getting naked, go to a private setting, create a romantic atmosphere, giving a massage, doing something special for the person, telling a person he or she is sexy, paying compliments, watching a sexually oriented movie, eye contact, tone of voice, kissing, "the look," dancing provocatively in a club, cuddling. As such examples show, much sexual communication is indirect. This avoids taking responsibility or seeming too forward and minimizes the risk of rejection, but being indirect also means ambiguity and more room for misunderstanding when you have to guess at what another person is thinking. Does provocative dancing or dressing mean that this person wants to have sex with you? Associated are feelings of uncertainty, uneasiness, confusion. Why don't we just ask right out? Uncertainty preserves some of the mystery ("will we or won't we"), prolongs the chase, makes the interaction more intricate, the game more interesting, and heightens the positive tension of anticipation. Indirect methods of initiating sex are sometimes also manipulative and controlling, with accompanying feelings of mistrust, apprehension, anger, and being used. Is a compliment sincere, or just a way of getting sex?

Socialization

Socialization is the process by which we learn to function as competent members of our society. Having identified certain patterns of conduct used to initiate sex, try to recall how and from what sources (e.g., family, peers, school, church) you learned these kinds of behaviors. The ways individuals have been socialized to think and feel about sex influences how they later initiate sex. What messages are we given about sex? What has our society taught us about sex that makes open communication so difficult sometimes? The United States appears to have a peculiar and distinctive cultural ambivalence about sexual matters, so we receive many conflicting messages.

While popular music, magazines, movies, and television often model and extol sexual activity, sex is not a likely topic of conversation at the dinner table when children are growing up. Sex is entertaining and sells books, but is not necessarily talked about in a comfortable way in conventional settings. Sex education is controversial in the United States. Ideally, healthy families would convey age-appropriate sexual information, generate discussion of sexual feelings and attitudes, and encourage problem solving in sexual as well as other matters. Yet adolescents report learning about sex mainly outside the family rather than from parents (Day et al. 1995). Parents do influence children's values and actions, though sometimes in unintended ways. Galvin and Brommel (1991) suggest that communication in the family about sexual issues often remains indirect, resulting in confusion or misinformation.

"The tampon talk" is an example of rituals parents create to avoid talking to their children about sex. When a daughter begins menstruating, her mother sits her down, hands her a box of tampons or pads, and a "So Now You Are a Woman" booklet, and tells her, "If you have any questions, just ask me." Father is assigned the task of having the father-son talk. Too little, too late! Such talks may be well intended but ineffective except to convey the message that sex is an awkward subject; the less said the better. Oblique, strained, vague, obscure, inaccurate, roundabout, rambling, or strictly admonitory ("don't") parental lectures about sex are variously described by adolescents as amusing, uninformative, embarrassing, uncomfortable, frustrating, and the like. Even sex education classes in schools are often less than ideal from the standpoint of facilitating communication. To avoid value conflicts, they may focus on biological aspects of sex rather than on the more personal psychological and social issues involved, and schools in many communities still segregate boys and girls when conducting sex education. What message does this send about talking to the opposite sex about sex? The author is reminded of a case of an adolescent girl seeking contraceptive information from Planned Parenthood after one unplanned pregnancy. Asked whether her sexual partner had used any protection, she replied, "I didn't know him well enough to ask." Apparently it was easier to have sex than to talk about it.

Gender

Have men and women in the United States been socialized differently? Part of what we learn about sex growing up in American society is that men and women are different sexually. If you had to fill in the blanks, what would come to mind if you were asked what men are sexually and what women are sexually? In classroom discussions, college students have come up with the following kinds of replies. Sexually, *men are:* initiators, aggressive, forward, insatiable, always ready, "studs," not very selective, perfor-

mance oriented, exploitative, willing, adventurous, physical, braggarts, boast-
ful, lacking control, selfish, thinking about it all the time, experienced,
dominant, nonmonogamous, irresponsible about birth control, keeping score,
conquest oriented, easily aroused, visually stimulated, able to have sex just
for sex. Sexually, *women are:* more emotional, inhibited, more considerate,
manipulative (my way or no way), relationship oriented, passive, more concerned with birth control, "a slut if you do, frigid if you don't," romantic,
pleasers, submissive, more committed, practical, play hard to get, less se-
cure/more self-conscious, monogamous, faithful, need more stimulation, can
take it or leave it, longer lasting, affectionate/like touching, expect more, re-
pressed, fearful, want to make love not just sex, worried about reputation,
moralistic, teasers, able to fake orgasm, choosier.

Discussions of this topic usually raise the points that (a) men and women
do not *have* to be this way, and (b) not everyone *is* actually like this. These
are stereotypes of what men and women are sexually. Yet there is a noteworthy
ease and consistency in the way the stereotypes are described by students in
college classes, year after year. Men and women may list the characteristics
of the opposite sex in different terms—sometimes more, sometimes less flattering—but essentially they agree. Even students who say they do not personally endorse the lists have no difficulty generating them and recognizing
which traits are "supposed" to go with which sex. In other words, the stereotypes are part of a shared cultural script. Social expectations (which may be
stereotypes) regarding what men are sexually and what women are sexually
are **social facts**. Not facts in the sense that they are necessarily true descriptions of men or women but facts in the sense that they can be shown empirically to be shared beliefs about men and women; the emphasis is on the social in social facts. According to classical sociologist Emile Durkheim
(1938), social facts have the defining characteristics of *exteriority* and *constraint*. Exteriority means that social facts exist outside any particular individual. Standards of conduct, like currency and language, belong to the
group. The constraint attributed to social facts arises because social standards are taught to the individual by the group (socialization) and, if not internalized, are backed up by social sanctions (rewards for conformity, punishments for deviance). The concept of social facts is another reminder of
the presence of society within the individual. It encourages us to stop and
consider how we may individually be influenced by social stereotypes about
what men and women are sexually, even when we try not to be. Consider a
personal example provided by a student:

> My boyfriend and I have been together for awhile, so I started to feel
> comfortable about initiating sex with him. Then I noticed he was be-
> ing more distant and not so affectionate as before. I asked him what
> was wrong, and if it bothered him that I was taking the lead sexually.
> He said he knew it shouldn't but that yes it did bother him. Now I just

find ways to let him know I want sex without coming right out and saying so. I give him a certain smile and raise my eyebrows, and then let him be the one to initiate sex.

Problems: Acquaintance and Date Rape

Given the stereotypic messages we receive about what men and women are sexually, the many indirect ways by which sexual interaction is commonly initiated, and the difficulties we may have talking to prospective partners about sex, problems arise between men and women. One is **acquaintance** or **date rape;** that is, sexual assault by someone you already know and with whom you may have a dating relationship. There is growing recognition of a wider range of "coercive sex" in dating, too, without overt physical violence but without mutual consent. Date rape can be addressed in various ways, but here our focus will be on how it relates to concerns about sex and communication.

The concept of date rape still meets with skepticism and denial, yet the experience itself is far from uncommon. The most widely known study of acquaintance rape is the national survey of college students conducted by psychologist Mary P. Koss with funding from the National Institute of Mental Health. This three-year survey of 6,159 students at thirty-two colleges in the United States was completed in 1985. Fifteen percent of the 3,187 college women surveyed had been raped; in 84 percent of these assaults the woman personally knew the attacker; over half were dating him (Koss, Gidycz, and Wisniewski 1987). Another 12 percent had experienced rape attempts in which penetration did not occur. These figures resulted in the statistic popularized by the media that *one in four* college women experience rape or attempted rape. Professor Koss later emphasized that these figures are similar to prevalence estimates of at least 15 to 25 percent reported in seven other large-scale studies between 1979 and 1990 (Koss 1992). Rape was defined in her national survey as unwanted sexual intercourse (or other penetration) because of threatened or actual use of physical force, or when incapacitated with alcohol or other drugs (Koss, Gidycz, and Wisniewski 1987: 165, 167). Because women often fail to think of forcible sex as rape, Koss asked behavioral questions about what the men had done, then used legal definitions to reach her final figures. Koss found that of those women who had actually been raped, one-fourth thought it was rape, one-fourth thought it was a crime, but were not sure it was rape, one-fourth thought it was serious sexual abuse but did not know if it qualified as a crime, and one-fourth did not feel victimized by the experience (Koss 1992). This type of uncertainty over what actually constitutes rape led journalist Robin Warshaw (1988) to title her book based on the Koss survey and a series of additional interviews, *I Never Called It Rape.*

Disparities in the reports given by male and female respondents were observed in the national survey. Nevertheless, the 2,971 college men in Koss's sample described themselves as enacting behaviors that constituted 187 rapes, 157 attempted rapes, 327 episodes of sexual coercion, and 854 incidents of unwanted sexual contact. Warshaw (1988: 85) notes that men's lower estimates on items such as force used, victim struggling, or defining incidents as rape is partially due to "the men's inability to perceive situations as being forceful that women find quite threatening and their inclination to interpret female resistance as less serious than it is."

Legal definitions of rape and sexual assault are included in each state's penal code, copies of which can generally be found at university and public libraries, especially law libraries. While jurisdictions vary in how sexual offenses are defined and prosecuted, basically sexual assault is penetration of another person without that person's consent. Lack of consent occurs when the other person is compelled by use of physical force or violence, or compelled by threatened use of force or violence which the other person believes can/will be carried out, or when the other person is drugged, unconscious, or physically unable to resist. Confusion over whether forced sex is "really" rape when it occurs in party or dating situations can be answered simply. Yes. Lack of awareness, misunderstanding, or deliberate disregard of a woman's reluctance to engage in sexual intercourse puts men at risk of committing criminal misconduct. Men are well advised to proceed with caution in the area of sexual consent.

We live in a society that in some ways "sets up" individuals for such problems. A **rape culture** refers to social norms, values, and beliefs conducive to nonconsenting sexual relations. Applied to the United States, examples would include the idea that when women say "no," they really mean "yes," that you can always tell when someone really "wants it," that certain women are sexually experienced or teases or economic exploiters or otherwise "owe" a partner sexual access, that dressing provocatively is "asking for" sexual assault, that men cannot control sexual impulses once they are aroused, and so on. These ways of thinking support, rationalize, justify, or excuse sexual assault. They shape and reflect a climate of social opinion that surrounds our behaviors and our evaluations of others (for example, when

Reprinted with special permission of King Features Syndicate.

we serve as jurors). Yet not all persons exposed to the same culture internalize it to the same degree. Why do some males act out sexual aggression while others do not? **Rape proclivity** is an acquired individual disposition to engage in coercive sexual contact; individual sexual aggression based on internalized elements of a rape culture and other personal attributes. Robin Warshaw (1988: 84) reviewed some characteristics of the college men in Koss's sample who had raped or attempted rape: alcohol use, violent family background, very frequently read sexually explicit magazines, view mingling of sex and aggression as normal, talk daily to friends about women (e.g., how particular women would be in bed), younger age at first intercourse, approve of sexual intercourse under any circumstances, regard women as adversaries, endorse sex role stereotypes, and see rape prevention as women's responsibility.

Which elements of a rape culture an individual adopts as his or her own depends on the individual's particular social experiences in the groups to which he or she belongs. Groups link individuals to the larger society. Social scientists use the terms **significant others** and **reference groups** to refer to other persons whom the individual uses as a comparison standard in evaluating his or her own conduct. Rape proclivity is known to be influenced by reference groups. Professor Sally Lloyd (1991: 17), discussing sexual exploitation in courtship, acknowledges the role the peer group plays "in sustaining norms concerning the acceptability of sexual abuse." Males with a sexually aggressive peer group are more likely to behave aggressively in a dating situation (Gwartney-Gibbs, Stockard, and Bohmer 1987). Box 3.2 describes some relevant findings from an article by Eugene J. Kanin (1985) that appeared in the *Archives of Sexual Behavior,* "Date Rapists: Differential Sexual Socialization and Relative Deprivation." One interesting aspect is the attitudes of the controls, even after the researcher removed prospective control group males who had themselves participated in date rape. Another is the concept of relative deprivation as a motivation for sexual aggression. Kanin also looked at family influences, in particular the role of the father.

An earlier study of male sexual aggression conducted by Kirkpatrick and Kanin (1957) asked women about their dating experiences. More than half (55.7%) of Kirkpatrick and Kanin's 291 female college student respondents reported being offended at some level of erotic intimacy; 20.9 percent of these by "forceful attempts at intercourse" (p. 51). Level of erotic intimacy ranges from kissing through petting to intercourse and is a useful concept for addressing sexual pressures more generally. At lesser levels of physical force or intimidation, men as well as women may experience sexual pressure in heterosexual dating. In a study of abuse in intimate relationships at a

Box 3.2. Date Rapists

Sociologist Eugene J. Kanin has published several articles in social science journals on date rape and the influence of reference groups on sexual conduct. One article described his conclusions from a study of seventy-one men who volunteered to be interviewed as possible date rapists, conforming to the legal criterion that penetration was accomplished on a nonconsenting female by employing or threatening force, and a "control" group for purposes of comparison that was made up of 227 students from fifteen assorted university classes.

The men studied were all white, unmarried college undergraduates reporting on their dating experiences with women. Thirty-six (13 percent) of the prospective control group members had to be excluded because they indicated they had engaged in heterosexual encounters with dates where they tried to gain intercourse by employing force or threats or did in fact succeed in forcing a female to have intercourse.

The rapes had all taken place on dates, and most of the men had sexually interacted with the women on previous dates. Only six had been reported to police. Neither weapons nor fists had been used in these incidents.

When Kanin's respondents were asked how frequently they attempted to seduce a new date, 62 percent of the rapists and 19 percent of the controls responded "most of the time." Approximately 86 percent of the rapists in this study as compared to 19 percent of the controls believed in the abstract that rape can be justified under certain conditions. Ninety-three percent of the rapists and 37 percent of the controls said their best friends would definitely approve of exploitative tactics for certain women: the "tease"; the economic exploiter; the bar "pickup"; and women with a "loose" reputation.

Rapists as compared to the control group had more sexual experience, were more persistent in seeking dates, were more exploitative in efforts to gain sexual access; in short, were sexually more "predatory." Efforts to gain intercourse included getting the woman intoxicated, false professions of love, promises of commitment, and threatening to leave her stranded.

Date rapists did not lack sexual outlets, yet were *less* satisfied with their higher levels of intercourse than controls were with their lower level of sexual activity. They more often experienced pressure from best friends to engage in sexual activity than the controls and placed a high value on sexual accomplishment. According to reference group theory, the rapists are less satisfied with their greater sexual accomplishments than the controls because they still feel deprived relative to the exaggerated performance standards promoted by their friends.

The rapists began their aggressive sexuality before coming to college, but found groups in college that reinforced their values. Far more than the controls, the date rapists reported high school friendships exerting "great and considerable" pressure for sexual activity (85 percent versus 26 percent). Rapists more often sequentially shared female partners and recommended sexually congenial women to friends.

Few of the men's fathers strongly encouraged them to pursue sexual intercourse; the rapists' fathers may simply have failed to discourage it. Fathers perceived to be "very unfavorable" were more likely to be those of con-

(continued)

(continued)

trol group males (72 percent) than rapists (28 percent). Kanin's interpretation was that the fathers' influence on a son's sexual activities was not in overtly encouraging sex but occurred when he took a strong position of disapproval.

High expectancy of sexual success left the rapists frustrated by rejection. They failed to recognize that a female's rejection of intercourse even after advanced sex play was primarily expressing her need to stabilize intimacy, not to exploit or tease the male partner. Disregarding her actions and displaying verbal and physical aggression led to "success" in obtaining intercourse, i.e., rape.

southwestern urban university, the author and two colleagues (Rouse, Breen, and Howell 1988) found that close to 40 percent of the female respondents *and* the male respondents in heterosexual dating relationships reported feeling pressured by their partners for sex "much more often than you would like." Interestingly, fewer of the women than men reported feeling sexually pressured by their dating partner, but when they did feel pressured, the women's partners were more likely to be seen as *highly* pressuring or angry if refused (37.9 percent) than the men's partners (11.4 percent). Malamuth (1982) reported a striking 35 percent of the college men he surveyed indicating that they might force sex on a partner if they were assured of not getting caught. Men themselves may be surprised to realize how frequently men do in fact express "rapist" attitudes and women actually experience attempts at rape.

Solutions

It is an oversimplification to describe acquaintance or date rape as a result of misunderstanding between partners, but sex stereotyping and lack of open, direct sexual communication contribute to this and other problems in marital and sexual lifestyles. Acquaintance and date rape are part of the reality of sex and singles. Sociological imagination helps us understand the nature of social facts and how our own attitudes and behaviors contribute to a "rape culture." Critically considering how we developed these attitudes and behaviors provides an opportunity to change the messages we give men and women in our society. **Empowerment** means to enable; permit; invest with power; to authorize. For women, this means becoming more assertive and taking responsibility for their own sexual choices (e.g., not saying "no" when you mean "yes" to put the burden of decision on the male partner to avoid appearing "easy"). Women today can choose to be sexually active or not. If a woman feels manipulated or maneuvered in a way she does not like, she can trust that this is the wrong person, time, or place. Part of having "good sex" is that you feel sure it is right for you. For men, empowerment means rejecting social pressures to define their masculinity in terms of sexual conquest. Men need to take "no" for an answer and stop there, no matter how far they have gone sexually with that particular partner before. Workshop leaders such as Mark Stevens argue that men have a responsibility to end violence against women. Let peers and sons know that "real men" prove themselves by never forcing sex. In dating, both men and women have to deal with alcohol and other drug use and with feelings of jealousy, rejection, disappointment, and insecurity in ways that avoid sexual coercion. Both men and women should be able to ask for and receive clarification of what the other person is thinking and feeling. The bottom line is that both men and women have a right without exception to say no *at any time* in a sexual encounter.

Box 3.3. Dating Situations for Discussion

One step in preventing date rape is discussion of the types of situations that might be encountered while dating, honestly reflecting on how we react and considering the possible consequences of our beliefs. Two examples are provided of descriptions that have been used for this purpose. The first is based on a video dramatization produced by Swarthmore students. The second example was suggested by Mark Stevens, a counseling psychologist.

1. Paul ran into his classmate Karen at a dorm party. She looked especially attractive to him as she shimmied in her artfully torn sweatshirt, and he offered to walk her home. He asked if they could stop by his room to get a sweater, and after they were inside, he paid her compliments and stroked her hair. Suddenly Paul pulled Karen toward him for a kiss, then pressed her down to the bed. Clearly intimidated by so much happening so quickly, Karen quavered, "I don't know if this is the right time, right now." Paul ignored this, as if her resistance were merely part of the dating game. Karen tried to push him away, but he was stronger, so she pleaded with him to stop. Paul replied angrily, "What are you, some kind of tease?" Karen struggled again briefly, then turned her head away as he reached toward his belt . . .

Is this rape? If so, who is responsible? What is going on in this situation with Paul? with Karen?

2. A woman visits a man's apartment after a date. They slow dance for a while to some music on the stereo. They sit on the couch and start hugging and kissing. She goes with him into the bedroom. They undress. They lie down on the bed together. She decides she does not want to have sexual intercourse, and says "no."

How should he react? What reasons might she have for her behavior?

CONTRACEPTION

According to Planned Parenthood, half of all pregnancies in the United States each year are unplanned. This statistic can be interpreted as largely due to ineffective contraceptive behavior. Having intercourse unprotected, chances are that 90 percent of healthy females of childbearing age will become pregnant within one year. This may be less surprising if one considers the number of sperm ejaculated by a healthy fertile male in one instance of sexual intercourse (100 to 500 million) and the number of sperm required for conception (1)! Without taking consistent precautions to protect themselves, most sexually active couples stand a high risk of pregnancy. With all the birth control information and the variety of methods available today, how can we explain contraceptive failure? Effective contraception is a complex, learned behavior. Consider the steps involved:

1. Becoming knowledgeable about pregnancy; overcoming ignorance; understanding the facts versus myths (e.g., cannot get pregnant the first time you have intercourse); realizing that "if I engage in intercourse, I (my partner) can become pregnant."
2. Taking responsibility for one's own sexuality: "I am sexually active."
3. Deciding whether or not pregnancy is desirable for you at this time: "I do not want myself (my partner) to become pregnant."
4. Deciding on an *effective* method of contraception: "What can I do to prevent myself (my partner) from becoming pregnant as a result of sexual activity?"
5. Obtaining the method of choice; e.g., going to the doctor or clinic to be fitted for a diaphragm or to get a prescription for pills and going to the store to buy condoms, contraceptive foam, film, or jelly. This takes time and money.
6. Actually *using* your preferred method without fail, without rationalizing: "Just this once . . ."

Effective contraception is the responsibility of both partners regardless of the particular methods used. The steps involved make clear that contraception requires active commitment from partners to avoid pregnancy. Deciding on which method to use involves finding out about the pros and cons of various methods, considering your own circumstances, and deciding which method is most appropriate. Some methods, like withdrawal or douching, are ineffective. Regardless of the known and relatively high effectiveness rates of many methods, none is 100 percent effective, and each has its own peculiarities. Even abstinence has a potential for failure if one is placed in circumstances of strong desire and does not abstain in every instance (see step 6). For a personal view of sexual abstinence, see Box 3.4.

Box 3.4. Born-Again Virginity

In the following comments, Mark, a college student, and Ann, a high school student, share some of their thoughts about their choice to abstain from sexual relations after having already been sexually active earlier in their lives.

Mark: I was raised in a fairly strict Christian home. When I went away to college I took advantage of my freedom to party and raise hell. I did a lot of drinking with friends and wanted sexual experience. I was dating a lot, not seeing anyone special. There were two pregnancy scares and I thought I had herpes. My grades went down and I was on academic probation. I started to wonder what I was doing. I talked to the campus minister and decided to change priorities. I'm swearing off sex for a while. Some of my friends joked that now I am a born-again virgin, but they are okay with it. I think that rather than "screwing around" I'm better off waiting until I can commit to a more serious relationship.

Ann: In high school I was running with kids who were getting into sex really early. I slept with my first boyfriend when I was fourteen. After he dropped me it just didn't seem to matter. Sleeping with other guys made me feel better about myself. I like sex but I had a few really bad experiences with guys and I got tired of it. I'm pretty strong willed. Now I let men know up front that I am not interested in a sexual relationship. If they don't like it, that's their problem. I am not getting back into sexual relationships until I am ready.

Religion appears to have contradictory effects on contraceptive behavior. Religious persons have lower rates of participation in premarital sex but are less likely to use contraception if they are premaritally sexually active. In a sociology masters thesis, Peggysue Sadeghin (1989) described the dilemma of "religion and reproductive roulette." Sexual socialization that is sex-negative and abstinence-based undermines the ability to take the step of acknowledging one's intention to be sexually active, since this would be considered wrong. Having sex makes one feel guilty ("sex guilt"). Taking precautions against pregnancy is *planning* to have sex; manifest evidence that participation in sex did not "just happen." The obvious advice for singles is that if it feels wrong to use contraception, it is wrong to be having sex. The problem is only compounded by being irresponsible and risking unwanted pregnancy.

SEXUALLY TRANSMITTED DISEASES

Sexually transmitted diseases (STDs) constitute a serious health risk for sexually active persons in the United States. The Centers for Disease Control (CDC) in Atlanta, a primary source of health statistics, estimates that *one in four* Americans now between the ages of fifteen and fifty-five will contract a sexually transmitted disease at some point in their lives. According to the American Social Health Association, about *one in every six* persons in the United States is presently infected with an STD (ASHA 1991). Public health officials describe STD rates as "epidemic," particularly among teenagers and young adults (Nass, Libby, and Fisher 1984; Nevid 1998). While AIDS has received the most attention in recent years, a variety of diseases (including those listed in Table 3.7) can be transmitted by sexual contact. Overviews of STDs are provided routinely in human sexuality texts and in some marriage and family texts (e.g., Kersten and Kersten 1988; Nass, Libby, and Fisher 1984; Nevid 1998). The following brief descriptions will give readers a general orientation.

Gonorrhea and syphilis may already be familiar to readers as "venereal diseases," an earlier term now encompassed by "STD." Gonorrhea ("clap") is still very common today, with at least 1 million new cases a year. Contracted by vaginal or anal intercourse and by oral-genital contact, typical sites of *Gonococcus* infection are the cervix, the rectum, and the throat.

Within one to seven days, men may experience a burning sensation during urination or a discharge. Women with gonorrhea often have no symptoms but nevertheless remain infectious (Nass, Libby, and Fisher 1984: 309). Gonorrhea can be treated with high doses of penicillin or other antibiotics, but resistant new strains have developed. Untreated, it can lead to serious and painful infections of the male and female reproductive systems, possibly resulting in scarring and infertility (Kersten and Kersten 1988: 561,562). Syphilis is caused by the spirochete *Treponema pallidum*, a small spiral-shaped bacterium. After entering the body, the disease goes through stages, beginning in nine to ninety days with a painless chancre sore. In the secondary stage,

TABLE 3.7. Examples of STDs, Type of Organism Involved, and Prevalence in the U.S. Population

STD	Type	Estimated New Cases Annually
Gonorrhea	Bacterial	1 million
Syphilis	Spirochete	30,000-35,000
AIDS (HIV)	Viral	60,000-72,000
Genital herpes (HSV)	Viral	200,000-600,000
Genital warts (HPV)	Viral	1 million
Chlamydia	Bacterial	3-10 million
Other vaginal organisms:		
Candida albicans	Yeastlike fungus	Common
Hemophilis vaginalis	Bacterial	Common
Trichomonas vaginalis	Protozoan	2-8 million
Pubic lice ("crabs")	Parasitic insect	Not known

syphilis can be spread by simple physical contact, including kissing. In the next or latent stage, the disease may not be infectious but invades internal organs, until the final late stage when its serious effects appear. Penicillin or other antibiotics can completely cure the disease in the first three stages (Kersten and Kersten 1988: 563).

AIDS, acquired immuno deficiency syndrome, is the deadliest STD. The cause, the HIV virus, breaks down the body's ability to fight off other diseases. By 1997, nearly 600,000 Americans had been diagnosed with AIDS, and more than half had died from the disease (Nevid 1998: 16). Most at risk in the United States are men who have sex with other men or persons injecting drugs, but the fastest-growing exposure category is male-female sexual contact, which already accounted for 10 percent of AIDS cases reported in 1994 (CDC 1995). Nevid (1998) emphasizes that it is not simply the risk group to which one belongs that determines outcomes but the behaviors engaged in (such as unprotected intercourse or sharing needles) and having sex with a person who is infected. A person with a history of other STDs is also more likely to have an HIV infection.

The incubation period for developing full-blown AIDS is very long—as much as ten to fifteen years after exposure. Since the initial flulike symptoms usually disappear within a few weeks, persons who have contracted HIV often cannot tell they are infected, may feel well, and can unintentionally transmit the disease. Many individuals carry HIV without having any symptoms at all, yet are contagious. Medical practitioners cannot say for certain in an individual case if and when AIDS will develop, but the prognosis in general is not good. As a result of the recent (in 1996) introduction of new drugs, doctors have been able to slow the progression of the disease and reduce the presence of HIV antibodies as well as treating the opportunistic infections. Although the disease has become more manageable, there is still no cure. AIDS must still be considered fatal and, so far, shows an average life expectancy after diagnosis of little more than a year (Nevid 1998: 24).

Screening tests for AIDS have been available since the mid-1980s. A simple blood test can determine if a person is infected with HIV by detecting specific antibodies. Determining whether a person has AIDS is more complicated, since the diagnosis depends on the presence of particular opportunistic infections and specific cell counts (Nevid 1998: 46-50). The only way to know whether you are infected is to have an HIV antibody test. People can show antibody response before they develop symptoms. Having blood drawn takes a few minutes, and the results are ready in a few weeks. However, antibodies may not show up for perhaps three to six months, or even longer, after initial exposure, so individuals have to test six months or more after possible exposure to confirm results. Apart from human error, false negatives occur in only about 3 out of 1,000 cases; positive initial test results for HIV can be checked against another type of test for a more definitive conclusion.

Other viruses are transmitted sexually. In the 1970s, genital herpes became more common and publically recognized; more recently, genital warts. Genital herpes is caused by a type of herpes simplex virus (HSVII) related to the virus that causes cold sores on the mouth (HSVI). Both strains appear in the mouth and genital areas; kissing someone with a cold sore and later engaging in oral-genital sex might transmit herpes. In active outbreaks of genital herpes, sores may appear on the external genitalia, inside the vagina or urethra or on the cervix, in and around the anus, and on nearby areas such as the thighs or buttocks. Herpes is highly contagious until sores disappear and just *before* they break out. Infections hide in the body, e.g., in nerve cells, and create periodic, recurring flare-ups. The virus's long period of dormancy means it can be transmitted without other recent sexual contacts. There are no precise statistics, but an estimated 5 million Americans already have genital herpes (Nass, Libby, and Fisher 1984: 311). Though not typically life threatening, herpes was the first widely noted incurable sexually transmitted disease around which support groups formed to address the sense of social stigma attached.

Genital warts are caused by the human papilloma virus (HPV), which also causes common skin warts. The virus may be transmitted through vaginal, anal, or oral sex. Warts can appear from three weeks to three months after exposure and are very contagious. They may not be painful but can spread easily into clusters of warts. Once persons have genital warts, they are more susceptible to getting them again. Genital warts are associated with an increased risk of cervical cancer (Nass, Libby, and Fisher 1984: 316). In women, warts inside the vagina or cervix or even around the anus may not be visible. In men, warts usually occur at the tip of the penis, occasionally on the shaft or scrotum. Warts are treated with topical ointments, by freezing, by burning, or with surgery. Perhaps because warts are often not visible but still highly infectious, 60 percent of the sexual partners of infected persons also get warts (Nass, Libby and Fisher 1984: 316).

There are also sexually transmitted bacterial organisms that may lead to more serious reproductive tract infections and unwanted complications such as internal scarring or infertility problems. Chlamydia, caused by the bacterium *Chlamydia trachomatis,* is the most prevalent sexually transmitted disease, with 3 or 4 million and maybe 10 million new cases each year. At any given time, up to 10 percent of all college students have chlamydial infections (Kersten and Kersten 1988: 561). It is initially a mild infection, often asymptomatic, but can lead to complications when it causes inflammation of the urinary tract in men or more severe vaginal infection in women. It is a leading cause of sterility among young women worldwide (Nass, Libby, and Fisher 1984: 309). In women PID (pelvic inflammatory disease) is a generic diagnosis for a condition of the uterus and/or fallopian tubes caused by a variety of infectious agents including *Chlamydia trachomatis* and gonococci. PID affects one in seven women of reproductive age and an estimated 15 to 30 percent of all women who seek treatment for infertility. In men, NGU (nongonococcal urethritis) is primarily caused by chlamydia. NGU refers to inflammations of the urethra due to sources other than gonococci and is three times as common in men as is gonorrhea (Nass, Libby, and Fisher 1984: 311). At least 10 percent of men with NGU are asymptomatic, but still can spead the infection to their partners. These infections are easy to treat, if detected, by doses of antibiotics (e.g., tetracycline daily for a week), but it is important to treat the sexual partners too so persons are not reinfecting one another.

Organisms ordinarily present in the reproductive tract multiplying in excess of normal levels can produce discomfort. Infections caused by these organisms can be aggravated in women by friction during intercourse, wearing nylon underwear, stress, diet, or menstrual cycles. Trichomoniasis ("trich"), for example, is caused by a one-celled parasite found in some men and 50 percent of women (Kersten and Kersten 1988: 564). Close to 3 million cases are estimated annually. Women may notice an unusual vaginal discharge, but often there are no symptoms. Men may feel irritation during urination or show no symptoms and still be carriers. *Trichomonas* can be transmitted sexually but also by moist towels, bathing suits, underwear and, yes, toilet seats! Trichomoniasis is treated with Flagyl, an oral medication. Again, to limit further spread, sex partners should be treated at the same time.

Several parasites also are spread through sexual contact as well as by nonsexual means. They can be transmitted by skin-to-skin contact or by items of clothing. Off the body they can survive for up to six days. Pubic lice ("crabs"), for example, are tiny parasites that attach themselves to the skin around pubic hair to feed on human blood. They can cause a rash and itching. To treat the lice and their eggs, special creams, lotions, and shampoos are used.

Comment

This description of STDs is necessarily incomplete. Readers are encouraged to seek more information from their local Public Health Department or Planned Parenthood community education hotlines. Physicians and nurses can provide more details on symptoms, transmission, and treatment options. National toll-free hotlines also provide information about STDs and make referrals to local resources (e.g., the American Social Health Association hotline, 1-800-227-8922). Publications from the National Centers for Disease Control in Atlanta give regular updates on prevalence rates, and SIECUS (the Sexuality Information and Education Council of the United States) in

New York City provides a clearinghouse for information on human sexuality. From what we have already seen in the section on STDs, there are some general messages:

1. Sexually transmitted diseases are varied and widespread.
2. Symptoms come and go, and may be undetected.
3. Untreated, even mild infections can lead to unexpected complications.
4. Treatment involves other persons.
5. One can be infected with an STD and not realize it.

Both women and men can pick up and spread sexually transmitted diseases, "even the nicest people."

Prevention is the first line of defense. Common sense dictates that if one chooses to be sexually active, reasonable precautions should be taken. Be informed about STDs and act responsibly. As happens with contraception, "getting away with it" many times reinforces an illusion of invulnerability. Many contraceptive techniques, including birth control pills and natural (animal membrane) condoms, do not prevent sexually transmitted diseases. Eventually, the odds catch up with us. The community health perspective also urges consideration of the effects of our choices on others. For example, sexually transmitted diseases can have serious ill effects on infants passing through the birth canal of an infected mother. Sexually active persons need to have routine medical checkups and discuss any possible symptoms with their doctor as early as possible. Another reason to protect yourself and your sexual partner(s) is an emerging issue of potential legal liability.

RESPONDING TO STDs

What we don't know can hurt us. Compared to other nations, the United States has a high rate of STDs (Shelton 1996). Psychologist Jeffrey S. Nevid notes that sexually transmitted diseases take an emotional toll and strain relationships as well as having physical effects. Part of the problem is lack of knowledge. In an informative book, *Choices: Sex in the Age of STDs,* Nevid (1998) includes an STD quiz (pp. 10, 11). Consider the following sample true-false items:

- Chances are if you haven't caught an STD by now you probably have a natural immunity and won't get infected in the future.
- A person who is successfully treated for an STD need not worry about getting it again.
- STDs are only a problem for people who are promiscuous.

- You don't need to worry about AIDs if no one you know has ever come down with it.
- The time to worry about STDs is when you come down with one.
- A person doesn't have to be concerned about an STD if the symptoms clear up on their own in a few weeks.

These statements are all false and serve as a reminder of the types of mistaken assumptions that encourage risky behavior. General awareness of STDs is not necessarily translated into safer behavior, especially among sexually active teens and adults with multiple partners. Annually, 3 million U.S. teens become infected with STDs (CDC 1990). Nevid (1998) notes that most fail to use condoms regularly, if at all. One study found that the older men were the first time they ever had sex, the more likely they were to use a condom at first intercourse with a new partner, but if the partner was taking birth control pills men were less likely to use a condom (Ku, Sonenstein, and Pleck 1995). Like effective contraception, STD prevention takes (a) conviction about the importance of following through on steps that should be taken and (b) open communication with prospective partners *before* becoming sexually intimate. "Couples often become sexually active without first discussing whether or not they should engage in sexual relationships (Drinnin 1993), let alone discussing the necessary precautions they should take to protect themselves from unwanted pregnancies and

---

Box 3.5. Sexual Conduct Norms

How should people behave in seeking sexual partners in the face of STDs? What social obligations do we have, if any? The cases below illustrate several individual reactions.

#1. How have things changed for me as a result of sexually transmitted diseases? The only change I have made is to use condoms as protection. But when I find a girlfriend who is really special I plan to be tested for AIDS. This will show her how much I really care and alleviate her fears (Nevid 1998: 47).

#2. One woman has brought guys she wanted to sleep with to the herpes support group meeting. She insisted that her lovers be fully aware of what they might be in for. Personally, I thought she was just trying to absolve herself of any guilt in advance. Sometimes I go to bed with a guy without telling him about it—but only when I know I don't have an active infection. One guy in the group objected and said he had herpes because a woman didn't think she was contagious but she was. He felt he should have had the opportunity to make a choice for himself. But he never had that chance, and now he has something else—herpes. I see his point but everyone makes his or her own decision. I do it my way. Sometimes it is not worth the emotional pressure required to tell someone about it (Freudberg and Emanuel 1982: 521).

STDs" (Nevid 1998: 5). The notion that sex should be a spontaneous event is fostered by sexual scripts portraying sex in the moment as a product of uncontrollable passions. An interesting reflection of how our mixed feelings influence behavior is the type of conversation Nevid (1998: 6) mentions in which "one partner will say to the other, *after* making love, something like, 'By the way, I hope you are not infected with anything, are you?' "

Sex still is an awkward subject for many people. No matter how frank television talk shows get, this is quite removed from the real social circumstances in which individuals consider engaging in sex. We worry that bringing up sex too soon may seem forward or presumptuous. Talking about contraception or sexually transmitted diseases may kill the romance or scare someone off. It seems too "calculated," and so on. We are not always sure what to say or how a partner will react. *That* is part of the adventure. Sex educators have come up with examples of how to handle such conversations and plenty of good advice; e.g., if your partner is pressing for unsafe sex and is inconsiderate of your feelings or concerns, you need to assess whether you really want to be with this person (Nevid 1998: 159). With the proviso that condoms have a failure rate as a contraceptive method of about 10 percent (Kersten and Kersten 1988) and do not prevent all sexually transmitted diseases (e.g., herpes sores may appear in uncovered areas), latex condoms are the most effective and widely used method of reducing exposure to STDs. Box 3.6 lists some ways to talk about condom use.

Unlike the Pill for birth control, use of a condom for STD protection requires cooperation from male partners. In the 1980s, with single women more sexually active and AIDS having increased public concern about sexually transmitted diseases generally, efforts had begun to market male condoms to women in purse-size containers and, in one version, with an additional outer sheath to guard against tearing (by women's longer fingernails). More recently, medical innovation has produced a female condom, the vaginal pouch. Journalist Ellen Goodman wrote a newspaper editorial in 1992 on the female condom after hearing the device announced and commended as a new form of empowerment for women. She commented on the new reality in which women do everything for themselves. Now they get to be responsible for both contraception and disease prevention, leaving men free to just have sex. Is this empowerment? Not according to Goodman. She thought instead this might be considered further demonstration of "women's *lack* of power in relationships" and continuing deficiencies in "male-female negotiations." She observed that "after all this time, it is still easier for many women to insert a condom than to assert themselves" and to simply say to a male partner, no, not unless you use a condom. In this respect, the female condom signifies "something new and something very, very old."

In the same editorial, Ellen Goodman mentioned the case of a thirty-year-old woman married to a hemophiliac with AIDS. He refuses to use

Box 3.6. Talking to Partners About Condoms

Talking to partners about condoms is not as difficult as people some-times think. In an article titled "Cutting the Risks for STDs," which appeared in the journal *Medical Aspects of Human Sexuality,* Grieco (1987) gives ex-amples, presented below with modifications. A man may put on a condom without comment or say, "I plan to use a condom. I hope you don't mind." Be-fore sex with a man, a man or woman might say, "I have a condom with me. If we are going to have intercourse, I want you to use it." What if the partner objects?

If your partner says:	You can reply:
I know I am disease free. I haven't slept with anyone in months.	I think I am too. But either of us could have an infection and not know it.
I can't feel anything when I wear a condom. It's like shaking hands with a rubber glove.	I know there's some loss of feeling and I'm sorry about that. But there are still plenty of sensations left.
Condoms are messy and smell funny.	But with a condom, we'll be safer.
Condoms are unnatural and turn me off.	There's nothing great about disease either.
Condoms destroy the romantic atmo-sphere.	They don't have to. Using one may be a bit awkward at first but that will pass.
When I stop to put it on, I'll lose my erection.	I'll help you get it back.
I'm insulted! You act like I'm a leper.	Nothing of the sort. I care about us and our relationship.
I love you! Would I give you an infec-tion?	Not intentionally. But most people don't know they are infected.
Let's do it just this once without.	Once is all it takes.
I don't have a condom with me.	Be prepared next time. Let's go get one.
I won't have sex with you if you insist on a condom.	Let's put it off then until we work out our differences.

condoms; she still has sex with him. He is less concerned about her life than she is about pleasing him. Sexual socialization that teaches women passiv-ity and indirectness, being nice and putting others' needs first, has its costs. Elizabeth Powell's (1991) book, *Talking Back to Sexual Pressure,* addresses women's need to be more assertive in sexual communication. Her classi-fication of types of "lines" used in dating to obtain sex is helpful to women (and men) in confronting sexual pressure tactics. Examples in-clude lines that:

- Reassure you about negative consequences ("Nothing bad will happen.")
- Challenge you to prove yourself ("Show me you love me" or "If you were a real man/woman you would want to.")
- Stress what you will be missing ("It will be so good; we will be closer than we've ever been.")
- Threaten you with rejection ("If you won't, someone else will.")
- Claim you owe it ("After all this time/money I have spent.")
- Put you down ("Are you frigid/impotent, or what?")
- Pretend to settle for less ("I just want to hold you.")

"Good sex," as defined in the introductory chapter, is fully voluntary as well as physically and emotionally satisfying to both persons participating. Ideally, one is comfortable enough with a sexual partner to express one's preferences with respect to sexual practices (what to do, when, where, and how) and provide specific feedback ("I like this" or "Let's try something else now"). Chapter 4 will take another look at how to talk to a partner about sex—at generally effective ways to convey one's desires without the other person becoming distracted or defensive. For now, consider that the kinds of interpersonal skills that facilitate discussion with partners about sexual pressuring, contraception, and STDs also make it easier to negotiate other aspects of sexual encounters.

THE INDIVIDUAL AND SOCIAL CHANGE

So much of what we bring to sexual encounters is the sexual scripts about men and women and sexuality in general that we form growing up in our society. Among sociologists, who study human society and social behavior, there has always been debate about the extent to which society shapes the individual and the individual shapes society. Emphasizing the influence of social forces sometimes obscures the fact that individuals can and do change their beliefs and behaviors and, in doing so, they can also change the groups and the society to which they belong. Culture is not static. It is "constantly being questioned, challenged and altered" (Charon 1995: 113). Sociologist Joel M. Charon observes that ideas about men and women, family life, and child socialization have changed dramatically in the past several decades; date rape, for example, was not even part of our vocabulary twenty years ago. As we enter new groups, take on different social positions, and expand our social experience, our viewpoint shifts. Socialization is powerful, "yet we also think and wonder about what we are taught, we apply it and test it out" for its usefulness in dealing with situations encountered in life (Charon 1995: 116). To return to the idea of cultural and personal scripts, like the text of a play they can also be rewritten if they do not work well in performance. We can change the lines, the characters, the sentiments conveyed.

A related concept from sociological theory, the **definition of the situation,** refers to understandings among social actors about the meaning and significance of the activities in which they are participating. Definitions of the situation frame a sexual encounter. Sex as conquest and sex as romance illustrate two different definitions of the situation. When we consciously try to change the definition of a particular type of social activity, we are making an effort to **reframe** it—to place it in a different frame of meaning. Discussions about date rape, contraception, and sexually transmitted diseases are efforts to change the perceived significance of stated beliefs and actions related to sex. When a partner is resisting cues to slow down in a sexual encounter, saying he or she is just too turned on by you, what interpretation will you give this behavior? One option: "Very flattering and convincing; if someone wants me this much, I guess I *am* irresistible; let's go for it." Another option: "Oh, sure, but this is immature and irresponsible; get a grip on yourself." These are alternate takes on the same action. Similarly, the conversational guidelines listed earlier (Box 3.6) are about negotiating a revised definition of the situation in a sexual encounter.

Critical examination of cultural scripts may also lead to **social movements,** which are organized collective efforts to bring about or resist social change (Benford 1992: 1880). When individuals perceive discrepancies between value ideals and social realities, they can work with others to express common interests and mobilize resources such as time, skills, and money to obtain media attention and exercise political influence. In an analysis of the women's movement, Suzanne Staggenborg (1996) notes that the success of a social movement is typically measured in terms of substantive reforms (e.g., in law, policies, or procedures), but social movements can also succeed in bringing about changes in collective consciousness. For example, the pro-choice facet of the women's movement changed the way many people thought about sexuality, health, and "reproductive rights." These changes, however, are still being contested by organized opposition to abortion.

Briefly, individual thoughts, words, and deeds in part follow and in part rewrite the scripts given within a particular historical and social context. As a result of continuing social experience and reflection, our personal sexual scripts change. We negotiate new understandings with partners in sexual interactions. And cultural scripts concerning sexuality can be modified over time by cumulative shifts in personal choices or by deliberate collective action.

Chapter 4

Marriage, Divorce, and Sex

MARRIAGE AND OVERALL WELL-BEING

The June 1995 issue of *Population Today* reported on remarks made by Linda J. Waite, professor of sociology at the University of Chicago, during her presidential address to the Population Association of America in April 1995:

> Waite pulled together evidence from a variety of studies to present a picture of the benefits to individuals of the social institution of marriage. Even taking into account background factors and the selection of more advantaged individuals into marriage, research shows that married people on average have better health, longer life, a better sex life, greater wealth and better outcomes for their children, qualified by some differences between men and women. The less committed alternative of cohabitation, she said, seems to extend some of the benefits of marriage, but not all. (*Population Today* 1995: 3)

Catherine Ross of Ohio State University investigated one explanation for such findings, **social attachment.** Social attachment was defined as the level of commitment in an adult relationship, from no partner to living with a married partner (Ross 1995). Her analysis of telephone survey data from a national probability sample of 2,031 adults showed that, adjusted for age, sex, and race, living with a partner in the same household (married or not) was associated with lower psychological distress than having no partner or a partner living apart. "Social attachment, emotional support and economic support significantly reduce distress and explain the positive effect of being married and negative effect of being single" (p. 129). Ross was careful to add that "although relationships generally improve well-being, unhappy relationships are worse than none at all" (Ross 1995: 129). This is illustrated in Figure 4.1, which shows results from a regression equation graphed as deviations from the mean depression (appearing as a zero baseline).

FIGURE 4.1. Depression Levels of Persons with No Partner and in Relationships of Varying Quality

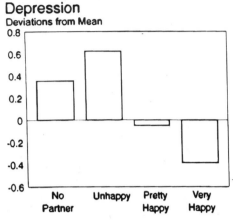

Source: Ross 1995: 138.

Lower quality relationships were identified as those in which people were more likely to report that they are unhappy with the relationship, would like to change many aspects of it, and often think about leaving. Individuals in lower quality relationships were more distressed* than those with no partner. Correspondingly, Wheaton (1990) suggested that separating from a partner, by divorce or in a nonmarital breakup, will not be uniformly detrimental to the individuals involved. For those in a poor-quality relationship, the long-term effects may be an improvement in well-being. It takes a good relationship to beat no relationship at all, but individuals in good relationships were least likely to experience symptoms of depression. Faced with the conflicts and strains of a poor relationship, individuals can attempt to improve the quality of the relationship, simply cope with the ill effects, or terminate the relationship.

The negative effects on personal well-being of being single or divorced can be offset by social attachment and emotional support (e.g., having someone to really talk to and people to turn to when things get rough); these are features of marriage that contribute to its beneficial outcomes. Ross found that being divorced rather than never married posed an added diffi-

---

*Psychological distress was measured by asking survey respondents on how many days in the past week (0-7) they: felt sad, were lonely, couldn't shake the blues, had trouble getting to sleep or staying asleep, felt that everything was an effort, felt they couldn't get going, had trouble keeping their mind on what they were doing, and (scored in reverse) felt hopeful about the future, felt happy, and enjoyed life.

culty relative to being married. Married people in her sample had the highest household incomes and the lowest perceived economic hardship. The divorced had lower household incomes than presently married persons and the highest reported rates of economic hardship (greater than singles). Controlling for family income and economic hardship, *being divorced, in itself, did not have a significant effect on psychological distress.* In other words, higher levels of depression among divorced persons primarily occurs when they lack supportive social attachments and/or experience economic hardship.

Differences between men and women, and similarities, are worth noting as these pertain to marital status and well-being. Sex differences in average level of social and economic support are most pronounced among divorced persons. Divorced women in Ross's study, for example, experienced higher levels of economic hardship (e.g., average income of $23,947 versus men's $35,545), while divorced men had the lowest average levels of emotional support of any group. "Men are just as distressed by economic hardship as women, but men have lower levels of economic hardship. Women are just as distressed by lack of emotional support, but women have higher levels of support than men" (Ross 1995: 138). Although women generally report higher levels of depression than men, the presence or absence of a partner significantly affects individual psychological distress for both men and women, and neither sex is immune to the adverse effects of poor relationships.

DIVORCE AS A SAFETY VALVE

Divorce is not only an individual solution to a poor marital relationship, it is an integral part of our family system. Consider this brief legend from nineteenth-century India, which was recounted by Adams (1980: 371):

> In the first year of the reign of King Julief, two thousand married couples were separated, by the magistrates, with their own consent. The emperor was so indignant on learning these particulars that he abolished the privilege of divorce. In the course of the following year, the number of marriages in Agra was less than before by three thousand; the number of adulteries was greater by seven thousand; three hundred women were burned alive for poisoning their husbands; seventy-five men were burned for the murder of their wives; and the quantity of furniture broken and destroyed in the interior of private families amounted to the value of three million rupees. The emperor reestablished the privilege of divorce.

When families are large and loose, arouse few expectations and make few demands, when they are less private and more open to the life of the community, when the life-span is short and family is necessary for economic survival, there is little need for divorce. But when families as small, isolated units become the center of social organization, with unrealistic goals concerning intimacy, divorce becomes the *safety valve* that makes the family system workable. Those who are frustrated or oppressed, those who fail can have a second chance. Remember that about four-fifths of those whose first marriage ends in divorce will remarry. Divorce is not an anomaly or flaw in the system but an essential feature of it (Adams, 1980: 372). Divorce became more common as the modern companionate family came to dominate in the United States during the nineteenth and twentieth centuries.

Legal statutes across the United States came to acknowledge simple incompatibility as an admissible basis for dissolution of marriage. State law defines when a partnership is recognized as a marriage, the nature of the marriage contract (the rights and duties entailed), and the circumstances under which a marriage can be legally dissolved. In Texas Family Code, for example, the first ground for divorce is *insupportability* (based on legislation enacted in 1969): "On the petition of either party to a marriage, a divorce may be decreed without regard to fault if the marriage has become insupportable because of discord or conflict of personalities that destroys the legitimate ends of the marital relationship and prevents any reasonable expectation of reconciliation" (*Texas Family Code* 1996: 13). In effect, the state recognizes the inadvisability of attempting to enforce continuance of marriage when the interpersonal bonds between the individuals involved are irretrievably damaged, and that under such conditions a marriage should be ended and divorce is, if not ideal, at least a regrettable necessity.

To say that divorce is functional is not to say that it is an "easy out." Just as it is unfeasible, and perhaps undesirable, to eliminate divorce from U.S. society and naive not to consider seriously the possibility of personally experiencing marital dissolution (through separation, divorce, or death of the spouse), it is also foolish to enter marriage cavalierly with the idea that the marriage probably will not work, but there is always divorce. Divorce is a major life change, not wise to romanticize. An end to the proximate cause of marital unhappiness, yes, and a new opportunity for freedom and self-discovery, but not a quick or sure end to stress or conflict. In "The Six Stations of Divorce," Paul Bohannon (1985) described six overlapping experiences involved in a divorce:

1. *Emotional divorce*—The spouses withdraw emotionally from the marriage; attraction, trust, commitment diminish; they feel more keenly ambivalent about the relationship, may question their love for the other person; they become more mutually antagonistic and have a sense of being "trapped" rather than positively interdependent.

2. *Legal divorce*—The courts are responsible for the formal dissolution of marriage. Legal divorce may be lengthy, expensive, adversarial, and unpredictable.
3. *Economic divorce*—The household as an economic unit is broken up. Assets are now divided, and new financial arrangements must be made. The courts may also be involved in this aspect, the property settlement.
4. *Coparental divorce*—Deals with any children involved in the marriage. In some ways, perhaps the most difficult because ex-spouses remain parents, often with diminished joint resources, continued emotional turmoil, and inadequate (if any) available positive social guidelines for coparenting after divorce.
5. *Community divorce*—A change in community attitude toward their new status as divorced rather than married persons; patterns of socializing change; friendship patterns are shifted, and the role of ex-inlaws is unclear.
6. *Psychic divorce*—The problem (or challenge) of regaining individual autonomy and recasting one's sense of self as a single person. People who have been married a long time tend to have become psychologically part of a couple or family; worse for people who married in the first place to avoid being on their own.

Bohannan (1985) summarizes:

> Divorce is an institution that nobody enters without great trepidation. In the emotional divorce, people are likely to feel hurt and angry. In the legal divorce, people often feel bewildered—they have lost control, and events sweep them along. In the economic divorce, the reassignment of property and the division of money (there is *never* enough) may make them feel cheated. In the parental divorce they worry about what is going to happen to the children; they feel guilty for what they have done. With the community divorce, they may get angry with their friends and perhaps suffer despair because there seems to be no fidelity in friendship. In the psychic divorce, in which they have to become autonomous again, they are probably afraid and are certainly lonely. However, the resolution of any or all of these various six divorces may provide an elation of victory that comes from having accomplished something that had to be done and having done it well. There may be ultimate satisfactions in it . . . (p. 311)

Comment

Careful consideration of what makes marriages work seems useful for a variety of reasons. Marriage remains the lifestyle of choice for most Americans at some time in their lives, and a majority of U.S. households will probably continue to include a married couple. Both married and cohabiting relationships appear to offer significant benefits for the well-being of participants by providing social attachment, emotional support, and economic resources. Poor relationships, married or otherwise, may be worse than having no partner at all. They are costly for both individual and society. Divorce, even when permitted by the state and desired by the couple, is a difficult process. Moreover, it frequently affects children as well as adults, and poses a new set of difficulties as well as ultimate satisfactions. Dating seems far from a foolproof system of mate selection. Participants may be as mystified as observers concerning why relationships that seem promising at the outset ultimately fail. Many factors contribute to successful relationships, but since sex is one key ingredient in successful marriage and cohabiting couple arrangements, the remainder of this chapter will simply focus on the part that sex plays in marital adjustment and how infidelity is related to marital dissolution.

SEX AND DIVORCE

Stan L. Albrecht and Phillip R. Kunz (1980) studied the decision to divorce among 500 already divorced persons identified through a short screening questionnaire sent to randomly selected households in eight Western states: Arizona, Colorado, Idaho, Montana, New Mexico, Nevada, Utah, and Wyoming. The five reasons respondents most frequently listed as why their marriages failed were: infidelity (255); no longer loved each other (188); emotional problems (185); financial problems (135); and sexual problems (115). Later, Janus and Janus (1993) asked the divorced persons in their national sample the "one primary reason" for the marital breakup. Emotional problems was the reason most often given by both sexes (31 percent of the 122 divorced men and 27 percent of the 127 divorced women). Sex was the reason given by 17 percent of the men and 5 percent of the women; infidelity was the reason given by 11 percent of the men and 22 percent of the women.

That infidelity is generally problematic for marriages may also be surmised from the prevailing public attitude toward extramarital sex. As shown in the previous chapter (Table 3.1), the 1994 General Social Survey (Davis and Smith 1994) found that opinion was highly unfavorable toward a married person having sexual relations with someone other than his or her spouse. Of the 1,330 respondents in this nationally representative sample of adult Americans, 80.2 percent characterized extramarital sex as "always wrong" and another 13.5 percent as "almost always wrong;" 4.4 percent said "wrong only sometimes" and only 1.9 percent said "not wrong at all."

Asked in a different way, the same attitude was clear in *The Janus Report* (Janus and Janus 1993). Samuel S. and Cynthia L. Janus presented reactions to a statement about how extramarital affairs were thought to affect marriage (see Table 4.1). Few respondents had no opinion, and the large majority (even more so in 1988-1992 than in 1983-1985) *dis*agreed that affairs do *not* seriously affect marriages, though some agreed (12 to 20 percent).

When Janus and Janus discussed their survey results and considered what they had also learned from the 125 in-depth interviews they conducted with a smaller random sample of these survey respondents, they painted the following picture:

> One after another, [divorced] interviewees told us that the major reasons for their divorce lay in the elements of a sexual relationship. When partners find each other too sexually demanding, or when one prefers to obtain sexual gratification in a way that turns the other off, there is bound to be antagonism in the bedroom . . .
> Conversely, interviewees told us that no matter what other problems beset them, when their sex life was excellent they rarely considered divorce. Instead they found ways to negotiate their non-sexual differences.
> Basic disagreement on such personal issues as a couple's preferred methods of sexual gratification can overwhelm other attributes needed for relating, such as trust, caring and feelings of security. The inability to feel unity with the marital partner sexually is so personal and profound that it may [override] otherwise good qualifications such as similar ages, religious attitudes, educational backgrounds and economic statuses.
> For some, sexual problems are seen as emotional problems, which may have inflated the category of emotional problems as a main cause of divorce as well as contributing to another reason for divorce, "rejection," reported by 12 percent of divorced men and women in this study. (Janus and Janus 1993: 194-195)

TABLE 4.1. Responses to the Statement "Extramarital Affairs Do Not Seriously Affect Marriages" (Percent)

	1983-1985 (N = 4,502)	1988-1992 (N = 2,759)
Strongly agree + agree	23	12
No opinion	3	5
Disagree + strongly disagree	74	83

Source: The Janus Report on Sexual Behavior, Janus and Janus, Copyright © 1993 John Wiley & Sons. Reprinted by permission of John Wiley & Sons, Inc.

Sexual problems in the marriage, extramarital affairs, or infelicitous attempts at sexually open marriage were listed as the primary reason for divorce by 29 percent of the divorced men and women in *The Janus Report*. (Open marriage was the primary reason reported by 1 percent of men and 2 percent of women.) Emotional problems or rejection were blamed as the primary reason for divorce by another 40 percent of the women and 43 percent of the men. The finding that emotional and sexual difficulties were major factors contributing to divorce is not surprising given contemporary motivations for marriage in the United States; a marriage is expected to provide emotional support and sexual gratification.

Family sociologists John Edwards and Alan Booth had earlier demonstrated a relationship between marital strain, coital frequency, and extramarital involvement. In a 1976 article in the *Journal of Marriage and the Family*, Edwards and Booth looked at correlates of sexual behavior in and out of marriage. Their sample consisted of 294 women and 213 men from a stratified probability sample of intact, white families living in the city of Toronto. Their results showed generally that "sexual behavior of both males and females is largely contextual, *determined to a greater extent by present circumstances than past background* [emphasis mine]. Specifically, it appears that the more severe the marital strain, the lower the frequency of marital coitus; and as the latter becomes more infrequent, the more likely is extramarital involvement to occur" (Edwards and Booth 1976: 73). Marital coitus was negatively affected by perceived decrease in love expressed by the spouse. Threats to leave home were positively associated with extramarital relations, a finding similar to Blumstein and Schwartz's (1983) observation that extramarital involvement was greater among respondents who were not certain that their relationships would last. In other words, infidelity was associated with less commitment to a future together. Modest levels of marital discord contributed to decline in coital frequency. More severe marital strain (as indicated by threatening to leave home) was related to engaging in extramarital relations. Edwards and Booth concluded that a negative perception of the marriage is related to sexual behavior in the marriage and to sexual involvement outside the marriage.

When social researchers attempt to explain outcomes such as frequency of sex within marriages or sexual involvement outside the marriage, they often use statistical techniques that provide estimates of **explained variance.** Explained variance summarizes how much of the differences (variability) from one case to the next in a measured outcome can be attributed to (explained by) the combined effects of the investigated possible causes. A complete explanation would account for all (100 percent) of the variability among cases; the difference between the explained variance and 100 percent is the **unexplained variance.**

For example, in the study conducted by Edwards and Booth, total variance explained for frequency of intercourse was 18 percent for wives and 32 percent for husbands; total variance explained for extramarital involvement was 12 percent for wives and 21 percent for husbands. The percentage differences indicate that the researchers were better able to explain husbands' behavior than wives' behavior and could account for more of what contributed to frequency of intercourse within the marriage than for whether or not a married partner would have sex outside the marriage. The magnitude of the percentages of variance explained, typical for survey research findings, still leaves a lot of variance *un*explained.

What we do know is that married partners who have sexual problems in their marriages are at risk for extramarital affairs, which become another reason for divorce. Although existing social attitudes are largely unfavorable toward extramarital sex, significant numbers of married persons become involved in extramarital affairs.

PARTICIPATION IN EXTRAMARITAL SEX

Despite increased permissiveness in attitudes in the United States toward *pre*marital sex, *extra*marital sex is clearly disapproved of by the majority, even among college students. Rates of actual involvement in extramarital sex, however, are higher than these attitudes would lead one to expect. Kinsey reported that half of the men and one-fourth of the women he surveyed acknowledged participating in extramarital relationships. In their book, *American Couples: Money, Work and Sex,* Philip Blumstein and Pepper Schwartz (1983) estimated that about one-third of husbands and wives will have extramarital sex sometime in the course of their marriage.

The Janus Report (Janus and Janus 1993: 195) included the figures reproduced in Table 4.2. In their sample, persons already divorced were clearly more likely to have had at least one extramarital affair. Among still intact marriages, 35 percent of the men (one in three) and 26 percent of the women (one in four) had been involved at least once, and 28 percent of the men and 18 percent of the women had been involved more than once in an extramarital affair. Janus and Janus (1993) commented that "apparently some extramarital sexual activity can occur within an otherwise stable marriage without causing a breakup" (p. 195), but outside sexual involvement is associated with greater risk of divorce.

TABLE 4.2. Responses to the Statement "I've Had Extramarital Affairs" (Percent)

| | Married | | Divorced | |
	Men (768)	Women (787)	Men (121)	Women (123)
Never	65	74	44	41
Only once	7	8	11	19
Rarely	14	11	24	27
Often	12	4	17	8
Ongoing	2	3	4	5

Source: The Janus Report on Sexual Behavior, Janus and Janus. Copyright ©
1993 John Wiley & Sons. Reprinted by permisson of John Wiley & Sons, Inc.

In an article in the *Journal of Marriage and the Family,* Thompson
(1984) discussed the emotional and sexual components of extramarital relations. This study distinguished between relationships that are *emotional
only* (in love but not sexual), *sexual only* (intercourse without emotional attachment), and *both sexual and emotional.* Thompson's respondents were
223 females and 150 males from a metropolitan area, about half students
and half randomly selected from the telephone directory, ranging in age
from eighteen to eighty, who were currently or previously in a committed
relationship (married or living together). Forty-two percent of the females
and 46 percent of the males indicated some form of intimate involvement
outside of their married or cohabiting relationships. Females were more disapproving than males of outside sexual involvement, more likely to feel they
detracted from the primary relationship, and less likely to pursue them.
Males reported significantly more sexual only involvement than females
(30 percent versus 16 percent). Differences between males and females in
emotional only or emotional and sexual involvement were not significant.
The total sample generally disapproved of all three types of extradyadic participation. Emotional and sexual relationships were rated as more wrong
than sexual only relationships. Sexual only relationships, in turn, were rated
more wrong than emotional only involvement.
   All types of extradyadic relationships were perceived by the overall sample to detract from the primary relationship in important ways, particularly
so in the case of emotional and sexual relationships, even among those who
had participated in them. Thompson (1984) concluded that "explanation of
extradyadic behavior seems to require an understanding of the process by
which behavior that is perceived as unlikely and undesirable becomes likely

and desirable (p. 41)." One possibility has to do with individuals having reference groups within which extradyadic relationships are more frequent. ("It's not 'desirable' but I see friends or acquaintances doing it.") Another line of investigation as to why individuals engage in extramarital liaisons focuses on dissatisfaction with the marital relationship. Glass and Wright (1992) found that men who had sex outside the marriage generally were seeking sexual excitement or novelty, while women were more likely to justify affairs as seeking love. Correspondingly, Patterson and Kim (1991) reported that men having affairs tended to like their wives better than their lovers, but women liked their lovers better than their husbands.

Most often, extramarital relations occur without the awareness or sanction of both partners (Hite 1976, 1981; Hunt 1974). There were some individuals in Thompson's sample, however, who did have an approving attitude and perceived extradyadic relationships as contributing in positive ways to a primary relationship. Also, the total sample estimated that 5 to 10 percent of married couples could work out agreements for pursuing outside relationships (Thompson 1984). These would be the "open marriages" in which a married couple decides to maintain sexual variety by allowing sexual encounters with persons other than the marriage partner. Given the difficulties of obtaining accurate information about unconventional lifestyles, it was interesting that the estimates made by Thompson's respondents correspond to the numbers of persons in Janus and Janus's survey who reported that they had in fact participated in an open marriage, about 5 percent of those who had ever been married. (Nevertheless, such figures are best regarded as rough estimates.)

OPEN MARRIAGE, SEXUALLY OPEN MARRIAGES, AND SWINGING

Marriages can be more or less open in a variety of ways. In sexually open marriages, both spouses have the opportunity to independently engage in sexual relations with outside partners. Swinging, or mate swapping, is a joint activity involving both spouses, together, with others.

Open Marriage

The concept of open marriage was popularized by Nena and George O'Neill, whose book by that title was a best-seller in 1972. Open marriage is an intimate lifestyle in keeping with our culture's emphasis on individuality, self-fulfillment, and personal growth. It is an attempt to overcome the problems caused by the isolation of the married couple in our society and the intense emotional demands we place on marriage. In a "closed marriage," the couple is turning exclusively inward to one another and expecting all their emotional needs to be met by the spouse or are forced to compromise these needs. In an open marriage the couple turns outward as well, seeking and maintaining other close personal relationships; the goal is "for two partners in marriage to accomplish more personal and social growth together than they could separately, without losing their own individual identities" (O'Neill and O'Neill, 1975).

Open marriage *does not necessarily involve sex* with outside partners. There are varying degrees of openness and different dimensions along which a relationship can be more or less open, as illustrated in Figure 4.2. With respect to *activities,* couples can as much as possible do everything together, or they can agree to do things on their own or with other people; such as going to movies, plays, concerts, athletic activities and sporting events, eating out, hobbies, or shopping. Regarding *emotional support,* the idea of a spouse being one's best friend and confidante is often mentioned as a characteristic of good marital relationships, but defining a spouse as one's one and only source of emotional support can be problematic. In a popular bestseller, *You Just Don't Understand,* linguist Deborah Tannen (1990) pointed out that men and women tend to have different conversational styles, which leads to misunderstandings between them in relationships. A same-sex friend may be more readily able than an opposite-sex partner to provide the kind of emotional support one is seeking. Too, some negative thoughts and angry feelings are better "vented" with a sympathetic, less involved outside listener and later discussed more calmly with one's partner. The trade-off is largely between being left feeling frustrated and isolated ("my wife/husband doesn't understand me") versus violating confidences or privacy needs ("airing dirty linen in public"). There is also the concern that emotionally supportive relationships with peers may lead to outside sexual attractions or romantic attachments.

FIGURE 4.2. Aspects of Relationships That Vary in Openness

	Closed	Open
Activities	/---/	
Emotional Support	/---/	
Sex	/---/	

Couples can decide together to have a marriage open to sex with other persons, as discussed in more detail below, but this is a distinctive lifestyle, not chosen by the majority of couples. In areas other than sex, the most practical advice for most married couples is to steer the moderate course. Marriages that are "too closed" leave partners unfulfilled and resentful, while marriages that are "too open" allow partners to drift very far apart, losing a sense of closeness and shared experience.

Sexually Open Marriages

Robert Whitehurst (1977) studied a nonrandom sample of thirty-five couples living in sexually open marriages. Sexually open marriage is a way of balancing the tension of wanting a secure, primary bonded relationship against the temptation of adultery. Couples in sexually open marriages experience monogamy as restrictive but want to avoid the secrecy and mistrust generated by clandestine affairs. They allow both partners to have outside sexual experiences. Stresses encountered in sexually open marriages include the following:

- The problems faced by those with any "deviant" lifestyle, protecting oneself against others' condemnation. (They rely on one another for mutual support and selectively associate with persons who are more accepting of their values and behaviors.)
- Time away from one another may cause loneliness for the person left behind. (Works best when both have strong outside interests.)
- Still have feelings of jealousy, possessiveness.
- May become used as an escape from the partner rather than just a means for new experiences.
- Is threatening and demanding, even described by some participants as painful, but they are willing to make the effort as a growth experience.
- Is more complicated than traditional marriage—not recommended for anyone looking for a tranquil lifestyle.

Participants in sexually open marriages recognized that this was a difficult lifestyle to sustain but felt one could work on the skills necessary to do so. They found many advantages in being married and did not want to jeopardize the stability of the marriage. They tended to feel that they had good marriages, strong enough to overcome the strains. Becoming sexually open will not help an already poor marriage!

Swinging

Swinging is one form of sexually open marriage. Regarded by participants as an answer to sexual monotony that is compatible with a conventionally structured marriage, the rules of swinging are designed to protect the marital relationship. It is a joint, shared activity, planned and discussed together (not done secretively or away from the other partner). Sexual ties with outsiders are brief and segmented (emotional entanglements with them are deliberately avoided); only sex within the marriage is viewed as romantic and loving. Ideally, the first loyalty is always to the mate. Denfeld and Gordon (1975) suggested that swinging and other forms of sexually open marriage might be viewed as functional in providing individuals who have a high need for sexual variety an outlet compatible with marriage. Swinging offers both partners sexual novelty, the thrill of the forbidden, and a taste of sex without entanglements or responsibility alongside love, marriage, and family.

Breedlove and Breedlove (1964), researchers who studied 407 swinging couples, estimated that 2.5 million couples in the United States exchange partners on a somewhat regular basis (more than three times per year). Couples meet at swingers clubs or bars, through personal reference or recruitment, and advertisements in swingers magazines. They guessed that the number of persons who had ever tried swinging was about 8 million, based on the observation that 70,000 couples had placed ads in the magazines, but only 4 percent of their sample of swingers had ever placed such ads. Most recreational swingers are relatively well educated, often in professional and white-collar occupations, basically "straight" and conservative in values—except for this sexual lifestyle!

In a review of research on nonexclusive marital relationships, David Weis (1983) noted that swinging had received considerable attention in the 1970s and reported that an estimated 2 percent of the American population had participated. Most studies of active swingers emphasized overcoming initial anxieties and effectively coping with strains to maintain the lifestyle successfully, but Denfeld (1974) also studied couples who had dropped out of swinging and entered counseling. As Weis (1983: 142) relates, "problems such as jealousy, guilt, emotional attachments, boredom and perceived threats to the marriage were common reasons for dropping out of swinging. Unfortunately, there has been no research identifying the factors that differentiate couples who are satisfied with swinging from those who are not." (Before concluding that swinging is a bygone attraction, see the supplemental material in Box 4.1, which reproduces a newspaper article that appeared on the front page of the *Star-Telegram* in Fort Worth, Texas, on Sunday, March 1, 1998.)

Box 4.1. Swinging in the 1990s

Swinging in Dallas: Couples gather to fulfill their fantasies where the black lights glow.

This article contains sexually explicit language.

By John Woestendiek
Knight-Ridder News Service

DALLAS—Two by two, dressed to the nines, they enter an unmarked warehouse indistinguishable on the outside from all the others in a quiet industrial district near downtown Dallas.

Inside, music pounds; cigarette smoke swirls under black lights; and, under the bemused stare of a huge nude in a mural that covers an entire wall, couples sit around the dance floor, scoping out the crowd.

They are regular people: doctors and lawyers, clerks and construction workers, in their 20s, 40s and even 60s. Some new to the scene, some veterans, many just curious, they are all gathered at a nightclub known as the Outer Limits for a swinging Saturday night.

But this ain't no square dance, partner.

They come to this club as couples, but they could be leaving as threesomes, foursomes, or maybe even moresomes.

Swinging—associated by many with leisure suits, gold chains and men who say "babe," thought by some to be a sleazy and dying remnant of the 1970s—is alive and well. And with a boost from the Internet, some say, it is more popular than ever.

Not just in Dallas, but from Bible Belt to Corn Belt, Sun Belt to Rust Belt, from glitzy Las Vegas—home of Hide-N-Seek, a 5,000-square-foot "couples playground"—to little Briar Hill, Pa., where the discreetly named Mountainview Retreat invites couples to frolic in a "spacious log cabin in a country setting."

Swinging never died, not even with the onset of AIDS. It just lay low, riding America's seesaw of morality, never becoming acceptable, never disappearing. Now, it appears to be, if not on the rise, at least more visible again.

There are magazines, Web sites, even travel agencies devoted to what practitioners call "the lifestyle." There are swingers' vacation tours and getaways. Last year's convention of the Lifestyles Organization, held in Palm Springs, Calif., drew 4,000 people.

Swinging, though it can take myriad forms, basically involves having "recreational sex" with spousal consent, but not necessarily with one's spouse.

An estimated 3 million Americans practice it, up from about 1 million in the 1970s, according to the North American Swing Clubs Association, whose founder, California psychologist Robert McGinley, sees mainstream American sexual attitudes as uptight and hypocritical.

"We can't sell a new Buick without sex. We can't sell cigarettes without sex. We're obsessed with it," he said. "Yet, if we catch somebody doing it, watch out!"

McGinley said that about 300 swing clubs operate across the country—not counting, he likes to add, "the White House and Congress."

(continued)

(continued)

It's a joke, but, to swingers, one with a point: With preachers, politicians and presidents getting caught up in sex scandals, maybe a more open approach to sex is not as unhealthy as some think. And, given that, what could be wrong with a "sensual evening" at a couples nightclub?

Open to couples on weekends, the Outer Limits charges a $10 temporary membership fee, and single men are generally not permitted. Customers give their names, sign in and take seats around a large dance floor. A disc jockey plays a mix of music, heavy on slow songs. As the evening progresses, the dancing gets dirtier, the petting gets heavier, and women, most of whom arrive wearing revealing outfits, strip down to even more revealing ones.

Among those in the crowd were Stu and Rita (not their real names), who have been married for nine years and swinging for four. They primarily practice "soft swing," which involves swapping mates for foreplay, then concluding the act with the original partner.

"Each couple is looking for something different," said Jim, who recently moved to Dallas with his wife of one year, Madeline (not real names, either; although open with one another, swingers say, they have public reputations to consider).

"Some are into trading, some enjoy having a third person join them in sex, some like to split up and each find another person, some like to have orgies of 10, 20 people or more, some are into filming, or watching. There is no end to the factors that come into play."

But, he added, many at the Outer Limits have yet to take the plunge; they are there mainly for the excitement of being in an erotic atmosphere where something COULD happen.

Although new to town, Jim and Madeline quickly learned about the clubs and made friends with other swingers over the Internet.

Although an increase in swinging cannot be substantiated, there is little doubt that the Internet, while revolutionizing communications, has revolutionized swinging as well.

Once limited to meeting people at private clubs and conducting correspondence through the mail, swingers now use Web sites, news groups and chat rooms to meet, screen and send zap photos to potential partners.

When they do meet face to face, it is often at places such as the Outer Limits: public enough to be safe, private enough to be naughty. It is one of five "off-premise" swing clubs in Dallas—the swingers' term for establishments where sex acts are not supposed to take place on the grounds. (Dallas also has at least five "on-premise" clubs.) One club has security staffers, known as the "sex police," who watch the crowd and warn couples who are going too far.

And many, at least in the eyes of the Dallas police, do go too far.

Nearly every year, police raid a swing club. Most recently it was the Jet Set, during a Halloween party.

As werewolves, nurses, devils and vampires mingled on the dance floor, men in ski masks ran in and ordered all those present back to their seats. It took a while for the crowd to realize it wasn't a joke.

Based on what undercover officers said they had observed, 15 customers were arrested on charges of public lewdness: seven accused of "deviate sexual intercourse," and eight accused of making "sexual contact with intent to arouse."

(continued)

(continued)

At least one of those arrested, an accountant, lost his job after the story hit the papers. Police said he was performing oral sex with a woman on the dance floor. It didn't matter that the woman was his wife.

"This happens every year or so when the police are having a slow night," said Steven Bankhead, a Dallas lawyer who represents four of those arrested and has represented others arrested in earlier raids. The most recent cases have not been resolved, but generally, those charged pleaded guilty to lesser offenses to avoid further publicity.

McGinley said that, nationally, such arrests are rare.

"Dallas is a very metropolitan area, but the laws are old," he said. "In Texas, it's illegal to put your hand on your partner's buttocks while dancing. It's illegal if a woman exposes her breast on the dance floor. Some people think that's worse than robbing a bank. This is the middle of the Bible Belt, and you've got people with religious views, and they press those views on authorities."

Police say they are just enforcing laws against public lewdness, and they consider the clubs public because they have liquor licenses.

Bankhead disagrees: It's not like having sex "in a public park where a bunch of Little Leaguers might stumble on you." It is behind closed doors.

Source: Woestendieck (1998).

MARITAL SEX

For the majority of married couples, what contributes to good sex and what creates distress? This section looks first at a clinical study of the types of complaints about sex in marriage that are likely to bring couples into counseling. It then considers known differences between men and women in sexual needs and desires. Next, an early article on factors contributing to female orgasm, using a sample of married women, is examined. Finally, guidelines are suggested for talking to one's partner about sex, to develop and maintain a good sexual relationship in marriage.

Sexually Distressed Couples in Counseling

Douglas Snyder and Phyllis Berg (1983) studied determinants of sexual dissatisfaction in sexually distressed couples using a clinical sample of forty-five couples seeking sex therapy. The couples were given a fifteen-item checklist (covering specific sexual dysfunctions and more general interpersonal difficulties) and a separate twenty-nine-item measure of overall sexual dissatisfaction.

For men, the most common complaint was too infrequent intercourse (87 percent), followed by failure of their partner to achieve orgasm (60 percent), and concern with their own sexual adequacy (58 percent). For women, five of the six most prevalent complaints, reported by 64 to 69 percent of the women, involved difficulty becoming sexually aroused or reaching orgasm.

For both sexes, specific sexual dysfunctions were less frequent than were more general interpersonal problems, and the most important determinants of overall sexual dissatisfaction included a partner's lack of response to sexual requests, infrequent intercourse, and lack of affection for the partner (Snyder and Berg 1983: 237, 241).

Note that the *greater prevalence of a particular complaint does not mean that it is necessarily the strongest predictor* of sexual dissatisfaction. For example, more of the men complained that the frequency of intercourse was too low than about anything else, but the partner's lack of response to sexual requests and her lack of orgasm were more strongly related to his level of dissatisfaction than the frequency of intercourse per se. By contrast, women complained most often about not climaxing during intercourse, yet this variable was not significantly related to their own sexual dissatisfaction; too low frequency of intercourse was. Box 4.2 lists the items most strongly predictive of overall dissatisfaction.

Such results suggest interesting points about sex in marriage. One is the likelihood that responsiveness to a partner's requests contributes to "good sex," particularly in long-term exclusive relationships in which what you do sexually you do with your partner or not at all. Another is the connection be-

---

Box 4.2. Sexually Distressed Couples

Factors contributing to overall sexual dissatisfaction among married couples in counseling do not necessarily represent the concerns of all married couples but give some indication of possible areas of disappointment. For the forty-five couples studied by Snyder and Berg (1983), the following items best predicted overall sexual dissatisfaction, listed separately for the men and women and in order of effect, beginning with the most important.

For the men:

- Partner's lack of response to sexual requests
- Partner is nonorgasmic
- Lack of affection for partner
- Frequency of intercourse too low
- Difficulty maintaining an erection

For the women:

- Frequency of intercourse too low
- Partner's lack of response to sexual requests
- Concern with own sexual adequacy
- Lack of affection for partner
- Dyspareunia (pain during intercourse)

These factors, collectively, explained a large portion of the overall sexual dissatisfaction expressed by the couples studied: 67 percent of the variance in the men's overall sexual dissatisfaction and 57 percent of the variance in the women's overall sexual dissatisfaction.

tween sex and general feelings of affection for a partner in a marriage. Lack of affection for the partner diminishes sexual satisfaction; likewise, sexual dissatisfaction may contribute to a loss of affection. Then too, wives' frequency of complaint about lack of orgasm and men's expressed concerns about wives' not climaxing, along with wives' mention of pain during intercourse (sometimes resulting from being insufficiently aroused), recommends more general attention to sexual technique and communication in sustaining long-term relationships. Readers are encouraged to consider what other issues raised by these couples may have broader implications, such as "frequency of intercourse too low" or "concern with own sexual adequacy," as related to marital and sexual satisfaction.

Gender Differences in Sexual Needs and Desires

Studies comparing men's and women's attitudes toward *foreplay* prior to sexual intercourse, sexual *intercourse* itself, and *afterplay* directly following sexual intercourse indicate significant differences between males and females in needs and desires. For example, one study reported that the "most important part of a sexual encounter" tended to be foreplay for the women (almost two-thirds) and intercourse for the men (over two-thirds). Only one in five of the men versus half of the women wanted to spend more time in foreplay. With respect to afterplay, about half the women indicated they would like "more time" while "over a third of the men said they would like to spend *less* time than they typically do" (Wadsworth-Denny, Field, and Quadagno 1984: 233, 243). Shere Hite (1976, 1981) had previously suggested that women were dissatisfied with the amount (not enough) and type of foreplay (e.g., not enough kissing or clitoral stimulation) and the abrupt ending of sexual interaction when the male climaxes (e.g., falling asleep, with no more touching or talking). For their part, men complained that women did not want sex often enough and were too passive in foreplay—expected it for themselves but did not reciprocate, even when asked—and during intercourse.

In a recent marriage and family text, author Robin Wolf (1996: 150-153) reviewed issues related to sexuality in marriage and midlife, including gender differences in sexuality:

> A number of sexual difficulties and complaints grow out of gender differences in attitudes toward sexuality. A frequent complaint among both married and single midlife men is that sex does not occur often enough. Men tend to equate what they see as an inadequate amount of sex with rejection by the partner. Midlife men also report they would like to experience more oral sex (Patterson and Kim 1991). The most common sexual complaint of both married and single midlife women is inadequate amount of sexual foreplay. For women, sex often hap-

pens too quickly. In addition, women often complain that after sex the man tends to roll over and go to sleep when a woman wants to snuggle and experience the afterglow of sex in a companionate manner (Patterson and Kim 1991). In sexual matters women tend to have a sensuous focus whereas men tend to focus on orgasm, . . . men become genitally oriented.

For married and cohabiting couples, researchers Sangra Byers and Larry Heinlein (1989) noted that, in general, men show more interest in sex and initiate sex more often than their female partners. Both men and women may take refusals as rejection. Byers and Heinlein found that giving reasons for refusals, such as simply being too tired or lacking time, helped to minimize negative feelings for both partners. Men have also expressed sexual dissatisfaction in marital relationships when they believe that frequency of intercourse is "too high" (Snyder and Berg 1983). The lesson is that not all women are alike and not all men are alike, but there are general ways in which men and women in our society differ in approach to sexual relationships. David Knox and Caroline Schacht (1991), authors of a marriage and family text, *Choices in Relationships,* say they ask students in their university classes, "What do you wish the opposite sex knew about sex?" If you had to make a list, what would you answer? Knowing what men and women most often say they wish you knew about sex would provide a useful starting point in initial sexual encounters, open to modification over time based on interaction with a particular partner.

Female Orgasm

Both clinical studies of sexual dissatisfaction in marriage and general observations of sexual differences between men and women, coupled with changing social expectations about women's sexuality, draw attention to female orgasm. What does it take to satisfy female partners? Figure 4.3 summarizes several relevant factors addressed by sex researcher Paul H. Gebhard (1975), based on data from lengthy interviews with married women conducted by the Institute for Sex Research.

Gebhard observed that a satisfying sex life is one factor contributing to marital stability. Good sex (operationally defined here as female orgasm) was positively associated with a woman's marital happiness and duration of marriage in a sample of married women. This may be because regularly experiencing orgasm causes women to be happier with their marriages and more likely to stay in them. Alternatively, the happier the marriage to begin with (the more successful in other areas of marital interaction), the better sex life a couple has, and the longer a marriage lasts, the more experience a couple has together, so the better the sexual adjustment. Wives who reached

FIGURE 4.3. Factors Related to Female Orgasm in Marriage

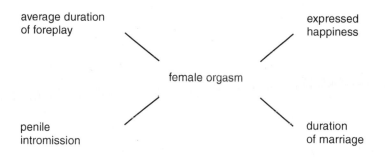

orgasm during 90 to 100 percent of marital coitus were found more commonly (59 percent) in "very happy" marriages than any other kind, and the percentage of coitus resulting in a wife's orgasm rose steadily with increased length of marriage (Gebhard 1975: 99).

Female orgasm was also positively associated with the duration of foreplay and penile intromission. **Penile intromission** is "the length of time the penis is in the vagina prior to ejaculation—after which most males soon cease pelvic movements and withdraw—a matter accorded great importance in our folklore as well as in our marriage manuals" (Gebhard 1975: 100). The highest percentage of females nearly always experiencing orgasm (90 to 100 percent of the time) occurs when foreplay lasts an average of twenty-one minutes or more (nearly three-fifths; 58.9 percent) and when intromission lasts sixteen minutes or more (two-thirds; 66.7 percent).

Duration of Foreplay

Table 4.3 shows the effect of average duration of foreplay on percentage of coitus resulting in orgasm for women in Gebhard's sample.

> Where 1 to 10 minutes of foreplay were involved, two fifths of the wives reached orgasm nearly always; 15 to 20 minutes of foreplay raised this percentage to half; and still longer foreplay resulted in nearly three fifths of the women achieving this high orgasm rate. Conversely, wives with lesser orgasm rates received shorter periods of foreplay, the 1-10 minutes category having the most cases. The women who never experienced orgasm constitute a separate phenomenon. While their number is small, it appears that many of the husbands (most of whom were also college educated) were protracting foreplay with the hope of inducing orgasm. (Gebhard 1975: 100)

In reading tables such as Table 4.3, keep in mind that the percentage results depend on how the variables presented are categorized and the number of cases in each category. The total number of cases in each category are called the marginal totals or, simply, the **marginals.** They are important because they tell us *how many persons in the sample fall into a particular category,* such as for foreplay, none, 1 to 10 minutes, 15 to 20 minutes, or 21 minutes or more. Examining the marginals, we see that in this table the majority of the women who were interviewed reported an average duration of foreplay in marital sex of 1 to 10 minutes, very few reported no foreplay, and the rest were about evenly divided between 15 to 20 minutes and 21 minutes or more. The other variable in the table, percentage of coitus resulting in orgasm from 0 percent to 90-100 percent, was categorized into four groups to basically compare those who never climaxed with those who did so sometimes (1 to 39 percent of the time), regularly (40 to 89 percent of the time), or nearly always (90 to 100 percent of the time). Looking closely at the categories presented in tables also serves as a reminder of measurement validity concerns. How accurately do you think people are able to report on matters such as "percent of coitus resulting in orgasm," "average duration of foreplay," or "average duration of penile intromission"?

Duration of Intromission

Gebhard (1975: 101) stated that all females with coital experience were questioned as to duration of intromission and "their responses appear to be reasonably accurate since they agree with the time measurements from a small but growing number of cases of observed coitus." Table 4.4 displays a portion of the complex original results. This table is based on over 1,000

TABLE 4.3. Female Orgasm Rate and Duration of Precoital Foreplay in Intact Marriages

Percent of Coitus Resulting in Orgasm	Average Duration of Foreplay in Minutes			
	0	1-10	15-20	21+
0	(2 cases)	3.9%	7.6%	7.7%
1-39	(1 case)	19.5%	12.6%	7.7%
40-89	(1 case)	34.6%	28.9%	25.6%
90-100	(2 cases)	41.9%	50.6%	58.9%
Cases	6	179	79	78

Source: Gebhard (1975).

cases but shows percentages of column totals only for those who said they reached orgasm always or nearly always (90 to 100 percent of the time). Gebhard found the original data "not easy to interpret" and speculated that the effect of duration of intromission may be "masked by other variables." Lengthy foreplay with brief intromission may be as effective for female orgasm as brief foreplay and lengthy intromission. Other variables such as manual stimulation may affect results. "Yet another complication is the probability of the husband's adjusting himself to the speed of the wife's response: a man with a highly responsive wife being less inclined to delay ejaculation" (Gebhard 1975: 101).

Gebhard's data did clearly show that penile intromission of less than one minute was insufficient to cause regular orgasm in most women, and the highest orgasm rate was associated with the lengthiest duration of intromission, 16+ minutes (see Table 4.4). "Where intromission is under one minute only slightly over one quarter of the wives achieved orgasm always or nearly always, while lengthier intromission (1 to 11 minutes) raises this proportion to roughly half, and where intromission is protracted beyond 11 minutes three fifths to two thirds of the wives reach this high orgasm rate" (Gebhard 1975: 101). Not to get too carried away, though, with our expectations for male sexual performance, 16-plus minutes for penile intromission is a lot. Check the marginals in Table 4.4. By far, most husbands in Gebhard's sample were in the 4 to 7 and 2 to 3.9 minute categories as reported by their wives.

FREQUENCY OF INTERCOURSE

Another issue of popular interest is the frequency of intercourse among married persons, coupled with folklore about the declining quality of sex in marriage. The frequency of sexual activity may decline over time for a variety of reasons, including age, overfamiliarity with one's spouse ("comfortable as an old shoe"), boredom with sex, and pressures from work or child care responsibility. Presence of children, particularly preschoolers, and larger numbers of children in the household are related to less frequent sexual activity. Nevertheless, when Janus and Janus (1993) compared married persons with never married singles and divorced persons, married couples

TABLE 4.4. Female Orgasm Rate and Duration of Penile Intromission in Intact Marriages

Percent of Coitus Resulting in Orgasm	Average Duration of Penile Intromission in Minutes						
	1	1-1.9	2-3.9	4-7	8-11	12-15	16+
90-100%	27.5%	51.2%	50.2%	51.6%	48.3%	61.6%	66.7%
Cases	40	160	255	308	89	73	39

fared well. As Table 4.5 indicates, married persons were *more* likely than the singles or divorced to report having some sexual activity daily or a few times weekly and *less* likely to report sexual activity only monthly or rarely. Most married respondents (85 percent) reported having some kind of sexual activity at least weekly; only 15 percent had sex less frequently. Both men's and women's perception of a positive marital relationship tends to enhance their sexual relationship (Oggins, Leber, and Veroff 1993). Sexual enjoyment can be associated with feelings of caring for the spouse and with perceptions of enjoying relaxing or exciting time with the spouse. Age and marital happiness were identified in another study as the two most important predictors of sexual frequency in marriage (Call, Sprecher, and Schwartz 1995).

In an article on sexually inactive marriages that appeared in the *Journal of Sex Research,* Denise A. Donnelly (1993) began with the observation that marriage is the formally and legally sanctioned avenue for sexual fulfillment in our society. Since married persons are expected to have sex, the notion of marriages without sexual activity strikes most persons as unusual and problematic. "Sexless marriages" may catch the interest of the media and talk shows but, according to Donnelly, little in-depth or large-scale research with such couples has been published in social science journals. Her objective, therefore, was to investigate the suggestion that lack of sexual activity is an indication of marital distress by looking more closely at the incidence and correlates of sexually inactive marriages.

A sample of 6,029 married persons from the National Survey of Families and Households was analyzed by Donnelly. The original survey was designed and supervised by Larry Bumpass and James Sweet at the Center for Demography and Ecology at the University of Wisconsin-Madison, with field work conducted by the Institute for Survey Research at Temple University. Sexual activity, as measured in this survey, referred only to the month previous to the interview, so the survey cannot distinguish temporary from longer term sexual inactivity. However, respondents are able to recall behavior more accurately over the past month than for longer periods;

TABLE 4.5. Frequency of All Sexual Activity (Percent)

	Married (1,552)	Single (815)	Divorced (246)
Daily	14	11	9
Few times weekly	44	32	33
Weekly	27	21	26
Monthly	8	17	10
Rarely	7	19	22

shorter time periods seemed insufficient, and previous studies used this same time frame. Also, the measure asked about the "frequency of sex," not frequency of intercourse. This broader measure recognizes that couples may stop having intercourse (at least for a time) without stopping all sexual interaction.

Sixteen percent of the marriages in this sample were reported to be sexually inactive during the month prior to the interview. Correlates of sexual inactivity in marriage identified in this study included: unhappiness with the marital relationship, increased likelihood of separation, lack of shared activity, the presence of preschoolers, increased age, and poor health. Donnelly concluded that although sexually inactive marriages are not uncommon, they are generally not happy, stable marriages in which the partners simply do not have sex. Lack of sexual activity appeared to be associated with other problems in the relationship and therefore may serve in many (not all) marriages as a warning sign.

TALKING TO A PARTNER ABOUT SEX

With sexuality an important component of a successful marriage, knowing how to address sexual issues with one's partner would appear to be an aspect of marital communication worth special attention. In *Human Sexuality* (Second Edition), William Masters, Virginia Johnson, and Robert C. Kolodny (1985: 332-333) offer the following advice on talking about sex:

- *Talk with your partner about how and when it would be most comfortable to discuss sex.* You may be surprised to find that your partner is also hesitant about sexual discussions and that simply bringing up the topic provides an opportunity to defuse tensions. Determine when it would be easiest to talk about sex. Some people prefer to avoid the "instant replay" analysis right after making love but others feel this is a good time since events and feelings are still fresh in your minds.
- *Let your partner know you are interested in feedback about your sexual interaction.* Then your partner will not be so worried that you will react to anything he or she brings up as though it was simply criticism.
- *Consider using books or media sources to initiate discussions.* This approach allows partners to discuss what they have read or seen and to relate it to their personal preferences or dislikes. The advantage is that the discussion is more abstract—in effect, a discussion of sexual ideas as much as sexual action—and doesn't sound so much like, "when you touched me here, it didn't feel good."

- *Remember that if your partner rejects a type of sexual activity you think you might enjoy he or she is not rejecting you as a person.* Individuals have different tolerances for sexual experimentation.
- *Be aware that sexual feelings and preferences change from time to time.* It's very tempting, on hearing that your partner likes to have his or her earlobes licked, to do this automatically every time you make love. Doing the same things over and over tends to get boring and sometimes downright unpleasant. The other side of this coin is that a partner who doesn't generally like a particular form of sexual stimulation, such as oral sex, may develop a yen for that activity on a given occasion. Be flexible.
- *Don't neglect the nonverbal side of sexual communication, since these often speak louder than words.* Don't be afraid of showing your partner just how you like to be touched; firm or feathery, vigorous or slow, consistent or alternating intensity. Since it is often difficult to express precise preferences in words, you might demonstrate. This also relieves your partner of the need to guess what you like.
- *Don't expect perfection.* Intimate relations can stumble if partners expect that sex should always be a memorable, passionate experience. Realize that just as moods can change or physical feelings ebb and flow, sexual experiences can range from ecstatic peaks to fizzled-out fiascoes. It isn't necessary to analyze what went wrong whenever sex wasn't superlative. Be sure both partners have realistic expectations.
- *Talking about sex with your partner isn't something you do once and then put aside.* Like all forms of intimate communication, this topic benefits from an ongoing dialogue that permits a couple to learn about each other and resolve confusions or uncertainties over time.

CONCLUSION

On the whole, married couples enjoy many advantages in well-being, but they are increasingly vulnerable to divorce. Although divorce can be examined as an individual experience, it makes greater sense against the background of changes in American society as a whole. Staying single, living together, marrying, and divorcing are matters of personal choice, but these decisions and their consequences are shaped by the kind of society in which one lives. The "sociological imagination" gives us a much broader perspective on divorce than we might otherwise have. You may remember that the sociological imagination, according to C. Wright Mills, is the ability to see a connection between biography and history; in other words, between private lives and social issues, the individual and social structure, or personal choices and social forces. Why we divorce in America today has a lot to do with why we marry. To summarize, family today: (a) performs fewer functions than it did in earlier centuries; though (b) the functions it does perform are more emotionally charged, with higher levels of expectation; (c) the main goal of marriage is personal fulfillment; and (d) marriage rests on individual choice based on feelings of love.

Sexual gratification for consenting adults in a socially sanctioned union is one of the functions of the family. Generally speaking, couples with a good sexual relationship are less apt to turn to outside partners and less often seek divorce. While some married couples are able to experiment successfully with sexually open marriage, these remain the exception. Extramarital relationships in the more usual form of clandestine affairs are widely regarded as negatively affecting a marriage. When Israel Charney and Sivan Parnass (1995) investigated the impact of extramarital relationships on the continuation of marriages, they found that out of sixty-two cases known to their informants, nine (14.5 percent) cases resulted in positive growth and improvement in the marriage while twenty-one (34 percent) resulted in divorce. In twenty-seven of the remaining cases (43.5 percent), the marriage continued but in a negative atmosphere; in the last four cases (6 percent) the future of the relationship was in doubt. They described the emotions of the majority of "betrayed" partners, male or female, as including damage to self-image, lowered self-confidence (personal and sexual), feelings of abandonment, loss of trust, attacks on their sense of belonging, rage, and a surge of justification to leave their spouse.

Sex is one way intimacy and a sense of connectedness are expressed in marriage. Morton Hunt (1974) observed that singles were not the only ones to have benefited from the "sexual revolution." Married couples reported an increase in rates of intercourse (from once a week to five times a month). In contemporary American society, we have moved away from the Victorian idea that only men are seriously interested in sex to a belief that both women and men have a desire for and right to sexual satisfaction in marriage. Neither men nor women today endorse as a model for marital relations the stereotypic "quickie" in which the man initiates and takes his pleasure while the woman passively accepts and does not expect much. Still, in heterosexual relationships, couples have to successfully negotiate common differences between men and women in sexual needs and desires. Women, especially in marriage, expect to express their own sexuality more openly and have the option of being the initiator. In general, they expect to reach orgasm, not necessarily always—sex can still be satisfying without—but frequently or regularly. They expect a lover/mate to take his time; in foreplay, during intercourse itself, and after (in ways that communicate affection).

Much more information about sex is available today through legitimate channels than in the past; e.g., you can buy *The Joy of Sex* in just about any bookstore or take college courses in human sexuality. In addition, there are counseling and support services for couples who run into problems and want outside help. Sexual problems can be physical, psychological, or interactional—that is, involving no particular individual emotional difficulties, just a different perspective on the issue. For example, how often should you have sex? One partner thinks three times a week is a lot; the other thinks six times a week is still sacrificing a lot of potential. Neither is right or wrong. Their task is to adjust individual expectations to reach a shared definition of what is appropriate for them as a couple. This takes communication and compromise. If sex generally is no longer looked on as shameful or sinful or "dirty," then sex in marriage does not have to be done in the dark, literally or figuratively. Both partners should be free to say what pleases them or what they might like to try, and both should be willing to make a genuine effort to please the other person (within the boundaries of their own personal values). Finally, decline in frequency of intercourse with age does not mean that satisfaction with sexual activity necessarily decreases. Patterson and Kim (1991) found the majority of married Americans quite satisfied with their sex lives.

Chapter 5

Sexual Morality and Sexual Hang-Ups

SEXUAL MORALITY

Sexual morality is a uniquely human characteristic. We not only behave, we evaluate our behavior in terms of "right" and "wrong," "good" and "bad," "proper" and "improper." These judgments reflect the values, beliefs, and shared standards of conduct, or **norms,** we have learned growing up in the groups and larger society to which we belong. As discussed in earlier chapters, viewing sexual practices in the United States as only an individual matter would be misleading. Every society regulates the sexual behavior of its members. Community standards provide the social context within which individual choices are made, and a standpoint from which we define and respond to sexual "hang-ups." Consider two extreme positions, one at each end of a continuum, with different degrees of social conservatism or permissiveness in between:

Straitlaced		*Libertine*
Sex is always wrong;	∧	Sex is always right;
"better to marry than to burn,"		"anything goes,"
St. Paul		Marquis de Sade

Concerning sex we often find human opinions running to extremes. One set of voices cry that sex is a lust of our lower nature, a base necessity for procreation. Then we have the voices who cry for sex and more sex; who bewail the institution of marriage; who think that most of the troubles of the world are traceable to sexual restrictions. (Al Anon 1976: 68)

Between these two extremes we exercise individual freedom of choice within normative guidelines. Human morality and ethical conduct is about the choices we make in our relationships with others, the principles of right and wrong we follow. In sexual matters, our impulses will be guided (e.g., encouraged, inhibited, modified, or redirected) by our social ties.

Sometimes the messages or social scripts we internalize will be relatively more straitlaced, as represented by the religious figure St. Paul. As a result, we acquire **sexual hang-ups,** defined as inhibitions, fear, rejection, or closed mind toward any particular sex act, due to religious beliefs, legal sanctions, or personal preference. The negative effects or dysfunctions of excessively prohibitive sexual values include hypocrisy (pretending to be what one is not), fear, guilt, shame, and an overall attitude that sex is "dirty." Examples of such effects are seen in the sex guilt that undermines effective contraceptive behavior and in the negative feelings about sex expressed by working-class wives interviewed by Rubin (1976).

The callous libertine's unrestrained quest for sexual gratification at the other extreme, represented by the historical Marquis de Sade, can lead to excesses that endanger one's social standing, physical safety, and/or psychological well-being. Looking critically at the libertine position suggests another definition of sexual hang-ups as *deviations* or *perversions,* which involve conduct believed to express an unnatural sexual preference or behavior deviating greatly from what is generally considered right or correct (deviating from stated expectations, actual practice, or both).

According to *Webster's College Dictionary,* what is natural is that which is present in or produced by nature in the expected order of things. It is inborn, not acquired; not artificial or man-made. It is inherent in human nature; part of our essential constitution. Regarding what is "natural" or "normal" human behavior, readers should keep several points in mind:

- A *range* of behavior is always found in nature.
- Human potential is always channeled in interaction with culture.
- What is normal varies cross-culturally, and changes over time.
- It is reasonable to talk about what is normal within a given society or social group during a particular historical period.
- Cultural relativism does not rule out consideration of individual psychopathology.

The discussion that follows does not take a position at either extreme. Recalling the social science objective of sorting facts from values, it tries to remain descriptive and analytic, not prescriptive. The focus will be on two related questions: What are some of the various forms of sexual expression, and how are they socially regulated?

Sexuality is an aspect of human experience very much subjected to social scrutiny and imbued with moral judgments about what should or should not be permitted. For better or worse, the topic provokes considerable difference of opinion. Opposing viewpoints related to sexual values (Cozic 1995) are heard in debates on issues such as: whether or not lust is a fundamentally "base" instinct; whether any involvement in sex before marriage is immoral;

whether homosexuality is normal; whether pornography is harmful to society; whether prostitution should be legalized; or, how, what, and by whom children should be taught about sex. One person's belief and practice may be someone else's idea of deviance.

Sociological perspectives on sexual deviance emphasize the importance of the social processes involved in defining or labeling certain behaviors as unacceptable (Bryant 1977, 1982). "A form of behavior becomes **deviant** when it is defined as violating the norms of some collectivity" (Gagnon and Simon 1967: 2). A **collectivity** refers to people as a whole, representing a society at large, social institutions, or groups within the society. Norms are enforced by **sanctions,** designated consequences that can be imposed by the group including punishments for deviance and rewards for conformity. Negative sanctions for sexual misconduct can be *formal,* as when one is excommunicated from the church or arrested by the police, or *informal,* as when one is no longer invited to social gatherings by former friends who learned of behaviors they find intolerable. The types of labels and sanctions applied to known incidents of deviance also vary with the *audience;* religious judgments may invoke sinfulness and damnation, the legal system criminality and incarceration, while medical and mental health practitioners respond in terms of illness and hospitalization or therapy.

Sexual behaviors that have been prohibited in the United States on one basis or another run the gamut from those most people agree are bad and very few engage in (e.g., sex with a corpse) to those that are widely disapproved of but many people do anyway (e.g., adultery) to those that people disagree about to begin with (e.g., premarital sex), and so on. This complicates social reactions. Too, the application of sanctions depends on detection, and sexual behavior is often private. Some types of sexual deviance are more socially visible than others. The man who exposes his genitals in public, for example, is more likely to be arrested than a married man who likes to dress up at home in women's clothes, but both are engaging in non-normative sexual expression.

Gagnon and Simon (1967) used the term **normatively integrated** to designate a community in which norms do not conflict much with each other and serve individual needs reasonably well. In this case, institutionalized norms (that is, laws), shared and internalized folkways and mores (norms), and actual behavior would be consistent. One way to analyze specific types of sexual behavior is as more, or less, normatively integrated. As Gagnon and Simon noted, there are many examples of inconsistencies in U.S. society, with masturbation cited as one example of a behavior widely practiced, not illegal, yet not publicly endorsed, while oral-genital contact is still a legal offense in some jurisdictions even though it is approved of and engaged in by many. Oral-genital contact also illustrates societal ambivalence about actively *enforcing* some laws pertaining to sexuality even when there is still resistance to repealing them. Prostitution and homosexuality are cases of legally prohibited sexual conduct where participation is voluntary but conventional morality remains opposed, and enthusiasm for legal prosecution is mixed. "The sheer persistence of relatively large numbers of persons engaging in such behavior is sufficient to constrain norm-enforcing agencies," so they largely attempt to regulate rather than effectively suppress the behavior (Gagnon and Simon 1967: 6).

Box 5.1 suggests an exercise for discussing sexual behaviors with the idea of normative integration (or lack thereof) in mind. The meaning of some of the listed terms that denote less well known sexual practices will be

---

Box 5.1. Sexual Morality Exercise

Consider the set of sexual practices listed below. On the left side, rate them from 1 to10:

"right," "good"..."wrong," "bad"

ACCEPTABLE 1   2   3   4   5   6   7   8   9   10 UNACCEPTABLE

On the right side, check to indicate that the behavior should be illegal.

_____nonprocreative sex   _____
_____masturbation   _____
_____nudity   _____
_____indecent exposure/exhibitionism   _____
_____adultery/swinging   _____
_____pornography   _____
_____oral sex (cunnilingus, fellatio, "69")   _____
_____sodomy/anal sex   _____
_____voyeurism   _____
_____homosexuality   _____
_____pedophilia   _____
_____zoophilia/bestiality   _____
_____rape   _____
_____incest   _____
_____abortion   _____
_____promiscuity/nymphomania or satyriasis   _____
_____fetishism   _____
_____frottage   _____
_____klismaphilia   _____
_____bondage   _____
_____masochism/sadism   _____
_____prostitution   _____

As you go, note any conditions you may want to attach to your response; e.g., in private versus in public, or one kind versus another, or felony versus misdemeanor, or other people versus for me.

covered in the following sections, which turn to three major social institutions that address sexual norms and deviant behaviors—religion, law, and mental health—and variation due to personal preferences.

INSTITUTIONAL PERSPECTIVES

Religion

The Christian church has strongly influenced Western attitudes toward sexuality. Its dominant view was that sexual behavior should be **procreative,** that is, tied to conception and childbearing, and between married persons. Sociologist Anthony Giddens (1996: 146) noted that today "traditional attitudes exist alongside much more liberal attitudes toward sexuality." Some people, influenced by Christian teachings, still take the conservative view that only sex in marriage is acceptable, and its purpose is having children. Premarital sex is fornication, a sin, and most forms of contraception are rejected. The Moral Majority, formed in the 1980s, is a political movement consisting primarily of Protestant fundamentalists seeking to further a socially conservative agenda. Giddens (1996: 290) described fundamentalism as intentionally promoting beliefs, values, and practices of the past, which participants fear are being lost. In reaction to changing social conditions, traditional family and sexual values are reaffirmed. The Moral Majority provides a conservative, religiously oriented standpoint for evaluating sexual expression.

Nonprocreative sex refers to sexual activities for purposes other than reproduction—e.g., for physical or emotional intimacy, pleasure, or recreation. Even between married persons, this sometimes conflicts with religious doctrines, as controversy among Catholics over use of birth control well illustrates. The church takes an official position not uniformly endorsed by priests nor necessarily followed by all practicing Catholics. This would be an example of a lack of normative integration. Some religious persons unequivocally reject a particular church teaching. Others act contrary to it but feel some degree of remorse, regret, or guilt; they retain hang-ups about nonprocreative sex. Secular society has become sufficiently liberal overall, however, to have redefined sexual expectations in marriage even for most religious persons to include a pleasurable and satisfying sexual relationship between husband and wife, not exclusively oriented toward producing children and allowing contraceptive use for family planning.

Attitudes about our bodies also reflect theological assumptions and teachings, one stream of which regards the body as "bad," e.g., a source of weakness and temptation, and sexuality as correspondingly dangerous and tainted (Wood 1968: 34). Frederic C. Wood Jr., a moral theologian and pastoral minister, observed that "a negative view of the body can lead to fears of sexual involvement and a negative self-image" and instead endorsed a body-as-good position (p. 35). Sexuality could be seen as a gift to celebrate, in a morally responsible manner; a perspective that "could not be called a popular or prominent attitude" (Wood 1968: 35). Shame and embarrassment about the body are feelings that can be learned from the social environment, traceable in part to religious influence. Parmelee (1966) cites several biblical verses emphasizing shame associated with nakedness, most notably from Genesis 3:7 concerning Adam and Eve: "They knew that they were naked; and they sewed fig leaves together; and made themselves an apron." Some people carry this shame to an extreme called *gymnophobia,* a dread of nakedness (Parmelee 1966: 64).

Adultery is a sexual behavior expressly prohibited by the church. Defined by *Webster's College Dictionary,* **adultery** is voluntary sexual intercourse between a married person and someone other than one's lawful spouse. As laid out in religious teachings, adultery violates one of the Ten Commandments. As Wood (1968: 111) characterizes adultery, whatever else it represents, given the institution of marriage, "adultery involves the breaking of a vow. It always betokens some loss of faith," hence use of the term infidelity. Judaism, which has a fundamentally positive view of sex as joyful and good apart from reproductive potential, also sees sex as primarily proper within marriage and forbids adultery (Masters, Johnson, and Kolodny 1992: 624).

Another moral issue that has received considerable recent attention is abortion. **Abortion** is deliberate termination of a pregnancy before the fetus can survive outside the uterus (Hoshii 1987: 87). In 1973, in the *Roe v. Wade* decision, the U.S. Supreme Court ruled in support of a woman's right to an elective abortion without state regulation in the first trimester and with medical restrictions in the second. Legality hinged on issues of individual right to privacy and whether the term "person" in the Fourteenth Amendment extends the right to life to the unborn. "For moral evaluation of abortion, the time when human life starts is of decisive importance," but this has proven elusive (Hoshii 1987: 104). Catholic doctrine holds that life begins at conception; many Protestant moralists believe true human life begins at "quickening," about three months into pregnancy when the child gives indications of life; and some Jewish scholars favor forty days after conception (Hoshii 1987). Public opinion is divided and sensitive to circumstances (e.g., generally more favorable if the woman's life is in danger or in cases of rape and incest). Many religious leaders continue to view abortion as wrong. The antiabortion or right-to-life movement strenuously opposes abortion; ironically, even resorting to violence, bombings, and killings at abortion clinics.

The abortion controversy also raises the more general point that judgments of legality and morality do not necessarily coincide, since the decision-making principles followed are not the same; differing ethics apply.

Ethics refers to a set of principles, precepts, or values about right and wrong that govern conduct and guide individual decisions. Many public debates about sexuality include concerns about the extent to which the state should or effectively can legislate sexual morality. The rules of civil society will impinge on persons with varied, often conflicting, religious beliefs and personal preferences.

Legal Sanctions

In the United States, substantive criminal law in each state defines various sexual offenses and the penalties attached. As summarized by Roberson (1996: 1), the Texas Penal Code, for example, states that the general purpose of the law is to deal with conduct that "causes or threatens harm to those individual or public interests for which State protection is appropriate." Reasonable persons may, of course, disagree on precisely what sexual conduct should fall within that category, but elected state legislators, representing their constituents and subject to political pressures, will make decisions determining the laws of their state. Offenses are "graded" with respect to the severity of the misconduct involved, broadly categorized as misdemeanors (lesser offenses) and felonies (more serious violations with greater penalties). Misdemeanors typically can result in fines or jail (e.g., up to $1,000 and one year in jail); felonies in larger fines and imprisonment, up to life. Box 5.2 provides examples of sexual offenses.

Laws vary from state to state, but there are commonalties concerning sexual offenses. Exposing the genitals, watching others uninvited, sexual contact with animals, oral-genital sex, anal sex, incest, homosexuality, sexual abuse of children, and rape are behaviors most widely identified as being legally prohibited. Of those offenses, some are backed by strong law enforcement, while with others we tend to look the other way (Dietz 1985: 32). Commenting on the application of criminal law, Paula Dietz (1985) noted that according to the circumstances involved, an act may be regarded as meaningless in one case, and in another the same act will be punished to the fullest extent of the law. For example, anal penetration between consenting adults would be overlooked, but committed during a rape would be charged against the attacker. Selective attention might also be paid to the same act if engaged in by same-sex participants rather than a married, heterosexual couple.

Normative integration on the felony sexual offenses would indicate substantial public consensus that the conduct involved does harm to individual or public interests and justifies state intervention. As indicated in Box 5.2, the most serious offenses involve use of force, as in sexual assault or sexual exploitation and abuse of minors. **Incest** refers to sexual relations, including intercourse, oral sex, genital manipulation, or other sexual contact, between close relatives. Between an adult and a child, these acts are considered

---

Box 5.2. Types of Sexual Conduct Prohibited by Law

Felony

- *Sexual assault:* Intentional penetration of mouth, anus, or vagina by any means without the other person's consent.
- *Indecency with a child:* Exposure of genitals to or any sexual contact with person under specified age (up to seventeen), or sex with prohibited relations (e.g., incest, including a stepchild or sibling).
- *Sexual performance by a child:* Involving a child in performances that include sexual conduct by the child. Also, *possession or promotion of child pornography.*

Misdemeanor

- *Public lewdness:* Sexual conduct in a public place or recklessly in the presence of others who would be offended or alarmed; including sexual contact, sexual intercourse, "deviate sexual intercourse," or sexual contact with animals.
- *Indecent exposure:* Knowingly exposing any part of the genitals to arouse or gratify sexual desire and reckless about whether another person present will be offended.
- *Obscene communication:* Making an "obscene" comment, suggestion, request, or proposal by telephone or in writing, knowingly, to harass, annoy, or embarrass.
- *Obscenity:* Intentionally producing or promoting distribution of "obscene" material or devices.
- *Prostitution:* Intentionally engaging in sexual contact for a fee (with higher grade offenses including felonies for third parties who promote or compel such activities).
- *Disorderly conduct:* Entering another person's property and looking through a window or other opening for lewd or unlawful purposes; using abusive, indecent, profane, or vulgar language in a public place.

Source: Based on Texas Penal Code.

---

abuses of a social position of trust and authority toward a minor. Though some differences of opinion do arise over an appropriate age of consent, violating even a sexually permissive norm that what *consenting adults* agree to do between themselves in private is their own business, the elements of coercion and child victimization in sexual conduct would be serious concerns for law enforcement.

Misdemeanor sexual offenses are more varied. Some are prohibited because of the public nature of the act or because it intrudes on another person's right to privacy. In these instances the state's obligation to protect public spaces or targeted individuals from offenders is widely acknowledged, though the potential harm done may be deemed less than in felony transgressions. Other sexual behaviors are prohibited because the conduct, judged by "severity of perversion," is regarded as inherently unnatural and improper. Punishment is sought through use of legal sanctions to affirm that the behavior is significantly deviant and offensive. Sex with an animal or sex with a corpse, accordingly, are prohibited. **Bestiality** refers to sexual contact between a human and an animal, which can include intercourse, masturbation, or oral stimulation. **Necrophilia** involves an erotic attraction to dead bodies that may lead to fondling or attempted sexual intercourse with a corpse. In neither of these cases can the behavior be characterized as being between consenting adults.

Obscenity statutes disguise complex, continuing social and legal controversies regarding how to define and prohibit what is "obscene" without unduly infringing on individual rights. **Obscene** means containing a "patently offensive description of or a solicitation to commit an ultimate sex act," including sexual intercourse, masturbation or oral sex, or a "description of an excretory function;" patently offensive "means so offensive on its face as to affront current community standards of decency" (Roberson 1996: 98, 100). In describing Texas criminal law, Roberson (1996: 100) outlines legal criteria used to identify obscene materials or performance:

1. The average person, applying contemporary community standards, would find that taken as a whole the work appeals to prurient interest in sex.
2. It depicts or describes
   a. patently offensive representations or descriptions of ultimate sex acts, normal or perverted, actual or simulated, including sexual intercourse, sodomy and sexual bestiality *or*
   b. patently offensive representations or descriptions of masturbation, excretory functions, sadism, masochism, lewd exhibition of the genitals, male or female genitals in a state of sexual excitation or arousal, covered male genitals in a discernible turgid state, or a device designed and marketed as used primarily for stimulation of human genital organs *and*
   c. taken as whole lacks serious literary, artistic, political and scientific value.

Even a cursory reading of these criteria suggests the ambiguities faced by the courts in enforcing such principles. Who is the average person? By what community standards? How is prurient interest demonstrated? Is there room for disagreement about what is "patently" offensive? What constitutes redeeming value? Interpretation may at times be quite difficult and contentious.

Among the misdemeanor sexual offenses are those that presently reflect a lack of normative integration because, while the law specifically forbids them and religious teachings may define them as sinful, public opinion and practice do not show consistent disapproval or rejection of these behaviors. For example, "deviate sexual intercourse" in the Texas Penal Code includes oral-genital contact, which is also prohibited in many other states, along with homosexual acts, adultery, premarital sex, and prostitution. Masters, Johnson, and Kolodny (1992: 606, 607) commented that "if current laws regulating sexual behavior were enforced in a strict and uniform manner, our prisons would have to accommodate the great majority of our population. . . . It's safe to say that in any 24-hour period, millions of ordinary Americans unwittingly engage in sex acts that are criminal and could lead to imprisonment." These laws are not being vigorously enforced because, generally speaking, our society has adopted the attitude that what goes on sexually behind closed doors is no one else's business. There is considerable social and political resistance to the idea that private sexual acts involving consenting adults should be subject to scrutiny by the state. Laws have been changed in many states or are simply not enforced but remain on the books and are selectively enforced in other states. Even misdemeanor prosecution for a sexual offense that does not result in conviction can be quite costly in time, money, stress, and public embarrassment for the accused.

Sexual Deviance and Mental Health

In addressing sexual deviance, the law judges and sanctions specific, overt acts according to community standards, but the role of the mental health professional is to help individuals "better understand their motives, anxieties and interpersonal stresses" (Strean 1983: 155). Sexual variations are examined in terms of self states and interactional consequences, while keeping the larger social context in mind. The rightness or wrongness of the behavior of a client who is indiscriminately having sex with many partners, for example, is evaluated in terms of how the person feels about the behavior, about himself or herself and any other persons involved, the motivation behind the behavior (why it is engaged in), and the resulting outcomes experienced. Consider, from a mental health standpoint, the question of what, if anything, is wrong with a shoe fetish. A **shoe fetish** refers to sexual arousal exclusively or primarily in the presence of selected shoes, which may be used for visual and tactile stimulation, accompanied by masturbation. It involves private conduct engaged in by a consenting adult, does not harm anyone physically, and is not a severe perversion of the sort that warrants explicit legal attention. If it feels good, do it? However, finding out that a friend, neighbor, or family member can respond sexually only to the stimulus of women's shoes is still likely to invoke feelings that the behavior is not quite "right" or "normal." It is often subjected to ridicule and makes people feel uncomfortable. Why? The issue of how *normal* and *abnormal* sexual behavior can be and typically are defined is addressed by Leonore Tiefer in Box 5.3. The text then discusses three related issues; the paraphilias, sexual addiction, and inhibited sexual desire.

Box 5.3. What Does Normal Mean?

In *Sex Is Not a Natural Act*, Leonore Tiefer (1005) raises the question, "What is sexual normalcy?" She suggests several possible approaches:

1. *Subjective*. Based on my own personal experience. I am normal, therefore behavior like mine is normal. Tiefer thinks that publicly we don't say so, but privately we often use this standard.
2. *Statistical*. Conduct a survey asking people what kinds of sexual behaviors they have engaged in and graph the results. The most common behaviors are normal, the more uncommon behaviors less so (e.g., both "too much" and "too little" sex are cause for concern).
3. *Idealistic*. Normal means perfect, an ideal to strive for. The ideal becomes the standard of comparison; anything less is unacceptable.
4. *Cultural*. In a given society, the prevailing shared standards of appropriate conduct. Normal is what is generally considered proper. Deviance is that which violates these standards.
5. *Clinical*. Based on scientific data about health and illness. Activity is considered clinically abnormal when research shows it is related to disease or disability.

Cultural standards often have a taken-for-granted quality and are assumed by adherents to be universal definitions of normalcy. However, cultural standards vary historically, cross-culturally, and even among subgroups within a particular society. According to Tiefer, applying the clinical standard to psychosexual matters is in some respects difficult. Is the absence of interest in sex, for example, abnormal? What sickness or disability befalls a person who avoids sex? "Clearly, such a person misses a life experience that [most people value] . . . It's not trendy, but is it 'sick'?" Tiefer cautions that clinical standards for sexuality may not be based only on valid, empirically sound standards of health and illness but may also reflect cultural standards. "Sexual habits and preferences that do not conform to a procreative model for sex are the ones considered abnormal in medicine and clinical psychology" (p.13).

A person's persistent interest in unconventional sexual expression and experience is often seen by clinicians as evidence of that individual's personality immaturity, poor judgment or extreme needs. Although I would agree that such patterns could be evidence of psychological problems, I would want corroborating evidence from other parts of a person's life. And I would want to see that there were negative consequences to the person's well-being other than a sense of

(continued)

(continued)

shame or guilt from being different. The problem is that the very existence of standards of normality breeds negative psychological consequences for those who deviate—that is known as the "social control"
function of norms. And once norms become clinical standards, it's
very difficult to identify those psychological problems that might not
exist if social conformity weren't so important. (Tiefer 1995:14)

The Paraphilias

The terms sexual deviations, perversions, and aberrations have been
used to label various types of sexual behavior that did not conform to society's standards. The neutral term presently used is **paraphilia,** derived from
Greek roots meaning "alongside of" and "love" (Masters, Johnson, and
Kolodny 1992). Robert Francoeur (1991: 529), a fellow of the Society for
the Scientific Study of Sex, defined the paraphilias as involving "chronic
dependency on an unconventional object or sexual stimulus for sexual
arousal and/or gratification." Masters, Johnson, and Kolodny (1992: 418),
too, note that in a paraphilia the unusual sexual experience "becomes the
principal focus of sexual behavior [and fantasy]. A paraphilia can revolve
around a particular sexual object (e.g., children, animals, underwear) or a
particular sexual act (e.g., inflicting pain, making obscene telephone calls)."
Major types of paraphilias include the following:

1. *Exhibitionism*—When an individual repeatedly exposes the genitals
uninvited to strangers to gain sexual satisfaction. Many exhibitionists or
"flashers" have difficulties in other heterosexual activities and an "uncontrollable urge" pushes them to this behavior; most tend to be young (averaging in their twenties), male, and to be described as "passive, shy and sexually inhibited" (Masters, Johnson, and Kolodny 1992: 422). Exposing the
male genitals is typically experienced as a demonstration of masculinity.
The behavior is most of concern "when it takes on elements of intent and
compulsion, . . . deliberately exhibiting the genitals to women or girls to interest, frighten or disgust them may signify anger toward women or fear of
relating to them directly" (McWhorter 1977: 104).

2. *Fetishism*—Sexual arousal is elicited by an inanimate object or specific body part, used during masturbation or assimilated into sexual activity
with a partner. Common fetish items and body parts are: women's stock-
ings, bras, underpants, negligees, shoes, or gloves; lace, leather, rubber,
silk, or fur; and hair, feet, legs, breasts, or buttocks (Masters, Johnson, and
Kolodny 1992). "Most people with fetishes are men," who tend to indulge
their paraphilia in private and are "usually not dangerous" (King, Camp,
and Downey 1991: 344), though sometimes the objects desired are taken
without permission or are preferred because they are predictable, yielding,

and can be ruined without penalties. Some individuals may *only* be aroused when the fetish is used or require its use in a certain way; sometimes the individual is simply less responsive without it but can use supporting fantasies for stimulation. Partners may be receptive, or resistant if they find the fetish intrusive, irritating, confusing, or disappointing.

3. *Obscene communication*—Most commonly, obscene communication has taken the form of habitually making sexually explicit, offensive telephone calls. Like exhibitionists and voyeurs, obscene callers are predominantly men with feelings of inadequacy in interpersonal relationships, who retain control by distancing themselves from the other persons involved in order to respond sexually (Greenberg, Bruess, and Haffner 2000: 548). They may also be gratified by shock, fear, or anger evoked in the recipient (Strong, DeVault, and Sayad 1999). Women receiving obscene phone calls typically do feel victimized, upset, annoyed, and fearful. Masters, Johnson, and Kolodny (1992) explain that a caller may boast of himself and describe his accompanying masturbatory activity in detail, directly threaten the recipient ("I know where you live"), or try to get her to reveal intimate personal details, e.g., by posing as a legitimate phone interviewer.

4. *Pedophilia*—Pedophiles are adults who achieve sexual gratification by persistently fantasizing about or engaging in actual sexual contact with children who have not reached puberty. Contact can involve anything from fondling to intercourse. Perpetrators are mainly heterosexual men; the most common victims of the pedophile or child molester are girls (two-thirds of cases) between the ages of about eight and twelve. Three types of pedophiles reviewed by Masters, Johnson, and Kolodny (1992) and King, Camp, and Downey (1991) are: the *personally immature* individual lacking in social skills who "courts" the child as a friend, gains trust, then engages in sexual abuse; the *regressed* individual who has a history of heterosexual relationships, but, at some point, as a result of stress, sexual inadequacy, or other factors, turns to impulsive sexual contact with children; and the *aggressive* individual who is more generally antisocial and more likely to assault child victims, causing severe physical injury.

5. *Sadism and Masochism*—Sadism refers to obtaining sexual arousal and gratification from deliberately inflicting pain; masochism likewise from being hurt or humiliated. Acts of S&M can range from mild spanking, loose restraint, and playing at dominance/submission to severe whipping, burning, trampling, torture, or lust-murder. Sadomasochistic interests and activities have given rise to a supporting subculture, with dedicated magazines, networking, personal ads, bars, and clubs. While many persons enjoy occasional sadomasochistic experiences, the genuine paraphilias are less common (Masters, Johnson, and Kolodny 1992). Box 5.4 describes a clinical case of a husband and wife involved in sadomasochistic sexual activities. Some sadists derive pleasure from hurting unwilling victims, but even

consensual participation in extreme, compulsive acting out of sadomasochistic fantasies is dangerous and requires clear, shared understanding of desired limits (Strong, DeVault, and Sayad 1999). **Autoerotic asphyxiation** is a form of sexual masochism "linking strangulation with masturbatory activity" in an attempt to heighten exhilaration at climax due to oxygen starvation (Strong, DeVault, and Sayad 1999: 308). Based on medical and police records, Strong, DeVault, and Sayad note that this practice results in up to 1,000, usually accidental, deaths annually.

6. *Transvestism*—"Cross-dressing" occurs in the form of a paraphilia when a person experiences an "irresistible" recurring need to dress as a member of the opposite sex (Francoeur 1991: 517) and achieves sexual gratification in doing so. Although cross-dressing is popularly associated with gays "in drag" and with the public performances of female impersonators, the "majority of transvestites are heterosexual men," who might secretly wear items of women's clothing or fully cross-dress in private or public, but are not sexually attracted to other men (Greenberg, Bruess, and Haffner 2000: 550). Too, not all cross-dressing is connected with sexual arousal; it may be used as a parody of gender roles, a political statement, or to pass as the opposite sex.

7. *Voyeurism*—The voyeur "is a person who obtains sexual gratification by watching others engaged in sexual activity or by spying on them when they are undressing or nude" (Masters, Johnson, and Kolodny 1992: 422). Like exhibitionism, voyeurism is mostly found in young men and attracts persons who have difficulty with ordinary heterosexual relationships. Voyeurs prefer "peeping" at women who are strangers, enhancing sexual excitement by the novelty and risk involved. Places where nudity is accepted, such as nudist beaches and camps or strip shows, are therefore not as appealing to the voyeur (Masters, Johnson, and Kolodny 1992).

8. *Zoophilia*—Bestiality denotes actual sexual contact with animals whereas zoophilia refers to the personal disposition for achieving sexual gratification through preferred and repeated contact with animals, even with other sexual outlets available (King, Camp, and Downey 1991; Masters, Johnson, and Kolodny 1992). Kinsey's (Kinsey, Pomeroy, and Martin 1948; Kinsey et al. 1953) findings on bestiality are widely cited, that 8 percent of adult males and 3.6 percent of adult females reported ever having at least one sexual contact with an animal. Further, rural males were two to three times more likely to perform an act of bestiality than those who lived in a city, signifying greater isolation and opportunity, not necessarily persistent fantasies about or exclusive sexual preoccupation with animals.

People are generally curious about the origins of paraphilic attachments. Recalling earlier discussions of the influence of social learning on the development of individual sexuality, humans are thought to be born with a broad

---

Box 5.4. The Experience of a Sadist and a Masochist

A married man in his twenties requested psychiatric help because he feared he would soon commit murder. Since adolescence, he had been excited by fantasies and pornography depicting women bound and tortured. During courtship of his wife, he introduced mild versions of his fantasy into their sex play, and in this manner only was able to proceed on to intercourse. Now, after eight years of marriage, they invariably have intercourse by first binding her tightly with ropes and then, with her still bound, having intercourse. She has noticed that gradually the binding has been less and less symbolic and more painful. On two occasions in the last year, binding around her neck choked her into unconsciousness. It is in the nature of the man's work to enter households of strangers to do repairs. He frequently meets housewives there, and the temptation to bind and torture them is becoming unbearable. So far, he has avoided doing so by going out to his repair truck and masturbating while looking at photographs of bound and tortured women. His fear of killing a strange woman stems not from a belief that such an act would be sexually exciting but rather that, having bound and tortured her, he would have to kill her to remove the witness.

The wife of the man described above found, during her courtship, that their first intercourse, under cramped conditions in a car, where her husband fixed her arms and legs so they could not move, was at first uncomfortable but soon aroused in her a feeling of "interest." In time, this progressed to mild excitement, and now, several years later, she is appalled to find herself greatly excited by being bound. She is frightened by her excitement and she is frightened by her experience of unconsciousness while being bound. She believes that her husband is dangerous, and at the same time she feels deeply that he loves her.

Source: Stoller 1977: 204-205.

---

capacity for erotic responsiveness and possibly some innate predispositions toward certain types of behavior. "After birth we develop the actual content of sexually arousing stimuli. During the preadolescent and early adolescent years, individual experiences are associated with sexual arousal and particular images or stimuli that trigger sexual arousal become programmed in neural pathways within the brain" (Francoeur 1991: 530). Francoeur (1991: 531) explains that specific unusual or traumatic events can "sidetrack or distort the development of eroticism and result in unconventional sexual turn-ons."

Formative early experiences can affix lasting sexual significance to events or stimuli that most individuals will not react to at all as sexually arousing or may find mildly erotic but not especially important in their overall sexual conduct. Francoeur gives the example of a child experiencing sexual arousal during an enema at a vulnerable period in development who becomes dependent for sexual excitement in adulthood on repeated enemas. This paraphilia is termed *klismaphilia*. Thus events such as being spanked or punished, exhibiting one's genitals, watching people naked, cross-dressing, wearing a mask, even urinating or feces can take on distinctive sexual importance to the individual. Another example is *frottage*. The frotteur is sexually aroused and may climax by deliberately pressing or rubbing up against nonconsenting persons in crowded places.

The central and repetitive, compulsive character of paraphilias means they can be highly resistant to change. The illicit, risky nature of some paraphilic behavior seems to be part of its continuing attraction; the behavior can also be associated with a rewarding sense of safety or feeling of power. Not only the conduct itself but the compelling urge to engage in such conduct has to be considered. Paraphilias cause problems when they are revealed to partners or to other persons who find the behavior unacceptable, or take the form of legally prohibited behaviors, or generate internal guilt and distress. However, "many persons with unconventional sexual orientations are comfortable with their lifestyle and have negotiated accommodations with their partners" (Francoeur 1991: 545).

Another curious feature of the paraphilias is that they appear to be far more common among men than among women (Francoeur 1991; Masters, Johnson, and Kolodny 1992; Strong, DeVault, and Sayad 1999). For example, in cases generally known to police and health professionals, child molesters, obscene telephone callers, fetishists, voyeurs, frotteurs, necrophiliacs, and rapists are primarily or exclusively men. The extent to which this indicates biological differences in propensity for "distortion" of sexual development and/or cultural factors (e.g., relating to gender socialization or differential detection) remains to be determined. Mainstream U.S. culture also appears to indulge certain sexual "variations," perhaps more so for men than for women. Examples might include using young adolescent or preadolescent girls in advertising in a manner that is sexually provocative, fetishizing women's breasts as an independent object of sexual arousal, or depicting peeping on unsuspecting women as a common male adolescent prank. Also, as movies become more sexually explicit, millions of viewers publicly watch and are "turned on" by images of other consenting persons engaging in simulated or real sexual acts; a case of open conformity versus private deviance.

Sexual Addiction

In April 1992, a Dallas-Fort Worth monthly magazine, *Recovery,* ran an issue on sexual addiction. In this issue, Marvel Harrison and Terry Kellogg discussed the application of an addiction and recovery model to out-of-control sexual behaviors. Sexual behaviors are viewed as an addiction when they cause a person's life to become unmanageable; the individual persists in behaviors that produce adverse consequences. Consequences may include loss of jobs, poor relationships, divorce, health problems, AIDS, arrest, and imprisonment. The behaviors may be compulsive masturbation, multiple heterosexual or homosexual affairs, indecent phone calls, anonymous sex, frequent use of pornography and prostitutes, voyeurism, exhibitionism, incest, or rape. Some of the behaviors involve criminal offenses; some do not. From Jimmy Swaggart's public fall from grace as a result of involvement with prostitutes to the private death by autoerotic asphyxiation of a man whose wife and daughter found him with a belt around his neck tied to the doorknob (and surrounded by pornographic magazines), addictive behaviors have a characteristic obsessiveness and inappropriateness. Box 5.5 lists signs of sexual addiction that also indicate why the behavior is problematic.

Compulsive sexual behaviors are estimated to affect 5 percent of all adult Americans (Rosellini 1995: 209). Harrison and Kellogg (1992) observed, however, that there is little public recognition of sexual addiction. (In fact, some counseling professionals also dismiss the concept of addiction as applied to sexual conduct.) The problem of sexual addiction runs against an inclination to see sex as pleasurable and to avoid dictating another person's sexuality. Unwillingness to confront sexual addiction as a social problem may also reflect denial of one's own compulsive sexual behaviors and/or personal victimization. Our culture reinforces some sexual addictions that, in effect, become the norm—as in public fascination with the president's sex life or fixation on women's breast size. Given beliefs that pleasure is good, more is better, life is short, and you only live once, an individual's focus on sex can be mistaken for self-confidence and athletic prowess; observers do not necessarily notice the desperate, callous, and exploitative element in sexually addicted behavior.

A main feature of compulsive sexual behaviors is the lack of options experienced. Addiction *decreases choice* and ultimately results in unsatisfactory outcomes. Sex is used for a release, to avoid tensions and feelings of powerlessness, but in a way that generates shame, numbness, and alien-

---

Box 5.5. The Signs of Sexual Addiction

1. A pattern of out-of-control behavior
2. Severe consequences due to sexual behavior
3. Inability to stop despite adverse consequences
4. Persistent pursuit of self-destructive or high-risk behavior
5. Ongoing desire or efforts to limit sexual behavior
6. Sexual obsession and fantasy as a primary coping strategy
7. Increasing amounts of sexual experience because current level of activity is no longer sufficient
8. Severe mood changes around sexual activity
9. Inordinate amounts of time spent in obtaining sex, being sexual, or recovering from sexual activity
10. Neglect of important social, occupational, or recreational activities because of sexual behavior

Source: Matousek 1993.

ation. One reformed sex addict observed that despite an "unceasing parade of lovers," intimacy was lacking. The habit had been formed of reducing oneself and others to objects, which left a feeling of loneliness and lack of connection no matter how frequently one had sex. Matousek (1995) theorizes that sexual addiction begins with a desire for love, not self-destructiveness. Sexual addiction is common among persons sexually abused as children, who therefore formed unhealthy associations and obsessions around sex. In "crazy" families, the child is left unable to distinguish between appropriate and inappropriate sexual expression, when desire is trouble and when to stop. He or she learns bad feels good and vice versa (Matousek 1995: 181). Matousek gave the example of a man who had been forced to perform fellatio on his father as a child, resulting in a sexual fixation compelling him to repeat the behavior with hundreds of men. Early abuse and bad models of sexuality at both extremes of overt demonstration and intense repression set the stage for emotional dissociation.

Recovery from sexual addiction involves a commitment to stop and participation in counseling or self-help groups. Twelve-step or other therapeutic programs that emphasize stopping destructive behavior and gaining spiritual strength can help sex addicts lead a normal life (Matousek 1995). The twelve-step addiction recovery model adds a spiritual interpretation alongside psychotherapy and behavior modification. Sexually compulsive behaviors are not defined as moral weakness or perversion, but are understood instead as a *replacement behavior*, reenactment of childhood abuse or misdirected efforts to compensate for needed love and spiritual connection. Though a period of celibacy is useful for self-evaluation, the solution for sexual addiction is not permanent abstinence, but a different form of "sobriety." Persons recovering from sexual addition struggle with acknowledging activities that are harmful to themselves and others, confronting sexual fears, and replacing destructive behaviors with healthier ones. Since sexual health, however it is individually expressed, is assumed to be vital for self-actualization, integration of sexuality within the self as a whole and "honorable participation in sex" is the goal (Matousek 1995).

Patrick Carnes (1990), PhD, author of a book on sexual addiction, *Don't Call It Love,* notes that we can all learn something from sexual addiction about healthy sexuality. In tracing the recoveries of 1,000 sex addicts and their partners over a five-year period, he found that they contrasted healthy sexual activity with their experience of addiction. **Addictive sex** "disconnect(s) one from oneself." A sense of unreality fosters "self-destructive and dangerous behaviors." Sexual excitement is associated with fear. One is frequently drawn into illegal and socially inappropriate activities; abusing trust and taking advantage of others. Based on domination, sex becomes predatory, manipulative, and deceitful. Addictive sex "feels shameful"; it demands a "double life," undermines values, and tarnishes one's image. Used to avoid pain and seek perfection, it does not satisfy, but becomes "routine, grim and joyless." *Healthy sex* enhances feelings of self-worth and "deepens life's meaning"; it "has no victims." Vulnerability, not fear, provides excitement in a context of trust and safety. Furthering one's needs mindful of others, healthy sex encourages responsibility, faces emotional pain, and allows personal growth. "Originating in integrity," healthy sex "is mutual and intimate. It presents challenges while integrating the most authentic parts of oneself. Healthy sex is fun and playful, and allows for the imperfect" (Carnes 1992. 20).

Inhibited Sexual Desire

> At first it was fun: feverish kisses in his red Chevy, giggly nights of passion in his apartment. But then came marriage, two kids, and suddenly her husband's hands on her flesh felt like tentacles, and the sight of him approaching made her stiffen with revulsion. Then the disagreements began, hurtful scenes ending with each of them lying wedged against opposite sides of the bed, praying for sleep. . . . (Rosellini 1995: 206)

Among clinical concerns about sexual expression, on the opposite side of sexual addiction is "inhibited sexual desire." Inhibited sexual desire is more common than sexual addiction or compulsive sexual behaviors and contributes to why many Americans are not satisfied with their sex lives, according to Lynn Rosellini (1995). While movies, television, and the music industry endlessly portray the pursuit of sexual gratification, in millions of bedrooms across the United States couples are not having sex because one, or sometimes both, just don't want to anymore. Not simply a matter of occasional lack of interest, thousands of Americans each year seek help from counseling professionals as a result of little or no sexual desire—often prompted by the rejected partner. Readers can imagine the effects of trying to initiate sex and being met repeatedly with resistance, excuses, or complete lack of interest, interspersed with occasions on which the partner forces himself or herself to have sex every few months or so to avoid worse consequences.

Low sexual desire is a more visible problem against the social background of newly raised expectations for sexual satisfaction since the 1960s. Cultural supports for female frigidity disappeared along with pillbox hats and petticoats, while men are still stereotyped as "always in the mood." Rosellini reported that inhibited sex desire may be clinically recognized, loosely, when a client has sexual urges, fantasies, and/or activity less than twice a month. More telling, clinicians consider whether there has been a definite drop in desire that does not rebound and if it is causing the patient some distress—feelings of guilt, anxiety, or worry. Rosellini (1995: 207) notes that inhibited sexual desire is twice as prevalent in women as in men and cites an estimate that 35 percent of women and 16 percent of men experience persistent lack of sexual interest.

Dr. Helen Singer Kaplan (1979, 1995) argued that, unlike sexual arousal concerns, inhibited sexual *desire* exists primarily in the mind and stems not from inability to perform but from lack of motivation. Inhibited sexual desire has varied causes. One is a past history of child sexual abuse. Persons may seek relationships but then find themselves frightened or distrustful and sex avoidant. Another cause is a sex-repressive upbringing in which sex is viewed as bad or evil and a child's sexual explorations are severely punished. Good girl-bad girl thinking about women also leads some men to have difficulty in marriage when they cannot respond to a wife and mother as an object of lust or passion. Unresolved marital difficulties that generate dislike for the partner, resentments, and anger also underlie sexual inhibition. Distractions such as work stress or family responsibilities may also result in depressed sexual interest. And sometimes, in perhaps 15 percent of the cases of inhibited sexual desire, an underlying medical problem is responsible. Rosellini (1995) concludes, optimistically, that encouraging adults to have more enlightened sexual attitudes and better educating children about sex will help avoid both sexual addiction and inhibited sexual desire. If we were altogether less "imprisoned" by public expectations (often not followed in actual practice) and less burdened with private shame, more couples would be more fully satisfied with their relationships.

PERSONAL PREFERENCES IN SOCIAL CONTEXT

Moral and legal reasons behind some of our sexual hang-ups, and mental health perspectives on problematic sexual variations, have been considered. A few additional sexual behaviors about which persons may be inhibited, and why, are examined in this section.

Personal preferences about bodily display are certainly influenced by socialization and social norms. Parmelee (1966) makes the case that children quite naturally like to show off and, if they have not been inhibited in their conduct by social pressures, like to do so naked; clothes seem a nuisance and an imposed constraint. He contrasts a temperate, judicious, and "genuine" modesty with "artificial" shame-driven modesty of varying intensity. On the whole, Americans are fairly restrictive about nudity and sensitive to potential offense given to viewers. Parmelee (1966: 72) mentioned a law enacted in Kentucky requiring that "nudist colonies must be licensed and surrounded by a wall of cement and birch at least twenty feet in height." Nude beaches, where they are permitted, are commonly posted to "warn" casual or unsuspecting visitors that they may encounter naked persons. Informally, comments about women breastfeeding in public places, when negative, emphasize that onlookers do not know how to react or "don't want to see that" in public because breasts have a private and sexual significance. Social feedback from friends, relatives, dating partners, spouses, or others commonly influences how individuals feel about displaying their bodies. Mass advertising and the entertainment industry may contribute to less restrictive standards of dress but also to greater self-consciousness about one's own physical imperfections.

Bodily self-exploration is another natural impulse. Children, even quite young, exhibit sexual responses to genital self-stimulation, and adolescents often experiment with masturbation. **Masturbation** refers primarily to "stimulation or manipulation of one's own genitals, especially to orgasm" but also denotes "stimulation, by manual or other means exclusive of coitus, of another's genitals" *(Webster's College Dictionary)*. In *mutual masturbation*, partners stimulate each other in such fashion. This is essentially a nonprocreative sexual activity that has in our society traditionally been "conceptualized as inappropriate, undesirable and unacceptable, . . . bolstered by both religious and medical rationales" (Bryant 1982: 162). Doctors wrote that masturbation would lead to "inevitable ruin," citing masturbation as a cause of insanity, impotence, shortened life, blindness, epilepsy, hairy palms, and more (Bryant 1982). In this social context, it would not be surprising if individuals avoided the practice or following masturbation felt guilty and worried about ill effects.

Supported by a freer social climate and consistent with results of several widely publicized sex surveys in the 1960s and 1970s, however, medical and moral objections to masturbation declined (Bryant 1982). Janus and Janus (1993: 31) reported that among eighteen- to twenty-six-year-olds in their national sample of adult Americans, 24 percent of males and 8 percent of females masturbated "daily" or "several times weekly"; 27 percent of males and 19 percent of females said "weekly" or "monthly"; the remaining 49 percent of males and 73 percent of females said "rarely" or "never." Fewer females than males in each age group (27 to 47 percent versus 47 to 62 percent) reported masturbating at least monthly. Overall, perceptions have largely shifted away from seeing masturbation as a misguided or harmful self-indulgence and medical problem to a matter of personal preference, even a recommended therapy.

In private and in moderation, and without replacing desire for sexual gratification as part of an interpersonal relationship, masturbation has been encouraged as a learning experience, routine tension reliever, more reliable means to climax for women, far less risky outlet for singles than casual intercourse, expanded lovemaking technique, fill-in for married partners with different levels of sex drive, or just for pleasure (Bryant 1982). Despite these changes, a degree of stigma is still attached to the practice. That a surgeon general of the United States could be criticized, even in the 1990s, and officially reprimanded for speaking frankly in public and endorsing masturbation as a safer sex practice is revealing of lingering social restrictions and hang-ups.

There are diverse opinions too on the practices of *fellatio* and *cunnilingus*. These are the oral stimulation of the penis and the female genitals, respectively *(Webster's College Dictionary)*. Some people regard these as unnatural and immoral acts; others find them enjoyable ordinary sexual activities. Simultaneous fellatio and cunnilingus, known as "69," is pictured in many human sexuality texts. Masters, Johnson, and Kolodny (1992: 371, 372) observed that "while oral-genital sex was avoided by large numbers of the married men and women who participated in the Kinsey studies, a majority of married people today include fellatio and cunnilingus in their sexual repertoires," along with increased time spent in foreplay and greater variety in positions used during intercourse. The prevailing social attitude appears to favor sexual versatility and playfulness between consenting adults, as they choose.

General orientation toward sexuality also determines individual openness to trying particular sexual acts. For example, Rice (1989: 280-283) reviews relevant philosophies, including *asceticism,* which values avoidance of physical pleasure, instead urging self-discipline, self-denial, and abstinence; *hedonism,* following the principle that pleasure is good and should be the aim of action, with sexuality unconstrained by morality; *legalism,* emphasizing strict adherence to the rules, so if an act is prohibited, do not do it (e.g., staying a virgin before marriage means no intercourse, no matter what else we do sexually); and *situationalism,* in which the morality of actions is evaluated by the variable effects on persons involved and not by absolute laws or rules about the acts themselves (e.g., divorce is not wrong if it protects a child or adult from abuse).

Individual preferences may coincide with social norms. Indeed, when socialization is most effective, norms are *internalized,* and doing what we want to do *is* doing what is expected. But the United States is a **pluralistic** society, offering more than one standard (Rice 1989), and this contributes to sexual diversity. Further, individual inclinations are not uniform to begin with, and consequently may run afoul of one or more such standards. A relatively uninhibited person who seeks sexual gratification with a variety of partners can be labeled "a free spirit" or "promiscuous," referring to indiscriminate sexual involvement with a large number of partners, depending on one's point of view. The more conservative observer is more likely to see such sexual activity as deviant. *Nymphomania,* applied to women, and *satyriasis,* applied to men (from ancient Greek myths of nymphs and satyrs), are terms which have been used to describe persons with high need for continuous sexual stimulation—excessive, "abnormal, uncontrollable sexual desire" *(Webster's College Dictionary)*—but the label nymphomaniac, especially, was indiscriminately applied to many women who were simply more sexually active than was socially acceptable. Labeling is a form of social control, stigmatizing the offender and establishing the boundaries of accepted activity.

Even more liberal observers find some sexual practices, usually the ones they do not engage in (see Tiefer, Box 5.3, on the subjective standard of normalcy), too "kinky." As *Webster's College Dictionary* defines *kinky*, the term refers to unconventional sexual behavior; also meaning eccentric, quirky, imperfect, flawed, or twisted. These include the limited practices, e.g., including coercion and violence, that appear more extremely deviant to most of the general population. *Bondage* is the practice of tying up or binding the arms and legs of a sexual partner to increase sexual excitement. The term also suggests being subjected to external power or control *(Webster's College Dictionary)*. Is this kinky sex? Strong, DeVault, and Sayad (1999: 290) describe *domination* and *submission* as "consensual acting out of sexual scenes in which one person dominates and the other submits." Although associated with S&M, sexual fantasy play does not require hurting the partner. That many "ordinary Americans," perhaps less inhibited than others, engage in such activities may be inferred from the Ann Landers column reproduced in Box 5.6. Contrast this behavior with the clinical case of sadomasochism described earlier.

Pornography, too, illustrates the range of personal preferences and the influence of social norms. According to the dictionary, *pornography* is visual or written material "intended to arouse sexual excitement," especially if considered to have little or no artistic merit *(Webster's College Dictionary)*. *Erotica* is literature or art dealing with sexual love; erotic also means "arousing or satisfying sexual desire." Pornography is about sexual content and about its impact on readers or viewers. "Fifteen years ago, the word pornography was a generic term for anything with a sexually explicit content"; now it increasingly refers to material with particular themes such as violence and coercion or exploitation of women or children (Francoeur 1991: 635). Hard-core pornography is more uncompromising and graphically explicit in depicting sex; soft-core is sexually provocative without being so explicit, thus less "lewd," vulgar, or offensive. Personal preferences vary in receptivity to and enthusiasm for seeking out such stimulation. Individuals who enjoy pornography see no harm in this. Yet pornography is considered objectionable by many persons, and some types of pornographic materials generally appear more offensive than others. Pornography is not illegal; obscenity is. While the First Amendment to the U.S. Constitution protects freedom of speech, this privilege is not extended to obscenity; e.g., possession of child pornography in one's own home may be prohibited by the states and prosecuted.

Box 5.6. Ann Is Surprised by Mail on Bondage

Dear Ann Landers:

Awhile back you printed a letter from a woman whose husband wanted to spice up their lovemaking. He insisted on tying her hands and feet with silk scarves. She refused, saying it was "sadistic." You called him "kinky." Bondage can be fun. My girlfriend and I have enjoyed it for years. Sometimes we reverse roles. She is the binder and I am the "bindee." There is no slapping, hitting or clothespins on the breasts. The key words are "mutual consent."

We play another game called "Make Believe." We take turns making up situations to act out. For example, I pick her up at a bar and pretend that she is a hooker. We play our respective roles and it's very stimulating. Another scenario: She is a lonely working woman who is spending yet another evening alone, wondering why romance has eluded her. An attractive man shows up to repair the furnace. Your imagination can take over from there. Granted, these games are not for everyone, but they can enhance lovemaking to an incredible degree. Sign me—Hedonist in Woodland Hills, California.

Dear Woody: The mail on that subject was mind-boggling. I had no idea so many people in the U.S. and Canada were tying each other up. The final word from here is—whatever turns you on is OK so long as there is mutual consent and no inflicting of pain.

Source: Landers 1989.

Social norms influence individual experience, but experience itself also shapes our personal preferences and perceptions of deviance. We know ourselves and persons who are most like us best, and tend to use this as a benchmark for evaluating sexual lifestyles. **Pluralistic ignorance** refers to a lack of knowledge about different standards, opinions, and practices other than one's own, in which case we are more likely to condemn them. True enough, as popular wisdom holds: Even if everyone else is doing something, that does not make it "right." Individuals still have to make their own moral decisions and choices. Sociologically, though, objective examination of "what everyone else is doing," that is, the diversity of actual conduct, beliefs, and values, gives a better picture of changing sexual lifestyles; what needs are served, what values are represented, among what segments of society. Mass media coverage is often quite selective and oversimplified. A few people who express their opinions openly and forcefully may seem to speak for others, the "silent majority," when what the majority in fact believes or does is not known, and is more complicated than simply being "pro" or "con" on a particular matter. Hence there is continuing fascination with and need for scientific social surveys.

CONCLUSION

Although societies often accept new ideas only slowly, significant changes have occurred in the United States in the past several decades. Many sexual practices that in the past were viewed as "deviant and/or manifestations of neurotic suffering" were later "championed as legitimate lifestyles" (Strean 1983: 151). Today's bikini beachwear would have been considered scandalous and "sick" exhibitionism in earlier eras and offensive enough to standards of public decency to warrant arrest. In the 1940s, even dictionary definitions of many sexual terms revealed cultural biases; fellatio was "an act of sexual perversion," cunnilingus "an abnormal practice," lust "an inordinate or sinful desire, as for gratification of sexual appetite," and masturbation "self-pollution," "sexual self-abuse," or "defilement" (Parmelee 1966: 21, 22). Male homosexuals are now called "gay"; a commune that consists of married and unmarried people practicing group sex is "the new surrogate extended family"; swinging is known as "comarital sex"; and living together without being married (a.k.a. "living in sin") is now simply "cohabitation," while nontraditional gender roles have also brought us "androgynous" marriages (Strean 1983: 152). Sexual attitudes and prevailing practices do change. What once were hang-ups become more common, accepted practices, and attention shifts to new hang-ups or inhibitions. Conventionality and deviance are redefined.

As the times change, we have opportunities to change with them. Specifically, in sexual relations, many more options are open today than in the 1950s. Between the straitlaced and libertine extremes, many individuals make room for some playful experimentation and acting out of fantasies. If we ask ourselves what our hang-ups are and why we have them, the picture of our own sexual preferences becomes clearer. We can then take a more objective look at what practices we have engaged in and also what practices we might be ready to try, with more information, a sense of adventure, and willingness to explore new avenues. Being comfortable with personal preferences is important. Otherwise, we will continue to have sexual hang-ups because of an overly repressive religious morality, legal sanctions, personal trauma, or emotional conflicts. That can be a different type of bondage; a bondage of self, experiencing less than our potential (Holland 1985).

Social institutions—including religion, law, and medicine/mental health—will continue to influence sexual attitudes and behaviors. These institutions provide various guidelines for individuals in making decisions about their own sexual conduct regarding what is going too far and what is not far enough. Religious teaching and doctrines are not uniformly against all nonprocreative sex. Within each religion are more conservative and more liberal interpretations of human sexuality. The law varies over time and by state (e.g., age of consent has ranged from seven to twenty-one). It basically addresses violations of social standards and threats to community welfare on the following grounds: public nature (e.g., exhibitionism) or invasion of privacy (e.g., voyeurism); "severity of perversion" (e.g., bestiality); and abuse involved/use of force and harm to victim (e.g., rape, incest, child sexual abuse), which violate the norm of sex between "consenting adults." Medical and mental health standards consider sexual behaviors and their consequences from the perspective of individuals' well-being. In the case of the paraphilias, an individual is dependent on an unusual or socially unacceptable stimulus for sexual arousal or climax; the stimulus becomes the preferred or required and habitual form of sexual expression. What is "wrong" with these cases, even when the behavior is not illegal, might be evaluated in terms of criteria such as compulsiveness, narrowness, may be degrading to self or to partner, may be physically dangerous to self, or falls short of the quality of "relationship" sex.

In human sexuality texts and professional literature, careful attempts are made to distinguish paraphilias from personal preferences, "ordinary" deviance, and transitory conduct. Strong, DeVault, and Sayad (1999: 293), for example, refer to a study by Templeman and Stinnett (1991), who (a) collected sexual life histories from sixty "normal" college men, (b) found that "65 percent had engaged in some form of sexual misconduct, such as voyeurism, obscene phone calling or sexually rubbing themselves against a woman," and (c) "concluded that young men were easily aroused to diverse stimuli, blurring the distinction between typical and atypical behavior." King, Camp, and Downey (1991: 346) pointed out that adolescents are known to make occasional obscene phone calls, but "their sexual arousal does not depend on making such calls. Compulsive, habitual obscene phone calling is indicative of a more serious sexual disorder."

Much variation and experimentation in adult sexual activity is motivated by curiosity and playfulness; seeking a challenge, a jump start, or just something new. Finding sexual arousal occasionally in, say, being spanked, wearing a costume, watching a partner undress or masturbate, exhibiting one's genitals to be admired, dressing in opposite-sex clothing, or using "dirty" words is not uncommon. In one amusing episode of the television show *All in the Family,* an adult character, Gloria, and her husband make love one time while she is wearing a wig. He likes it so much that he keeps asking her to put the wig on in bed, and she finally refuses, saying he is in love with the wig, not her, and he is having an affair, with her as the other woman; "that's sick!" What if you always find black leather pants a turn-on, or get excited reading romance novels, or cannot get aroused unless your partner is very good looking, or find yourself sexually stimulated by the feeling of rubbing your partner's underpants against your body? Masters, Johnson, and Kolodny (1992: 418) suggest that only when these acts are "magnified to the point of psychological dependence" and become a persistent preoccupation might they operate as a paraphilia. The American Psychiatric Association (1994) identifies symptoms of the particular paraphilias as mental health concerns in terms of recurrence, intensity, distress, and impairment (Greenberg, Bruess, and Haffner 2000).

So people have varied sexual fantasies, urges, and behaviors. Distinguishing in practice between an occasional indulgence, a personal preference, a paraphilia, and a social offense is subjective and not always clear cut. Overall, perhaps the best course is to err on the side of tolerance. The "fears, anxieties and cruelty sometimes promoted by stigmatizing the deviant generates non-rationality in social policy and inability to study and understand the general human experience" (Gagnon and Simon 1967: vii). Particularly in a society that values personal freedom and individuality, there is an inherent tension between the goal of maintaining community standards and the costs of invading privacy, restraining liberty, and repressing sexual expression. *Censorship* of pornography ("official examination for the purpose of suppressing or deleting objectionable material," according to *Webster's College Dictionary* illustrates the difficulties. Recall that one feature of normative integration is that a particular norm does not conflict with other norms and values. Issues of sexual morality, connected with fundamental value conflicts, continue to generate controversy and provoke ongoing political and social debate.

In lieu of absolute social dictates, the "new sexual morality" that emerged in the 1960s assigns the challenge of responsible decision making to the individual and calls for honest, careful, and well-informed consideration of alternatives. Pastoral counselor Frederic Wood Jr. (1968), a college chaplain, characterized U.S. society in the 1960s as both sex-saturated *and* sex-starved; starved for "real sexual involvement," partly because it was so inundated with "sexual superficiality." Today, business and mass media still routinely exploit sex while family members do not communicate effectively about their own sexuality, and schools are permitted to teach sexual biology but not to openly discuss values. The new morality "does not prescribe the form and detail of what you do in given situations . . . is instead what might best be called an ethical attitude . . . [that] encourages (literally, 'gives courage for') both moral freedom and moral responsibility" (Wood 1968: 12, 13).

Sexuality—its promises and uncertainties, drives and consequences—is part of human striving for personal meaning and fulfillment and, as such, should be judged by "the appropriateness and naturalness of particular acts for the actors themselves" (Wood 1968: 113). Insofar as sexuality also has wider social significance, each society devises its own commentary on what will or will not be tolerated, under what circumstances. Decades ago, Simon and Gagnon and Simon (1973) urged that social scientists studying sexuality and sexual lifestyles need to view sexuality not as a segregated domain of existence but as part of our total social selves. More research is still needed (a) with representative samples, allowing a more complete picture of diverse segments of U.S. society; (b) in which reported sexual acts are more clearly situated with respect to their psychological, interpersonal, and social context so their significance to persons involved can be better understood.

Chapter 6

Homosexuality

Homosexuality is another facet of variability in human sexual expression, one that remains controversial in our society. This chapter will first review traditional concerns about homosexuality, including its nature, causes, and prevalence. Perceptions of homosexuality as a clinical condition that can or should be "cured," and public attitudes in the United States toward homosexuality generally, are also examined. The term **homosexuality** refers to sexual attraction or behaviors directed toward persons of one's own biological sex. In current usage, the terms **gay** and **lesbian** tend to carry additional connotations of social identity and political activism, bringing homosexuality closer to the notion of an alternate lifestyle. Accordingly, the second part of this chapter looks at contemporary lifestyle issues for gays, lesbians, and bisexuals, reflecting the changing focus of more recent scholarship (Hunter et al., 1998). Difficulties and successes in same-sex couple relationships are viewed against the background of continuing societal obstacles, or heterosexism. **Heterosexism** is defined as prejudice and discrimination, social stigma (or "disgrace"), and oppression against persons on the basis of homosexual involvement. Homosexuality and the family will be discussed with particular emphasis on three topics: "coming out," couple relationships, and parenting.

THE NATURE OF HOMOSEXUALITY

Homosexuality appears in cultures all over the world and throughout history, although its extent, forms, and acceptance vary (Robertson 1987: 240). Historically, there is more evidence of male homosexuality and less information about female homosexuality. Cross-culturally, when homosexuality is disapproved of, it may be reacted to with only disbelief and ridicule or more severely; in the extreme, Rwala Bedouins considered the death penalty an appropriate response (Robertson 1981). More often, homosexuality is tolerated, if not approved, and sometimes even "required," in limited particular circumstances. "The Aranda of Australia, the Siwans of North Africa and the Keraki of New Guinea required every male to have exclusively homosexual relations with adults during adolescence but to be bisexual or heterosexual thereafter; ... in ancient Greece an elaborate system of sexual and spiritual relationships between adult men and male youths was apparently more highly valued than heterosexuality"; and among the Chukchi of Siberia, marriage between men was permitted in the case where one, dressing as a woman, adopted "the social role of wife, while the husband was regarded as a normal heterosexual" (Robertson 1987: 240, 241).

Clellan Ford and Frank Beach (1951), early on, observed that homosexuality was never the *predominant* type of sexual activity in the societies they studied, but some homosexuality, more commonly among men than women, appeared in nearly all. Animal behavior studies also suggest that homosexual behavior is not uncommon among primates. Young monkeys and apes "indulge in a variety of homosexual games which may include manipulation of the genitals of a like-sexed partner and may even involve attempts at homosexual coitus. Adult male monkeys with ample opportunity for heterosexual intercourse may nevertheless indulge in homosexual contacts; in some cases, carrying on hetero- and homosexual alliances concurrently (Ford and Beach 1951, reprinted in Skolnick and Skolnick 1971:162). In other species as well, atypical mating responses are sometimes displayed, as when adult females mount other females in the manner of males, or males attempt to copulate with other males. Ford and Beach's perspective on sexual behaviors generally was that among humans (and other mammals to a lesser extent), all males and females possess an inherited capacity for erotic responsiveness to a wide range of stimuli, but the tendencies leading to sexual relations with individuals of the same sex are not as strong in most individuals as those leading to heterosexual relations.

In human societies, individual expression of homosexuality may involve behavior, desire, self-identification, or some combination of these. Correspondingly, studies of homosexuality can vary in focus depending on the researcher's basic perspective and objectives. Homosexuality has been seen as an "underlying sexual orientation," with *desire* for and interest in people of the same gender treated as more fundamental than behavior (Marmor 1980). With the lesbian and gay rights movement in the 1970s, sociological, historical, and social psychological research began to examine *identity* issues such as the process of "coming out" in the context of an emerging lesbian and gay community (Herdt 1992). **Coming out** refers to the development of self-consciousness and a relatively public homosexual, gay, or lesbian identity. At the same time, AIDS-related health concerns focused attention on specific sexual *behaviors,* regardless of public or private identities. Survey respondents are found to place themselves at different points on separate scales of sexual behaviors, fantasies, emotional preferences, and overall self-labeling.

The etiology and nature of homosexuality continue to be debated. What causes homosexuality? When and how homosexuality originates are still unanswered questions. Not enough is known to pinpoint the causes with certainty. Probably many different factors enter in, and they may be different for different people. Some of the possible explanations that have been explored are that homosexuality is an *inborn trait,* that it results from *disturbed family relationships,* or that it is a *lifestyle of choice.* Returning to the theme of diversity, it is probably most useful to acknowledge variability in the paths that lead individuals to express sexual feelings and identities in different ways at different times, "rather than assuming that homosexuality is a single, uniform trait with the same underlying causes and the same outcomes in all people" (Laumann et al. 1994). Homosexual acts (overt actions) and desires or fantasies can be simply part of adolescent experimentation for one individual, while for another it is part of a process of "finding oneself" as a gay or lesbian. Homosexuality can be a passing phase or a master identity, accepted or rejected by the individual and/or others, with associated feelings of certainty or confusion, pride or shame, excitement or fear. Development of a social identity as a homosexual, gay, or lesbian person and the manner in which this is lived out depends on the configuration of personal and social resources the individual has available.

Bisexuality complicates the picture. It challenges the popular conviction that the world can be divided into "them" (homosexual) and "us" (heterosexual) and generates criticism from the gay and lesbian community about ideological backsliding and denial of one's "true" homosexual orientation. Theories of lesbian and gay identity formation initially saw bisexuality as a transitional stage, but are shifting toward recognizing bisexuality as a distinctive sexual orientation (D'Augelli and Patterson 1995). Bisexuality is still less well developed as a social identity than either heterosexuality or homosexuality (Blumenfeld and Raymond 1993). In *Chasing Amy,* a popular movie and video release, the heroine is an openly lesbian woman who is pursued by a man with whom she ultimately falls in love and enjoys sex. When this particular relationship ends, for a variety of reasons (including the man's difficulty coming to terms with her previous *heterosexual* adventures), she returns to the lesbian lifestyle and takes a new woman lover. This example reinforces the idea that sexuality is an ongoing process, influenced by available social scripts and by changing personal experiences. Individuals' sexual careers generally may not be as simple as we often suppose.

Most Americans nevertheless tend to think in polarities of homosexual versus heterosexual, despite Kinsey's early finding that many individuals who were not exclusively homosexual had engaged in homosexual activities (Kinsey, Pomeroy, and Martin 1948; Kinsey et al. 1953). Kinsey's research is widely regarded as having established that homosexuality and heterosexuality are *not* mutually exclusive categories. Kinsey observed that "the human mind invents categories and tries to force facts in them, but the living world is a continuum. . . . The sooner we learn this concerning human sexual behavior, the sooner we will reach a sounder understanding of the realities of sex" (Gould, 1986: 17). So whatever readers may think of homosexuality in a moral sense, homosexuality challenges us intellectually to come to a better understanding of human sexuality in general. Although questions are often raised about what causes homosexuality, one of the implications of Kinsey's work is that we might just as well ask, what are the causes of heterosexuality? As long as we take heterosexuality for granted, we cannot step back for a clearer picture of the mechanisms involved and still, correspondingly, do not understand causes of homosexuality very well.

Sociologists are apt to argue that both homosexual and heterosexual behavior are social in origin; yet many gay rights advocates make the case for homosexuality as an inborn sexual orientation, not a casual, revocable choice. Sex researchers and therapists William Masters and Virginia Johnson (1979) were criticized for taking even the position that that there is no simple, empirically demonstrated relationship between a genetic/hormonal factor and homosexual conduct. Considering both viewpoints, Figure 6.1 suggests a way of thinking about the combined effects of biology and society. Because heterosexuality favors species reproduction, and if Kinsey's respondents (see Box 6.1) can be taken as a guide, biological predisposition will be biased toward heterosexuality while also accounting for a consistent, smaller percentage of individuals exclusively homosexual in orientation.

FIGURE 6.1. Nature and Nurture Shape Sexual Expression

**Social
pressures,** ⟶
largely toward ⟶
heterosexuality ⟶
e.g., from family,
school, church,
and state

              4-10%   ~50% –

/------/----------------------------/-----------------------------------/

         Exclusively   Exclusively
         homosexual   heterosexual

Biological foundations and predisposition

Box 6.1. Kinsey's Findings on Male Homosexuality

The following statistics were presented by Kinsey, Pomeroy, and Martin (1948: 650-651) in their report on sexual behavior among American men.

- Approximately 50 percent of all males have neither overt nor psychic homosexual experience after the onset of adolescence.
- 37 percent of men have at least some overt homosexual experience to the point of orgasm between adolescence and old age.
- 25 percent of the male population has more than incidental homosexual experience or reactions (i.e., two to six) for at least three years between ages sixteen and fifty-five.
- 10 percent of the males are more or less exclusively homosexual for at least three years between the ages sixteen and fifty-five.
- 4 percent are exclusively homosexual throughout their lives after the onset of adolescence.

Like Ford and Beach, sex researchers John Gagnon and Bruce Henderson (1977) assume that humans begin with a capacity to respond to a wide variety of sexual stimuli. We do some experimentation as adolescents, but over time most of us are conditioned to respond in conventional ways. These response patterns become part of our personal identities; then, they come to seem "natural," inevitable, and morally correct. Consequently, it may be difficult to look at other forms of sexual expression in an objective way.

To the extent that sexual behavior is learned, many questions remain about how this occurs. With conventional socialization pressures strongly encouraging heterosexuality, in what way are homosexual behaviors or desires learned? Sociologist Ian Robertson (1987: 244) favored self-labeling theory as an explanatory framework. Adopting a homosexual or heterosexual identity depends on self-definition, usually forming in late childhood or adolescence. Again, given the flexibility of the human sex drive, an adolescent may experience sexual interest in a same-sex person. This attraction and, if acted on, corresponding behavior may still be interpreted as a not very important event in the life of a heterosexual or as signifying attraction to both same *and* opposite-sex partners (bisexuality) or as revealing a core underlying homosexuality ("I must be gay"). How one's feelings and actions are *understood* and *given meaning* by the individual is a social process. One learns both what gay is and how to be gay in a particular culture. Existing social scripts are not uniformly conventional, and experience exposes us to a variety of marital and sexual lifestyles, through direct observation, conversation, books, television and movies, electronic communication, and so on. We use social information, images, and models to "recognize" and enact our sexuality. The extent to which social identities at odds with felt attractions can be constructed and maintained over time is still being investigated and debated.

Ideally, social scientists attempt to keep an open mind and evaluate conclusions about the nature of homosexuality on the basis of scientific merit. Because homosexuality does deviate from the conventional expectation of heterosexual relations, there is a certain social stigma attached. As a result, before the gay liberation movement, homosexuality was mostly kept hidden to avoid sanctions from the disapproving majority. It was not until 1973, in response to pressures from the gay liberation movement, that the American Psychiatric Association decided to remove homosexuality from its list of mental disorders in the *Diagnostic and Statistical Manual* (DSM-III). Some homosexuals are, coincidentally, mentally ill; some are driven to despair by social condemnation; and some homosexual behavior may reflect psychological disorders (e.g., engaging in homosexual behavior due to intense fear or hatred of the opposite sex resulting from childhood sexual abuse). But homosexuality *in itself* is not a mental disorder. With respect to issues of social definition of sexual behaviors, we have a curious spectacle. In 1972, if you were gay, you were officially mentally ill; in 1974 you were not. Beliefs and practices not only vary cross-culturally but over time within the same society. Norms change, and our lives change with them. In this example, they change not only as larger societal conditions change but also in response to specific collective efforts to redefine sexual morality. (Other examples of political activism in the arena of marital and sexual lifestyles include the women's movement, right-to-life versus reproductive choice, and anti-pornography campaigns.)

CAN HOMOSEXUALITY BE "CURED"?

The question, can homosexuality be "cured," reveals something about underlying social attitudes; it *presupposes* that homosexuality is a sickness. Psychotherapist Carlton Cornett (1995) contends that belief in homosexuality as a form of emotional illness is relatively recent and predominantly American. In response to a letter from an American mother who wanted her son "cured" of his homosexuality, Sigmund Freud wrote in 1935: "Homosexuality is assuredly no advantage, but it is nothing to be ashamed of, no vice, no degradation; it cannot be classified as an illness" (Cornett 1995: 140). Although the American Psychiatric Association removed homosexuality from its list of personality disorders in 1973, many psychiatrists (64 percent in an AMA survey) continued to believe in the pathology of homosexuality (Nass, Libby, and Fisher 1984: 153). The notion that homosexuality can be cured remains alluring. Irving Bieber (1962) concluded, as did Masters and Johnson (1979), that a heterosexual shift is possible for homosexuals who are strongly motivated to change, but it is not clear whether the reported success of such efforts in a number of cases refers to change in fundamental feelings and desires or to restriction of overt behavior to contacts with opposite-sex partners (Cornett 1995).

Psychoanalyst Charles W. Socarides (1994) also reported successes in "reorienting" gays who desired change (Stalcup, 1995). In a *Washington Times* article on July 5, 1994, Socarides described his concern that the new political correctness of homosexuality would discourage persons who "already have a homosexual problem" from finding their way out of a self destructive lifestyle into more conventional participation in society. Adolescents, "nearly all of whom experience some degree of uncertainty as to sexual identity," may prematurely and mistakenly adopt a homosexual identity (Stalcup, 1995: 149). Unconscious determinants of same-sex object choice that originate in childhood deficits can be addressed in therapy. High rates of attempted suicide, alcoholism, sexual compulsion (manifest in large numbers of sexual partners), and sex with strangers have been interpreted as evidence of serious disorder associated with homosexuality. However, Socarides also acknowledged nonclinical forms of homosexual behavior, variously described as situational, experimental, or ideological, not constitutional, and presumably a matter of choice.

Therapists, striving to relieve individual pain over homosexuality in a social context of disapproval, could attempt to help a person live out a heterosexual lifestyle or, instead, to accept his or her homosexuality and to cope more effectively with outside social pressures. Suicide, alcoholism, depression, and sexual compulsions can be attributed to society's prejudices and unwillingness to support stable gay relationships (Stalcup 1995: 150) rather than to inherent disorders associated with homosexual experience. Moreover, clinicians in practice typically do not encounter the many individuals who are already well adjusted to a gay or lesbian lifestyle. The idea of "repairing" homosexual persons faces strong professional and political opposition on grounds that psychotherapy cannot change one's basic orientation and attempts to do so reinforce social oppression, increase feelings of shame, undermine self-esteem, and alienate a person from "the genuine feelings, wishes and desires that form the true self" (Cornett 1995: 144).

Since the 1970s, newer approaches to counseling gay or lesbian clients have come to be described as *affirmative practice,* helping these clients accept and value their sexual identities while living in a heterosexual society (Hunter et al. 1998). The lifestyles and personal issues of gay and lesbian clients are understood from the perspective of participants, with existing theories and interventions modified accordingly. "Every major mental health profession eventually adopted statements regarding professional responsibility to offer treatment to lesbians and gay men based not on homosexuality as an illness but on the individual's needs," and without prejudice (Hunter et al. 1998: 174). Hunter et al. (1998: 177) noted that fewer adults today wish to change their sexual orientation and there is "no persuasive data that therapy, religious experience or heterosexual marriage can successfully result in anything other than short-term, superficial change." Fassinger (1991) suggests that clients asking for change may really be seeking acceptance and validation of their worth. The National Association of Social Workers (1984, 1996) agrees that exploring with gay and lesbian clients the adverse effects of heterosexism on their life experience and self-attitudes is more appropriate than efforts to convert sexual orientation.

PUBLIC ATTITUDES

As late as 1970, homosexuality was disapproved of by 86 percent of respondents in a nationwide sample of 3,000 persons interviewed by the Kinsey Institute for Sex Research. Two-thirds viewed homosexual relations as obscene and vulgar. Nearly four-fifths were reluctant to associate with homosexuals. In 1977, a Gallup poll showed less than half (43 percent) of Americans surveyed thought homosexual relations between consenting adults should be legal, with little change by 1982 (Nass, Libby, and Fisher 1984); only 14 percent thought homosexuals should be able to adopt children. Such survey results reflect a generally negative view of homosexuality in our society. At the same time, Americans have opposed various kinds of discrimination against individuals based only on their sexual orientation (Laumann et al. 1994).

Recall that a General Social Survey has been conducted regularly since 1972 by the National Opinion Research Center in Chicago. Table 6.1 shows results for 1985 and 1994, based on 1,484 and 1,545 adult respondents respectively, when an attitude item asked, "And what about sexual relations between two adults of the same sex—do you think it is always wrong, almost always wrong, only sometimes wrong, or not wrong at all?" Within a continuing overall social context of disapproval, gay and lesbian individuals have to decide whether to be relatively more open or closed about their sexual orientation in conventional settings such as school or workplace versus more informal settings; in public versus in private; and in the larger straight society versus within the gay community.

TABLE 6.1. Attitudes Toward Homosexuality (Percentage)

	1985	1994
Always wrong	75	70
Almost always wrong	4	4
Only sometimes wrong	7	7
Not wrong at all	14	19

Source: Davis and Smith (1986; 1994)

Negative public attitudes are also reflected in legislation against homosexuality. To a much greater extent than most readers are initially aware, individual sexual practices, even in private and between consenting adults, can be and often are prohibited by law. Homosexuality offers an example. Laws vary by state, and jurisdictions vary in the consistency and enthusiasm with which they are enforced. Opponents of change in laws (e.g., against sodomy) argue that homosexuality is unnatural and immoral and that relaxation of laws proscribing such behaviors may lead to greater sympathy with homosexuality and as a result might seriously threaten the central role of the family in society. The Wolfenden Committee in England and the American Law Institute in the United States have recommended that private sexual behavior between consenting adults should be removed from the list of crimes regardless of how it is morally considered. Decriminalization of private homosexual acts did not lead to an increase in homosexuality in Holland or England.

A book on human sexuality published by Greenhaven Press (Stalcup 1995) as part of a series of "opposing viewpoints," devoted several sections to homosexuality. On the question of what sexual norms society should uphold, two viewpoints were offered: Society should not tolerate homosexuality versus society should celebrate all forms of sexuality. Homosexuality, in the first argument, is viewed as invariably disrupting the family and contributing to the moral decline of society. In the second, with reference to Native American cultures that recognize "two-spirited" people—e.g., Nadle among the Navajo or Winkte among the Lakota—homosexual persons are accorded distinctive and positive roles within society. Societywide, homosexuality is a minority position that may be appreciated as such rather than punished as a threat to more conventional values and practices. According to Terry Tafoya (1995), a Native American and psychology professor, the term "medicine path" connotes a combination of destiny and free choice in enacting one's individual behavior in everyday tribal life based on a specific spiritual vision. Two-spirited persons are understood and valued as flexible, able to transform themselves toward greater masculinity or greater femininity, and as having a uniquely useful blended perspective.

A contemporary play, *The Twilight of the Golds,* also raises interesting questions about social attitudes toward homosexuality. The Golds are a family consisting of a mother and father, a married daughter, and a gay son. The daughter decides to terminate her pregnancy when a newly developed diagnostic test confirms that the child will definitely be born homosexual. The ensuing drama reveals to the gay son/brother the depth of ambivalence and negative attitudes other family members have toward him, and he must decide how to react. Clearly, attitudes toward homosexuality as well as other alternate lifestyles are more complex than simply being viewed as always, nearly always, only sometimes, or not at all wrong. For example, there are differences on the conservative side between not agreeing with, actively disapproving, rejecting and avoiding, fearing or hating (homophobia), and violence toward homosexuality. On the liberal side, too, there are differences between tolerating, acknowledging, accepting, respecting, and valuing a particular lifestyle, which results in a qualitatively different impact on those toward whom such attitudes are directed. Readers examining their own attitudes thus might consider the nuances conveyed by the language they tend to use to describe their own opinions on such matters.

PREVALENCE OF HOMOSEXUALITY

The extent of homosexual behavior has not been fully established, but existing estimates make clear that it occurs widely in our society. Kinsey, Pomeroy, and Martin's (1948) volume on the sexual behavior of the human male, based on a large but unrepresentative U.S. adult sample, remains a point of reference for many subsequent discussions of the prevalence of homosexuality (see Box 6.1). Regarding the incidence of homosexuality among men in the United States, Kinsey and associates found that 37 percent of their respondents had experienced at least one homosexual contact to the point of orgasm and another 13 percent had experienced homosexual desires but had not acted on them. The percentage who were lifelong exclusively homosexual was a much smaller 4 percent. The incidence of homosexuality among women was lower, with corresponding figures of 13 percent, 15 percent, and 2 percent respectively.

In their comprehensive representative national survey of sexual behavior, Laumann et al. (1994) divided questions concerning homosexuality into three basic dimensions: behavior, desire, and identity. Behavioral questions always referred to specific time frames, while desire and identity items were asked in terms of respondents' current state of mind. They interviewed 1,749 women and 1,410 men.

Attraction. Women were asked, "In general are you sexually attracted only to men, mostly men, both men and women, mostly women, only women?" For men, the same question was used but reverse ordered. The percentage of respondents reporting any same-sex attraction was 6.2 percent for the men and 4.4 percent for the women.

Self-identification. Respondents were asked, "Do you think of yourself as heterosexual, homosexual, bisexual or something else?" (Persons who answered "something else" but described themselves as gay or lesbian were coded as homosexual.) Altogether, 2.8 percent of the men and 1.4 percent of the women reported some level of homosexual or bisexual identity.

Behavior. The proportion of respondents who reported having a same-sex partner "at any time since puberty" was about 7.1 percent of the men and 3.8 percent of the women; "in the past five years," about 4.1 percent of men and 2.2 percent of women. At the end of the interview, when specific sexual behaviors were asked about rather than "partners," the researchers obtained their highest estimates: 4 percent of women and 9 percent of men reported having engaged in at least one sexual activity with a same-sex person.

Differences were noted in the way same-sex sexuality was experienced by men and women. Given that a person reported any same-sex partners, "women were much more likely than men in any time frame longer than a year to have had male as well as female partners" (Laumann et al. 1994: 312).

Further, *place of residence* will change the percentage and visibility of persons expressing homosexual attraction, identities, and behaviors. For example, Laumann et al. (1994: 307) found that "nine percent of 18-59 year old men living in the largest central cities in the U.S. currently identify as either homosexual or bisexual, fourteen percent have had male sex partners in the past five years and about sixteen percent report some level of attraction to men." Further, within gay communities, in cities such as New York, San Francisco, Chicago, or Dallas, a higher proportion of persons encountered would self-identify as gay.

Janus and Janus (1993) asked their respondents, "Have you ever had homosexual experiences (yes/no)?" Of the 1,335 men, 22 percent said yes; of the 1,384 women, 17 percent said yes. Correspondingly, 78 percent of the men and 83 percent of the women said they had not. The level of participation among those who answered yes is shown in Table 6.2.

As a percentage of all men and all women (not just those who have had some homosexual experience), this amounted to "active" participation among 9 percent of the men and 5 percent of the women. Regarding self-identifica-

TABLE 6.2. Frequency of Homosexual Activity Among Respondents Who Have Had Homosexual Experience (Percent)

	Men (294)	Women (235)
a. Once	5	6
b. Occasionally	56	67
c. Frequently	13	6
d. Ongoing	26	21
"Active" = lines c+d	39	27

Source: The Janus Report on Sexual Behavior Janus and Janus. Copyright © 1993 John Wiley & Sons. Reprinted by permission of John Wiley & Sons Inc.

tion, the persons who had reported engaging in homosexual acts either "frequently" or "ongoing" almost equally identified themselves as homosexual or bisexual (Janus and Janus 1993: 71). When asked to "check off the response that is correct for you: heterosexual, homosexual or bisexual," Janus and Janus's respondents answered as shown in Table 6.3.

Like Laumann et al. (1994), Janus and Janus expressed some reservations about categorization of persons as heterosexual, homosexual, or bisexual, given the different levels of participation in homosexual activity and the fact that persons had sex over time with both male and female partners, regardless of how they labeled themselves. "As we have noticed in other areas of sexual involvement, there is often a looseness of labeling relative to any particular sexual activity" (Janus and Janus 1993: 70). Heterosexual individuals sometimes have homosexual experiences; homosexual individuals have heterosexual experiences yet may not regard themselves as bisexual.

Regardless of the self-labels embraced, individuals engage in homosexual behavior in a variety of situations, from brief, casual encounters to longer term, committed relationships. How open individuals will be about their sexual orientation and some of the relationship issues confronted by lesbians and gay men are considered in the remaining sections of this chapter.

HOMOSEXUALITY AND THE FAMILY

Socially conservative groups in American society have characterized lesbians and gay men as antifamily, but this is a misleading portrayal. Certainly, lesbians and gay men are involved in family life. In traditional families, a son or daughter, a parent, sibling, cousin, or other family member may be gay or lesbian. They are not deliberately acting "against" their families. However, family members who are heterosexual, especially when they also hold strong religious convictions or personal beliefs opposed to homosexuality, may find themselves with an uncomfortable conflict of loyalties

TABLE 6.3. Self-Identification (Percent)

	Men (1,333)	Women (1,411)
Heterosexual	91	95
Homosexual	4	2
Bisexual	5	3

Source: The Janus Report on Sexual Behavior Janus and Janus. Copyright © 1993 John Wiley & Sons. Reprinted by permission of John Wiley & Sons Inc.

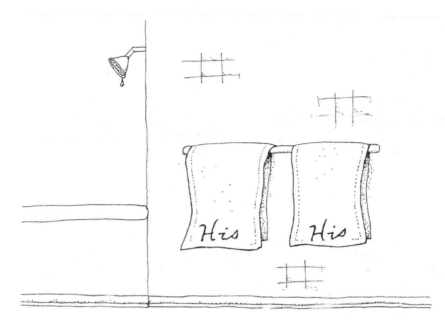

Illustration by Tom Urquhart.

when confronted with a family member's homosexuality. How do traditional beliefs and values weigh in against attachment and commitment to one's own kin? Further, lesbians and gay men seek social affiliation, emotional connection, and physical intimacy with others in couple relationships, friendship networks, and larger communities (Bozett 1989). Recall that alternate lifestyles arise when existing social institutions fail to meet individual needs. Socially approved marital and sexual relationships and the traditional path of dating, engagement, marriage, and children—which assume heterosexuality—do not meet the needs of lesbians and gay men. Gay persons and couples more often experiment with a variety of different social arrangements. Given the still marginal status of even heterosexual cohabitation relative to marriage, live-in partners will typically be denied medical care, insurance coverage, inheritance, and social security benefits. For same-sex couples legal marriage is not available as an option. As Bozett (1989) discusses at greater length, the legal system, the workplace, religious institutions, and social custom ignore or more often oppose and seldom support gay families. Consequently, gay and lesbian persons stand both within and outside conventional families.

Coming Out to Family Members

If, when, and how families learn of an individual member's unconventional sexual orientation, and with what results, is an issue of growing interest as increasing attention is paid to lifestyle diversity. Coming out is an ongoing process of accepting and revealing to others one's sexual orientation. One is not simply out, once and for all. First, there is coming out to oneself, acknowledging a "different" sexual orientation and determining what that means. Then, coming out is a decision about disclosure ("Should I tell?") made in each new social setting, not knowing what the reaction will be. Too, other persons' reactions unfold over time in unpredictable ways.

Parents are not necessarily the first to know about a son or daughter's homosexuality. Lynn Sutcliffe (1995), who published a collection of coming-out stories titled *There Must Be Fifty Ways to Tell Your Mother,* described herself as a lesbian activist receiving increasing media coverage, "out to the whole world, except my mother" (p. 2). Because we have a unique social relationship with family members, telling them is a significant and risky event for most lesbians and gay men. Reactions in the family run the gamut from hostile and violent to understanding and supportive. Various parental and sibling responses over time to disclosure of a child's homosexuality are described in the stories presented in Box 6.2.

Box 6.2. Coming Out Stories: Family Reactions

The following are adapted from Lynn Sutcliffe (1995), *There Must Be Fifty Ways to Tell Your Mother.*

Tony. My Mom found a letter I had written to a boyfriend. Later, while we were all watching TV, she told my Dad, who said it was "debased debauchery," and they took me to a psychiatrist. When the psychiatrist said they had the problem, not me, they ignored him, got angry, cried, and tried everything. Now my Mom has gotten to a stage where she'll say, "Wish [my current lover] a happy birthday from me." It took ten years for them to realize it wasn't a phase.

Ann. My mother and I were out shopping. She turned to me and asked whether I'd ever had a boyfriend. I said I didn't think I ever would actually. She looked puzzled and asked what I meant. I was embarrassed and just repeated what I had said, hoping she would get it. She asked me why and I was trying to make her guess, so she said, "Well, it's not like I think you're a lesbian, if that's what you mean." "But that *is* what I mean." At that point we ran into a friend of the family and just pretended nothing had happened. After a week with neither of us saying anything, she came to my room and told me she hadn't slept for three nights for worrying. "I don't think you'll ever be happy if you don't marry and have children." I tried to explain but she wasn't

(continued)

(continued)

listening. She came out with every cliché about lesbians you can think of. Basically we couldn't really talk about it. I came out to my brother shortly after. He was very supportive. I gave him a book about having a gay child to give to my mother and he said he'd talk to her. She said later the book helped her understand.

Dave. My mother told me not to tell my Dad but he must have overheard something because he took me aside and in a strangely calm voice said, "It's okay if you are gay, you just have to leave this house and never come back. Are you gay?" I denied it. Twelve years later when I finally managed to tell him the truth, he was more reasonable, saying it was just the dressing up he didn't understand. I guess he thought all gay men were transvestites. I told my brother I am gay and he said I made a lot more sense to him now. I was very reassured by his acceptance.

Beth. I was having sex with girls in my class but none of us talked about it. I came out during a family meal. "You know my friend Susan?," "Please pass the potatoes," "Well, Susan and I are both lesbians," "What does that mean, dear?," "We love each other and we have sex." Mother: "Oh." Father: "Get out." So I went upstairs, packed and moved out. I didn't speak to them for six years. Recently, I called my mother. She said she missed me and felt bad she didn't even know where I live. We are trying to build a new relationship, but it will take time. My sister was married with children when I finally came out to her. She met me and my partner in a quiet bar and said, loudly, "I know, you are going to tell me you are a lesbian. Is this your girlfriend? Oh, she's wearing a skirt ..." My sister wants each new partner to be "the one," so I will be settled down. When a cousin came out later some of the family blamed me, like she was just copying me.

Christy. My mom found out from a friend of hers but didn't let on. Then one day when we were having an argument she threw it up to me. I didn't know whether to try to deny it or admit it. I told the truth. She couldn't look me in the face after that. She was really angry and upset because she believes if you are gay you are completely mental and should be locked up. Later in a fight she pushed me down a flight of stairs. The situation became unbearable. A best friend I came out to though was great. She said she isn't gay but it's fine with her.

Ben. I knew I was definitely queer. I never felt sexually attracted to a woman. I decided to tell my older brother and led into the conversation with some stories about boys at school. He suddenly stopped me. "I hope you are not trying to tell me you are gay because that will kill me and I will have to beat some sense into you." He was very angry and I was frightened. I couldn't believe his reaction. For years I just never mentioned it again. This was one in a series of family rejections. My Dad's reaction to the idea of homosexuality was "maybe gay people need understanding but I can't give them that and I don't care." He said he was "definitely worried about my friends at school and you know what I am talking about." It was menacing. I knew there would be trouble if I told him so I didn't but as I got older I could not collude in their self-deception. I just have no contact with them now.

(continued)

(continued)

Alex. I tried and tried and couldn't say it, then finally blurted it out when my Mom kept asking, "What? What are you trying to say?" She went really over the top after I told her. My sister's baby was being christened and the whole family was over at our house. She got everyone's attention and said she had an announcement: "Alex and I had a chat and he's told me he is a homosexual, so if anyone has any problems with that speak up now, I don't want any gossiping." I was mortified but everyone started being ridiculously nice saying, "Oh, are you? I thought maybe you were. Okay then." That sort of thing. After that, the christening was completely forgotten and it became my family coming out party. I came out with a boom. It was really good.

Marla. My mother must have remembered a program we watched on TV about a woman in South Dakota whose six children all turned out to be gay. When I came out to her, right away she telephoned my brother and sister and made them come out to her as heterosexual, "just to be sure how many I have to get used to."

Patrick. I had a boyfriend so I decided to tell my family over break. My mother picked me up in the car asking a lot of questions about college like whether I was seeing anyone. I blushed. She asked me what her name was and what was she like. I kept blushing. After a long pause she asked, "Is it a boy you are going out with?" I told her. She cried all the way home, which I found stressful. We decided not to tell anyone else in the family—my Dad because he would have a bad reaction and my brother because he was a tough, sports-minded kind of guy. The next time I talked to my brother on the phone, though, he said, "I know. You're my brother and I love you." My Mom had told his girlfriend, who told him, but he was fine.

Ed. One day my mother just yelled from the kitchen, "Hey, are you gay?" I said I was and we went on from there. I blame her sudden awareness of the issue on Oprah Winfrey, who had been doing a show on gays and lesbians.

Steve. After going out with a man for awhile, I finally told my Mom he was my boyfriend. She went up the wall and smashed the mug she was holding and started shouting insults at me. I felt angry at her for the first time. She stormed out of the room and I was just stunned. A few minutes later she came back, crying. She told me she was fearful of AIDS and she thought my father would kill me, but she was going to tell him. I was terrified, and cried. He came into the room. I had picked up a sports magazine, his favorite, and was pretending to read it. All he said was that he knew I'd been miserable and noticed a change for the better since I had been seeing the man I was with. He said being gay wasn't a big deal. He even gave me a hug. My Dad was perfect.

Kate. I was home for a weekend and wanted to tell. I stuttered and stammered and said I thought I might be a lesbian. My mother fainted straight away. When she came to she was calm but insisted I could still get married; "everyone finds relationships with men difficult, you just have to keep trying or maybe you could just not have sex." I thought that was unfair. I felt a need to justify myself and I wasn't ready to do that. She was also afraid I'd break

(continued)

(continued)

my father's heart but he took it okay. Nowadays she is fine about it and has even met my girlfriend. Later, looking back at my childhood, my mother said they suspected something from a very young age.

Vicky. My mom called me and asked if I had something to tell her. "No, not really." "When are you coming out?" "Excuse me?" "There's a book here on my library card called *Coming Out: A History of Homosexuality.*" "School project." "Well, it's overdue and I can't show my face in that library now; they'll think I'm a queer." I don't think I'll ever tell my parents now. We only get together once in a while and they seem to enjoy themselves a lot when we do. They won't understand and the longer I wait, the harder it gets. What can I say to them—I've been out in the gay community for years and have been lying to you for ages? They would be upset remembering incidents in the past where I had deceived them. That won't make them feel like loving parents which they very much are except for this. They were really horrible and homophobic to my brother when they thought he was gay, and he's not. I could have come out before and I chose not to; now it seems impossible.

As the issue of sex education already suggested in an earlier chapter, most parents are not keen on discussing their children's sex lives in the first place. Further, confronting the ways in which one's children are different from oneself on important matters may be difficult anyway. Add that homosexuality is not a conventionally accepted lifestyle and may not be well understood by parents. Parents, compared to peers, are more likely to feel responsible, guilty, disappointed, ashamed, or worried about their children and, depending on the child's age, to feel entitled to try to change them. A wide range of reactions are encountered, many negative:

- "Spare me the details; just be careful."
- "People will look down on me because you are gay."
- "If you have these unnatural feelings, the decent thing to do is just get married anyway and get on with your life."
- "No, you're not gay."
- "No queer is any son/daughter of mine."
- "Swear you will never see anyone like that again and we'll never mention it."
- "You can't be; it would make me sick."
- "I guess I'll probably just have to learn to accept it."
- "I'll pray for you."
- "I just thought you were sensitive/assertive, not necessarily gay."
- "But you used to go with girls/boys. I don't understand."
- "Where did I go wrong?"
- "I knew we shouldn't have let you play with dolls/trucks."

- "I don't want to see you old and lonely when you are fifty."
- "Well, as long as you are happy."

Even parents with accepting attitudes toward homosexuality in general have sometimes described early suspicion and denial, later shock and anger when finally confronted with their own child's homosexuality. One famous recent example was Chastity Bono, daughter of entertainers Cher and Sonny Bono. *The Star,* a tabloid newspaper, disclosed her sexual orientation for worldwide scrutiny. Her experience received a great deal of media attention and was described in detail in a book titled *Family Outing* (Bono and Fitzpatrick 1998). In the 1950s, a family outing might have meant a Sunday drive in the country with the family. In the 1990s, the phrase signified revealing to parents a child's gay or lesbian lifestyle. **Outing** refers to disclosure of one's sexual orientation by others, when one is not necessarily ready or intending to do so. In a televised interview about her daughter's lesbian lifestyle, Cher described in a humorous way the adjustment she had to make in giving up her previous plans for her daughter, that "she would grow up, get married, get divorced and live happily ever after like everyone else." Comedian Ellen Degeneres, another public figure, came out on television and discussed mixed family reactions. Her mother's concerns included the difficulty of letting go of expectations for her daughter's marriage and having grandchildren, and fears about her child's safety, well-being, and happiness. Homosexuality is "different." At the least, family members have to formulate new understandings of what their children's lives will be like. Parents should keep in mind that "there are worse things than being gay." It doesn't change who someone is as a person, and that person is still your son or daughter (Bono and Fitzpatrick 1998).

Despite the uncertainties, one of the main motivations for coming out is the strain of deception involved in living a lie. Staying "in the closet" (that is, hiding one's sexual orientation) requires constant vigilance and generates a sense of inauthenticity. As one of Sutcliffe's (1995) interviewees put it, "Before I came out I spent most of my life in fear and panic trying not to be found out, skillfully deceiving family, friends and work mates to ensure they didn't discover the 'other' me" (pp. 91, 92). In such circumstances, individuals feel guilty and worry that they will let their parents down or embarrass them. Adolescents and young adults are dependent on parents and realistically fearful about parents withdrawing financial and/or emotional support. Sometimes they simply do not feel close enough to parents to share this aspect of their lives. In many cases, family members "know" but are afraid to ask outright, because then there is no ignoring the fact. This type of denial still communicates that something is wrong with being gay or lesbian. Children will be reluctant to tell parents as long as the fear of rejection outweighs the benefits of disclosure. A positive reaction from family members, however, is important to most individuals even as adults. "If my parents accept me," one of Sutcliffe's (1995: 64) female informants reports, "there is no one I need to apologize to for who I am." Other interviewees explained that coming out gave them more confidence and courage to do other things; "people accepting you gives you strength" (p. 102); and being visible as a gay or lesbian individual brings a positive role model to others.

Same-Sex Couples

Increasing attention by social scientists to close relationships in general was demonstrated by the appearance in 1984 of the *Journal of Social and Personal Relationships*. Psychologist Lawrence A. Kurdek (1991: 177, 178) later proposed several reasons for scientific interest specifically in "homosexual couples and their differences from heterosexual couples": Gay and lesbian relationships develop and are maintained with a relative lack of role models and without institutional support (e.g., legally recognized marriage); they are less focused on procreation and may reflect different attitudes toward fidelity; partner selection may be more restricted by numbers or exhibit different dating and mating patterns; and they exist in a social context of homophobia (Kurdek 1991: 177-178). When family sociologists Katherine Allen and David Demo (1995) reviewed sociology journals that publish family research, they found few studies pertaining to lesbians and gay men. Overall they judged that the topic was neglected and merited further investigation. Studies of lesbian and gay families (including same-sex couples or one lesbian or gay adult rearing a child) were seen as contributing to improved knowledge of families in general. The limited existing research has, in fact, begun to address same-sex partnerships and romantic relationships as well as parenting issues—a needed shift from the public view of homosexuals as deficient individuals to instead examining "the familial and social contexts in which lesbians and gay men live" (Allen and Demo 1995; Laird 1993).

In comparing same-sex and heterosexual relationships, there will be both differences and similarities. Living in a predominantly heterosexual society, individuals in same-sex couples experience some unique problems as well as benefits (McWhirter and Mattison 1984). First, all gay and lesbian couples are not alike. For example, types of couples might include:

1. Individuals who live together much like heterosexual married couples.
2. Two men or women living apart but describing themselves as a couple, spending most of their free time together and sharing job and family concerns.

3. Partners, one of whom is in a heterosexual marriage. One partner maintains a home while the married partner lives with the wife or husband and children.
4. Brief relationships lasting less than a year. Moving from one relationship to the next can become a lifestyle.

Too, lesbian and gay male couples may differ. Social psychologists Wiggins, Wiggins, and Vander Zanden (1994) noted that earlier findings from studies of romantic relationships among both heterosexual and homosexual couples led Peplau (1981) and Blumstein and Schwartz (1983) to conclude that "gender is a more important determinant of the nature of couple relationships than is sexual orientation. Owing to gender socialization, the fact that lesbian couples consist of two women and gay male couples consist of two men may be expected to significantly shape their partnership" (Wiggins, Wiggins, and Vander Zanden 1994: 352).

Like heterosexual couples, same-sex couples come together after an initial process of getting acquainted. The search for a prospective partner can be more difficult for persons with an unconventional sexual orientation but is facilitated by access to an openly gay community, clubs, formal organizations, or informal social networks. Gay and lesbian couples can and often do establish stable, long-term, committed relationships based on mutual caring, generosity, creativity, love, support, and nurturing. This may be more difficult insofar as gay and lesbian individuals are presented with mainly heterosexual models for partnership, including their own families of origin, which they may try to emulate but find unsuitable. Common elements in same-sex and heterosexual relationships include issues of trust and respect, communication, decision making, managing conflict, physical affection, sexual intimacy, relationship values, and social ties (Mackey, O'Brien, and Mackey 1997). Yet many features of same-sex relationships are unique.

Same-sex couples do not approach roles, finances, ownership, and social obligations in the same way heterosexual couples do. Heterosexual couples are directed by society's norms and expectations while lesbian or gay couples have greater freedom to explore alternatives. Neither the social roles nor the implicit power dynamics of traditional marriages apply (Gilbert 1993). Research on gay and lesbian couple relationships indicates that they generally avoid traditional male and female roles in favor of equality and reciprocity (Kurdek 1991). However, lack of clearly defined roles can also lead to disagreements over matters such as household division of labor or whose job takes precedence. Gay male couples are likely to have an economic advantage as a result of joint male incomes. Social obligations are influenced by how "out" individual partners are about their couple relationship. Concerns about acceptance by their respective families are the rule for lesbian or gay couples, who struggle with issues of disclosure to parents, friends, employers, and others. As a result, lesbian and gay couples tend to derive less support from their parents and other family members and to rely more on friendship networks than do married heterosexual couples (Gilbert 1993).

Nass, Libby, and Fisher (1984: 169) suggested the possibility of heightened sensual pleasure in homosexual relationships due to more sympathetic intimacy based on similarity. For gay women, however, too much likeness may necessitate working out issues of separation and comfortable distance in the relationship (Kreston and Bepko 1980), and finding a balance between social isolation and insecurity about other attachments. Gay and lesbian couples confront jealousy in a new form, since same-sex friendships now have erotic overtones. Outside sexual activity is more commonly accepted among gay male couples but remains consistently disapproved of by the majority of heterosexual couples and not highly valued by most lesbian partners (Kurdek 1991). Many gay males do form long-term relationships, even without relevant visible role models, in which they expect mutual emotional dependability with a partner, but fidelity differs with their individual attitudes about sexuality and exclusivity (McWhirter and Mattison 1984).

Sexual activities within same-sex couples appear to be varied and adaptable. McWhirter and Mattison (1984) and Blumstein and Schwartz (1983) reported that "gays were versatile in their sexual behavior and did not assume male and female roles. Reciprocity in doing and receiving was the norm" (Kurdek 1991: 179). Blumstein and Schwartz (1983) and Kurdek (1991) found that quantity and quality of sex were related to overall satisfaction with the relationship for gay and lesbian couples as well as for married and cohabiting heterosexual couples. Gay males reported equivalent levels of relationship quality in sexually exclusive and sexually nonexclusive relationships. Like participants in heterosexual open marriages, gay males in sexually nonexclusive relationships did not value sexual fidelity and typically engaged in sex outside the relationship with each other's knowledge. Among lesbian couples, like heterosexual married or cohabiting couples, fidelity was more strongly related to relationship satisfaction, prompting the observation that fidelity may generally be a more important aspect of relationship quality for women in committed relationships than for men (Kurdek 1991).

Antihomosexual attitudes—ignorance about homosexuality, prejudice, and homophobia—influence lesbian women's and gay men's lives and relationships. Same-sex couples repeatedly deal with these situations. Successful same-sex couples have to overcome both oppression from others and internalized self-oppression and resolve possible differences between themselves in ways of dealing with issues such as disclosure. Heterosexuals experience social pressures to be "coupled," but gay and lesbian couples are pressured to be apart, "to deny the reality of their sexual intimacy with one another" (Krestan and Bepko 1980: 284). Despite the difficulties, gay and lesbian couples form household and alternate family units that contribute significantly to society. Many participate actively in civic, neighborhood, church, and political life alongside nongay neighbors and friends who accept them as individuals and as couples (McWhirter and Mattison 1984).

Finally, questions of whether and how to rear children involve different issues and realities for lesbian and gay partners than for heterosexual couples. Societal expectations that marriages should produce children do not apply; same-sex couples raising children are typically regarded with disapproval (Slater and Mencher 1991). "Moreover, the *how* of having children, which typically goes unquestioned by heterosexual partners, is complex for same-sex partners and requires resources as well as sources of support outside of the relationship" (Gilbert 1993: 123). Family and health care benefits are not usually extended to gay and lesbian partners. Obtaining accommodation at work for parenting is likely to be more difficult and will also raise concerns about risks of disclosing same-sex relationships to employers and coworkers.

Gays and Lesbians As Parents

Implicitly, there seems to be a contradiction between being gay and being a parent, as if these two social statuses are mutually exclusive. Consequently, gays and lesbians have been largely invisible as parents. The *Harvard Law Review* (1990:119) reported, however, that "approximately 3 million gay men and lesbians in the U.S. are parents, and between eight and ten million children are raised in gay or lesbian households." Reviewing statistics from seven studies of gay men, Harry (1983) concluded that on average 20 percent of gay men (one in five) have been in a heterosexual marriage. Just over half of these marriages were estimated to result in one or more children. Lesbian women were found even more likely to have been heterosexually married, about a third (one in three), with half of their marriages also resulting in children. As compared to gay men, lesbian women are also more likely to have custody and live with their children (Laird 1993). Most gays and lesbians who become parents do so in the context of heterosexual intercourse (alternatively via medically assisted conception); a reminder of Kinsey's wise observation that conventional thinking about homosexuality and heterosexuality in either/or terms obscures the greater complexity of actual experience.

Ironically, support for parenting from the gay and lesbian community also appears to be problematic. Gay fathers confront an unexpected lifestyle dilemma, finding themselves a minority within a minority, inasmuch as "typically, gay culture is singles oriented" (Bigner and Jacobsen 1989: 164). Recall that singles versus married persons place greater emphasis on personal freedom and autonomy, but gay fathers, like heterosexual men who are single parents, have social, financial, and emotional responsibilities and obligations toward their dependent children. Gay fathers may feel marginalized both among heterosexuals and among gay men (Bigner and Jacobsen 1989). While the gay community validates their sexual orientation, it generally ignores or rejects child-rearing issues. Likewise, researchers have reported that "lesbian mothers may have more in common with their heterosexual counterparts than with lesbians who are not parents" and that they "felt more accepted as a family with their own families of origin and among their associates and friends than by the lesbian community" (Hare 1994: 27, 32). Hare's interviews with twenty-eight lesbian couples involved in child rearing highlighted perceived challenges and benefits. Challenges included those associated with being an unconventional family and those arising from parenting itself, such as how to identify themselves as a "family," custody issues, and providing a male role model for their children. Perceived benefits of being raised by a lesbian couple included the additional love and nurturance a child received (as compared to living in a single-parent household) and the tolerance for diversity that children developed in these circumstances.

Gay and lesbian parents remained concerned about social disapproval of homosexuality and how this might affect their children, who would be vulnerable to adverse comments or behaviors from others. Parents developed strategies to help their children deal with this: e.g., discussing with them whether to tell and how to respond to negative reactions; reminding the children that they had a loving family, were good persons, and were not responsible or at fault; and reinforcing that their worth does not depend on others' reactions. As children grew older and confronted prejudice regarding an unconventional family structure, their parents' hope was expressed by one interviewee as follows: "People have different views. I want [my children] to appreciate that what should influence our behavior is what we believe about ourselves, not what other people believe about us" (Hare 1994: 33).

Given the difficulties, why do homosexual men and women enter heterosexual marriages and have children? Some are the same reasons heterosexuals marry: societal expectations of marriage; particular pressures to marry from a dating partner, her or his family, or one's own; genuine affection or love for the person one marries; to escape loneliness or disappointing past relationships; and desire to have children. Motivations are complicated, however, by conflicts over sexual orientation. In their discussion of why homosexual men marry, Ortiz and Scott (1994) recognize both conscious and unconscious efforts to cope with *social scripting* that simply assumes heterosexuality or actively rejects homosexuality. To function more "acceptably and productively," individuals "deny, ignore or minimize desires which are different from the norm." They may be unaware of or confused about their homosexuality; e.g., viewing their homosexual experiences before marriage as "experimentation, a phase, or only something they did when they were drunk," or they might consciously choose heterosexual marriage to hide, deny, compensate for, or "cure" their undesirable sexual orientation (Ortiz and Scott 1994: 68). Bozett (1989) noted that individuals who resisted identification with a gay or lesbian lifestyle may already have married and had children before coming out to themselves or others. Other individuals may desire the parental role despite an established, openly gay or lesbian identity because children anchor them in a positive way to a familiar, conventional responsibility and provide them with a role that enhances their life experience.

Considerable prejudice and discrimination presently exist regarding gay and lesbian couples or persons as parents. For example, in Florida and New Hampshire, legislation prohibits gays and lesbians from adopting children or providing foster care. Yet several reviews of previous research studies found no evidence that children reared in households in which one or both adults are homosexual are harmed or compromised in comparison to being raised by heterosexual parents (Bozett 1987; Patterson 1992, 1994; Hunter et al. 1998). Moreover, children who themselves are gay would probably benefit from being reared by a gay or lesbian parent or couple; having positive role models can temper the guilt and pain many homosexual adolescents experience over nonconventional sexual identities (Bozett 1989: 194). Gay and lesbian parents are likely to teach acceptance, not blanket dismissal of homosexuality, but will not turn children disposed toward a heterosexual sexual orientation into homosexuals. Most gays and lesbians, after all, are "produced" by heterosexual, not homosexual, parents. Their common goal in parenting is to raise productive, well-adjusted members of society. The same elements contribute to their success; accepting the parental role, being dependable, spending time with their children, enjoying activities together, good communication skills, consistent discipline, respect and affection, and so on.

A priori dismissal of gays and lesbians as parents creates a lack of accurate information about what effects parental homosexuality has on child, adolescent, and adult sociopsychological development and sexual identity. In what ways do these families function? How do they manage particular strains and difficulties? What are their unique strengths? Bozett (1989) argues that before one can identify and treat dysfunctional family dynamics, baseline information is needed to describe and understand "typical" or "normal" gay and lesbian families that already have positive outcomes for participants.

CONCLUSION

Disclosure to parents, siblings, and other relatives brings homosexuality home; it is no longer just a matter of opinion about what "other" people do, right or wrong. Coming out in the family is a much more personal confrontation between an unconventional sexual orientation and expectations regarding family attachments and loyalties. If parents were generally better informed about homosexuality, beyond obvious stereotypes and negative attitudes, and able to imagine a gay or lesbian lifestyle as a happy and rewarding one, some of their distress might be alleviated.

Public opinion at large remains that homosexuality is wrong. By the 1994 General Social Survey, nearly 20 percent of adult Americans responding indicated that sexual relations between two adults of the same sex is "not wrong at all" but 70 percent still said "always wrong." Negative messages conveyed by family, peers, mass media, schools, church, and the law complicate self-identification and personal adjustment for gays, lesbians, and bisexuals. As described in one of Sutcliffe's (1995) interviews:

> At school being called gay was an insult. All the associated images had a negative connotation. At 15 I remember thinking "but I still want to marry and have kids"(pp. 24, 25). I couldn't imagine telling my parents. My dad might be physically sick. When I was younger my mom used to say "I'm glad you're not *that way.*" I wouldn't tell them unless I had some specific news or if they asked I might think maybe they were ready to hear. I'm happy but feel that I am living a lie.

A student in the author's class, who said he knew very early on that he was attracted to other men, added: "Nature or nurture, I am what I am. You go on from there. All the negatives don't change your sexual orientation, they just make you have to work harder to feel good about yourself." Social psychologist Charles Horton Cooley (1983: 183-185) used the concept of the **looking-glass self** to explain how individuals are influenced by social feedback: "Each to each a looking glass, reflects the other that doth pass." We formulate opinions of ourselves based on how we imagine others appraise our appearance, manner, character, and behavior, with associated feelings of pride or shame, satisfaction or regret. In unconventional marital and sexual lifestyles, individuals find validation from significant others who do not subscribe to the more negative general opinion; e.g., gay and lesbian communities, supportive heterosexual coworkers, friends and relatives, or "out" media figures.

Growing recognition of lifestyle diversity in the United States has prompted closer consideration of the meaning of marriage and family. Beyond legal definitions (with family typically described as a group of people related by blood, marriage, or adoption), "more and more individuals are beginning to define family in functional terms" (Tully 1994: 77). The basic functions, or purposes, of family are increasingly being provided by different types of structures. For example, whether or not legal marriage is ever extended to encompass same-sex couples, these "domestic partnerships" do provide commitment and interdependence, companionship, economic cooperation, and emotional support. And they do so despite the considerable obstacles, summarized by Brian Miller, a psychotherapist in private practice (Bozett 1989: xii):

> Like their heterosexual counterparts, gay couples have conflicts, about privacy, power, jealousy, intimacy, freedom, definitions of friendship (including sexual friendships), searching for a balance between "I" and "us." In addition we struggle against a society that believes these relationships are not valid or lasting; they are not blessed by the church or recognized by the courts as families. A homophobic society also instills self-hatred that sometimes sabotages gay relationships from within.

To explain the full range of marital and sexual lifestyles, social scientists must challenge conventional biases, both personal and societal. As discussed in Chapter 1, existing public debates can be examined to disentangle "statements of value" and "statements of fact." Empirical research, oriented by sociological theories, can help to frame a more accurate, comprehensive, and detailed understanding of homosexuality in social context. Family sociologist Katherine Allen (Allen and Demo 1995) suggests, for example, that the *life course perspective* (applied in Chapter 2 to dating and mate selection) raises many relevant questions about the various paths to gay, lesbian, and bisexual identities; the stages, transitions, and significant events in their couple relationships and parenting experience; and how these are given personal and social meaning. "In addition to illuminating the rich diversity of lesbian and gay families, a life course framework highlights the interplay of historical, demographic, and social structural influences in shaping family experiences, as well as the dynamics of intergenerational relations" (Allen and Demo 1995: 123). Future studies of marital and sexual lifestyles in family sociology can be expected to provide fuller description of what people are doing in what types of relationships, with what consequences or implications for themselves, their partners, other family members, and society at large. With an emphasis on social process (that is, on what goes on within various social systems), we will also learn more about how individuals adapt to existing social scripts and how these social scripts change over time.

Chapter 7

Marital Relationships:
Men, Women, and Children

Participants in a marriage commonly think of their relationship in personal terms, as a unique pairing of two individuals. But individuals relating to one another both as men and women and as a married couple do so in ways shaped by societal expectations. The experiences of men and women in marriage, as in other social settings, reflect culturally prescribed roles and socially defined identities. Since most married couples will also have children, marital relationships typically are connected with child-rearing responsibilities, which tend to reflect traditionally different roles for fathers and mothers. Children's lives are directly affected by parental work and family arrangements. The divorce trend, in particular, has had distinctive consequences for children and for society, including a growing number of single-parent and stepfamily households.

GENDER ROLES

To appreciate how society influences men and women in marital relationships, consider the concepts of sex roles and gender. Sex simply denotes the biological fact of a person's being male or female. **Sex roles** are shared social expectations concerning appropriate conduct for men and for women; *learned* expectations that define the ways members of each sex should think, feel, and behave. Sex role analysis emphasizes our social identities as men and women as distinct from the biological fact of being a man or a woman. Sex roles are *not* innate, not "natural," not directly determined by our biology—though they do reflect a social interpretation of biological differences. Social roles in general define the rights and obligations that are understood in a given society or social group to accompany particular social positions and serve to guide a person's interaction with others with reference to these positions. For example, husband and wife are social positions with associated rights and obligations affirmed by custom, law, and public opinion; we learn shared ideas about what marital partners can expect from and owe to one another. Like other social roles, sex roles denote *patterned social expectations,* *not simply individual attitudes.* In other words, sex roles are a "social fact," with the characteristics of exteriority and constraint, influencing us through processes of socialization and social control. From the moment of birth (or now, even before birth, as we scan the sonogram) when we ask the question, "Is it a boy or a girl?," each new generation confronts existing beliefs about what boys and girls, men and women "are." Individuals are categorized socially as male or female and responded to based on a set of assumptions about what it means to be a member of one category or another.

Gender, sociologist Margaret Anderson (1993: 31-34) explains, is a different but related concept, distinguished from sex roles by its broader connotations. Gender encompasses "the complex social, political, economic and psychological relations between men and women" in society as a whole. Sex roles (or, in this context, gender roles) are patterns through which gender relations are expressed, but gender cannot be reduced to specific roles. Gender is "experienced through" but is more than a matter of interpersonal interaction. It includes the socially learned behaviors and expectations that are associated with the two sexes, but gender, like race and class, is best understood in terms of *structured inequality.* Gender is located in wider social institutions and involves the distribution of power and resources in society at large. **Patriarchy** is a term used to describe a system of dominance relations in which men rule. Men's traditional position as head of the household did not simply arise naturally in each family but was determined and sustained by a social system providing men with the legitimate authority and social resources needed to enforce their rule. For example, in England, under the common law doctrine of *coverture,* a married woman lost her individual identity and became a legal nonperson, not entitled to make contracts, keep her own wages, or control her own property (Weitzman 1977). Similarly, gender inequality in the United States has worked against women becoming equal partners in marriage; e.g., in the 1950s married women were not legally permitted to secure credit in their own name.

The concepts of gender and gender roles are useful tools for analyzing society and acquiring some important insights about ourselves—why we think, act, and feel the way we do as men and as women. Gender profoundly influences our personal lives, often in ways we do not realize. In the 1960s, the women's movement slogan that "the personal is political" displayed sociological imagination in recognizing the connection between private lives and public issues. What happens in the family is related to other social institutions and to social structure and trends in American society as a whole. Feminist scholars, focusing on women's issues, have demonstrated that gender is one of the central organizing principles of society. Later scholarship also addressed men as men, that is, as "gendered beings" (Kimmel 1996; Kimmel and Messner 1998). Individual experience of what it means to be a man or a woman in the United States is shaped by gender roles, a feature of the larger social context. Studies of gender clarify the processes that transform biological males and females into gender-socialized men and women.

Our sense of what is possible in relationships between men and women is limited by the taken-for-granted nature of gender roles. Change may be resisted when we assume uncritically that "men will always be men and women will always be women." What does that mean in practice? One early investigation of the influence of culture on how men and women behave was conducted by anthropologist Margaret Mead (1935/1969), and reported in a book titled *Sex and Temperment in Three Primitive Societies*. Mead used three New Guinea tribes, the Arapesh, the Mundugamor, and the Tchambuli, to illustrate how particular societies raise men and women to exhibit the traits desired in that culture. Two of these societies exhibited less sex role differentiation than the United States. **Sex role differentiation** refers to the extent to which a society expects men and women to differ in attitudes and behavior. Among the Arapesh, both men and women were raised to be cooperative, gentle, and nurturing; among the Mundugamor, by contrast, both men and women were aggressive, hostile, and suspicious. In the Tchambuli she found a case of *role reversal;* men exhibited more "feminine" traits and women more "masculine" traits than we popularly expect based on our own society's interpretation of sex differences. The range of possibilities may be bounded by biology, yet room for considerable cultural variability remains. The extent and types of sex differences we have endorsed in character and behavior are not inevitable. Some of the expectations we have assigned to men and women are unnecessary, others actually damaging.

In *Measuring Sex Stereotypes*, psychologists John E. Williams and Deborah L. Best (1990) distinguish between two relevant concepts. **Sex role stereotypes** are beliefs concerning the general appropriateness of various roles and activities for men and for women; **sex trait stereotypes** are a set of psychological traits considered more characteristic of one sex than of the other. In each case, sex stereotypes are uncritical, oversimplified beliefs about males and females which are then applied to individuals; e.g., that women are passive, weak, dependent, nurturant, and belong in the home while men are active, strong, independent, competitive, and should focus their lives on work outside the home. Williams and Best (1990: 15, 16) note that sex roles are often "explained" by reference to sex trait stereotypes—as in, women make good nurses because they are gentle and caring while men make better business executives because they are strong and competitive. Gender analysis suggests that sex trait stereotyping may as much follow from and serve to rationalize gender roles as to create them. In part, the harm in sex stereotypes is that they deny to both sexes the opportunity to explore and develop all one's individual interests and talents. From society's point of view this is a waste of human resources.

A man is perceived as "masculine" and a woman as "feminine" to the extent either displays the sex-stereotyped traits associated with their own sex. Williams and Best's own cross-cultural research used a lengthy adjective checklist to determine empirically what traits were more associated with men than with women and what traits with women more than men. Their instructions to survey respondents acknowledged that not all men are alike nor are all women alike but asked respondents to consider the *typical characteristics of men and women in our culture*. Men and women answering this type of question show a high degree of agreement in their adjective ratings. For a more detailed look at the particular traits associated with men and women in the United States as reported by Williams and Best (1990: 22) and others, see Box 7.1. What do you conclude from the two lists of traits?

A problem with such sex stereotyping is that the roles and traits of men and women are not only different, they are unequal. Specifically, the qualities assigned to women are regarded as inferior. It is not just a matter of who does what; it is a matter of how, as individuals and as a society, we *value* the

---

Box 7.1. Sex Role Stereotyping—Masculine and Feminine Traits

"Masculine" means: "snips and snails and puppy dog tails"

adventurous	determined	logical	steady
aggressive	dominant	noble	stouthearted
ambitious	enterprising	paternal	strong
analytical	farsighted	profound	tough
assertive	forceful	rational	undaunted
bold	frank	realistic	unemotional
brave	hardy	resolute	unfeminine
confident	heroic	rough-natured	unwomanly
courageous	independent	self-sufficient	upright
daring	intellectual	stable	virile

"Feminine" means: "sugar and spice and everything nice"

affectionate	flirtatious	masochistic	superficial
appreciative	fragile	maternal	sympathetic
attractive	frivolous	meek	tactful
cautious	gentle	mild	talkative
chaste	girlish	modest	tender
delicate	home-loving	monogamous	timid
dependent	hysterical	nagging	weak
docile	impulsive	prudish	whiny
emotional	intuitive	self-sacrificing	
envious	lacking foresight	sensitive	
excitable	lacking self-	sentimental	
fickle	confidence	submissive	

relative contributions of men and women. It is possible to imagine a social division of labor in which the contribution of each sex, while different, is equally respected, but that has not been the reality of gender in U.S. society. For example, housewife ranks below dog trainer in occupational prestige. There is a difference in the social status granted to men and women. Given the lower status associated with feminine traits and "women's work," it is not surprising that women have been more strongly motivated than men to challenge traditional gender roles. **Sexism** refers to prejudice and discrimination on the basis of sex and an ideology (fixed set of beliefs) used to justify both. For women, sexism means devaluation of their abilities and a narrowing of opportunities; for men, the relentless pressures and life-shortening performance demands of masculinity.

Sociologist Michael Kimmel's (1996) book *Manhood in America: A Cultural History* traces the changing social scripts that have defined what it means to be a man in our society. Masculinity is problematic in one way that femininity is not. Masculine trait stereotypes emphasize action and demand accomplishment for validation of "manliness." Masculine traits are more highly valued but more difficult to attain than feminine traits; to a greater extent they must be *earned* by physical, sexual, or economic performance. In terms of social identity, they pose the corresponding threat of potentially losing one's manliness. Note that the masculine trait stereotypes in Box 7.1 include avoidance of appearing womanly. When students discuss the difference between a girl being a tomboy or a boy being a sissy, they are quick to observe that a girl gains status by being more bold, adventurous, and active while a boy loses status by being "like a woman." Further, they expressed the thought that a girl can easily grow out of the tomboy stage and become feminine, but a sissy boy might never retrieve his masculinity. This interpretation says a lot about gender in our society. Accordingly, it does appear that masculine traits are more highly valued and rewarded in our culture but are more difficult to attain, and their violation is regarded as more "serious," with whatever underlying anxieties and defenses that may entail for individuals attempting to develop and maintain a socially validated sense of self.

Gender Identity and Marital Interaction

Gender identity is the degree to which a man or woman incorporates traditional masculine and/or feminine role definitions, including dominant and subordinate statuses, into his or her own self-concept.

Gender identity influences marital interaction. In traditional marriages, the husband is the key provider and ultimate authority while the wife plays a subordinate, supporting role in the family. In such marriages a husband's predominantly masculine and wife's predominantly feminine gender identity are assumed to provide the best fit with expected marital roles. **Androgynous** gender identities combine both types of traits, masculine and feminine, in the same individual. The person's overall self-concept is less tied to being specifically masculine or feminine. When both husband and wife are more androgynous than traditional in gender identity, they will adjust marital roles to fit their own sense of what is appropriate given each person's particular strengths, weaknesses, and character. This will take some innovation insofar as traditional family roles cannot simply be followed; new definitions of what a husband and wife should do will have to be negotiated during the course of everyday interaction in the marriage. In cases where the husband is androgynous but the wife's gender identity is predominantly feminine, difficulties may arise. She may see her husband as weak or indecisive or unreliable if he is not sufficiently masculine. Conversely, when the husband is predominantly masculine and the wife is androgynous, he may see her as challenging his position of authority and thereby threatening his "manliness." Well-intended partners in these marriages are often frustrated by their unexpected incompatibility. Another pattern that sometimes occurs is a reversal in gender identity—masculine wife, feminine husband. That this pattern is uncommon and tends to produce an unstable relationship says something about the effectiveness of gender socialization and the lack of social support for such departures from expected gender identities.

Gender roles and identities influence *task allocation* (the division of labor) in a marriage. Couples face many practical tasks that have historically been assigned on the basis of assumptions that they are best suited to either men or women: Who disciplines the children? Who takes the children to the doctor? Who prepares the meals? Who is in charge of paying the bills? Who does minor household repairs? Who does the housework? Who washes the car? Who mows the lawn? And so on. How these questions are resolved raises issues of *power relations* and *styles of decision making* in a marriage. Who gets to decide, and on what? Because gender identity encompasses notions of dominance and subordination, it affects satisfaction or dissatisfaction with how decisions are made, who is more likely to compromise, and who ultimately gets his or her own way. While traditional male authority promotes a husband-dominant pattern, in practice women often had authority in designated domestic spheres (e.g., "Okay, you know what is best for the children"). A wife-dominant marriage is not the societally preferred form; jokes and ridicule for "henpecked" husbands serve to sanction men who appear to be letting their wives get "out of control." Other options include joint decision making in all matters pertaining to the marriage and family welfare (e.g., discuss everything and decide together), independent decision making (e.g., separate checking accounts), or less sex role stereotyped separate spheres (e.g., she knows more about cars, he decides about grocery purchases).

Uneven change over the last three decades in gender role expectations has generated conflicts for men and women who find themselves with divergent views. In marriage, dating, and sexual relationships, sometimes the strains created by disagreement over the proper roles of men and women are obvious. Other times the influence of gender is more subtle; e.g., in the questions we do not even think to ask. Why do people refer to a young unmarried mother as having "gotten herself pregnant"? Why should women be "grateful" if a man "helps around the house"? Why should he be pleased with himself if he "lets" her go back to work or to school? If she earns a lot more money than he does, why may one or both feel "funny" about it? In predicting marital stability, the key element appears to be **role congruence.** Couples with compatible gender identities and similar sex role attitudes tend to report higher marital quality and satisfaction than couples whose attitudes do not correspond well. In other words, whether both partners are traditional or both are modern in sex role orientation, they are more likely to have common goals and to agree on the basic rules of the relationship than couples in "mixed" marriages.

WORKING WIVES

In the introductory chapter, we looked at U.S. household composition in 1977. Recall that about 15 percent of all households consisted of families in which the wife was a full-time homemaker, while in 18 percent both parents were in the paid labor force. Correspondingly, sociologist Peter Stein (1981) reported that families with two wage earners constituted roughly 53 percent of all intact families. By 1986, about 62 percent of all married women were working outside the home, including 48 percent of married women with children under age six. By 1992, the figure for married women with children under age six in the labor force had increased to nearly 60 percent, the majority of whom were employed full-time (Gilbert 1993). Lucia A. Gilbert, a professor at the University of Texas in Austin, noted that the proportion of intact families in which the husband is the sole breadwinner had by this time dropped to 20 percent (less among minority families). Further, government statistics show that working wives in the United States are contributing a substantial share, 40 percent, to total household income (U.S. Department of Labor 1991).

Today, many women who might otherwise prefer the role of full-time homemaker do not see this as a feasible option. When the author interviewed a local minister about the types of conflicts that bring couples to him for counseling, he mentioned that ten years ago he typically saw couples arguing because the woman wished to work outside the home and the husband was opposed, while more recently he has counseled couples having conflicts because the wife wanted to stay home full-time but the husband wanted her to seek paid employment, to "go out and get a job." Further, a high rate of divorce over the past several decades has impressed upon many women the need to obtain job skills and to remain employable. Looking at the challenges confronting families today, social historian Stephanie Coontz (1997) emphasizes that this trend of married women in the paid labor force is crucial in maintaining the standard of living of American families and will not be reversed. Wishful thinking will not bring back the mythical happy homemaker of the 1950s (Coontz 1992).

The reasons are primarily economic. Nevertheless, studies of working women also find many women reporting they would work even if they did not have to because as a result, they feel more useful and recognized, less isolated, less dependent, and more equal in the marriage. Still, most working wives take on outside employment in addition to carrying the major burden of household labor. Hochschild's (1989) look at "the second shift" called attention to the notion that domestic responsibilities are sufficiently demanding to be considered a second job. The traditional ideal of a full-time housewife implies that taking care of a home, especially when children are present, already is a full-time occupation. How women have tried to combine work and family demands is discussed later in this chapter. Ultimately some adjustments in family responsibilities have to be made. How willing were men to take over a greater share of domestic chores? See Box 7.2 for excerpts from a humorous essay by Pat Mainardi on the politics of housework. In the 1980s, Hochschild found that the majority of

---

Box 7.2. The Politics of Housework

"The Politics of Housework" is the title of an essay written by Pat Mainardi for *Notes from the Second Year: Women's Liberation,* published in 1970. Its radical premise was that women are not destined for housework by immutable natural law. Rather, who does housework reflects the politics of gender. She opened her essay with an observation by John Stuart Mill to the effect that failing to recognize the collective power of husbands as a privileged group, each woman is left to complain about her own particular husband and private division of household labor. Mainardi identified herself primarily as a housewife, though she was also a writer and social activist. Since both she and her mate worked for pay, she thought that he should share the housework. While not turning her down outright (he was too "hip" for that), he appeared less than enthusiastic about the prospect of being responsible for household chores such as planning, shopping for, cooking, and cleaning up after meals or cleaning clothes, floors, bathrooms, and so on. His arguments and her interpretations included the following:

"I don't mind sharing the housework, but I don't do it very well. We should each do the things we're best at." MEANING: Women have had hundreds of years of experience doing domestic chores. It would be a waste of manpower to train someone else to do them now. AND: I don't like the dull stupid boring jobs, so you should do them.

(continued)

(continued)

"We have different standards, why should I have to meet yours? That's unfair." MEANING: I know women feel guilt over a messy house and believe household work is ultimately their responsibility. (If anyone visits and the place *is* a sty, they are not going to leave thinking "he sure is a lousy housekeeper." You'll take the rap.) I can outwait you. ALSO MEANING: I can provoke innumerable scenes over the housework issue. Eventually, doing all the housework yourself will be less painful than trying to get me to do half. Or I'll suggest we get a maid to do my share.

"I've got nothing against housework, but you can't make me do it on your schedule." MEANING: Passive resistance. I'll do it when I please; dishes once a week, laundry once a month, floors once a year. If you don't like it, do it yourself oftener, then I won't have to do it at all . . . and don't try to do anything else while I'm doing my jobs. I'll annoy you until you'd rather I quit.

"Housework is too trivial to fight about . . . I hate it more. You don't mind it so much." MEANING: It's even more trivial to do. Housework is beneath my status. My purpose in life is to deal with matters of significance. It's degrading and humiliating for someone of *my* intelligence to do it. But for you . . . (Mainardi 1975: 28, 29)

Mainardi has some advice for women trying to share housework. Insofar as men gain time, ease, independence, or liberty from women's domestic labors, they lack incentive to change. People generally are more interested in how they are oppressed, not in how they oppress others. Understandably, individuals in positions of privilege rarely wish to give up the benefits, nor even to acknowledge them, but "the measure of your oppression is his resistance." Why would he want to do housework—which Mainardi describes as a form of unpaid monotonous repetitive work that "never results in any lasting let alone important achievement"—if he can avoid it? That does not automatically make it your job. Reach a fair division of labor in the household and stick to it. Historically, as other forms of race and gender domination have fallen, concerns were expressed about the end of civilization (e.g., what ills could come of freeing slaves or extending the right to vote to women). Life goes on. Society will not crumble if men take a turn at the dishes.

men she studied "did not share the load at home." Differences between men and women in extent of participation in household labor continued to be reported in research studies through the 1990s.

Dual-Career Couples

The increase in working wives, now the norm, includes but is not the same as dual-career couples, a less common and still "deviant" lifestyle. Because a career is more than a job, the effects on couples and families are more far reaching. A career is viewed as intrinsically more important to the individual and more satisfying. The motivation is not only economic necessity but has more to do with self-fulfillment and advancement. Careers require a higher degree of commitment, energy, and attention and have more open-ended time demands than a "9 to 5" job.

Dual-career couples are more often middle class in family of origin, have higher average levels of education, marry later, are more likely to be childless, and more often find themselves in "commuter marriages" for at least some of their married lives. Like participants in other nontraditional lifestyles, dual-career couples experience *role ambiguity* and corresponding strains. With normative guidelines lacking, unclear, or contradictory, participants in dual-career marriages have to think through each new decision on their own; they can't just do what is "expected." Under stress, dual-career couples tend to revert to traditional sex roles. Two major stresses are career moves and children. The traditional solutions are that his career takes priority and the children are her responsibility.

How couples adapt to the demands of two careers can vary over time and changing circumstances. Generally speaking, there are several possible approaches for balancing the demands of family and career. Both partners can be career driven and agree to give their careers priority over marriage and family, creating a relationship that requires minimal maintenance. Alternatively, both can still be strongly committed to family and agree to make career decisions with what is best for the marriage in mind. A third strategy of trying to maximize both family and career outcomes for both partners, requires high energy, optimism, and good luck, and is most likely to require modification as unanticipated obstacles are encountered. Finally, couples may opt for complementary priorities; that is, both partners will have careers but one partner (not necessarily the female) will set a higher priority on marriage and family activities, the other on career requirements. In the latter strategy, couples may reverse positions for periods of time when a particular career requires more intensive time and focus at one stage than another.

Job seeking is difficult for anyone who is serious about his or her work but is especially difficult for the dual-career couple. Dual-career couples face the task of obtaining *two* positions that will ideally permit them to: live in the same geographic area; coordinate their schedules so child care tasks and necessary household chores get done; have the same free time to spend with one another for sex, recreation, meals, and conversation; get what they want from the present job; satisfy their long-range career goals; decide to their mutual satisfaction how to manage their money; and be physically and emotionally available to their children.

For successful partnerships, dual-career couples particularly need trust, tolerance, independence, open communication, flexibility, conflict resolution skills, imagination to create new roles, and determination to make time for the relationship. It is important to try to understand as much as possible from the beginning one another's career goals and likely working conditions. Talking to persons already in the same careers about their personal as well as professional lives is recommended. Box 7.3 illustrates some of the kinds of questions couples should consider even before marriage.

Box 7.3. Dual-Career Couples

With support from the University of Texas at Austin, researchers Lucia A. Gilbert, Suzanne Dancer, Karen M. Rossman, and Brian L. Thorn studied individuals' perceptions of how work and family roles could be integrated. They published some of their findings in a 1991 article in the professional journal *Sex Roles*. Several items from their survey questionnaires, used to measure young men and women's attitudes, are reproduced below (from Gilbert 1993: 63-67). Respondents were asked to indicate their level of agreement with a particular statement from 1 = "not at all" to 5 = "very much." How well do these items capture your own sentiments about work and family? Persons contemplating dual-career marriages should certainly discuss these kinds of issues with their partners beforehand.

A. Orientation to Occupational-Family Integration

	Not at all				Very much

Female Traditional (for women)
* After marriage I see my spouse as being the major financial provider and working full-time.   1 2 3 4 5
* After marriage I see myself working part-time and taking primary responsibility for raising the children.   1 2 3 4 5

Male Traditional (for men)
* I see my spouse pretty much taking responsibility for raising the children.   1 2 3 4 5
* I see my spouse's income as providing extra money.   1 2 3 4 5

Role Sharing
* I see my spouse and I both working full-time and sharing the financial responsibility continuously throughout the marriage.   1 2 3 4 5
* With or without children I see myself and my spouse to a great extent sharing the day-to-day responsibilities for maintaining the household—like food shopping, cooking, cleaning, laundry and money management.   1 2 3 4 5

B. Essential Characteristics of Spouse

How important to you?   Not at all   Very much

(continued)

(continued)

Career Success Traits
- Someone who pursues their own needs or interests.   1   2   3   4   5
- Someone who is able to be independent financially.   1   2   3   4   5
- Someone who is strong and confident.   1   2   3   4   5

Emotional/Relational Traits
- Someone who puts me first.   1   2   3   4   5
- Someone who is warm and nurturing.   1   2   3   4   5
- Someone who makes me feel needed.   1   2   3   4   5

Views of Family Life
- Someone who shares daily household tasks.   1   2   3   4   5
- Someone who will alter their daily work schedule   1   2   3   4   5
  for parenting.
- Someone who holds traditional views of men's roles.   1   2   3   4   5
  (reverse scored)

EGALITARIAN RELATIONSHIPS

In 1972, Pat Schroeder, a lawyer by training, married and the mother of two, was elected from Colorado to a seat in the U.S. House of Representatives. Over the next twenty-four years she participated in national debate and legislation, and helped to forward the role of women in politics. In addition to serving on the prestigious House Armed Services Committee, she brought attention to issues such as pay equity, the Equal Rights Amendment, research on women's health, and family leave. She retired undefeated. In 1998, she published a book about her life in politics, titled *24 Years of House Work . . . and the Place Is Still a Mess,* in which she described the rewards and challenges of her political career, and how she balanced her public and private lives. She remembers being told repeatedly that she could not be an effective mother, wife, *and* politician. In Box 7.4, her reflections on what she had been taught about how to be a good wife provide a description of marital relationships as envisioned in the 1950s.

For working wives and two-career couples in the twenty-first century, the 1950s role prescription for a good wife appears quite incongruous. Women who work outside the home as an economic necessity or a matter of choice have less time and energy to devote to pampering the working husband. The women's movement in the 1960s also voiced a different ideal: marriage as a partnership of equals, not a relationship of dominance and subordination. Even wives who worked part-time were freed of complete economic dependence and, with increasing participation in higher education, women were more likely to aspire to a profession, not simply a job. As women entered the paid labor force, men and women could be both providers and homemakers. As Gilbert (1993: xi) observed, dual-career couples poten-

Box 7.4. How to Be a Good Wife

Former Democratic member of the U.S. Congress Pat Schroeder reminisces about the rules of marriage she was taught in the 1950s in her high school home economics class:

Have dinner ready. Plan ahead, even the night before, to have a delicious meal—on time. This is a way of letting him know you have been thinking of him and care about his needs. Most men are hungry when they come home, and the prospect of a good meal is part of the welcome needed.

Prepare yourself. Take fifteen minutes to rest so that you are refreshed when he arrives. Touch up your makeup, put a ribbon in your hair. He has just been with a lot of work weary people. Be a little more lively and interesting. His boring day may need a lift.

Clear away the clutter. Make one last trip through the main part of the house just before your husband arrives, gathering up schoolbooks, toys, paper, etc. Then run a dust cloth over the tables. Your husband will feel he has reached a haven of rest and order, and it will give you a lift too.

Prepare the children. Take a few minutes to wash the children's hands and faces if they are small, comb their hair, and if necessary change their clothes. They are little treasures, and he would like to see them playing the part.

Minimize all noise. At the time of his arrival, eliminate noise from the washer, dryer, dishwasher or vacuum. Encourage the children to be quiet. Be happy to see him, and greet him with a smile. Don't greet him with problems and complaints. Don't complain if he is late for dinner. Count this as minor compared with what he might have been accomplishing that day.

Make him comfortable. Have him lean back in an easy chair or suggest he lie down. Have a cool or warm drink ready for him. Arrange his pillow and offer to take off his shoes. Speak in a soft, soothing and pleasant voice. Allow him to relax and unwind.

Listen to him. You may have a dozen things to tell him, but the moment of his arrival is not the time. Let him talk first. Make the evening his. Never complain if he does not take you out for dinner or entertainment. Instead, try to understand his world of strain and pressure, his need to be home and relax.

Your goal: Try to make your home a place of peace and order where your husband can renew himself in body and spirit.

Source: 24 Years of House Work . . . and the Place is Still a Mess © 1999, 1998 by Pat Schroeder. Reprinted with permission of Andrews McMeel Publishing. All rights reserved.

tially represent a "dramatically different view of how to accomplish work and family goals. It is a view that assumes certain changes in women's and men's self-concepts as well as in social norms and structures." When Rhona Rapoport and Robert Rapoport (1969) introduced the term dual-career family, they were describing a revolutionary alternative lifestyle. The two-career family concept was met, according to Gilbert, with both excitement and skepticism. Excitement because it promised to retain the best of love and intimacy between married partners while freeing them from traditional gender roles. Skepticism because, even if this was considered desirable, it was difficult to imagine how such a departure would actually be possible given "proper" male-female relationships under patriarchy, as described below in a passage from Alfred Lord Tennyson's (1902) poem "The Princess":

> Man for the field and woman for the hearth;
> Man for the sword and for the needle she;
> Man with the head and woman with the heart;
> Man to command and woman to obey;
> All else confusion.

> Historically, women depended on men economically and were not taken seriously as providers, even in those instances when they were able to achieve necessary education and credentials. Women were not supposed to have "independent means" because men were their eventual and natural benefactors. The notion that a person could pursue a career and actively be involved in family life was not considered an option. Overall, the occupational structure has been highly resistant to recognizing workers' family obligations. The demands of careers were structured by men for men, and men's freedom to pursue careers came from having women in their lives to sustain their ambition and attend to the domestic details of their lives. Women's freedom to pursue a career usually came by avoiding marriage and family altogether. (Gilbert 1993: 7, 8)

Consequently, much of the strain experienced in two-career families, and in all families with working wives to a lesser extent, arises because *structural supports are inadequate,* as when quality affordable day care, employer receptivity, and favorable public policies are lacking. Pleck (1994) described, for example, how employers' leave policies inhibit men's participation in parenting. Dual-career couples try to negotiate a private understanding and maintain an egalitarian relationship in a larger society that still sees men and women as fundamentally different and men as superior. Gender theory sensitizes us to the reality that "women and men act out their private roles as spouses, parents and homemakers within the larger world of institutional and occupational structures" (Gilbert 1993: 10). We suppose we can have any kind of marital relationship we choose based on our own unique personalities, goals, and wishes. Yet privately held principles of equality "may prove inconsistent with social institutions that embody the values of male authority over women." Meanwhile, the prevailing ideology attributes difficulties associated with changing gender roles to the inevitable ill effects of "going against nature," not to sexism itself.

Further, gender theory proposes that power-based conceptions of men and women's relationships are internalized as a result of gender socialization. When socialization is effective, socially defined expectations tend to be taken as given. They shape our sense of how the world is, how relationships are conducted, and who we are. **Self-concept,** the set of beliefs and feelings we have about ourselves, is engendered. We form culturally based ideas about who we are as men and as women and how we should interact. As part of a sense of self, these beliefs are experienced as personal, familiar, comfortable, and "right." If we frame our experience in stereotypic ways, other ways become literally unthinkable. We have difficulty conceiving other possible selves in another type of relationship. Aspirations to attempt egalitarian relationships as well as persistence in overcoming obstacles are compromised when we feel threatened. As one male student phrased his concern, "If women don't need us as protectors and providers, what do they need us for?" Insofar as men's standing in marriage has been defined through the role of protector and provider, women's equality can be perceived as fundamentally challenging their masculinity and worth. Gender role changes *are* disorienting and unsettling in a very immediate and personal way. In egalitarian marital relationships, the revolution hits home.

What constitutes equality between the sexes and a democratic relationship in marriage? Dictionary definitions associate the word "democratic" with a social condition of equality and respect for the individual within the community. Equality, according to the *American Heritage Dictionary,* denotes "having the same capability as another; having the same privilege, status or rights; of similar value; deserving or worthy; having the requisite strength, ability, determination and the like, as in 'equal to the task.'" Women have pushed harder than men for more egalitarian relationships because traditional gender biases devalue women (so women have fewer incentives to perpetuate them) and because changes in American society in the past three decades have had a greater impact on women. Men resist, for all the reasons Mainardi's essay suggested. Men's relative insensitivity to issues concerning integration of work and family has been demonstrated in studies of occupational aspiration and future plans (Gilbert et al. 1991; Ganong and Coleman 1992). Men may lack insight into the difficulties women experience in marriage, the necessary coping strategies, and the resentments that working women feel, because men do not typically see these issues as personally relevant; for them there is little anticipated or ongoing conflict between work and family.

Even among dual-career couples, arrangements vary from more conventional to more egalitarian. As described by Gilbert (1993), in *conventional* two-career families the wife still assumes responsibility for running the household and for child care. Particularly if the husband earns a large salary, her work involvement is seen as her choice, in support of which she will have to work out the necessary accommodations. In *participant* two-career families, men play a more active part in parenting, role specialization is less rigid, and male dominance is muted, but the wives remain responsible for household labor. Only in the **role-sharing** two-career families defined as those in which both partners actively involved in all aspects of family as well as outside employment, is egalitarian marriage endorsed in principle and in practice. Gilbert (1993: 87) reported that "only 1/3 of heterosexual two career families fit the egalitarian model; another 1/3 are conventional; the remaining third are intermediate." She added, however, that marital satisfaction does not necessarily differ across the three types. Satisfaction depends on the perceived fairness of whatever arrangements are worked out in the marriage as experienced by each partner. Perceived fairness will depend on factors such as desired level of work involvement, requirements of the particular careers chosen, general attitudes about family life, expectancies about marriage, gender identity, emotional support from the partner, and available family and community resources.

Recall that the Rapoports initially made a case for dual-career families as a transformative social experiment that would defy traditional gender roles and permit equality of partners in marriage. That most working wives today do not have careers in the first place and that perhaps only about one-third of all heterosexual two-career couples can be categorized as having egalitarian relationships underscores that the egalitarian marriage remains a "deviant" lifestyle. Nevertheless, women today who can provide for themselves economically are more likely to want partners who see them as equals and are willing to participate in role sharing, not simply task sharing. Pleck (1992) and Barnett, Marshall, and Singer (1992) called attention to the psychological and physical benefits for partners who are both involved in occupational work and family life. Men's family involvement appeared to be increasing in the 1980s and 1990s. The U.S. Department of Labor (1989) reported that greater numbers of men refused longer work hours, sought flexible schedules, and made time for family-related responsibilities. For example, Pleck (1994) found husbands in more than half the families he studied taking off from work an average of about seven days to spend time at home after the birth of a child. This often meant using up vacation time and sick days where no paternity leaves were available, a case of individual innovation in the face of limited normative and structural support.

Comment

For individuals contemplating egalitarian marriages, it is probably useful to keep in mind Lucia Gilbert's (1993: 57) observation that "little historical precedent exists for relationships in which both partners involve themselves in continuous careers and family life." This is a significant departure. Not many role models of successful egalitarian relationships are present even today. Most couples work out some kind of intermediate arrangement that they accept as fair under the circumstances they experience. Changes are occurring in the workplace, but slow in coming. Gender remains a significant factor contributing to inequality in U.S. society at large, which confronts individuals with existing social structures and dominant values that impede or complicate efforts to create egalitarian marriages. Traditional expectations for husbands and wives were clearly defined with respect to patriarchal authority and the "best" division of labor. Tennyson's warning that all else is confusion underscores the challenges generally faced by participants in any alternate lifestyle and especially the demands of reinventing gender roles and relations.

What makes such change possible? Gender roles never were uniformly reproduced in every American household. Individuals adapt cultural scripts according to their own personal perceptions and needs (and social expectations varied to begin with across different groups in the society). In an earlier chapter, alternative lifestyles were viewed as arising when existing institutions fail to meet individual needs. As the U.S. economy changed over the past three decades, and married women entered the workforce in greater numbers, role strains associated with traditional gender roles increased. Correspondingly, individuals experiment with new arrangements, despite uneven external support and while still contending with beliefs they have internalized as a result of early gender socialization and continuing social sanctions. Recognizing that gender is socially constructed and not immutable may inspire willingness to venture beyond our initial individual comfort levels in examining gender-based assumptions about competence, entitlement, and self in our marriages. Change is also desirable insofar as the perception of a fundamental injustice or unfairness in a marriage, even when not openly acknowledged, is potentially corrosive. Marital satisfaction is improved, at least, by mutual affirmation of each partner's personal worth and contribution, within a reasonably shared framework defining how gender roles are to be understood and enacted.

EXPECTATIONS OF PARENTHOOD

Marital and sexual lifestyle decisions influence not only the adults involved but, significantly, also affect any children they may have.

Most persons in the United States expect to have one or more children. Over the past ten years, students in the author's family courses have responded to a survey question asking, "How many children do you plan to have?" Consistently, very few students (3 to 5 percent) were planning to have no children, and not many students (about 10 percent) wanted to have only one child. The most frequently reported plan was to have two children and, in fact, women in the United States ages fifteen to forty-four who had children as of 1995 had an average of two children each (U.S. Bureau of the Census 1999).

Preparation for the parenting role is limited. Although students in the family courses generally believe they have the skills necessary to be good parents, an earlier study of women undergraduates reported that 94.6 percent expected to become parents but 53.1 percent felt inadequately prepared (Knaub, Eversoll, and Voss 1983). How many persons put at least as much time, thought, energy, and training into preparing for their role as parents as they do for jobs? Typically, formal education does not emphasize skills necessary for effective parenting. While algebra, history, and languages are all required college courses, child development is not. Is parenting so easy or obvious that anyone can do it, and do it well? What *is* successful parenting? In an article, "Transition to Parenthood," sociologist Alice Rossi (1977) compared the roles of parenting, marriage, and work. She argued that **role clarity**—the degree of certainty characterizing the expectations attached to a particular social position—was lowest, and **role ambiguity**—uncertainty, vagueness, or lack of clarity—was highest for parenting. The wide appeal of Dr. Benjamin Spock (whose book *Baby and Child Care* was first published in 1946, is still in print in revised form, and has sold tens of millions of copies) and, more recently, Dr. T. Berry Brazelton (media personality and author of another national best-seller on children's emotional and behavioral development) attests to the enduring concerns and insecurities parents have had in the United States about "proper" child care.

Although most Americans expect to have children, fewer feel adequately prepared, and little serious effort is put into socialization and training for parenting. On the whole, U.S. society provides inadequate guidelines and social supports for effective conduct in the parental role. Perhaps, since every adult was once a child, they are presumed able to raise one of their own, until proven unfit. At the same time, trends of increase in divorce, single-parent households, stepfamilies, and women in the workforce have created new challenges for parents.

In two-parent households today, both adults are more likely than not to work outside the home. With the majority of married women in the United States entering the paid labor force since about 1977, the resulting conflicts between work and family have generated numerous social science research studies and much debate, both private and public. Priorities concerning work and family are continually being reevaluated. In the 1980s, for example, newspaper columns, such as those by Joan Beck and D.L. Stewart (described in Box 7.5) illustrated issues raised, for men as well as women. Socialization for career performance is still one of the outstanding features of male identity in our society (Pleck 1975). Sociologist Peter Stein (1981: 308) noted that much has been written about the general importance of work as a source of well-being for men—"work as a life purpose, prized self-image

Box 7.5. Journalists Reflect on Work and Family

I. Columnist Joan Beck: "Working Moms Face Backlash"

The controversy that generated Beck's column was over a weekend news anchor in Chicago, a woman, who turned down an important assignment that required her to be away four nights from her toddler, even though she could afford good substitute child care, and her husband was also available. She was criticized by female co-workers who felt this reflected poorly on all women trying to succeed in competitive professional fields.

The column called attention to conflicts between career women who were willing to commit themselves entirely to the job and working mothers trying to balance the demands of the job with the needs of their children. Beck observed that women who succeed in highly competitive jobs have had to "play by men's rules, which makes no allowance for the demands of mothering. Any concessions working mothers ask for are perceived as an admission of sexual differences, which translates into weakness, which becomes a justification" for holding all women back.

Are the answers better day care, longer maternity leave, and more help from husbands? Beck thinks "it's not that simple." Pushing children into daycare "as if they didn't exist so their mothers can give full-time-plus-overtime devotion to employers is not a solution women should accept."

Maternity leaves disregard the fact that the needs of children are not confined to a preset timetable.

Nor is it feasible to push women back into the home full-time—women workers have become too essential to the national, and family, economy and millions of them have worked too hard for their professional skills. And though many husbands have yet to learn to do a full share of parenting, most of them are caught in the same job pressures.

The workplace—the times and places and ways in which work is done—should be changed to fit the workforce that has changed so drastically . . . [e.g.,] flex-time, professional level part-time work, telecommuting, shared jobs make it easier to combine parenting with employment . . . are cost-effective for employers and should be more widely available.

What also must be changed is the value system that insists both mothers and fathers put the widget company first, that demands a totally work-centered life as the price of success. Women have come a long way in recent years. But they will be making a bad mistake if they settle for a society that lets them have a good job only if they have no children or are willing to push their children into a small corner of the lives.

As men have typically done before.

Source: Beck (1985)

(continued)

(continued)

II. D.L. Stewart: "Busy Parent Misses Joys of Fatherhood"

Stewart had recently talked to a friend who called long-distance about "the things men usually talk about over the phone"; namely, work, and sports and the weather. Just to be polite, he asked the friend about his family. "Everybody is fine . . . the baby is really growing up fast. I love him but sometimes get tired of my wife nagging me to do things with him . . . take him places and give him baths and stuff like that. I just don't have that much time. I'm working really long hours."

Stewart says that was when he wanted to hit him; "but some lessons only experience can teach you and only the lucky learn them in time. I wish I had." He explains that he has not been a bad father; maybe not great but definitely better than his own father. He provided well, so his children had the things they needed, and he spent time with them: fed them sometimes; bathed them occasionally; read them bedtime stories once in a while; and took them to the circus once a year.

"But I really couldn't do all the things their mother seemed to be forever nagging at me to do with them. I just didn't have that much time. I was working long hours. A lot of evenings I was just too tired for feedings and baths and bedtime stories. Anyway, there would be plenty of other evenings to spend with them. If I didn't do those things today, I always could do them tomorrow. And then, of course, I ran out of tomorrows."

They stay our children, but they grow up and grow away from us. Stewart says he wonders now about all those evenings, the missed opportunities. Was it really such a chore to feed them? So tough to fill a tub with water and bubbles and toy boats? So much effort to sit on the edge of a bed and read a story? Were the baseball games he watched instead so important? He hardly remembers the scores.

Instead, he remembers evenings spent wrestling on the living room floor; times carving pumpkins, trimming trees, and dyeing eggs; "quiet moments when they climbed on my lap, warm and soft in their sleeper bags, and we just sat there, being close. . . . Those are the rewards of fatherhood and, for the life of me, I can't imagine why it took their mother's nagging to make me accept them, . . . why I let so many of those moments get away. Sometimes the lesson is learned too late, and it is not until opportunity has passed that it hits you. Right between the eyes."

Source: Stewart (1986)

and validating experience." Fathers who choose to take a more active role in parenting are enlarging the scope of their family participation beyond breadwinner, disciplinarian, and handyman. As a result they may also experience corresponding conflicts between work and family. For example, men who become custodial single parents "more often reduce work hours, report passing up promotions that would mean relocating, and choose work with the demands of child care in mind" (Stein 1981: 308).

WORK VERSUS FAMILY: A HISTORICAL OVERVIEW

Parenting takes place in a larger social and historical context in which social structures and cultural values shape individual assumptions, opportunities, and constraints. Social scientists have tracked and documented some very broad and dramatic changes in the United States over time in the ways family and work intersect. Keeping in mind that the picture varies for different social groups within U.S. society and that in any case this is an oversimplification, Box 7.6 provides a very broad overview of the connection between work and family as it pertains to parenting.

In the early U.S. colonies and through the period of westward expansion, agriculture was the primary occupation for most Americans. The farm was a center of family life as well as a means of economic production; work and home were not physically separated. While there was a division of labor in tasks assigned to husbands, wives, and children, all family members participated together in the everyday routine of making a living. Family members had the bond of **occupational cohesion,** being kin but also co-workers. Children participated as fully as they were able according to their abilities and were regarded more as small adults than set apart as children.

By the nineteenth century in the United States, industrialization and urbanization were well underway. In 1850, for the first time more Americans lived in urban than rural areas (with urban areas defined as population centers of 10,000 persons or more). The factory system for mass production created a separation of work and home; adults in the paid labor force would now leave home in the morning and go to work. The ideal husband-wife roles among those with sufficient economic means became husband as breadwinner and wife as full-time homemaker. The wife's job was to create a home, an "island of affect in the sea of impersonal relations" that was

---

Box 7.6 Historical Overview of Work and Family

	Work (Public)	Family (Private)	
1650-1750	Work/Home *men, women, and children*		"Occupational cohesion"; children as small adults
1850	Work *men*	Home *women and children*	Sex role segregation and the "generation gap"
1950s-1980s	Work *women* *men*	Home *children*	Women in the labor force; "latchkey kids"
2050	???		

emerging with the competitive capitalistic system of economic production. Children were left at home in the care of their mothers. This separation of everyday living into two domains, with men's social role predominantly vested in the public arena and women's social role in the private domestic sphere, can be described as **sex role segregation.** Into the twentieth century, as the economy came to be more complex and the number of specialized occupations grew, children were involved in productive labor less early. The main preoccupation of children came to be their schooling, which set them apart from working adults and contributed to a **generation gap** insofar as the lives of children and adults substantially differed. Adolescence emerged as a separate, socially recognized stage of life between childhood and adulthood.

After World War II, women who had been drawn into the workforce to support the war effort were encouraged to vacate their jobs and return to the home. The postwar economy provided an incentive for consumer spending, reestablishing a sense of national security and prosperity. In the1950s family, a successful working-class or middle-class male breadwinner could support a wife and children and sustain the American dream of home ownership and a "good life." An inflationary economy in the following decades, however, nudged women back into the labor force with support from the women's movement and began a remarkable transformation in American society. With men's identities and efforts still firmly anchored in the workplace and women increasingly trying to straddle the worlds of work and home, new concerns were raised about children. For a time the mass media featured **latchkey kids,** school-age children who came home after school and let themselves into the house, unsupervised until their parents arrived from work. How this picture will look in 2050, another century later, remains unclear. Today, parents still struggle to balance the conflicting demands of work and family, experimenting with various ways to handle "the second shift" (Hochschild 1989)—the job working parents do before they get to the office and after they return home.

EFFECTS OF DIVORCE

How Divorce Is Changing America was the title of a television documentary reported by Jane Pauley in 1986 (NBC 1986). It looked at the personal and social consequences of the increase in the U.S. divorce rate, with a focus on children. Divorce has been changing the way children grow up in the United States as more and more children experience single-parent households and stepfamilies, with whatever benefits and strains these lifestyles entail. Each year over a million American children experience their parents' divorce.

Women usually get legal custody; they have the primary responsibility for child rearing both before and after divorce. About 90 percent of all single-parent households consist of women and children. Many of these families face poverty when women must support themselves and their children on inadequate incomes. Single-parent families have just one wage earner, and women on average earn less than men. Sometimes even providing the basics becomes a struggle. Most women (about 85 percent) are not awarded *alimony;* those who receive it find on average that the amounts are insufficient and last only a short period of time, about two years (Weitzman 1985). Women are now assumed to be independent, self-sufficient, and able to make the transition out of marriage quickly. Younger women can launch a career or remarry, but women who are older, have less education, have long been out of the paid labor force, or are inexperienced in financial management are at a disadvantage.

In an era of widespread divorce, family sociologist Lenore Weitzman (1985) urged a closer look at how marital property is defined in divorce settlements. More than just homes, cars, and stereos, **career assets** are "investments in ourselves and our human potential." They include college degrees, trade and professional licenses, and benefits of employment such as pensions, medical insurance, and enhanced earning capacity. A spouse who invests full-time in homemaking and child care may find in the wake of divorce that the ex-partner walks away with the major economic benefits of the years of marriage. Men should understand that changing laws in many states recognize this principle and are at least open to arguments in favor of compensating the spouse for lost earning capacity. Hardly romantic, but marital and sexual lifestyles do have economic ramifications.

Without directly participating in decisions such as divorce, children nevertheless experience the resulting social, economic, and emotional disruption. Average court-ordered *child support* payments are low to begin with, and single-parent households often do not actually receive even these amounts. As many as 50 percent of absent fathers do not pay the full amount, and 24 percent pay nothing; in one study, 80 percent of men at all income levels stopped their support by the end of three years (Weitzman 1985). Nonpayment of child support has become a national problem, some say "disgrace," leading to enactment of special legislation. The Uniform Reciprocal Enforcement of Support Act (URESA) provides a mechanism (through district attorneys' offices) for pursuing child support claims at no expense to the custodial parent against the noncomplying parent who resides in another state.

As the documentary (NBC 1986) described the situation: "So we have nearly three million divorced fathers in effect stealing from their own children at the rate of three billion dollars a year, and getting away with it." Failure to pay court-ordered child support is a crime in every state. Enforcement is difficult because the caseload is overwhelming, individuals can move from state-to-state, and methods of attachment (e.g., taking the money out of wages or tax refunds) take time to put into place. Underlying the practical difficulties of seeking legal remedies is a sociological insight: *The state is trying to enforce a social obligation that socialization and informal social controls have failed to accomplish.* The internalized norm, a personal sense of responsibility for one's children, is, for many, not strong enough to overcome self-interest and other barriers to meeting those obligations. Some fathers complain that it is not all about money; they may be resentful about the divorce, miss being with their children, disagree with the ex-spouse's child care decisions, and want a larger voice in the child's upbringing. Fathers who were not well off financially to begin with have a harder time meeting child support obligations but may still want to play some part in their children's lives. Others just walk away.

Children contend with their own feelings of being deprived, poorly treated, abandoned, at fault, and uncertain about the future. Dr. Neil Coulter of the University of Michigan estimates that 20 to 30 percent of children whose parents divorce will experience "serious" problems, manifested in behaviors such as poor impulse control and interpersonal aggression. He also indicates that children who experience parental divorce are 50 percent more likely to get divorced themselves. Coulter developed the "Divorce Club" as an in-school preventive intervention program. In several Michigan elementary schools, kids whose parents were divorced were encouraged to meet, list questions they had when they found out about the parents' divorce, and discuss their concerns. **Preventive interventions** try to help people recognize and talk about their feelings, or offer other forms of social support *before* potential problems arise.

Young children may not fully understand the decision to divorce. What *is* a "divorce"? They have many questions about the reasons for the divorce ("Why? Was it my fault?") and its consequences ("Will I still see the parent who is leaving? What else will change now?"). One youngster interviewed for the television documentary commented that "kids feel a lot in the matter; they are afraid to show it though." Children sometimes express feelings of uncertainty or sadness in artwork or play. Suppose a child in a single-parent female-headed household begins to draw animals crying and, when asked, says they are crying because their mother left them. A parent or other adult then has an opportunity to address the feelings expressed and possible underlying questions: If you lose one parent, how can you be sure you won't lose the other? Who will take care of you? If your parents used to love each other and now they don't, will they still love you?

Adolescents too face special problems in connection with parental divorce. In the documentary (NBC 1986), Judith Wallerstein argues that the effects on adolescents are more serious because the decisions they make are "for keeps"; in other words, the consequences are longer lasting. As executive director of the Center for Families in Transition, she has been involved in studying the psychological effects of divorce, especially on children, and in providing treatment and counseling. Many need help. Adolescents may show serious depression, drop out of school, run away from home, use drugs to escape, drink and drive, get involved in juvenile crime, move too quickly into sex, or consider suicide when they are troubled. Wallerstein notes that truancy and school failure leading to not graduating is "hard to undo." Or, if a young woman becomes involved sexually with a lot of men "it is difficult to go back and retrace her steps over those relationships."

Kim Long, as director of a Center for Children of Divorce in Washington, DC, was also interviewed for the *How Divorce Is Changing America* broadcast (NBC 1986). She remarked that divorce is "probably a child's most painful experience; when one parent who has been a part of their lives is gone." The Center for Children of Divorce was experimenting with a puppet show, a preventive intervention program in which puppets expressed the feelings children are believed to have, notably that "divorce is a grown-up problem, with kids caught in the middle of it," thereby helping them deal with their fears. This sentiment was also reflected in the name of another center, in St. Louis, Missouri, called Kids in the Middle, which treated youngsters from preschoolers to teens for the "trauma" of divorce. Wallerstein went so far as to express the view that "if children had the right to vote, there would be no divorce." Not everyone would agree.

A fair summary of current opinion is probably that being raised in a happy home with both parents present is the first choice, but better a stable household with one parent than the conflicts, sadness, and tensions of a household with a bad marriage, physical violence, sexual assault, or verbal abuse. Routinely, a few outspoken students in the author's family classes testify that even as young children they were satisfied that the parental divorce was an improvement for them in family climate; "I was *glad* they got divorced." One caution is that children's needs may be neglected in the aftermath of divorce. At best it is an unsettling experience. As a result of divorce, children today face a higher incidence of poverty and greater uncertainty about relationships. They have a right to continued financial support and to as positive a relationship with noncustodial parents as circumstances allow. Minimally, it seems important to recognize that children may have difficulties with divorce and to provide them with needed social support.

Single Parents

The number and proportion of single-parent households out of all U.S. households and families has risen considerably in the past three decades. By 1981, sociologist Peter J. Stein noted that children in the United States have about a one in two chance of spending part of their lives in a single-parent home. A decade later, a population bulletin compiled by Ahlburg and DeVita (1992) also estimated that *half of all children by age eighteen will experience the breakup of their parents' marriage.* Moreover, they reported that about 44 percent of white children and 66 percent of black children who experience the breakup of their parents' first marriage will also see the end of a parent's second marriage.

Like different types of singles (never married, separated or divorced, and widowed), there are different types of single parents based on how they enter this lifestyle. Roughly, 75 percent of single-parent households occur as a result of divorce or separation, 15 percent due to death of a parent, and 10 percent are cases of parenthood without marriage ("unwed mothers"). Noncustodial ex-spouses, unless remarried, are "single" parents too—as are "unwed fathers," who have received little attention.

Initial adjustment to single parenting includes dealing with the trauma of divorce or death or, for those who never married, the stigma of an "illegitimate" birth. Longer term, negative aspects of single parenthood include **role** and **task overload,** trying to care for your own and your children's physical, emotional, and social needs, without help and usually under strained economic circumstances. Another long-term issue in single parenting is having to deal with the ex-spouse as a parent. Dissolution of a marriage does not necessarily allow the adults involved to walk away from one another in the same way as when no children are present. (In some states an ex-spouse can sue for custody every thirty days after the last court decision.) Single parents frequently feel stress as a result of role overload, often complain of missing adult company and find themselves in an odd social status (not married, not exactly single).

One way to escape role overload is to remarry. *The strains of single parenting are the pushes toward remarriage.* But it is harder for single parents than for other singles to find a new partner. Dating is awkward. It is harder to find time. The other person has to accept you *and* your children. And some single parents may not be ready to remarry. In Kohen, Brown, and Feldberg's (1981) sample of thirty divorced women with children, based on detailed interviews one year after divorce, only seven out of thirty were seriously interested in remarriage, ten were ambivalent, and thirteen were disinclined. Over time the majority of divorced mothers do remarry, but expecting them to simply find a new partner is not an appropriate societal response to growing numbers of single parents. There are also some benefits of single parenting. In Table 7.1 these are considered relative to both individualism and communalism.

The strains of alternate lifestyles can be addressed in various ways. Adaptations can be made at the levels of individual adjustment, marital and family relations, and institutional or societal changes. With respect to internal family dynamics, seven themes of successful family functioning emerged from research done by Olson and Haynes (1993), which can be used by individuals or by counseling professionals as guidelines for single parents. They are listed in Box 7.7. How can society help single parents? Considering responsibility, task, and emotional overload, "we can link personal troubles to social issues by developing the kinds of social policies necessary to reduce overload and provide social support for single parents" (Stein 1981: 284). Kohen, Brown, and Feldberg (1981) note that the social resources available to men—money, power, rights, recognition—enable them to head families, so we need social policies recognizing women as legitimate heads of households and making necessary resources available on the basis of equal merit. Men as single parents also face task overload, jeopardize their work role, receive less social encouragement and have fewer guidelines to follow as exclusive child caretakers.

Sociologist Robert Staples (1977) observed that conservative ideals concerning marriage and family have some backlash effects. Promoting traditional families has the unintended consequence of hurting individuals who do not conform. For example, values opposed to child care outside the home because children "belong" with their parents (i.e., the mother) have reduced incentives to provide quality, affordable day care for working parents. Opposition to sex education because adolescents should "just say no" contributes to unwed motherhood among teenagers. Reluctance to support single-parent households because they are not "real" families undermines their effectiveness. Single parenting works, with social support. Public policies can be designed with recognition of the diversity of family experience, granting persons the right to

TABLE 7.1. Benefits of Single Parenting

Individual (freedom, privacy)	Communal (attachment, belonging)
+ What you do have is all yours	+ Companionship; less lonely than single and living alone
+ Regain autonomy/independence	+ Challenging; keep busy
+ One authority figure	+ Have children in common with most married persons
+ Make your own decisions	+ Special closeness and bond beween single parent and children
+ Self-respect (getting the credit)	+ Extended family; new kin if ex-spouse remarries
+ Children learn early the value of diversity—there are different kinds of families	+ Adult friends and neighbors are like family; serve as role models

---

Box 7.7. Advice for Single Parents

Myrna Olson and Judith Haynes (1993) conducted in-depth interviews with twenty-six single mothers identified as "successful parents," based on a family health model. Successful single parents showed the following characteristics:

1. *Positive attitude toward parenting and life*—accepted their responsibilities and the challenges that come with single parenting.
2. *Prioritization of the parent role*—sacrificed time, money, and energy because they viewed their goal at this stage of life as raising their children.
3. *Use of consistent, nonpunitive discipline*—employed a democratic discipline that calls for logical consequences of behavior.
4. *Open communication*—encouraged open expression of opinions, thoughts, and feelings; as a result a trusting relationship emerges.
5. *Emphasis on independence and individuality*—cultivated within the family unit.
6. *Self-nurturance*—took time and trouble to nurture themselves physically, emotionally, and spiritually.
7. *Establishment of routines and rituals*—followed daily routines, engaged in weekly or monthly family activities, and observed seasonal or holiday rituals.

---

pursue happiness in their own way. The types of policy options suggested by Staples include the following:

- Sex education to prevent unwanted pregnancies
- Better enforcement of child support orders
- More focus on noncustodial parenting
- Quality day care at reasonable expense
- After-school programs/community centers
- Flexible work hours
- Divorce counseling
- A less adversarial divorce system
- Single-parent groups to share concerns with other single parents
- Attitude change to create a positive social environment (single-parent family versus "broken home")

Stepfamilies

Since the majority of persons who marry will have children, a large number of divorces and a high remarriage rate in the United States over the past decade have led to an increase in the number of stepfamilies, sometimes also called "reconstituted" or "blended" families. Most divorced single parents become legally or socially remarried. In addition, there are previously unmarried single parents who later marry and experience a stepfamily situation. The **remarried family** is a two-parent, two-generation unit that comes into being with the legal remarriage of a widowed or divorced person who has biological or adopted children from a prior union with whom he or she is regularly involved. (Husband or wife or both may have children who live elsewhere but interact with the remarried couple on a regular, sustained basis.) Sometimes a couple is not legally married but lives together with his or her children from a prior union "as if" they were married. These families are often referred to as live-in arrangements or socially remarried families.

One of the problems facing stepfamilies is learning to negotiate a new variety of relationships. Stepfamilies have only the nuclear, biological unit to pattern themselves after, but comparing their new relationships to traditional parent-child bonds is probably a mistake. Stepfamilies are different! The stepfamily that tries to function simply as a "natural" family may set up unrealistic expectations. For example, one difference is that in first marriages there is usually a period of privacy and adjustment to the marriage before children are born. Also, stepchildren have to cope with the residue of divorce or death of a parent. A stepparent may not automatically like the children of his or her new spouse. The taken-for-granted attachments of the biological family are not present in step relationships. Another issue is whether to add new children to the stepfamily. Problems may arise, for example, if a childless woman marries a man who is the father of children from a previous marriage with the expectation that she and her husband will have a family of their own. He may not share that expectation, since he already has children.

The law is not always clear on the rights of a stepparent; in most cases the biological parent has priority. Stepparents are sometimes resentful that they seem to have obligations without rights. They are burdened by myths such as the wicked stepmother in Cinderella, favoring her own daughters at the stepchild's expense. Stepparents have to negotiate their role; e.g., father's wife could be treated as the new mother (e.g., when a child is over mourning for lost parent), a friend, or the "other" mother. Stepmothers appear to have more difficulty establishing good relationships with children from a previous marriage than do stepfathers. Authority, discipline, and punishment are often troublesome issues. Stepchildren accuse stepparents of favoritism, overstrictness, trying to monopolize the parent, and rejection. Authority is best established by leading rather than commanding and balancing discipline with affection.

The way a previous marriage ended is an important determinant in the quality of relationships between children and their stepparents. The age of the child when entering a stepfamily situation is also important. (Adolescence is reputed to be the most difficult time; both younger children and near adults appear to make easier adjustments.) For stepfathers, a special problem is with sexuality and female stepchildren. On the positive side, the stepfamily offers the opportunity to develop a larger number of relationships and support systems for adults and children than is available in the nuclear family.

Research Studies

Over the past several decades, interest has grown in the problems that confront stepfamilies and in how best to systematically study them. Andrew Cherlin (1978) published an article in the *American Journal of Sociology* that first described remarriage as an *incomplete institution* because social guidelines were lacking as to how participants should conduct themselves, particularly when children were involved. Fifteen years later, Kay Pasley and Marilyn Ihinger-Tallman (1994: xi) observed that high rates of divorce and remarriage "ensure that a large proportion of American adults and children have experienced or will experience stepfamily living at some point during their lives," and some common patterns are beginning to emerge from continuing research on this topic. One pattern, unfortunately, is now well known—the higher rate of breakup of second marriages than first marriages (Booth and Edwards 1992).

Early efforts to identify problem areas facing remarried couples suggested the following for further research (Furstenburg 1979):

- Consequences of previous marital experience on likelihood and quality of remarriage
- Changes in conjugal role from first to second marriage
- Impact of former spouse relationship and noncustodial child care arrangements
- Child rearing in the remarried household
- Extended kin alignments

Another area of interest has been the implications for children of being raised in stepfamily settings (Ganong and Coleman 1984). Outcomes considered are variables such as: self-esteem; academic success and achievement; overall well-being; behavior problems, including drug use and sexual involvement among adolescents; child abuse; and timing of leaving the nest (Pasley and Ihinger-Tallman 1994).

Single-parent and stepfamily structures typically produce stress in that they confront members in all participating families with some inherent difficulties, such as role overload for single parents or the ambiguity of the stepmother and stepfather roles. *Differences across families* help to explain their more or less successful adjustment to these lifestyles. For example, recall that discipline is frequently a problem in stepfamilies. Using data from the National Survey of Families and Households, social researchers Fine, Donnelly, and Voydanoff (1991) reported that children's adjustment was connected with parents' particular styles of discipline. Higher use of rewards, lower use of punishment, consistency, and consensus between parents about child rearing were associated with more positive outcomes.

Children also are expected to make better adjustments in stepfamilies when they are assisted in coping with parental divorce and remarriage. Correspondingly, their relationship with the noncustodial parent, and this parent's attitude about the divorce, may be expected to influence children's outcomes. For example, Bray and Berger (1990) found that continued contact and a good relationship with the noncustodial father facilitated boys' initial (six-month) adjustment to a new stepfamily household.

Note that sex of children and sex of stepparent are recognized as also playing a part in stepfamily dynamics and adjustment. According to Vuchinich and colleagues (1991) and others, families with stepdaughters had more problems than families with stepsons. And research studies continue to report that the stepmother's relationship to stepchildren is more difficult than the stepfather's (Pasley and Ihinger-Tallman 1994).

The manner in which parents handle family conflicts is important. Conflicts between parents are frequently cited as adversely influencing children's outcomes. In stepfamilies this potentially extends to relations involving nonresident biological parents as well as the married adults in the current stepfamily household. One consistent research finding noted by Pasley and Ihinger-Tallman was that marital quality among remarried couples is strongly related to quality of the relationship between stepparent and stepchild. Hobart (1990, 1991) found no significant difference in first married and remarried couples in frequency of marital conflict, but while first married couples had more conflicts over household tasks, remarried couples had more conflicts over children.

Finally, understanding of stepfamilies will be improved by development of more comprehensive, better integrated, and empirically referenced theoretical models of stepfamily dynamics to guide continuing research and counseling practice. Generally, such models should help to clarify the connections between family structure (e.g., intact two-parent, single-parent, or stepfamily) and family functioning.

Counseling Issues

Jeannette Lofas of the Stepfamily Foundation was asked in an interview on *How Divorce Is Changing America* (NBC 1986) what the chances were that a stepfamily would succeed. Her thought-provoking reply was, "With or without counseling?" Lofas added that without counseling, 70 percent will fail. She advised individuals contemplating a stepfamily to plan; "plan the marriage, plan the step relationships . . . and when you are in love, that's the time to plan!" Box 7.8 presents a set of recommendations for improving stepfamily relations that have been made with the unique conflicts and stresses of stepfamilies in mind. Having an optimistic outlook and rejecting myths about stepfamilies are also factors that influence marital and parental satisfaction in these situations (Kurdek 1990). Aside from the quirks of individual participants, a stepfamily's basic structural complexity and ambiguity of roles make it challenging:

- A new partner's ex-spouse becomes the "other" man or woman. Even though a remarried partner is already legally divorced, he or she remains connected to the ex-spouse as a parent of their child. In this way, former spouses actively intrude into the new marriage as coparents or can simply be "present" in the children's mannerisms, appearance, and memories as a reminder of the former spouse.
- Children from a previous marriage link a new marriage partner to an expanded set of relatives. He or she is confronted not only with in-laws but also ex-in-laws who remain a stepchild's grandparents, aunts and uncles, and cousins. What obligations and rights, if any, the new marriage partner's own kin have toward stepchildren is also unclear.
- Stepparents might hope for recognition and respect from the non-custodial parent and other relatives of a stepchild; acknowledgment of what they are contributing in raising the child despite the difficulties they encounter. This may not, in fact, be forthcoming. Likewise, appreciation from a stepchild may be tempered by the child's own ambivalence about the overall situation. Child rearing in such circumstances may seem to be a particularly thankless task.
- Remarried couples with stepchildren often have a sense of divided loyalties. They are vulnerable to feeling guilty about neglecting either the needs of their children or a new spouse in favor of the other. Both spouse and children may wish to come first in one's affections. Stepchildren may be jealous when a stepparent enters the scene or have an allegiance to the absent parent that hinders their new relationship with a stepparent. Remarried couples also can have children residing with ex-spouses whose lives they wish to be a greater part of. In effect, they are raising someone else's child instead of their own.
- Stepparents may not accurately foresee or really be prepared for the extent to which their lives are changed by a ready-made family. Especially if they have never had children but even because stepchildren

can be unexpectedly different from their own, stepchildren can seem very intrusive and difficult. Providing emotionally and materially for stepchildren can be harder than anticipated. Also, remarried couples many times have responsibilities toward children not in their own household; they will be contributing to supporting two families. Correspondingly, strained finances contribute to the breakdown of remarriages.

The news is not all bad. Some general ways to cope with stepfamily issues include minimizing the problems that cannot be resolved, maintaining good communication with your spouse, and understanding your own limitations. With stepchildren, just staying in the picture and taking time in getting to know them is needed, not rejecting them or blaming the children for all the problems. For the married couple, support from one another is crucial. Their success as stepparents depends on their effectiveness in making joint decisions, backing one another up, setting boundaries, negotiating crises, and generally confronting the uncertainties of stepfamily relations.

Box 7.8. Advice for Stepfamilies

Sharon Turnbull and James Turnbull (1986) provided the following guidelines for counselors seeking to assist stepfamilies and facilitate their adjustment to the unique circumstances of this family form. They have used these ideas as a basis for discussion with stepfamily members in individual, family, and group therapy.

Ten Commandments of Stepparenting

1. Provide neutral territory.
2. Do not try to fit a preconceived role.
3. Set reasonable limits and enforce them.
4. Allow an outlet for the children's feelings about the absent parent.
5. Expect ambivalence—it is normal.
6. Avoid confrontations at mealtime.
7. Do not expect instant love.
8. Do not take all the responsibility for the relationship.
9. Be patient.
10. Maintain the primacy of the marital relationship.

Chapter 8

Growing Older and Improving Relationships

GROWING OLDER

Probably the last thing on most students' minds is growing older, but with any luck we will all get there. Developing in advance an understanding of the problems that may be faced, and a positive attitude, will be immensely beneficial in later years. The effects of aging on marital and sexual lifestyles are closely related to individuals' prior attitudes and behaviors. What part sexuality plays in the well-being of the elderly is discussed in the first section. The debut issue of *Sex Over Forty* (a publication described in the second section) makes clear that the effects of aging may also be felt earlier in the life cycle. The next section provides some additional notes on marital lifestyles and aging. A final section in this part of the chapter offers an overview of the challenges and opportunities of later life.

Sex and Aging

The elderly are defined as persons age sixty-five or older. According to the U.S. Census Bureau, the elder proportion of the U.S. population was about 12 percent in the 1990s but is projected to reach 20 percent by 2030 (Thompson 1994); one in five persons in the United States will then be elderly. Counting from 1945, baby boomers will already begin reaching age sixty-five in 2010. Whatever concerns surround aging, including marital and sexual lifestyles in later years, we can expect to hear more about them in the twenty-first century as the United States undergoes a remarkable change in age composition. From 1900 to 1990, life expectancy increased by twenty-five years or more (depending on sex and race). Persons now increasingly live to age eighty-five and older, resulting in new distinctions being made between the younger and older elderly. Both the arbitrary selection of age sixty-five to mark becoming "elder" and recognition of new "categories" of older persons serve as reminders that aging, like gender, involves socially constructed interpretations of human biology.

Isadore Rubin (1968), an early editor of *Sexology*, called attention to one socially constructed image of the elderly, the stereotype of "the sexless older years"; potentially damaging because it acts as a **self-fulfilling prophecy.**

233

Social attitudes shape individual behavior, thereby creating the expected outcomes. If older persons feel guilty or awkward about expressing their sexuality because the culture appears to believe they are sexless, they may suppress their desires and restrict their own behavior accordingly. Rubin (1968) argues that sexual interest, needs, and abilities play an important part throughout our lives—there is no automatic cutoff point, and this applies to single and widowed persons as well as those who are married. If carrying on sexually is seen as a youthful preoccupation, older persons risk feeling uncertain, rejected, or ridiculous about their own passions. Rubin emphasizes that the harm done by denial of sexuality in older persons goes beyond their sex life to their self-image, social relationships, and institutional responses to the elderly.

In a text on marriage and family experience, Bryan Strong, Christine DeVault, and Barbara Sayad (1998: 194) remark that "sexuality is one of the least understood aspects of life in old age." In U.S. society, we associate physical attractiveness and sexuality with the young and discount sex among the elderly. In this social climate, it is not surprising that Kellett (1991) concluded after reviewing relevant research literature that a decline in sexual activity among aging men and women is more a result of culture than biology. Masters, Johnson, and Kolodny (1982; 1992: 263) observed that "while American cultural myths continue to suggest that people over forty are 'over the hill' sexually, the truth is that with reasonably good health and an interested and interesting partner, sexual activity can continue for decades as a pleasurable pastime for both men and women." Yet there are changes in sexual functioning over time. Box 8.1 summarizes some early findings from Masters and Johnson's clinical research.

Other researchers have studied rates of self-reported interest and participation in sex at different ages. **Longitudinal** studies question the same individuals over again after some period of time, while **cross-sectional** studies simply compare people of different ages who are all surveyed at the same time. At Duke University, researchers conducted a longitudinal study of several hundred men and women, ages sixty to ninety-five (Palmore 1981; Walker 1997). Initially, two-thirds of the men were still sexually active; four-fifths expressed interest in sex. Ten years later, men were still as interested, but sexual activity had dropped considerably. The women were less interested and less sexually active to begin with, and stayed about the same after ten years. Data from the same study showed a shift in the frequency of sexual behavior from once a week to once a month for men and a similar trend for women, among those who were sexually active. Nearly 70 percent of the over-sixty-five women did not engage in sex at all. Aiken (1982) proposed that this was due to reduced opportunity, which largely reflects changing marital status. There are more unattached elderly women than men, so fewer men are available to marry, and a widow's remarriage may

---

Box 8.1. Age and Sexual Functioning

William Masters and Virginia Johnson's research (1966), reported in *Human Sexual Response* included sixty-one women ages forty to seventy-eight and thirty-nine men ages fifty-one to eighty-nine whose physiological responses during sex acts were monitored.

Concerning women, they found:

- Older women need more time to become sexually aroused, but lubrication can generally be produced in one to three minutes.
- The vagina becomes smaller and the vaginal walls lose thickness, which can cause discomfort during intercourse.
- Orgasms develop in a way identical to younger women, but are somewhat less intense and shorter in duration (four to six versus eight to twelve contractions).

Concerning men, they found:

- The older the man, the longer it took for penile erection.
- Penile erection may be maintained for "extended periods of time," as the urge to ejaculate is not present on every occasion (every two to three times).
- Orgasmic contractions are fewer and less intense; fluid expelled is less in volume and pressure.
- Erection is lost more rapidly after climax and once lost will not return for hours.
- Some secondary impotence.

---

jeopardize financial benefits or provoke resistance from relatives. Older women are more inhibited about sex outside of marriage; they may also be embarrassed about their adult children's reactions and share stereotypes about the sexless elderly. Also, women for whom sex had been an unwelcome obligation in marriage can use age as an excuse not to pursue it. In a more recent longitudinal study, Hallstrom and Samuelsson (1990) interviewed nearly 700 middle-aged women who were interviewed a second time six years later. Just over one-fourth of the women studied experienced a decline in sexual desire, about two-thirds experienced no change, and 10 percent experienced an increase. The increase was attributed to improvements in troubled marriages and accompanying mental health gains.

Sexual history and attitude make a difference. Kinsey, Pomeroy, and Martin (1948) had already noted that individual males who were sexually active in adolescence remained sexually active into their fifties. One basic principle, affirmed by Masters, Johnson, and Kolodny (1992) and others, is: use it or lose it. The best way of maintaining sexual functioning is continued sexual activity, including manual and oral stimulation by a partner as well as masturbation. As Rubin's (1968: 89) article also suggested, the premature cessation of sex leads to aging as much as aging leads to less sex. Senior citizens comment: "If your vision is fading, you don't see his wrinkles"; "His stroke left his speech impaired (aphasia), so he lets his hands do the talking." One eighty-four-year-old grandmother said she and her boyfriend do lots of kissing and hugging when they are fishing or playing shuffleboard. They don't worry about the end result; they just enjoy themselves along the way. This gets the point across that sex is more than just intercourse. Noncoital physical intimacy is important in validating participants' feelings of being attractive, needed, and loved and in maintaining overall well-being.

Sex Over Forty

In June 1982, the premier issue of *Sex Over Forty* appeared, a "practical, authoritative newsletter directed to the sexual concerns of mature adults." Edited by medical and social work professionals and hailed as the first of its kind, the newsletter discussed physiological changes in sexual functioning in clear, direct language. Articles covered topics such as how a man can satisfy his partner when he cannot get an erection, use of lubricants, the special role of oral sex after forty, comfortable sexual positions, sex in the morning, overcoming a female partner's inhibitions, how to actively fondle and caress your partner, maintaining your sexual abilities, and a surgical procedure to have erections at any age. Concerns addressed for men, for example, included that men become slower to obtain spontaneous erections and require more direct physical stimulation as they get older. This calls for corresponding changes in sexual interaction with partners. Other changes described included erections not being as hard as when a man is younger, erections maintained longer without a climax, less frequent need for ejaculation, diminishing force of ejaculation, erection fading more quickly after climax, and needing more time before getting another erection (longer "refractory period").

One noteworthy feature of the promotional materials for the newsletter was a section on how the publisher would protect the privacy of subscribers:

> Sex is a private matter, so no further mail sent to you will have the words SEX OVER FORTY on the envelope. Instead it will have the symbol S/40 which will tell you (and no one else) that you are getting a new issue. Credit card charges will be registered to S/40 (*not* SEX OVER FORTY) and checks can also be made out to S/40.

Thinking about this sociologically, what inferences might you draw about why such precautions were taken? Why would subscribers not want to receive *Sex Over Forty* mailings? In class discussions, students readily ascribed such reluctance to the combined effects of not wanting anyone to know you are over forty, interested in sex, or need help—a reflection of the general cultural ambivalence in the United States about aging, sexuality, and therapy.

Yet embarrassment and ignorance about sexuality, and especially sex and aging, too often detracts from intimacy in relationships. *Sex Over Forty* discussed social and psychological consequences. Physiological changes in both men and women after forty can cause fear and self-consciousness during sex. Unless both people are sensitive to what is going on, their relationship may suffer. The following cases were presented, with the comment that many people like Bill and Martha run into the same kinds of problems—and rather than facing them go through years embittered by lack of intimacy (*Sex Over Forty* 1982):

> Bill M., 45, notices he no longer gets erections as easily as he used to. He develops fears about his aging and his continuing ability as a sex partner. In time, he has trouble attaining any erections because of his anxiety.

> At 52, Martha S. begins to lubricate less quickly. The walls of her vagina lose some of the stretch that allowed her to accept a penis comfortably. Afraid that her partner will notice her physical changes and find her less attractive, Martha begins to avoid sex.

It is not always just intercourse that is avoided. Reconsider in this new context the many indirect ways we initiate sexual relations that caused misunderstandings in dating relationships. Couples who have been together long term come to identify certain gestures as a prelude to sex. Compliments, a back rub, a special meal, or a hug and kiss, when interpreted as signals that the partner is "in the mood," now become fraught with anxiety. To avoid confrontations over intercourse, distressed individuals begin distancing themselves from their partners long before they get to the bedroom. In this way, inability to address sexual problems reverberates in other aspects of the relationship.

Sex is more stressful if men start trying to force themselves to a full erection or to climax because they feel they have to, but it does not work. Wives wonder what they are doing wrong and why they are no longer attractive. When they were younger he was aroused just to see her naked; maybe it's her. He remembers that she never used to have problems getting lubricated; maybe he no longer turns her on. If they misunderstand naturally occurring shifts in physiological reactions, they may give up on sex. Instead, they can think of these changes as encouragement to experiment with different ways of stimulating a partner, and their relationships can even improve.

Sex and aging offers lessons about gender and sexuality in earlier years as well. Men's greater focus on intercourse, on performance, and on "more is better" are not well adapted for growing older. Women's sexual inhibi-

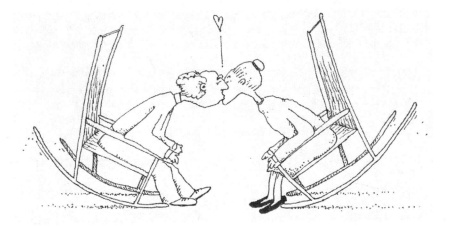

Illustration by Tom Urquhart.

tions, passivity, and indirect communication also make adjustment to aging
more difficult. Men would be well served to fully appreciate sooner in life
that sex is about more than physical release and to shift attention away from
genitals to the overall sensory and emotional experience. Women, for their
part, could take a page from men's sexual script in being more assertive and
adventurous. Over recent decades, there has been wider approval for women's
more active sexual participation (in a greater variety of activities, positions,
places, times of day, and so on). Less investment in gender stereotyping
gives individuals a broader range of options to draw on as they confront predictable changes over the life course.

Effects of Aging on Marital Lifestyles

Divorce is not the only means of losing a mate. Historically, until the
1960s more marriages were ended by death than by divorce (Cargan 1985:
294). Since then, the rapid rise in the divorce rate has drawn attention away
from the continuing significance of death as a cause of marital dissolution.
Being widowed in later life reduces the likelihood of remarriage, particularly for women. There are almost 150 older women for every 100 men, and
many of these men are already married (Stein 1981). Thompson (1994: 10)
noted that nearly 75 percent of men over sixty-five are married and living
with the spouse as compared to fewer than 40 percent of older women; in
1992, about one-third of all women sixty-five to seventy-four and half of
those seventy-five and older lived alone, versus only 13 percent and 22 percent of men. Since an elderly person's sexual activity is most strongly influ-

enced by health and the availability of a partner, older widowed women confront more difficulty in meeting intimacy needs. To try to convey the sense of longing for intimacy among many of the elderly, Jane Porcino (1985) quoted from a poem, "Minnie Remembers," by Donna Swanson: "How long has it been since someone touched me? Twenty years? Twenty years I've been a widow, respected, smiled at, but never touched." As years pass, never being "held close" can leave individuals with a profound sense of loneliness.

As one solution, Porcino recommended strengthening and nurturing friendships among women; to share trust and confidences, express feelings, hug, and touch in a loving way whether or not greater sexual intimacy is involved. Collective living is also a possibility; small groups of women "can join together to share living space, incomes, experiences, companionship, thoughts and tasks in a supportive environment. Women are successfully doing this throughout the country" (Porcino 1985: 152), though most of us have probably not thought much in advance about how to make such arrangements into a satisfying lifestyle. (The weekly television show *Golden Girls* was a positive model of this type of arrangement.) A **family of affinity,** a voluntary living arrangement that functions as a family, that includes both sexes might also serve similar purposes, in a less conventional way. Participants could share housework, thus lightening the burden, tend one another in illness, cook more adequate meals and have mealtimes regain social atmosphere, pool finances, take more interest in personal grooming, meet sexual desires, and feel less lonely or depressed.

Widows face grieving over the loss of a life partner, adjusting their relationships with other family members, acquiring new skills for independent living, dealing with their own health issues, negotiating a new social identity, making new financial and other practical arrangements, coping with loneliness, and going on with their lives (Walsh 1999). Women are not the only ones to experience the loss of a spouse. A *Newsweek* article, reprinted by Pocs and Walsh (1985) reported that

> "men show less tolerance for widowhood. More dependent on a nurturing wife and less willing to do without sex, they are apt to begin dating and remarry sooner—but in continued widowhood they also die sooner. A Johns Hopkins University study of more than 4,000 widowed persons showed the mortality rate for widowers was 26 percent higher than for married men, and 61 percent higher in the 55 to 64 year age group." (p. 154)

Men are more reluctant to grieve openly and to seek counseling or social support. "When a man is widowed," a sixty-one-year-old retired Navy pilot explained in the article, "9 times out of 10 his men friends give him a strong handshake and a steely look in the eye and say hang in there. And women friends hesitate to give close emotional support because of the sexual hang-up. So, a man goes without the hugs" (Pocs and Walsh 1985: 155).

Cohabiting Couples and the Never Married in Later Life

Sociologist Albert Chevan examined cohabitation among older persons. Although still a small proportion, the 2.4 percent of unmarried persons age sixty and older who were cohabiting in 1990 is expected to rise in coming decades as cohorts more experienced with and more favorable in attitude toward cohabitation grow older (Chevan 1996: 656). Cohabitation among the elderly already tripled in one decade from 1980 to 1990. Among those who are dating and over age fifty-five, cohabitation is favored as much as marriage (Bulcroft and Bulcroft 1991). Reasons behind such shifts are as yet unclear, but Chevan speculates that some motivations among older persons may differ from those of many younger persons, since cohabitation among the elderly is less likely to be a phase before marriage. Economic motivations to cohabit rather than live alone have been suggested. For older couples there is also less legal and social pressure to marry for purposes of child rearing. Research on predisposing individual characteristics and on the social context of later life will help clarify who chooses cohabitation as a lifestyle, with what benefits and strains.

Never-married singles present another lifestyle that is growing in numbers. How does aging affect them? Research provides as yet an incomplete picture, but diversity among the never married is recognized. Older never marrieds include men from impoverished backgrounds with low educational and occupational attainment (making family responsibilities difficult to undertake), career-oriented women of high education and occupational attainment who never quite found the time or the right partner, and gay or lesbian men and women of varied social class statuses.

Never-married singles generally are already experienced in living alone, being independent, and coping effectively. Gubrium (1975) found that the never marrieds in his study were not especially lonely in old age. They were more like the married elderly than like divorced or widowed aged persons, having avoided the trauma of bereavement and maintaining a more positive outlook. However, as noted by Braito and Anderson (1980), plans the never-married make for aging and retirement will not include options such as moving in with their children. Retirement may hit singles harder if they have focused more exclusively on their work roles than on family roles. The extent to which the friendship patterns of older singles differ, if at all, for never marrieds as compared to other singles is not known. More data on living arrangements among the never-married elderly would also be helpful to begin to develop social policy recommendations as the proportion of elderly in the U.S. population increases and a greater number of individuals remain never married.

Challenges and Opportunities

Recent work on the family life cycle brings new perspectives on individuals and families in later life (Carter and McGoldrick 1999). Countering the bleak picture of illness, neglect, and poor quality of life often associated with aging, Walsh (1999) points out that families remain important in later life, providing assistance in caregiving, emotional support, and social interaction. For those who are still married, the spouse provides companionship, connection, and satisfaction, as can contact with children and grandchildren. Siblings often become more important in adulthood (Cicirelli 1995). Friendship networks, church groups, and voluntary associations also contribute to the well-being of elders. Only 5 percent of the elderly live in institutions such as nursing homes. Most older Americans prefer to live in separate households while maintaining regular contact with family members. Research has found that frequent contact with others, mutual support, and reciprocal emotional ties increase longevity and the quality of life (Litwin 1996).

The life course perspective regards the negatives of aging as "challenges" and emphasizes possibilities for continued growth and meaning. Retirement, becoming a grandparent, physiological changes, illness, death of loved ones, living on after losses, and confronting one's own mortality are significant life transitions. Altered social roles and relationship alignments can be beneficial as well as problematic. Failing health does require increased support from caregivers, creating routine strains and sudden crises for them as well as for the elderly. The majority of primary caregivers (three-fourths) presently are women, who take this task on in addition to their other responsibilities.

"Studies of normal adult development and family functioning indicate that a variety of adaptive processes contribute to successful later life adjustment," but one feature is whether or not individuals develop "a sense of purpose and structure for making life choices and decisions" (Walsh 1999: 319). As Walsh describes the "opportunities" of growing older, later life opens possibilities for integration and reconciliation. Qualities such as humor, compassion, continued growth, and commitment contribute to resiliency in the face of obstacles. Aging can be defined in terms of personal and spiritual evolution: forgiving past imperfections, continuing to learn and to seek meaning in life, forging a coherent sense of self and self-worth, and staying connected with a social network of significant others.

IMPROVING RELATIONSHIPS

The rest of this chapter addresses how we can improve relationship, at any age, looking first at the basic nature of couples counseling and what motivates people to seek therapy, or inhibits them. Then, three theoretical approaches for understanding relationships, the psychodynamic, behavioral, and cognitive, and their practical application in therapeutic interventions are described. Myths about relationships and examples of what researchers have learned from studying couples in long-lasting happy marriages are also considered. Lastly, some of the unique issues in sex therapy are discussed.

Marital or Couples Counseling

Marital or family counseling/therapy is the systematic application of techniques intended to modify maladapted relationships. It is directed at the couple, not just one partner or the other. Outcomes of counseling depend on the goals and motivations of clients. **Conjoint** marital or couples counseling means that both partners participate together. Most principles of marriage counseling also apply to couples who are cohabiting or even dating long term. The single most important factor may be *reciprocal commitment;* both partners genuinely want to continue the relationship. No matter how much one person is still committed, a relationship takes two. If the relationship is over for either partner, it is over. However, counseling can be successful even if a couple does not stay together. It can also assist couples in ending a relationship constructively.

Do not overlook **premarital counseling.** Although many persons seem to feel that getting divorced is too easy today, maybe, instead, getting married is too easy. After all, the single biggest cause of divorce is marriage. Lack of communication *before* marriage is a factor contributing to divorce. Consider writing up a marriage contract with a prospective spouse. Discuss careers, number and timing of children, money, religion, recreation, division of labor, in-laws, holidays, sex, and mutual grounds for divorce. Regardless of the particular topics covered, such an exercise gives couples an opportunity to examine their values, expectations, styles of communication, and how they handle conflicts. Existing inventories of questions such as Olson's (1991) PREPARE serve to facilitate premarital counseling. Feedback sessions with a counselor help motivate couples to enrich their relationship by exploring both strengths and areas for possible improvement (Olson and Hawley 1992). A review of questionnaires used in premarital education and counseling indicated that PREPARE has good reliability and validity—"predicting with 80-90% accuracy which couples were separated or divorced from those who were happily married" (Larson et al. 1995).

Directional counseling is helpful when couples feel something is wrong but cannot see what their underlying problems are or do not yet know exactly what they might want from therapy. Directional counseling involves clarifying issues and setting goals, and can be a short-term way of seeking some outside guidance. One underlying relationship problem that couples often do not recognize or do not know how to deal with constructively is **power struggles.** A client's presenting complaint might be "we don't communicate," but what the person means is "my partner won't do what I want him/her to!" Or, a counselor asks, "What do you want to change?," and the client replies "my husband/wife." Each person in a relationship might expect the counselor to fix what's wrong with the *other* person, but essentially what is wrong concerns who is or is not getting their own way. Another general issue in relationships is **unfinished emotional business;** unmet needs left over from the past. Unfinished emotional business often appears in couples counseling as blocks that undermine behavioral therapy. If two people who supposedly love each other and want to live together cannot negotiate, compromise, and make desired changes, there may be hidden feelings— e.g., fear, anger, hurt, loneliness—that need to be confronted.

Marriage and family counseling also addresses preconceived ideas that come from our original families **(family of origin).** Initially we learn to be husbands and wives, mothers and fathers, by watching our parents. Our task in growing up is to become our own selves, not necessarily like our parents, but a great deal of our early programming stays with us. Much more than we are typically aware, early socialization generates our basic assumptions about the "right" answers to many questions of everyday living: Are dishes meant to be towel or air dried? Who takes out the trash? Are crossword puzzles properly done in pencil or in ink? Should toilet paper roll over the top or under? In relationships, are arguments best settled emotionally or calmly? Is it important to touch a lot? To eat at least one meal a day together? Is love best expressed by words or deeds? And so on. Individuals bring to relationships their own unique cultural heritage, family values, and lifelong attitudes which influence how they think, feel, and act toward each other. An implication of family of origin theory is that one person's assumptions about how people should properly conduct themselves in a marriage may not be shared by the partner, whose background is likely to be different in some important respects. Successful couples are able to understand and work out differences in family background, past experience, and personal styles. How well prepared to do this are people entering relationships that they hope will last for the long term?

Consider your own marriageability. **Marriageability** refers to the social and personal qualities predictive of marital success. Examples include age at first marriage, emotional maturity, empathy (perceiving other persons accurately and being genuinely concerned for their well-being), adaptability, problem-solving skills, and the happiness of one's parents' marriage. Notice that this listing of qualities includes different types of variables. With respect to family background and personality dynamics, Lawrence Maltin, MD, a psychiatrist, and Joan Atwood, director of a marital and family clinic, state that "the degree of nurturance and acceptance, appreciation and sense of emotional security which individuals experience in childhood largely contribute to how they respond to their partners over time and the level of intimacy they will allow" (Maltin and Atwood 1992: 117). Their description of individual qualities contributing to relationship success as aspects of "maturity" included flexibility, sensitivity, a basically positive self-image, confidence, self-reliance, ability to give without feeling depleted, a balance of reasoning and emotion, and ability to accommodate changes in a partner without feeling rejected or diminished. They note too that more secure individuals recognize their own limitations and reach out to others for help when needed.

Individual personality dynamics thus constitute one type of variable predicting relationship outcomes. Another is *interactional processes* that evolve within a couple or family unit. These are factors such as communication styles, role compatibility, and decision-making and conflict management patterns. There are *social and cultural variables* that also make a difference. Social homogamy, for example, is not only a feature of mate selection but also predictive of marital outcomes, as when similarity of religion, age, education, and lifestyle preferences contributes to shared values and similar expectations for marriage. *External resources* is a contextual factor that should be considered as well. Support or lack of support experienced by a particular couple from friends, family, and community influences marital stability. Structural facilitators or stressors such as employment opportunities, health benefits, or availability of day care alter the context within which couples try to function.

Family life educators and professors of family science at Brigham Young University Jeffry Larson and Thomas B. Holman (1994) concluded that predictors of marital satisfaction and stability could be organized into three major categories: *background and contextual factors,* including family of origin dynamics and sociocultural factors; *individual traits and behaviors,* including self-esteem, interpersonal skills, and conventionality; and *couple interactional processes.* Research on satisfaction in marriage has encompassed individual, interpersonal, and contextual level variables, which are interrelated in complex ways (Mackey and O'Brien 1995).

So, clearly, contributing factors are many and challenging. Mate selection is an imperfect process, and we are not always well prepared to undertake relationships successfully. Moreover, some things we learn only as we go, by trial and error. Relationships themselves provide a setting for growth and development by confronting and overcoming obstacles. When couples run into difficulties along the way, they have the option of turning to outside resources for help.

Seeking Counseling

What prevents people from seeking outside help? In class discussions, students suggested a variety of reasons: It is inconvenient, time consuming, and expensive; it is unfamiliar; you have heard of or have had bad experiences with a counselor before; denial ("no problem here"); self-reliance ("I can deal with it"—but you don't); accountability ("I might find out the problems are my fault, and I'd rather not"); stuck in the anger; it is hard to trust someone else with your problems; don't know what's wrong; think counseling is only for people with "really" bad problems, or don't believe yours can be fixed.

Bringle and Byers (1997) discussed intentions to seek marriage counseling in an article in the journal *Family Relations*. In reviewing earlier work, they noted that the majority of divorcing couples do not consult a professional prior to the divorce. In class discussions, students say they would seek professional counseling if their marriage was in trouble, but most of the evidence points against this. Resources such as counseling services are widely available, yet couples fail to take advantage of them (Bowen and Richman 1991). A main reason given is because "it was too late." To seek marital counseling, people have to realize they need help and decide to get it. Interestingly, about 45 percent of students surveyed in my own family classes say that problems should be kept between the couple and not discussed with friends or family. Additionally, women are frequently more willing to seek health care, including counseling, than men. Women in Campbell and Johnson's (1991) study of couples seeking therapy had higher expectations for therapy; the men they studied were more inclined to minimize the seriousness of many problems and to be ambivalent about (not necessarily opposed to) counseling.

Normative influences are seen in individual help-seeking behavior. Bringle and Byers (1997) found that intentions to seek marriage counseling were influenced by **subjective norms,** what persons believed "significant others would expect them to do" (p. 302). Social support or, conversely, social stigma for help seeking is a factor contributing to individual intentions and actual conduct. The perceived attitudes of others do not have to be accurate to influence our behavior. Another issue raised by Bringle and Byers was the question, from a consumer perspective, of what *types* of problems "would propel couples or individuals to consider marriage counseling." The respondents in their survey of 222 married volunteers recruited from an introductory-level college course at an urban commuter campus in Indiana identified only two marital problems that were described by both males and females as making marriage counseling "significantly likely." These were abuse and thinking about divorce. Women, but not men, believed counseling was warranted for problems related to depression, communication, conflict, stress, and extramarital affairs. Men and women agreed, however, on many problems that they viewed as *not* warranting counseling, such as housework, in-laws, having children, and money. Other problems that they were ambivalent about or disinclined to seek counseling for included jealousy, sex, and child rearing (Bringle and Byers 1997). This was not a random sample and the findings are not generalizable, but the reluctance to seek counseling that was in evidence is thought provoking. People may not be seeking outside help for most of the types of everyday stresses and resentments that actually contribute to relationship failure. The privatization of family life and an individualistic, self-reliant culture help to explain why couples get too little help, too late.

THEORETICAL PERSPECTIVES IN COUNSELING

Marital therapy reflects a variety of theoretical orientations that guide interventions by counseling professionals. Three of the approaches outlined by Sharon Brehm in *Intimate Relationships* are the psychodynamic, behavioral, and cognitive (Brehm 1985: 371-380).

Psychodynamic

Psychodynamic theories propose that how we select and interact with a partner reflects *unconscious motivations* and conflicts that originate with childhood experiences in our families of origin, our own parents and siblings. In therapy, individuals try to gain insight into their unconscious motivations with the idea that greater awareness and understanding of why they feel and act as they do frees them to feel and act differently. For example, a couple's conflict over household tasks may reflect issues of masculine identity underlying a husband's refusal to participate (based on what he saw growing up), or the intensity of a recurring argument about one partner opening the other's mail can be a result of childhood experiences (feeling like a child again with parents snooping in all your things versus feeling left out as when older siblings were sharing secrets but keeping them from you). When rational negotiation fails, understanding the unconscious sources of threat may help. Partners can then better understand intensity of reactions and be more open to alternative ways to meet their own and others' basic needs.

Psychodynamic theories call attention to how transference and defense mechanisms can interfere with intimate relationships. **Transference** is a largely unconscious process in which images or interpretations from past experience come to bear on present relationships. For example, if a young child's parents die, he or she may later enter many relationships to try to fill that emptiness or may simply avoid relationships because the risk of abandonment associated with closeness seems too great. In both these reactions, early feelings are transferred to later interactions so that current behavior is highly influenced by childhood fears or wishes, often to a degree we are not aware of. The closeness we missed and desire may nevertheless feel threatening and evoke anxiety, fear, and even panic, so we find ways to protect ourselves. **Defense mechanisms** are ways we shield ourselves from unwanted or painful aspects of our thoughts, feelings, and experience. We can disguise unconscious feelings by intellectualizing, projecting, displacing, or repressing them. See Box 8.2 for an example of how defense mechanisms, which originally developed to protect ourselves from anticipated harm, unpleasantness, or rejection, may come to be maladaptive and cause problems in relationships. Psychodynamic theorists examine the particulars of how individuals unconsciously contribute to undesirable outcomes and try to intervene in these cycles. Patience, acceptance, and noncritical evaluation of interactional patterns originating in early coping strategies, validating that they reflect reasonable early reactions and strategies, is part of a therapeutic intervention that brings greater compassion, lowered defenses, and "healing" to couples.

Behavioral

The behavioral approach views poor relationships as involving a "low level of reinforcing exchanges between the partners. Because they do not reinforce positive behavior toward each other, the partners either withdraw from the marital interaction or attempt to control each others' behavior in coercive, punishing ways" (Brehm 1985: 375). In behavioral therapy, participants systematically observe and record their interactions, and target particular behaviors for change. Box 8.3 provides an example of what such a record might reveal. Verbalizations as well as actions are treated as behav-

---

Box 8.2. Dysfunctional Defenses

In an article on the "tasks and traps" of relationships that appeared in the *Journal of Couples Therapy,* Lawrence Maltin and Joan D. Atwood (1992) provided an example of the effects maladaptive defense mechanisms can have on relationships. *Withdrawal* is the defense mechanism featured in this case.

A boy whose mother is chronically unhappy feels he is somehow at fault but is helpless to change what is wrong. In a later relationship, his partner's sadness triggers those feelings of unworthiness. He withdraws from her to protect himself. As a result, he fails to provide empathy and support, and she feels more sad and unhappy, but the more she calls attention to her unhappiness, the more he pulls away. Neither really understands why: "Why can't he just listen?" "Why do I keep doing this?"

Professional counselors who understand how such processes operate can untangle puzzling recurring behaviors and conflicts in relationships, redirecting attention and energies so clients can repair earlier hurts in more positive, productive ways.

iors. The effects of such communication are then open to scrutiny; problem solving can be facilitated by avoiding unproductive behavior. Behavioral counselors often suggest clients work out written contracts to perform certain behaviors so the couple remains focused on their objectives and observant of changes.

Research studies in social psychology also support the idea that successful couples "have learned a different form of interaction than dissatisfied couples. Satisfied partners tend to reciprocate each other's rewarding behavior, but they tend not to react in kind when a partner acts in an unrewarding fashion. In contrast, unhappy partners react unpredictably when one of them acts positively but tend to reciprocate negative action" (Wiggins, Wiggins, and Vander Zanden 1994: 365). Box 8.3 illustrates both positive

---

Box 8.3. Behavior Modification Exercise

The two charts below illustrate a husband and wife's observations about the partner's desirable and undesirable behaviors, and their own reactions.

Chart 1 — *Husband's Observations* — Date: _____

Wife's Desirable Behavior	Wife's Undesirable Behavior	Your Response to Her Behavior
	Nagged me about mowing lawn, picking up bathroom, etc.	"Shut up."
	Refused intercourse.	"I can get it elsewhere."
	Threw away my favorite shirt.	Emptied her top drawer on floor.
Served a great meal.		Suggested we go to a show.
Was ready to leave on time.		"I can't believe you're ready."

Chart 2 — *Wife's Observations* — Date: _____

Husband's Desirable Behavior	Husband's Undesirable Behavior	Your Response to His Behavior
	Did not turn off lights before coming to bed.	"How many nights is that now?"
Said he enjoyed dinner.		"It's about time you liked something."
	Said he hated my cat.	Slammed door.
Called to say he would be late.		"Thank you for calling. See you later then."
Told me I am a good wife.		Smiled and hugged him.

and negative behavioral responses, the probable long-term effects of which are not difficult to imagine.

Cognitive Theories

Cognitive theories refer to our beliefs, what we "know" or think we know, whether factually accurate or not. Brehm suggested two basic cognitive processes that are useful to consider in marital therapy: unrealistic expectations and causal attributions. Failure of experience to match expectations generates emotional reactions of disappointment, sadness or anger, rage, and despair. In therapy, hidden beliefs are raised and challenged; more realistic expectations are encouraged.

Causal attributions are our everyday understandings of why people do what they do. We assign responsibility for actions to internal or external and fixed or variable causes. In distressed marriages, participants frequently assign behavior to unchangeable factors within the person (a fixed, personal disposition: "that's just how he/she is"), offering no possibility of improvement. In therapy, couples are asked to consider other possible explanations, such as variable, situational causes that can be addressed and modified in the relationship. Clients are also encouraged to credit partners for the changes they are making instead of discounting their motives ("you only did that because you were embarrassed, not because you really care about me").

Though some problems are deep-seated, long-standing, and complex enough to require professional intervention, the theories that inform counseling are not entirely arcane knowledge. Earl Ubell (1984), writing for the Sunday *Parade Magazine,* for example, presented examples from cognitive psychology of "twisted logic" that can undermine relationships with other people. Emotionality leads us to mix feelings and beliefs together, as when anxiety convinces us something bad has to happen. Mislabeling involves painting a picture of what we want or fear rather than reality, as when a second date means "this must be love." Consider the listing and descriptions in Box 8.4. All of us are vulnerable to these types of **cognitive distortions** that influence feelings and conduct, often in undesirable ways. These thought patterns can easily undermine relationships. Controversy within a couple over a minor point is magnified in its consequences when thinking runs along the following lines: "You always disagree with me, when you should be supportive. Okay then, either do what I ask or don't bother me at all. I know exactly what you are thinking, and I don't appreciate it. This will be a disaster—the next thing we'll be divorced." The quick fix: Think twice! Be open to other possible interpretations and do not leap to conclusions.

Often we are not only being illogical, we do not realize that we are and resist accepting this. That is another kind of twisted logic: "I can't make mistakes." Ubell (1984) mentions an interesting relevant experiment conducted by Dr. Aaron T. Beck, a professor of psychiatry at the University of

Box 8.4. Twisted Logic Impedes Relationships

Cognitive Distortions	Definition	Comment
1. All or nothing	You see things in terms of extremes; no in-between.	Real people and situations. tend to be complex, not "all good/right" or "all bad/wrong."
2. Catastrophizing	Everything is viewed as a catastrophe (combines overgeneralization with negativity).	One gray hair means you are old; one argument signals the end of your relationship.
3. Mind reading	You are sure you know what someone else is thinking, no matter what they say.	You stop really listening.
4. Negativity	Looking at just the negative in a situation.	Child or spouse does most of what you asked, but you focus on one thing he or she did not do.
5. Overgeneralization	Based on one or two instances, you conclude this happens every time.	Partner is late getting ready for an event; you think he or she is *always* late (which increases your annoyance).
6. Rejecting positives	Distrust or discount compliments or friendly overtures.	Puts up barriers, discourages others from closeness.
7. Selfism	It's all about me.	Ubell (1984: 12) notes: "Most occurrences have more than one cause, the least of which is probably you."
8. Shoulds	A kind of perfectionism; shoulds and musts set up standards that seem absolute, not flexible	When self or other is unable to meet the shoulds, you react with great disappointment or disapproval.

Source: Based on Ubell 1984.

Pennsylvania. Beck videotaped confrontations between couples and later asked them to write down any good things the other person had said. They were unable to because they did not remember any. Yet the video replay demonstrated that the partner's comments had not been entirely negative. Such is the power of twisted logic that it alters our perceptions and recollections of events. This example also indicates how an outsider's perspective may prompt reevaluation and change.

Many principles that can improve relationships are readily available, but we need to actively apply them to our own lives. Instead we often sabotage our own relationships by clinging to our misplaced motives, "bad" behavior, or faulty beliefs. The commonsense question is, "How well are these strategies working for us?" If they are not, we need to change.

MYTHS ABOUT RELATIONSHIPS

Chuck Hillig, a licensed marriage counselor, has noticed in his professional dealings with people having problems in their relationships that many couples entering therapy believe in the same three common myths (Hillig 1985):

- Other people can *make* you feel some emotion.
- You should always know and be able to explain why you have certain feelings.
- Your partner should know what you want without having to be told.

These myths can damage relationships. For example, when we attribute the source of our feelings to someone else ("you make me so happy/angry") we lose a sense of control over what we feel and a sense of choice about how we react to events. And we often use this an excuse for our own misbehavior. We give away responsibility for our feelings and blame others. "If you hadn't made me so angry, I would not [fill in]; so it's your fault, not mine." Trying to make someone else happy is also a very popular and, maybe surprisingly, misguided notion. It suggests we are directly responsible for another person's emotional responses and to blame whenever they are not happy. A partner can become dependent, passive, and resentful waiting for you to fulfill this obligation. We do what we think would make someone else happy (often based on movies, television, or our own past experience) and get annoyed if it does not work since we have put in a lot of effort. Instead of spending our lives in misery or feeling justified in punishing someone else for disappointing us, perhaps a more reasonable objective in relationships is to contribute positively to the conditions under which another person can make his or her own happiness and to take responsibility for our own feelings.

Hillig also points out that the problem with the second myth arises when people find, as they often do, that they do not understand and cannot justify their feelings, so instead they keep them inside and try to deny them. If the emotion is still with them, however, it may find expression in indirect ways. Hillig uses the example of a man who begins to feel jealous over his mate's financial success. He has an excellent job but at some "deeper level" feels threatened. Rationally, this seems foolish to him, so he tries to repress the feeling, but the "jealous energy" leaks out in withdrawing from the partner or picking quarrels over small issues. Better to simply acknowledge and allow ourselves to experience (not necessarily act on) the emotions of the moment, no matter how outrageous or unreasonable. Our feelings are what they are; they do not necessarily have to be justified, understood, defended, or explained (Hillig 1985: 183). A related idea is to look behind puzzling behaviors for what "unreasonable" (or unconscious) feelings they are actually expressing.

Finally, much mischief arises from the belief that a partner should know what the other wants or needs without being told, "if you really loved me or cared about me." The danger is in automatically concluding that if the partner does not give you what you want, he or she does not love you or care about you. Accordingly, when "rejection mechanisms get triggered inside us," they open the door to growing resentments and hostility. In class discussions, students commented that telling the other person what you want "spoils" it, especially for women. One example given was having to remind your husband repeatedly of your anniversary or birthday, or he ignores it. In this case, the spouse is failing to respond to the wife's expressed need for recognition and acknowledgment. Hillig is talking about something else, a desire to have our wishes magically fulfilled that may be unconscious, going back to infancy. As an adult, expecting our partners to anticipate and fulfill needs the way parents seemed to in early childhood is unreasonable, and sets us up for feeling betrayed and disappointed. When we dismiss our responsibility to explicitly communicate our needs to others, we "unfairly place on them the impossible burden of reading our minds. When they fail to pick up on our signals or if they misinterpret our wants, it becomes easy for us to justify feeling hurt and angry" (Hillig 1985: 184).

Why do we persist in believing myths? Sometimes we just do not know better. We have been socialized to believe them and still see such myths extolled in popular culture (which we selectively tune in to). Many relationship myths also seem more convenient and appealing than simply being accountable for ourselves.

Communication and Conflict

Another difficulty in relationships is that individuals can be sincerely expressing their positive regard for a partner but in ways that do not have the same meaning for the other person as for themselves. Sarah Matthews, a sociology professor and contributor to a book in a series on men and masculinities, presented the following example of differences between men and women in how they express love. In an earlier study, a husband was told by the researchers to increase his affectionate behavior toward his wife. Accordingly, he decided to wash her car. He was surprised and perplexed when neither his wife nor the researchers regarded that as an affectionate act. Matthews found that older men's positive feelings toward kin were often expressed by taking over some task or responsibility. They showed love by doing, not saying, by sharing their time and expertise. She notes that sharing expertise would not typically be an element of how social scientists define closeness, and few women would choose this as a way of describing their affectionate feelings (see Matthews 1994: 180). Still, the husband in this example was not wrong, he was misunderstood. The difficulties inherent in trying to make someone happy by doing what you *think* they want are clear. A popular interpretation of this dilemma is that what we have here is a failure to communicate; but good communication alone is not enough.

Add another myth to Hillig's list: Good communication is all you need. Does it seem reasonable to expect in all instances that if you just tell someone clearly enough what you want, you will get it? Consider that good communication is a necessary but not sufficient factor in good relationships. What can happen when couples discuss things in an open way is that they find they have a fundamental difference of opinion or conflicting needs and desires. Good communication does not ensure that couples will not have conflicts. A **conflict** is a disagreement, being at variance with or in opposition to another person's actions or opinions. I want to vacation in the mountains; you want to go to the beach. I want sex every night; you want sex once a week. I want to invest this year's tax refund in our child's college funds; you want to replace the roof. I want you to do something or stop doing something; you do not want to. And so on. It is obvious that no two people are likely to agree on every one of the countless decisions they will be confronted with in the course of a relationship. All couples have conflicts, so the ability to handle conflicts constructively is an essential element contributing to success in relationships. *Constructive conflicts* move couples forward developmentally, providing "opportunities for personal and marital growth," if spouses are ready and able to change; *destructive conflicts* lead instead to deterioration in the relationship, stimulating defensive behaviors that generate more conflict and estrangement (Mackey and O'Brien 1995: 51). Like effective communication skills, principles of constructive conflict resolution can be learned. Consider the guidelines presented in Box 8.5. When you know what you should be doing but still do not do it, you are sabotaging your relationships. That is when therapeutic interventions can help.

Communication skills themselves are based on putting some basic ideas into practice. Clear communication requires effective expression of intentions and feelings on the part of the sender and a receptive listener. Listening does not mean judging or interrupting to give your own opinions. Listening, in itself, conveys respect and concern for the partner. *Active listening* involves checking with the other person to learn whether your impression of what is being said is accurate, so you are not drawing mistaken conclusions. This also gives the partner a chance to improve transmission if what you heard is not what he or she meant to say. What is being conveyed to another person depends, of course, not only on what is being said but on how it is being presented. Communication in a couple relationship is weakened at both extremes, when the manner of presentation is critical, aggressive, and competitive or when individuals are passive, withdrawn, and secretive. Viewing a partner as genuinely caring increases willingness to risk self-disclosure, while low self-esteem creates anxieties that interfere with communication. In short, being aware of and following principles of effective communication can increase the sense of closeness, participation, and satisfaction in relationships.

Box 8.5. Guidelines for Effective Conflict Resolution

All couples have conflicts. The ability to handle conflicts constructively is an important factor contributing to successful relationships. Make it a win-win situation.

1. *Identify the issue.* Couples often don't know what they are really arguing about. Consider underlying issues and decide what is actually bothering or upsetting you in this instance.

2. *Stick to the point.* The art is to define an issue and not get sidetracked or overwhelmed with a replay of every old grievance; deal with one problem at a time.

3. *Understand the other person.* Competitively, we get vested in the idea that winning is everything. Maybe in football—not in relationships. We are not trying to defeat an opponent; the goal is to understand more about our partner. Ask questions.

4. *Don't hurt the other person.* Restrain the impulse to retaliate when your feelings are hurt. In close relationships we know just what buttons to push, but this is a violation of trust. Getting back at the other person is not the best outcome.

5. *Be willing to compromise.* In a relationship, one person cannot have his or her way in all matters. Give a lot, get a lot. Look for alternative solutions, outside the my-way-versus-your-way box.

SUCCESSFUL RELATIONSHIPS

Keeping in mind that most Americans will marry, what is a "successful" marriage? From the point of view of society, marriages are a key element in the family system and are successful when they enable basic functions of the family as a social institution to be performed. From the point of view of the individual, success is the degree to which the personal goals of participants are met. Self-interest in interpersonal relationships is restrained, however, by norms of reciprocity and by a practical need to ensure that the partner's goals, not just your own, are being met so that the relationship will continue to be attractive to him or her. **Maximum joint profit** (MJP) is one way to express the principle involved. In the social exchange model of interpersonal relationships, some degree of perceived "profit" (rewards minus costs relative to investments) must be experienced in the long run to motivate participants to remain in a given relationship, especially when there are other partners and alternate lifestyles available.

While much media attention is given to the high divorce rate, successful marriages are typically not in the news. But imagine the headline: Millions of marriages successful! In fact, there *are* millions of marriages in the United States that work well for the couples involved, who manage to stay together long term. Family researchers and counseling professionals make a distinction, though, between stable marriages and happy marriages. Stability simply refers to whether a relationship continues over time, as in marriages that do not end in divorce. Happy marriages additionally have a high level of mutual satisfaction of participants and quality of relationship. In or outside of marriage, good relationships contribute to individual satisfaction and well-being. But couples who stay together do not always have a good relationship. One or both may resist divorce for religious, social, or financial reasons. They may fear confrontation, change, independence, or loneliness. As discussed in earlier chapters, even though a relationship falls below the *comparison level* of what we think we deserve, it can remain above the *comparison level for alternatives,* as when the alternative of divorce and singlehood is perceived as less attractive than the bad relationship.

Scholarly studies of couples in good relationships are less numerous than research on marital problems and divorce but do offer relationship suggestions based on successful couples who responded to survey questionnaires or in-depth interviews (e.g., Lauer and Lauer 1986; Kaslow and Hammerschmidt 1992; Mackey and O'Brien 1995; Wallerstein and Blakeslee 1995). Lauer and Lauer (1986) pointed out that *reasons given for divorce do not highlight the same qualities as direct investigation of successful marriages.* Counseling professionals, too, try to identify the characteristics of good relationships. For example, a professional conference in 1990 suggested nine "basic dimensions" of healthy families (*Family Therapy News* 1990):

1. *Adaptability* to deal with routine change, stressful events, and crises
2. *Commitment* to the marriage and family
3. *Communication* that is open, clear, and frequent
4. *Encouragement* for individual development and sense of belonging
5. *Appreciation* expressed in words and actions
6. *Religion* or other spiritual orientation
7. *Social connection* provides support from family, friends, and community
8. *Role clarity* so family members have a sense of rights and responsibilities.
9. *Shared time* with mutual involvement in enjoyable time together

Lists of the qualities contributing to marital success are varied. Mackey and O'Brien (1995) noted four relational values that were repeatedly identified in scholarly and popular literature as important for marital stability and happiness: trust, respect, sensitivity, and understanding. Robert and Jeanette Lauer (1986) sampled 351 couples married for fifteen years or more. In long-term, happy marriages, mates viewed each other as a best friend and a person who was liked as well as loved. Good conflict management skills were in evidence in these relationships, even when not listed specifically by participants as a significant factor in their marriage.

Kaslow and Hammerschmidt (1992) studied twenty couples married twenty-five years or longer to identify the "essential ingredients" of these relationships. Some of the factors satisfied couples themselves believed contributed to their success were: love and commitment; mutual respect; trust and honesty; shared interests and values; good communication; give and take of compromise; sensitivity to needs of spouse; closeness and expressed affection; fun, humor, and playfulness. "Having and sharing interest in their children was cited by all couples as important in their lives together but only by *un*successful couples as a reason for the longevity of their marriages. The most satisfied couples stayed together because they wanted to be with each other, and not for the sake of the children" (Kaslow and Hammerschmidt 1992: 29).

Maltin and Atwood (1992: 114) outlined relational development tasks necessary for a couple to remain together in the face of modern social, economic, and personal pressures:

1. Continuing to grow as separate individuals while maintaining interdependence
2. Combining romantic love with long-term nurturing
3. Balancing own needs with partner's needs, without resentment
4. Agreeing on a mutually acceptable division of household labor

5. Adjusting to children, meeting their needs without losing sight of the marriage
6. Managing conflicts while allowing both to express thoughts, feelings, and needs
7. Maintaining sexual interest, with partner as primary sexual and emotional bond

"Research also supports a consensus about the importance of *intimacy* to the vitality of marital relationships, though there is no general agreement about its definition" (Mackey and O'Brien 1995: 75). Features they consider include vulnerability: lowering boundaries, allowing personal disclosure, and exposing a self usually kept from others. Intimacy is both physical and psychological (emotional, intellectual, and social). It involves feelings of warmth, closeness, and safety based on being able to rely on each other for understanding and support. Handling differences through discussion rather than avoidance nurtures psychological intimacy, which is an important resource when coping with tragedy and crisis (Mackey and O'Brien 1995).

Various other characteristics may contribute to successful long-term relationships as well, such as the following:

1. Sharing a meaningful sense of the relationship; it includes you, me, and "us"
2. Respecting the other person's goals, needs, feelings, ideals
3. Cooperation and courtesy
4. Dependability; not making promises you cannot keep
5. Honesty, not to be confused with tactlessness or verbal aggression
6. Enthusiasm; expressing appreciation, happiness, excitement, and positive attitude
7. Operating on the assumption of permanence, with patience through rough spots
8. Not dwelling on past grievances but being in the present and optimistic about future

Mackey and O'Brien's (1995) study of lasting marriages showed that while the frequency of sexual intercourse declined as people got older, the quality of psychological intimacy was enhanced. Good sex does not necessarily mean just a lot of sex. Long-term couples experience a blend of sex and love, a mix of conjugal and romantic love that depends on a particular couple's relationship style. **Conjugal love** is defined as calm, solid, and comforting; **romantic love** as urgent, exciting, self-absorbed, and mysterious. A small number of Wallerstein and Blakeslee's (1995: 22) couples were predominantly the romantic type, which "has as its core a lasting passionate sexual relationship." These couples retain and revisit memories of a sensual, exciting first meeting and courtship, and share a sense of being destined for one another. By contrast, even from the beginning, some lasting couples are drawn to one another not primarily as sexual partners but as companions. In most long-term, live-in relationships, the primary ingredient is conjugal love, with room for recurring affirmation of romantic attachment. Further, in most of the happy and stable long-term marriages studied, a renewal of interest in each other after grown children had left home was reported by participants.

Nick Stinnett (1985) urged greater attention to the qualities of successful families to provide a more balanced view of family problems and strengths. First on his list of qualities, based on a study in Oklahoma, was *appreciation*. Since we like to interact with people who let us feel good about ourselves, a way to improve relationships is to identify and comment favorably on the strengths of one's family and its members. Second, strong families spend *time together*. It does not just happen; they set aside time to have for one another. Third was good *communication*, which is facilitated by time together. Fourth, *commitment*. Given that contemporary life offers an array of activities drawing people in different directions, strong families critically evaluate their activities and deliberately make choices about what is most important with their families in mind. Fifth, *religiosity* in strong families gives them a sense of higher purpose and motivation to maintain family ties. Sixth, they are able to *respond positively* to crises, based on trust in and support from other family members. Stinnett recommended extending investigation of strengths to a variety of family forms, such as single-parent families or ethnic group variations, and concluded that family life succeeds best when it is given high priority, personally and socially.

What do we make of such lists? Satisfaction is subjective; couples have different ideas about what constitutes happiness, with some common elements. Researchers have noted that partners in satisfying relationships do tend to agree with one another about the important characteristics of their own relationship. Box 8.6 outlines Wallerstein and Blakeslee's (1995) version of the tasks involved in building a good marriage. They found a fit between partners in conscious and unconscious needs and wishes across different types of good marriages, which they called romantic, rescue, companionate and traditional. In each type, both individuals and the marriage underwent changes over time as they engaged in the challenges of the tasks listed. This required continued negotiation, compromise, and adjustment. Accordingly, *the same couple can experience several different marriages over time.* Long-term success is not just a matter of initial adjustment. Some qualities of relationship partners are evident from the first; others emerge only as people get to know one another better over time (Mackey and O'Brien 1995). Making a marriage or other long-term relationship is a gradual, ongoing process.

Box 8.6. Nine Tasks for Building a Good Marriage

Judith Wallerstein and Sharon Blakeslee (1995) conducted interviews with fifty couples in long-lasting, happy marriages entered into during the 1950s, 1960s, 1970s, or 1980s. For a couple to be included, both husband and wife had to consider the marriage a happy one. Based on these interviews, psychologists Wallerstein and Blakeslee identified nine tasks contributing to good marriages:

1. Separating from the family of origin
2. Building togetherness and creating autonomy
3. Adjusting to parenthood
4. Coping with crises
5. Making a safe place for conflict
6. Exploring sexual love and intimacy
7. Sharing laughter and avoiding boredom
8. Providing emotional nurturance
9. Preserving a double vision (idealization of youth and realities of aging)

Couples in good marriages were not happy all the time, even admitted there were times they had wanted out, but on balance each person believed *they had a "fit" in what they wanted and expected from the relationship, in what they perceived and valued in the other person, and in their shared sense of themselves as a couple* that enabled them to remain together through their difficulties.

SEX THERAPY

Sexual counseling is difficult for many couples to seek because sex itself is viewed as a particularly embarrassing subject. Since there is not one ideal right way to be sexual, sexual "problems" in a marriage or other couple relationship occur when whatever is or is not happening sexually causes the persons involved to be unhappy, distressed, and concerned. Diagnostic classification of sexual disorders recognizes problems with desire, physiological arousal, orgasmic response, and physical pain associated with intercourse. Professionals offering therapeutic interventions related to sexuality include physicians, psychiatrists, social workers, pastoral counselors, and clinical psychologists. Generally speaking, counseling for sexual dysfunction involves consideration of physical problems, outside stress factors, knowledge (e.g., myths, poor technique, lack of communication), values related to sex, and psychological factors such as performance anxiety or fear of rejection. Basically, if you can (a) rule out physical causes, you begin (b) working on behavioral changes, and (c) as needed address psychological issues (present and past; relational and individual). Psychological issues might include, for example, questions about the connection between sexual dysfunction and other problems in the marriage or whether there is a history of sexual abuse that underlies resistance to sex therapy.

William Masters and Virginia Johnson (1970) developed a distinctive approach for treating sexual dysfunction. Their treatment program typically involved couples, not simply individuals, since partners are always affected by sexual problems. Information was obtained from both participants, and their cooperation enlisted in support of the techniques used for overcoming sexual distress. Extensive physiological and psychological data were obtained and considered in treatment. Masters and Johnson favored use of two counselors, a man and woman, working together as cotherapists in an intensive short-term treatment program. Couples were seen daily for about two weeks and given exercises to complete on their own in between sessions.

In *Human Sexuality,* Masters, Johnson, and Kolodny (1992: 555) review several salient treatment concepts:

- The couple's own values and objectives determine what is done.
- Sex is assumed to be a natural function; treatment focuses on identifying and overcoming obstacles that block effective sexual function.
- Performance fears and other anxieties that take partners out of the moment are addressed by the therapists in discussion with the couple and via assigned exercises.
- Determining fault is counterproductive; the therapists encourage participants to explore what feels good and comfortable to themselves rather than training one person to do sex "right."
- Sex is just one component of their relationship, neither to be neglected nor overly concerned with.

As the Masters and Johnson program continues to influence sex therapy, their **sensate focus** exercises are used to shift attention away from genital intercourse and emphasize a wider range of pleasurable sensations. In a series of structured exercises, participants are initially asked to avoid the genitals and refrain from intercourse. Reactions to various levels and forms of bodily touching in the exercises are discussed in sessions with the cotherapists. Specific methods to treat particular sexual dysfunctions are also included as needed. *Premature ejaculation,* meaning the man ejaculates more quickly than a couple would like, is treated by introducing the *squeeze technique.* After erection occurs, the partner briefly and firmly applies pressure with the thumb and two fingers on opposite sides of the ridge below the top of the penis, front and back. During coitus the man can also employ a similar squeeze at the base of the penis, with the objective of delaying ejaculation. Proper timing is learned. *Vaginismus* is an involuntary reflex spasm some women experience that contracts the vaginal opening, preventing penile insertion. Treatment involves the use of plastic dilators of increasing size and teaching the woman how to contract and relax muscles in this area. Exploration of related psychological issues is tailored to the particular circumstances presented. Masters and Johnson also treated erectile dysfunctions in men. *Primary impotence* describes cases in which a man has never had an erection; *secondary impotence,* more common, refers to men who already have a history of prior erections. Ogasmic dysfunction in women, *anorgasmia,* also includes cases where a woman has never had an orgasm as well as women who have been stimulated to climax before, but not in intercourse with the current partner.

Intensive sex therapy requires sufficient willingness and confidence in the therapists to explore one's sexual functioning in an open way. For couples who are committed to trying such a program, however, improvement rates which have been reported for the Masters and Johnson Institute are good (Masters, Johnson, and Kolodny 1992: 563): vaginismus, 98 percent; premature ejaculation, 94 percent; secondary impotence, 80 percent; anorgasmia, 75 percent; primary impotence, 68 percent. Improvement was lower for inhibited sexual desire, nearer 50 percent. Inhibited sexual desire is likely to have more varied causes and is generally regarded as more difficult to treat (Rosen and Leiblum 1995). Some couples present complicated cases and mixed motivation to overcome their problems. Others prefer less concentrated sessions with a single therapist, which may be more accessible for practical reasons and can also be effective. Rosen and Leiblum (1995: 10) note that beginning in the 1980s, increasing attention has been paid to biomedical approaches, especially for erectile dysfunction, with "men opting for medical rather than psychological solutions" to sexual problems. Examples include implants, vacuum pumps, injections, and pills. Viagra is probably the most widely known such intervention.

Many marriage and couples counselors can also address sexual problems. One caution raised by Masters, Johnson, and Kolodny (1992: 566) is that, in itself, "sex therapy is an unregulated profession," so there are deliberately fraudulent, unqualified, or simply ineffectual therapists who practice sex therapy. Improper therapy can cause further problems, so they urge couples to discuss with a prospective therapist his or her education, training, counseling orientation, and plan for therapeutic intervention. Directories of therapists are also available from the Society for Sex Therapy and Research in New York City or the American Association of Sex Educators, Counselors and Therapists in Washington, DC. As another resource, Box 8.7 lists some of the most influential professional journals in the area of marital and sex therapy.

Case studies often mention a client's previously unsuccessful attempts at therapy, both individual and marital, but this cannot be attributed simply to poor skills of counseling providers. Clinical experience cannot be reduced to one simple formula. The therapist's task is to help people investigate the personal meanings of their own desires and conduct. As described by Levine (1995: 97), "Clinicians' work depends on their ability to synthesize the complex interaction of numerous factors in their patients' lives." In contrast to empirical social science that seeks to draw probabilistic generalizations about patterns of human social interaction, clinical practice is an enterprise that defies statistical methods of ascertaining in advance precisely what is required to assist a specific client. Within a framework of professionally shared ethics, knowledge, training, and techniques, a good therapist always takes into account the sensibilities of individual clients, and outcomes depend to a great extent on what clients themselves bring to the process of change.

One final observation is about the close connection between marital and sex therapy. Therapist Sandra R. Leiblum describes sex therapy as "a complex psychotherapeutic process that incorporates ongoing exploration of intrapsychic conflicts, couple dynamics and transference issues. Marital therapy is an intrinsic part of treatment, as is individual psychotherapy" (Rosen and Leiblum 1995: 253). A similar view, expressed by Arnold Lazarus (1995: 82) based on his own experience as a therapist, is that "it is rare to find harmonious marriages wherein all goes well except for some specific sexual problems. Typically there is an inextricable link between the couple's interpersonal ambiance and what goes on in the bedroom. Thus the need to integrate marital and sexual interventions is fairly standard" (Rosen and Leiblum 1995: 82). Although there are no easy and instant cures for relationship problems, marital or couples counseling and sex therapy can be very effective. Therapeutic gains in sexual functioning are likely to be associated with improvement in other areas of a relationship, and vice versa.

Box 8.7. Marital and Sex Therapy Journals

Professional journals such as those listed below address research, theory, and practice issues related to couples counseling.

American Journal of FamilyTherapy
  Annual Review of Sex Research
Archives of Sexual Behavior
Behavior Therapy
Behavior Research and Therapy
Cognitive Therapy and Research
  Family Process
Family Therapy
International Journal of Family Therapy/Contemporary Family Therapy
Journal of Consulting and Clinical Psychology

Journal of Family Therapy
Journal of Marital and Family Therapy Psychotherapy
Journal of Psychology and Human Sexuality
Journal of Sex and Marital Therapy
Journal of Sex Education and Therapy
Journal of Sex Research

Chapter 9

Looking Ahead

A main objective of this book is to help readers understand ways in which social structure and social change influence individual experience. The growing diversity of marital and sexual lifestyles in the United States over the past half century has resulted in an imposing array of options confronting the individual. Understanding our society as a whole and various groups within it, as well as making the right lifestyle choices and decisions for ourselves, requires adequate information. In reviewing definitions of family life education, Myers-Walls (2000: 361) cited one that seemed particularly apt in this context; **family life education** is "the study of individual roles and interpersonal relationships, family patterns and alternative life styles, emotional needs of individuals at all ages, and the physiological, psychological, and sociological aspects of sexuality" (Herold, Kopf and deCarlo 1974: 365). Becoming better educated about the many aspects of marital and sexual lifestyles discussed in this book (and then some) can contribute to successfully negotiating the possibilities offered in our society today. This concluding chapter takes a final look at several topics raised earlier, turns to consideration of appropriate social policies, and offers a few parting comments.

MARITAL LIFESTYLES: DIVORCE AND COHABITATION TRENDS

When students in the author's classes reflect on what they learned and conclusions they reached about marital and sexual lifestyles in the United States, one concern sometimes expressed is for the future of the family—especially after looking at an increase in divorce since the 1950s, the effects of divorce on children, and the difficulties faced by both single parents and

Excerpts from *Our Sexuality Update Newsletter,* Winter 1990: "How Shall We End the Century? Behavior and Sexually Transmitted Disease" by Thomas Britton from *Our Sexuality,* Fourth Edition, by R. Crooks and K. Baur, Benjamin/Cummings Publ. © 1989. Reprinted with permission of Brooks/Cole, an imprint of the Wadsworth Group, a division of Thomson Learning, Fax (800) 730-2215.

stepfamilies. Students tend to focus less on the increase in cohabitation, but it has received considerable research attention in recent years. Both trends appear relevant to continuing concerns about marriage in our society.

Divorce

It is really quite striking that, according to data from the United Nations' (1995) *Demographic Yearbook,* the United States may presently have the world's highest divorce rate (Eshleman 1997: 527). Family sociologist J. Ross Eshleman notes, however, that a high divorce rate is *expected* to accompany a high level of "socio-economic development and female labor force participation, with an erosion of traditional patriarchal patterns and a heavy emphasis on the individual and small nuclear family in contrast to an emphasis on extended kin" (Eshleman 1997: 528). Does this mean that the divorce rate has been steadily increasing in recent decades and will continue to climb, with dire ultimate consequences?

Consider first that the divorce rate is a statistic that can be calculated in several different ways, each of which provides a somewhat different picture, and all are subject to some degree of error. The necessity of giving careful attention to how statistics are calculated and interpreted was raised before, in Chapter 2, in discussing cohabitation. Earlier in that same chapter, Table 2.2 served to caution readers about extrapolating trends. It showed that while median age at first marriage steadily increased for men and women from 1970 to 1995, it did not change much between 1950 and 1965, and from 1890 to 1948 had been *declining.* Ability to accurately grasp the fundamental patterns behind such numbers is important; ignoring or glossing over statistical data can lead to mistaken interpretations of social change and its causes. To return to the particulars of divorce, Table 9.1 shows the number of divorces and associated rate of divorce (indicated by divorces per 1,000 married women age fifteen and up) from 1955 to 1995. The divorce rate in 1955 was slightly higher than it had been three decades earlier but was down from a previous upward rise that peaked in 1946.

Note that the rate of divorce in the United States is *no longer increasing;* instead it has been relatively stable, even declining slightly, from its high in the 1980s. This may be more readily apparent when the same information is charted as in Figure 9.1, another way of showing patterns of change over time in social phenomena. Social trends are, after all, connected with other social changes and may end or pause when a new balance of social forces is attained. For example, Leigh (2000: 79) suggests that "decline in marriage rates has been offset by the increase in cohabitation, and this trend may have prevented the divorce rate from continuing its pre-1980 increase. It is estimated that about 20-24 percent of unmarried American adults between age 25 and 34 are cohabiting (Waite 1995)."

TABLE 9.1. Estimated U.S. Divorce Rates

Year	Number of Divorces	Rate per 1,000 Married Women
1955	380,000	9.5
1960	393,000	9.2
1965	475,000	10.5
1970	708,000	14.9
1975	1,030,000	20.2
1980	1,189,000	22.6
1985	1,174,000	21.3
1990	1,175,000	20.9
1994	1,191,000	20.5

Source: Adapted from Eshleman 1997: 531, based on U.S. government statistics.

FIGURE 9.1. Overview of U.S. Divorce Rate, 1955-1995

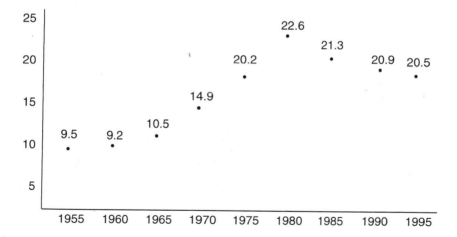

Source: Adapted from Eshleman 1997: 532, based on U.S. government statistics.

Note: Per 1,000 married women fifteen years of age and up.

Cohabitation

U.S. News and World Report recently included an article about more and more Americans opting for cohabitation, claiming "most Americans are still unaware of the extent or significance of cohabitation, even though more than half of today's newlyweds live together before tying the knot, compared to about 10 percent in 1965" (Tolson 2000: 48). Jay Tolson, the author, remarked that we are "still a long way from Sweden, where unmarried couples—who have all the rights, benefits and obligations of married partners—make up about 30 percent of couples sharing households" (p. 48). For the now over 4 million cohabiting couples in the United States, Tolson reported that this arrangement is likely to be transitory, with 55 percent marrying and 40 percent ending the relationship within five years.

Marriage is not going out of fashion, but it is part of an increasingly complex overall picture of marital and sexual lifestyles in the United States. Promotional material for *The Ties That Bind,* edited by University of Chicago professor Linda J. Waite (2000), commented that "at the same time marriage rates are declining, it is clearer than ever that marriage matters to Americans. Those who do marry report better health, higher incomes, more sexual satisfaction and higher levels of well being than those who are single." Scholars address questions about the formation of marriages and other intimate unions, their timing, and the various forms these relationships take. They also examine factors explaining the dramatic changes in union formation observed over recent decades. Their answers demonstrate that there have been "powerful forces reshaping marriage and intimate unions and that *the confluence of these factors rather than any single factor has brought us to where we are today*" [emphasis mine] (Waite 2000).

The increase in cohabitation and decline in marriage is similar to what has happened in other countries but is not as prevalent in the United States as in Sweden or Guatemala, for example (Leigh 2000: 80). Research by Prinz (1995), looking at the United States and other nations, suggested an interesting path of social development for cohabitation that may relate to other marital and sexual lifestyles as well. Beginning as a "deviant" phenomenon with only a small percentage of the population participating (Italy), cohabitation is next viewed as a prelude to marriage (Germany); then as a possible alternative to marriage as attitudes toward marriage change (France); and finally, as a legitimate type of union (slowly, in Sweden) considered acceptable in itself by a larger proportion of the population. In the United States, cohabitation is primarily, though not exclusively, a "trial marriage" without the ceremonial, social, or legal commitment (Leigh 2000). Among young never marrieds, however, cohabitation is more often terminated by separation than marriage, and has not been demonstrated to result in better marriages. Box 9.1 reviews some other facts and figures about cohabitation today.

Box 9.1. Cohabitation Facts and Figures

In a chapter, "Cohabiting and Never-Married Families Across the Life Course," Geoffrey K. Leigh, a professor at the University of Nevada, reviews research that provides us with baseline information on cohabitation as we enter the twenty-first century. According to Leigh (2000: 82-85):

- The greatest incidence of cohabiting is still among young adults.
- Cohabitation is increasingly occurring in older age groups.
- About 40 percent of cohabiting households include children (Bumpass, Sweet, and Cherlin 1991).
- These children are economically better off than children in single-parent households; less well off than children in married couple households (Manning and Lichter 1996).
- Children of cohabiting unions are more likely than others to cohabit themselves.
- There is general approval of cohabitation among young adults today (Axinn and Barber 1997; Sweet and Bumpass 1992).
- Dissolving these unions is emotionally similar to the ending of other close couple relationships.
- Cohabitation reflects varying personal motivations.
- Never-married persons who *expect* to cohabit are more accepting of divorce, less likely to think it is better to be married, and more egalitarian than those who do not (Sweet and Bumpass 1992).
- For previously married persons, nearly two-thirds of second partnerships begin as cohabitation.

Keeping in mind the very small base from which cohabitation has grown over the past several decades, it does provide an interesting example of an alternate lifestyle arising as existing social institutions failed to meet individual needs. Although personal motivations for cohabiting vary, sometimes by social characteristics such as age, race, and marital status (nevermarried versus formerly married), participants may share a perception that, at least for a time, cohabitation is more beneficial than either being married or living alone. In the social exchange framework, the relative balance of rewards and costs offered makes cohabitation a more suitable option in which to invest one's efforts than the available alternatives; cohabitation seems to better meet one's needs overall. Individuals may have a negative attitude toward marriage based on past experience, regard a particular partnership as too costly or insufficiently rewarding to formalize with a marriage, or simply not see marriage as necessary. For example, disillusioned divorced persons or elderly individuals experiencing loneliness may seek emotional and physical intimacy in a living together arrangement without feeling strongly motivated to marry; in other words, individuals can be seeking the relationship rather than the status of marriage. For gays and lesbians, the existing institution of marriage is not available as an option. More likely than official extension of the social status of marriage per se to gay and lesbian couples in the next several decades is the prospect of growing recognition of cohabiting partnerships that involve long-term commitment and warrant some increasing legal and social protection as well as acknowledgment.

SEXUAL LIFESTYLES: CONTINUING CONCERNS

The winter 1990 issue of *Our Sexuality Update,* a newsletter for human sexuality instruction, raised several concerns about how we would end the twentieth century. Thomas F. Britton, MD, noted that "by the age of 20, up to 85% of young people will have had premarital intercourse, frequently with more than one sexual partner" (Britton 1990: 1). At least through the 1980s, a steady increase in the number of sexually experienced teens and a drop in the age of first intercourse was observed (see Table 3.5 in an earlier chapter). Recall that Janus and Janus (1993) found that 21 percent of males and 15 percent of females in the eighteen to twenty-six age category reported having first intercourse by the time they were fourteen years old. "While some analyses have indicated a possible leveling off in these rates, there are still enormous numbers of young people initiating sexual activity. And while these relationships may not include very frequent intercourse, they still represent a significant risk for unintended pregnancy and sexually transmitted diseases" (Britton 1990: 1). In the 1960s and 1970s, twenty-to twenty-four-year-olds had the highest STD rates, but "by 1982, teenagers for the first time showed the highest rates of infection" (Britton 1990).

Among related public health worries, teens are found to delay seeking medical attention and, though use of condoms may be increasing, application of preventive methods is not consistent. Surveys show teens have more knowledge today about sexually transmitted diseases but do not necessarily translate facts into behavioral change; "the latest suggestion from peers will often outweigh the fact-filled health lecture when it comes time for personal decision making" (Britton 1990: 1). At any age, impulsivity and a sense of invulnerability increase risks taken. More detailed discussion of STDs in an earlier chapter highlighted some of these risks. In the United States, there are now as many as possibly 10 million new cases of bacterial chlamydia infections annually; another 2 million cases of gonorrhea. Genital warts affect millions of men and women in the United States, and the connection between genital warts (an HPV viral infection) and cancer is more widely recognized. "Over 100,000 cases of AIDS have been diagnosed in the U.S.; the background rate of incubating infection may be 1-2 million individuals" (Britton 1990).

AIDS strikes about 40,000 Americans every year and, while there is still no cure, a recent news update by Dr. Isadore Rosenfeld (2000: 4) noted that "patients are living longer and more enjoyable lives thanks to several new drugs that attack the virus itself, as well as more sophisticated testing." Most people who become HIV positive do not develop symptoms of AIDS for about ten years, during which time the virus can be influenced by treatment "hitting hard" in this silent stage (Rosenfeld 2000). Early detection is important. New tests register not only T4 helper cells (which inhibit infection and cancer) but also "viral load" (direct concentration of virus in blood), thereby helping to judge effectiveness of treatment. Drugs that attack the virus itself also help to better manage the disease and slow down the rate at which it replicates. The downside is that the new drugs are expensive, potentially toxic, and are not a cure; symptoms almost always recur.

The double standard is another lingering concern about contemporary sexual lifestyles. Specifically, the gender-based social script of "token resistance" (Muehlenhard and Hollabaugh 1988) has an unintended consequence of increasing the risks of date rape, unwanted pregnancy, and sexually transmitted diseases in heterosexual encounters. If women are going to be sexually active but still feel compelled to defend their virtue by not appearing too interested, frank discussions with partners and effective decision making is all the more difficult. Take the example of a woman providing a condom for STD prevention. How much time will be given over to worrying that she will seem too "easy," "fast," or "loose" if she brings a condom with her on any date that just might involve sex? The idea of sex guilt and reproductive roulette discussed in an earlier chapter emphasized that effective contraception, as well as disease prevention, requires up-front acknowledgment of and comfort with one's own decision to be sexually active. How can women protect themselves if sex has to "just happen" to be right? How can "no" mean no, if sex is supposed to be a matter of a man just persisting until the woman gives in, and men *expect* to have sex with women who are passive or initially refuse their advances? A sexual double standard reinforces rape proclivity among men and, by undermining women's assertiveness, encourages cases such as the thirty-year-old woman married to a hemophiliac with AIDS described earlier in the book. He refuses to use condoms and she still has sex with him because "she is more reluctant to hurt his feelings than he is to endanger her life." The double standard stacks the deck against "good sex," which means, for *both* women and men, sex that is freely chosen and responsible about pregnancy and sexually transmitted diseases.

Thinking about marital and sexual lifestyles in the century ahead, sex education ultimately seems a very important issue. Surveys of students in the author's college classes asking how they learned about sex showed TV/movies, peers, and personal experience ("trial and error") far ahead of parents, church, and even school. Sex education in the school is still controversial in many communities and often fails to effectively address interpersonal relationships and value conflicts. For adolescents, emerging sexuality nevertheless remains a significant aspect of the transition from childhood to adulthood. Sexuality continues to be highly visible outside the home, exploited by the mass media and entertainment industry, now by electronic networks as well, and we still cannot talk about it at the dinner table. Our culture remains remarkably ambivalent about sexuality, and decades after the so-called sexual revolution of the 1960s, our society still seems both sex saturated *and* sex starved—saturated with "sexual superficiality" and starved for "real sexual involvement," as described in an earlier chapter. Whether in future our collective sexual morality can embrace comprehensive sexuality and family life education, beginning with youth in their formative years, remains to be seen.

FACTS, VALUES, AND SOCIAL SCIENCE REVISITED

Issues such as divorce, premarital sex, cohabitation, sex education, and gender roles certainly generate differences of opinion and interpretation. Scientific study of marital and sexual lifestyles requires a well-developed sense of the difference between facts and values, as addressed in Chapter 1. Recall that statements of value have to do with the basic standards individuals apply when judging the *desirability* of particular situations or courses of action. Values are prescriptive judgments of what "should be." Statements of fact involve assertions about the *actual occurrence* of events. They may be accurate or inaccurate. Social science research methods are designed to appraise factual assertions, based on empirical observation. As social scientists, sociologists attempt to systematically and objectively gather information about the incidence of events, their causes and consequences; to describe their occurrence and investigate their connections with other events. They follow explicit procedures for gathering and analyzing their observations (data). Social scientists do not focus on whether people should or should not engage in particular lifestyles; they try to determine what people actually do, why they do it, and what happens as a result.

The patterns sociologists explore are not only in individual lives but in "social facts," which include rates of behavior and other regularities in groups and societies considered as a whole. Divorce is an example of an outcome that is both personal and social. We may investigate the subjective individual experience of divorce but can also look at rates of divorce as they are related to other social variables. Further, social scientists recognize that multiple forces, or variables, act together to produced observed outcomes. For example, the rate of divorce is related to societal-level economic development, individualism, companionate marriage, and female labor force participation. These illustrate the kinds of larger social forces that influence our personal lives. Sociologists contribute to our knowledge of ourselves and society by *distinguishing between facts and values,* by providing a conceptual framework for *understanding social facts* as well as individual motivation, and by reminding us that complex *multivariate models are needed* to explain human society and social behavior.

Recall that sex education was used in the chapter on research methods as an example of common, everyday confusions of fact and value in debates about marital and sexual lifestyles. Now consider another example, with divorce as the topic of discussion. A woman participating in the discussion comments, with great conviction: "There are too many divorces today because women are too aggressive and don't know their place. If the husband cannot feel like a man anymore, the marriage does not work. A man should be head of the household." What are facts here, what are values? The final statement is clearly a value judgment. *Should* husbands be head of the household? Students in the author's college classes asked this question on a written questionnaire were divided in opinion, with nearly 30 percent agreeing while 70 percent disagreed, a division reflecting variations in individual experience and social influences such as religion and ethnicity.

The original comment about divorce, however, did not allow for legitimate value disagreement and also made assertions of fact. Is it true that the high U.S. divorce rate is caused by women not knowing their place? This is certainly an oversimplified analysis of divorce with respect to ignoring multiple causes. How much of the variation in divorce would actually be explained by this variable? Do all, most, or some men not "feel like a man" unless there is a traditional division of labor in the household? If one man contributing to the discussion says he cooks and cleans up and still feels like a man, is he representative? How his experience and attitudes compare with those of other men in the United States is open to empirical investigation. Examples such as the divorce discussion serve as a reminder that facts do not speak for themselves. How they are presented and interpreted depends on the values of persons discussing them, and values are sometimes based on or defended with factual assertions that may not be accurate. An educated ability to sort out facts and values is quite useful. Empirical testing of propositions about marital and sexual lifestyles with *valid* measures also requires clear definitions; e.g., what does "too aggressive" or "not knowing one's place" mean operationally? The potentially limited *generalizability* of observations is another important methodological caveat and bit of practical wisdom. In drawing conclusions about what works best, we cannot safely assume everyone else's experiences, motivations, and values are the same as our own.

DIVERSITY

In attempting to draw an overall picture of changing marital and sexual lifestyles in the United States over the second half of the twentieth century, earlier chapters may have succeeding in calling attention to certain kinds of diversity, but others have been neglected, including race, ethnic, and class differences. Acknowledging such differences, *The Family,* a sociology text written by J. Ross Eshleman (1997), offers three separate chapters to describe social-class variations, lifestyles among African-American families, and lifestyles among Hispanic-American, Asian-American, and Native American families. Demo, Allen, and Fine's (2000) *Handbook of Family Diversity* likewise includes a separate section on class diversities and another on racial, ethnic and cultural diversities in families, specifically African American, Latino and Asian American. There are differences not only *across* these social types but, as current research increasingly emphasizes, *within* these groups. For example, Chapter 1 mentioned a book by Harvard sociologist Charles Vert Willie (1988), *A New Look at Black Families,* which used case studies to explore "patterns of variation in the lifestyles of affluent or middle class, working class and poor black households" (p. 1).

Reaffirming the obvious, not all single-parent families are alike; nor are all stepfamilies, same-sex couples, or older adults and their families (Demo, Allen, and Fine 2000). So too for participants in other lifestyles. Acceptability of and actual rates of participation in cohabitation or unmarried childbearing, for example, vary by race (Leigh 2000). Moreover, the lower marriage rate among African Americans is not just a matter of personal preference but reflects demographic and social factors such as an imbalance in the sex ratio (more available women than men) and economic constraints. *Intersecting categories* of social experience contribute to lifestyle diversity, where race, class, gender, age, sexual orientation, religion, and physical characteristics meet in persons' lives. As sociologists Stephen Marks and Leigh Leslie (2000) ask, what is it like to be Hispanic, middle class, male, and elderly as compared to African American, poor, female, and fifteen years old or white, wealthy, middle-aged, lesbian, and disabled? How can we best frame individual experience, taking into account subjective personal identities and objective social forces?

To understand contemporary U.S. society, cross-cultural and historical comparisons are also revealing. In *The Family,* J. Ross Eshleman (1997) used the examples of the modern Swedish family and the traditional Chinese family (an extended kinship system in a communal culture) to highlight both similarities and differences. Such comparisons help counter ethnocentrism, suggest alternative choices, and demonstrate the "close linkage between families and the larger social/cultural context within which they operate" (Eshleman 1997: 144). Readers of this book have already encountered material on human sexuality as viewed cross-culturally and historically, in the introduction, and the unique perspective this provides on the otherwise taken-for-granted features of our own sexual values and behaviors. Chapter 5, on sexual morality, also indicated how findings from social surveys have generated greater awareness of variations in sexual beliefs and practices within the United States and help to reduce "pluralistic ignorance."

Myers-Walls (2000: 376) raised an interesting observation about diversity, which, as sexual lifestyles demonstrate, is not always as obvious as gender, race, or age: "Diverse characteristics may be visible or invisible, chosen or inherent, shared by many people or only a few, and associated with acceptance or rejection by others." Demo, Allen, and Fine (2000: 441-443) concur that "diversity is broader than how it is typically presented," but not so far as to be completely idiosyncratic because it is "intertwined with social context." The socially constructed idea of diversity has come to play an increasingly prominent role in public consciousness and debates regarding marital and sexual lifestyles over the past several decades. Respect for diversity is, in itself, a visible theme in contemporary U.S. society, as reflected in attitudes of "openness and acceptance of difference and a more critical stance toward social mores [regarding] what is 'normal' family life" (Demo, Allen, and Fine 2000: 443).

As outlined in earlier chapters with respect to sexual morality, this does not mean that now "anything goes." As Demo, Allen, and Fine represent their views on diversity, there is a lot of territory between the one-form-fits-all-families standpoint and the conclusion that all family structures, behaviors, and processes are "equally effective," inherently adaptive, or good. Value judgments will still enter into discussions of marital and sexual lifestyles with reference to desirable goals for individuals, families, and society. Future scholarship in family sociology will continue to refine our understanding of lifestyle diversity and provide improved guidance for individual decision making. The more we know about how social forces influence individual experience, the broader view we have of our own life prospects, the greater our insight into lifestyles other than our own, and the better prepared we are for life in a pluralistic, complex modern society.

SOCIAL POLICY

Efforts to help individuals and families occur not only at the level of face-to-face therapeutic interventions but in social policies as well. For example, an earlier chapter listed policy options suggested by sociologist Robert Staples (1977) that would serve to support single-parent families. With respect to sexual expression, the law and its administration reflect social policy, as is evident in discussions about the functions of criminal law relative to private morality and general social welfare (Goldstein and Goldstein 1971), also considered in a previous chapter. "Family values," how best to preserve them, and what they are to begin with, feature prominently in continuing political debates. What is the proper role of government and other social institutions in sustaining family life and controlling sexual conduct? What policies should be followed? Lerner, Sparks, and McCubbin (2000: 380) describe public policies as representing standards for individuals, organizations, and institutions representing what we, as a society, value, believe, and think of as in our best interest.

A **policy** is a definite course of action adopted and pursued *(Webster's College Dictionary),* as by a government or business. Further, policies typically will be justified by those who make and follow them with regard to prudence or expediency. Expediency refers to actions deemed fit or suitable for their purpose, seeming proper and advisable, while prudence implies wisdom in practical matters or provident management of resources, with foresight, providing carefully for the future *(Webster's College Dictionary).* What constitutes **family policy,** and how best to define it, has been debated both among academics and politicians. According to Kohler and Zimmerman (2000: 231), "just as policy in general is concerned with the problems of individuals in relation to society and *social* policy with the problems of different groups (the elderly, children, the poor, etc.) in relation to society *family* policy is concerned with the problems of families in relation to society" and attempts to promote family well-being. In its broadest sense, family policy refers to everything that governments do that affects families, directly or indirectly (Zimmerman 1995), a domain made up of many separate individual policies.

Julie Kohler and Shirley Zimmerman (2000) suggest a few basic terms and concepts useful for thinking about family policy issues and provide examples of policies that affect family formation, child rearing, and later years (see Box 9.2). Family policy goes beyond policies that have clearly identified family-focused *goals and objectives.* Sometimes the family goals or objectives are explicitly stated; more often they are not stated but implicit. "An example of explicit family policy is federal legislation requiring insurance companies to provide 48 hours instead of only 24 hours of hospital coverage for new mothers and their babies. An example of *implicit* family policy is state legislation requiring the school attendance of school-aged youth" (Kohler and Zimmerman 2000: 230).

Policies have consequences for families that may be *direct* and *indirect; positive* and *negative; intended* and *unintended* or unforeseen. For example, in 1996 Congress enacted the Personal Responsibility and Work Opportunity Act, intended to "encourage the transition of parents of families receiving welfare to work" but with the possible unintended effect of increasing need for out-of-home placement of children because mothers working out-

---

Box 9.2. Family Policy

In a chapter on "Policy Issues and Families Over the Life Course," Julie Kohler and Shirley Zimmerman (2000) offer examples of policies that influence marital and sexual lifestyles.

Family Formation

Marriage is governed by laws defining who can marry whom. Restrictions can pertain to minimum required age, number of partners permitted, whether first cousins can marry, race (when interracial marriage was prohibited), and heterosexuality. In 1996, the U.S. Congress passed the Defense of Marriage Act (DOMA), defining marriage as "a legal union between one man and one woman." States can invalidate same-sex couple relationships, with wide-ranging effects (e.g., on inheritance and authority to make medical decisions when a partner is ill).

Adoption of children of one race by parents of another race is a controversial policy area. In 1994, Congress passed a Multiethnic Placement Act (META) explicitly aiming to reduce the time children wait for adoption, prevent discrimination in placement of children in adoptive homes on the basis of race, color, or national origin, and also make more same-race adoptive and foster parents available through tax incentives.

Child Rearing

Access to affordable quality day care and family leave time are two major policy areas. The 1996 Temporary Assistance for Needy Families (TANF) legislation limits financial aid for poor mothers with young children to two years (lifetime limit five years), making availability of *child care* more important. For all families, a 1997 White House Conference on Child Care highlighted presidential recommendations including federally funded scholarships for child care training, background checks on child care providers, and use of AmeriCorps volunteers in after-school programs.

Employer practices affect families. Based on legislation originally introduced by Congresswoman Pat Schroeder in 1984, and after several vetoes by President Bush, the Family Medical Leave Act (FMLA) was passed by Congress and signed into law by President Clinton in 1993. Employees of businesses with fifty or more workers were thereby entitled to up to twelve weeks of job-protected, unpaid leave to care for a new child, a seriously ill child, parent, or spouse, or their own serious health problems.

Later Years

Care of elderly family members will be an increasing concern, often complicated by financial constraints. Costs for long-term nursing home care can easily exceed $35,000 per person each year; in-home or community-based care, $15,000. Resource availability will be greatly affected by Social Security, Medicare, and Medicaid policies. Medicare is a federally funded program financed through payroll deductions. It does not cover most long-term nursing home care, for which families need supplemental insurance or Medicaid, designed to serve only very poor Americans. Future solvency of these entitlement funds will be determined by ongoing political debate and decision making. State and local regulation of nursing homes, other care facilities, and related services will also have a significant effect on the well-being of older Americans and their families.

side the home were then unable to be with them. How good a policy is "depends on how such policies are perceived by those families most directly affected by them, by the public at large who might be less directly affected by them, by various interest groups and political elites who have a stake in promoting one particular policy approach over another and sometimes by researchers trying to evaluate their effect on families" (Kohler and Zimmerman 2000: 231).

Kohler and Zimmerman's overview of family policy shows some of the "ways various policies affect families as they interact with systems in society—the educational, health care, social services, workplace, legal system and various levels of government," and helps conceptualize "connections between families and government via the policies that are enacted and implemented" (p. 230). This is yet another example of a point made in many different forms in previous chapters of this book, that marital and sexual lifestyles are lived in the context of a larger society that influences individual choices and outcomes.

Sociological theories and prior research findings contribute to formulation of social policies and design of programs. Existing knowledge and practical experience allow researchers and lawmakers to anticipate likely results and minimize adverse unintended consequences. Still, theories alone are not enough; systematic empirical observation is used to test the actual consequences of their application. *Policy research* and *program evaluation* are designed to assess the effectiveness of planned intervention programs and policies in achieving their intended objectives. Integrating basic and applied research, social scientists use their methodological skills in data collection and analysis to understand how individual lives, families, surrounding communities, and society are changed by a particular program. Programs represent field experiments, albeit with limited generalizability which require appropriate outcome comparisons (controls) to interpret results. *Participatory evaluation procedures* stay anchored in the everyday lives of those persons targeted by a policy or program, asking whether it promotes well-being of individuals in a particular lifestyle as experienced and perceived by participants themselves. In turn, development and implementation of policies and programs including evaluation research components provides "critical feedback on the adequacy of the conceptual frame" according to which the program was originally designed (Lerner, Sparks, and McCubbin 2000: 397).

Family diversity complicates the issues facing policy makers. Whether pertaining to variation in family structure and functioning, religious affiliation, ethnic identification, individual health status, lifestyle preferences, or dynamic changes over the life course, social interventions must be designed accordingly (Demo, Allen, and Fine 2000). One type of intervention does not necessarily fit all families, so efforts are made to take into account the real variety of experience: families with or without children, infants, or adolescents, young, middle-aged, or older adults, first family or stepfamily, with married couple present, single-parent household or custodial grandparents, in good health or with chronic illness or disabilities, financially well off or poor, Asian, Latino, African, Native American, and so on. "Policies and programs that are fit and effective for one social, racial or ethnic community or cultural group may be irrelevant, poorly suited or even damaging to families with other characteristics" (Lerner, Sparks, and McCubbin 2000: 395).

CLOSING COMMENT

Family experience today is definitely more varied than the idealized "traditional" white, middle-class, suburban family of the 1950s, a biological first (and lifelong) family unit consisting of a breadwinning husband, homemaking wife, and their dependent children. Today's high rates of divorce and remarriage mean Americans in large numbers enter, leave, and reenter marriage, then frequently find themselves single again. An increasing number, though proportionally still a minority, of all adult Americans will enter and leave cohabiting relationships. Some will choose to remain cohabiting couples. With the increase in age at first marriage, more persons are remaining single for longer periods of time. Social attitudes and structural supports make being single and living alone more feasible today. Same-sex couples may reside in separate households or together as cohabitants. Family variations among racial and ethnic groups in the United States feature shifts in household composition, interactional dynamics, and values. While millions of married women are "stay-at-home" wives and mothers, the majority of married women, even with children, today hold jobs outside the home in addition to their family roles. Sexual values and behaviors, too, show differences across households, e.g., in preferences regarding premarital sex and permissible activity within marriage.

Accordingly, a cross-sectional view of U.S. households shows considerable diversity in structure, roles, and values, which will require increased knowledge and flexibility in future policy making. Not only will different segments of the American population have different types of marital and sexual lifestyles as *different people at the same time* are doing different things, but the life course perspective reminds us that *the same people at different times* are doing different things (Macklin 1987). A couple may, for example, have a sexually open marriage for three years but not before or after. A particular husband and wife's labor force participation, marital satisfaction, and decision-making style may be different when they have children present in their household than before or after. From the perspective of the individual, it makes increasing sense to think not only about fixed "types" of families or relationships, but of varying *relationship paths*—how they unfold over time, why, and with what likely consequences (Leigh 2000). Similarly, the idea of *sexual paths* helps to conceptualize the emergence of adult sexual behaviors more clearly than simple categorical descriptions (see earlier discussion of paraphilias in Chapter 5 or bisexuality in Chapter 6). Observers of contemporary marital and sexual lifestyles have to consider that "two or three marriages over a longer lifetime along with periods of cohabitation and single living are likely to become more common, creating enlarged and more complicated family networks in later life" (Walsh 1999: 308).

The lives of children and adolescents as well as adults are altered by these circumstances. Going through divorce and entering new family forms are significant transitions in children's lives, and single-parent households and stepfamilies pose challenges as ongoing lifestyles. The financial, social, and emotional stresses experienced by adults influence their children's well-being. Millions of children and U.S. society as a whole would benefit from greater attention to child welfare and adolescent adjustment, and stronger social supports for both family planning and parenting—to enhance children's lives in the care of persons who have them and want to have them. As suggested in Chapter 8, single-parent and blended families can succeed with structural supports and greater insight into their unique needs. Another child-related issue is men's changing role as parents. In a chapter devoted to single-parent households headed by men, Kissman and Allen (1993) discussed men's increasing participation in parenting. As more married women entered the paid labor force, questions have been raised about the traditional gender-based allocation of domestic tasks. As women choose smaller family size and contemplate voluntary childlessness, "men have begun to think of child care, home activities, and relationships as acceptable domains for their lives. As a result, we are seeing a trend toward greater involvement by fathers" in both intact marriages and in the 10 percent of single-parent households headed by men (Kissman and Allen 1993: 109).

With so many single-parent households resulting from the high U.S. divorce rate and an increase in children born outside of marriage, a surprisingly neglected aspect of marital lifestyles is *noncustodial parenting*. Except for the social problem or, some say, "national disgrace" of nonpayment of child support (which has led mainly to legal remedies), the parental role for individuals who do not live with their adolescent or younger children has received little attention. In *Nonresidential Parenting,* Depner and Bray (1993) covered some preliminary conceptual distinctions and terminology, demographic origins/influences, and implications for family relationships. They noted a change in U.S. society not previously detailed in this book, "a general upward spiral in births outside marriage" that resulted in 26 percent of all babies born in the United States in 1988 being born to unmarried mothers

(Depner and Bray 1993: 5). For unwed or divorced men who are interested in being or staying in their children's lives, few social guidelines currently exist, leaving individuals much to learn by trial and error about how best to maintain an ongoing relationship via visitation. Using nationally representative sample data, Seltzer (1991) found that 25 percent of previously married fathers had contact with their children at least once a week, while 18 percent had not visited with them during the past year. For fathers not previously married to the mother, fewer saw their children once a week (20 percent), while 40 percent had no contact in the past year. Both the place of noncustodial parents in the larger scheme of family life and the parent-child relationship from the viewpoint of children who do not live with their parents clearly warrant further research.

At the other end of the life course, growing scholarly interest is connecting with U.S. demographic trends in the area of aging. In industrialized nations today, people live longer in better health. What does this mean for U.S. society? See Box 9.3 for information from a *Population Today* bulletin on aging (Treas 1995). Improved diet and exercise, self-awareness, and opportunities for social involvement have been shifting social identities for older persons. A Sunday newspaper feature on a seventy-eight-year-old grandmother who is a competitive bodybuilder suggests the raised bar for fitness expectations. The younger elderly are portrayed in advertising today as healthy, well off, fit, and fun loving. Conceptions of "modern maturity" have also been influenced by the changes in sexual lifestyles over the past several decades. Less support in general for sexual self-denial and widespread use of contraceptive technology have made room for nonprocreative sex, which redefined the function of sex for the elderly or middle-aged who have finished with childbearing. Too, the baby boomers are a unique cohort. They and later cohorts raised in more sexually permissive times (compared to persons who are already sixty-five or older) are likely to have different expectations of aging.

Without crystal ball gazing or speculating too far ahead into the twenty-first century, some prospects are already in sight. The broad overview provided in this book of where we were by the 1990s and how we got there from the 1950s provides a guide, especially for the immediate future. Meanwhile, U.S. society continues to be transformed by technology. Among the changes influencing marital and sexual lifestyles are certainly those in medicine that increase health and longevity, improve sexual functioning, and facilitate control over reproduction (whether enhancing contraception or fertility). Additionally, computers are extending the reach of our social networks, providing a way of staying in touch with distant kin or meeting people for dating as well as possibilities for alternative electronic relationships. It is by now a well-worn observation that a full understanding of the personal, social,

Box 9.3. Trends in Aging

In *Population Today*, a publication of the Population Reference Bureau, Judith Treas, professor of sociology at the University of California, Irvine, described the outlook for older Americans (Treas 1995: 1, 2):

> We started the century young, but we are ending it old. In 1900, . . . there were only 3 million people age 65 and older—less than 1 in 25 Americans. In 1995, almost 34 million Americans have lived past their 65th birthday—fully 1 in 8 Americans. . . . After the first of the baby-boom generation turns 65 in 2011, the ranks of the elderly will swell. After 2030, the rate of increase of the elderly population will slow. Nevertheless, by mid-century there will be 80 million people age 65 or older, roughly *1 in 5* Americans. . . . U.S. life expectancy is at an all-time high. A person age 65 can look forward, on average, to another 17.3 years of life. Those who survive to 85 have an average of 6.0 years of remaining life.
>
> The growth and change of America's older population may rank among the most important demographic developments of the 20th century. Fewer children per family and longer lives have transformed the elderly from a small component to a significant part of the U.S. population. A sizable segment of all consumers, voters, homeowners and family members are older adults. Older people are living a lifestyle that few could have envisioned in their youths. . . . Active retirement has emerged as an idealized lifestyle that encompasses social engagements, travel, hobbies, volunteer activities, independent living, Sunbelt migration and even part-time jobs. Today's elderly benefit from government income and health care programs, private pensions, and the postwar prosperity that permitted them to own homes and save for their later years. They tend to have more assets than younger people. . . . Older people also enjoy substantial political clout.

Growing numbers combined with high rates of voter registration and actual voting make senior citizens an important factor in election outcomes.

"The increasing diversity of the U.S. population will alter the racial and ethnic composition of America's older population. Changing family patterns—particularly the trends toward smaller family size, childlessness and divorce—mean that, while today's elderly typically have several grown children to turn to in times of need, the baby boomers themselves will have far fewer family resources" when they age (Treas 1995: 2).

Poverty is already a reality for 12 percent of all elderly, more so for older African Americans and Hispanics. Social Security is the biggest single source of income for older Americans, many of whom also rely on Medicare for health insurance. For U.S. society, growth of the population age sixty-five and older will affect the costs of Social Security, private pension programs, Medicare, Medicaid, and a host of other services and programs for the elderly. Perhaps the most serious concern is the potential need for expensive long-term care for elderly persons with declining health. Vulnerability of the elderly to changes in government policy can be appreciated by considering that "if Social Security and other government payments were not counted, the poverty rate for the elderly would be four times higher and half of all persons age 65 and older would live in poverty" (Treas 1995: 2).

and legal implications of technological innovations lags well behind the technology itself.

What does this emerging picture of marital and sexual lifestyles require of us as individual participants and observers? Change seems to be a constant, diversity a theme. Among scholars and the general public, a new perspective is beginning to develop that no longer uses the "traditional" family as a baseline for defining alternate lifestyles but rather begins with variability as the ordinary state of affairs. By various paths, we arrive at particular lifestyles, with differing degrees of popularity in which we stay for some period of time, long or short—perceiving the experience as more or less successful ("it works/doesn't work for me"). Americans today see and more readily accept that individuals do not necessarily grow up to live one lifestyle by one path only. Too, while we have examined alternative lifestyles as representing individual options and choices, often they happen without being quite intended or anticipated. For example, no matter how high the divorce rate, being divorced is not a condition we typically aspire to when we marry, nor is single parenting in the wake of an abusive relationship or as a result of contraceptive failure or the death of a spouse. Usually we do not screen dating partners with the goal of gaining entry into a stepfamily, though such a partnership may come to be a satisfying part of our lives. Persons may drift into cohabitation not as an ideal but as a reasonable accommodation to circumstances; other persons who believe cohabitation is acceptable may not find the right person or opportunity for such an arrangement. A couple who would prefer traditional roles may find a husband's unexpected job loss or low wages pushing his wife into the workforce. Sexual orientation is less a matter of choice than are the ways we shape a personal identity and live out our lives as heterosexual, gay, lesbian, or bisexual. Paraphilias as a response to formative sexual experiences and sexual compulsions are not exactly chosen, nor is being the "cheated on" partner in a marriage. Sometimes we do not know what we want. Sometimes we do not get it. And, always, what are seen as purely personal choices are heavily influenced by culture and social structure—existing social scripts, contextual parameters, and strains not directly of our own individual making (as when the demographic sex ratio affects chances of marriage).

An individualistic society gives us room to grow and express ourselves, to make mistakes and change course; to pursue "the right to life, liberty, and happiness" in our own ways (within the normative boundaries drawn by our society at a given point in time). The United States becoming more sexually permissive has not given us unrestrained license, and freedoms carry with them responsibilities, but greater openness does make it more apparent that other people do and believe in things we may not do and perhaps strongly disagree with. Making sense out of the overall result is a formidable task, facilitated by employing a shared historical, statistical, and conceptual framework. Knowledge about various types of lifestyles, the advantages and disadvantages of each, the possibilities and risks, provides a basis for understanding other people and for making the best of the lifestyles in which we find ourselves, by choice or happenstance—minimizing the strains and maximizing the benefits. Further, familiarity with the psychological, interpersonal, and social dynamics of variations within categories of lifestyles, which are increasingly being investigated by family scholars, helps refine our knowledge.

Individuals come to the study of marital and sexual lifestyles with their own emotions, beliefs, values, and past experiences that shape their sense of good or bad sex and proper or improper family arrangements. We know a lot about our own families and much less about other families, yet we often make assumptions and overgeneralize from our own experience. Beliefs we hold can be inaccurate, inconsistent, or *decontextualized* (disconnected from the overall picture of actually unfolding social events). That is where social science and the sociological imagination are useful. For coping with diversity, family life educator Myers-Walls (2000: 359) also urges that while growing in awareness of diversity, we should not lose sight of similarities; we dream different dreams but we all dream, and we all have experiences of being set apart in some way that can be used to bridge differences and develop empathy. Understanding lifestyles other than our own does not mean we have to embrace or agree with them; we simply have to set our biases aside long enough to see a lifestyle from the point of view of participants. Living together in a pluralistic society requires identifying the common ground in what determines a violation of social standards and otherwise showing tolerance; permitting others the same latitude of choice, without being stigmatized, we wish to enjoy ourselves.

In the end, despite all the changes in U.S. society, Americans still have an impressive attraction to marriage and family. Far and away the majority of all Americans will marry at some time, and millions will have satisfying, lasting marriages. Increasing longevity offers prospects for couples to remain together a long time. As Macklin (1987) indicated, *legitimizing alternative lifestyles should not obscure the need to provide supports for marriage.* Much is expected of contemporary companionate marriage and, though rewarding, child rearing is also very demanding. Yet family continues to be important at every stage of the life course. For older adults, "families provide most direct care giving assistance, psychological support and social interaction" (Walsh 1999: 308). Both longevity and quality of life are linked to social contact and support. Persons remaining single will still turn to others for intimate relationships. Sibling relationships and close friendships are also important bonds for unmarried adults. Secure attachment to others, as being in a committed marriage or, to a lesser extent, a cohabiting relationship, predicts better health, happiness, and overall well-being. Recall, however, that having no relationship may well be preferable to having a bad relationship. Poor relationships erode self-esteem and are associated with greater stress, anxiety, and depression, and generally poorer mental health outcomes. When sociologist Stephen Nock (1998) looked at marriage in men's lives and psychologist Ruthellen Josselson (1996) followed women's lives from college to their middle years, their observations converged in suggesting two themes underlying satisfying personal identities in contemporary U.S. society. "Identity resides at the intersection of *compe tence* and *connection;* this is where people feel most fully themselves": we strive to be effective in doing things we consider worthwhile and we seek to "connect" emotionally with the people we choose to make important in our lives (Josselson 1996: 178).

To address questions about how to sustain good long-term relationships, scholars are likely to pay closer attention to relationship dynamics over time and to long-lasting happy unions. Martin Whyte's (1992) finding that no aspects of dating he studied, such as timing of sexual intimacy or number of dating partners, actually predicted later marital success may indicate that marital outcomes depend on what couples do in the here and now to make a relationship last. As couples move through different experiences over time, the conflicts they encounter (about sex, money, children, gender roles, and so on) create opportunities for personal and relationship growth. Effectively managed conflict leads to *adaptive change,* not deterioration of the relationship, if both partners are willing (Mackey and O'Brien 1995). Individuals and couples can make use of professional therapy and other counseling to sustain long-term relationships. Social policies also make a difference in resources available for coping with family and life changes. The still-developing principles and practice of divorce mediation suggest how to avoid or ease the transition out of a marital relationship, to improve long-term adjustment. Marriage and parenting enrichment programs offer ways to strengthen families without waiting for a crisis to prompt seeking outside guidance. Box 9.4 provides an example of one marital enrichment program. Even the idea of an annual relationship "checkup" does not seem too fanciful, since a marriage might benefit more from a bit of constructive self-assessment than from a Hallmark anniversary card and flowers.

Psychologist Arnold A. Lazarus (1995) used the analogy of a "carburetor adjustment" in describing one case of a clinical intervention in marital and sex therapy to suggest that briefly addressing a few pivotal issues can result in significant improvement in functioning for couples who are willing to make changes. (It may also say something about our priorities if we in fact pay more attention to car maintenance than to "tuning up" our relationships.) A therapeutic approach can be used that emphasizes "education rather than healing and growth rather than treatment. . . . When clients realize that overcoming emotional and sexual problems is an educational pro-

Box 9.4. Marital Enrichment

Marital enrichment programs are typically intended as educational programs, not as therapy. They are designed to keep a good marriage strong or make it better by taking time out to focus on the primary relationship. Often they involve a group experience with other couples and a workshop leader, but Richard Mason (1985) presented a "do-it-yourself" version that can be used to illustrate the types of exercises one might try. His fourteen-day plan focuses on increasing intimacy "through mutual self-disclosure and acceptance." It emphasizes positives, not complaints, feelings, not reasons. Participants are told not to analyze or evaluate the feelings a partner expresses; just acknowledge and accept them. Be honest, and stay mostly in the present. Each partner uses a notebook for written exercises.

- *Active listening* to be sure we hear intended messages. One partner speaks, while the other listens, then feeds back what he or she has heard. The partner who spoke first then confirms or clarifies. Reverse roles and repeat procedure.

- *Expressing feelings* by replacing "you" messages, which invite negative responses, with "I" messages. Pick a positive feeling toward the spouse and convey in this form: "I feel ... when ... because I ..." Take a few alternating turns.

- *What I like about this marriage.* Both partners write down five things they like about their marriage, then take turns reading them to each other.

- *Write a love letter.* Imagine you are separated for a month or more; write your partner a love letter. Stamp it and mail it to your partner.

- *Levels of support.* Write in the notebooks about a time your partner (a) supported you all the way, (b) was "there" to just listen and talk, and (c) really didn't agree but let you do your own thing anyway. Then write a statement expressing your feelings of about these times, and share it with your partner.

- *Qualities of a successful marriage.* Refer to a list of qualities necessary for a successful marriage (e.g., see Ch. 9). Pick three qualities present in your marriage and write down specific ways your spouse exhibits the qualities. Read these to each other.

- *Discovering common interests.* Each partner lists ten or more things he or she (a) used to enjoy doing, (b) has always wanted to do, or (c) would like to do more often. Read the lists to each other. Maybe do one of the things on each list now.

- *Sexual feedback.* Write down what sexual activities please you most or turn you on. Be specific. Read this to your partner.

- *Appreciating flexibility.* Think about a time your partner was flexible in order to meet your needs; e.g., moved to a new house, changed jobs, took the children out, watched your choice of movie. Tell your partner how much and why you appreciated that.

cess, the concept of self-education is easily understood" (Lazarus 1995: 82). Some of this can be done on one's own or a professional counselor can be asked to recommend or "prescribe" particular self-help books, a technique described by Lazarus as bibliotherapy. Sexual or marital problems that "rest on (or coexist with) extreme anxiety and insecurity, abject misery, hidden agendas, accumulated resentments, malignant misperceptions and pernicious demands are *not* apt to respond to didactic rehearsals and specific readings" (Lazarus 1995: 89), but most of our everyday problems are potentially responsive to preventive interventions and enhancements, not focusing on analyzing what is wrong but on trying something new.

Marriage is a remarkably adaptable social institution. Today, if people marry it is less because they have to, more because they want to, and staying together is something of an achievement. Diversity within marriage means not all happy relationships are the same (there is no single best way), and different marriages can be tailored to meet the changing individual needs of both parties. Consider, too, that marriage is not just a matter of *finding* the right person; it is about *being* the right person. Marital happiness does not occur by chance; it depends on what you bring to a relationship. If no one else can make you happy, you have to come to terms with your own needs and limitations and address your own bad habits, insecurities, and goals. Your partner is not responsible for fixing you, and marriage will not basically transform anyone's personality. A lasting relationship is made up of many, varied ingredients: struggle and achievement, success and failure, unexpected disappointments and joys, the bad and the good. It does not remove us from vulnerability to life's difficulties but does offer unique opportunities to work on intimacy, competence, and connection.

This concluding section has summarized and reflected on changes we have seen in marital and sexual lifestyles in the United States since the 1950s. Social scientists and counseling professionals have identified (a) many features of U.S. society that will profoundly influence our individual marital and sexual lifestyle experiences and (b) various factors that contribute to more (or less) successful relationships. Familiarity with such information can lead to improvement in our own personal lives and interpersonal relationships and in the larger society to which we belong. Effectively applying this knowledge to your own marital and sexual lifestyle ventures will be an ongoing challenge—the chapter that remains to be written.

Appendix

Sample Survey Items

General Social Survey

The GSS has been conducted regularly since 1972 by the National Opinion Research Center in Chicago (Davis and Smith 1994). It includes the following items:

1. "There has been a lot of discussion about the way morals and attitudes about sex are changing in this country. If a man and woman have sexual relations before marriage, do you think it is always wrong, almost always wrong, wrong only sometimes or not wrong at all?"

___ Always wrong
___ Almost always wrong
___ Wrong only sometimes
___ Not wrong at all

2. "What about a married person having sexual relations with someone other than his or her husband or wife—is it always wrong, almost always wrong, wrong only sometimes or not wrong at all?"

___ Always wrong
___ Almost always wrong
___ Wrong only sometimes
___ Not wrong at all

3. "And what about sexual relations between two adults of the same sex—do you think it is always wrong, almost always wrong, wrong only sometimes or not wrong at all?"

___ Always wrong
___ Almost always wrong
___ Wrong only sometimes
___ Not wrong at all

Attitude Items

Attitude items often take the form of asking respondents to indicate their level of agreement or disagreement with a general statement.

	Strongly agree	Agree	Slightly agree	Slightly disagree	Dis- agree	Strongly disagree
1. Sex without affection should always be avoided.	1	2	3	4	5	6
2. A woman who has sexual intercourse with a lot of men is immoral.	1	2	3	4	5	6
3. Both men and women are equally free to initiate sexual advances in dating.	1	2	3	4	5	6
4. The man should be the one to initiate sex in a marriage.	1	2	3	4	5	6
5. A man who has sexual intercourse with a lot of women is immoral.	1	2	3	4	5	6
6. It is acceptable to have sexual intercourse without being in love with the person.	1	2	3	4	5	6

Vignettes

Brief descriptions of particular cases (vignettes) provide another approach for studying attitudes. Family sociologist John Cuber (1975) used items such as the following in his research:

1. Bob and Helen want to get married soon. They have been engaged for about a year but cannot get married for another two years at least. Bob and Helen have already had complete sexual relations a number of times. They don't see anything wrong with this.

____ Strongly agree/approve
____ Agree/approve
____ Disagree/disapprove
____ Strongly disagree/disapprove

2. Mike and Linda are dating regularly. Sometimes they go out with other people as well, but they do care about each other and are open and honest with one another. They both feel it is good to have sexual experiences before marriage and want sex to be a part of their relationship. They are not engaged and are not considering marriage because they know neither of them is ready for a lifetime commitment. They are, however, careful to practice effective birth control methods.

___ Strongly agree/approve
___ Agree/approve
___ Disagree/disapprove
___ Strongly disagree/disapprove

3. Jerry and Donna have been married six years. They have no children. They agree to spend their vacations apart. Jerry says, "It gives us a chance to get away from each other, see new people, and have new experiences. We both look forward to these vacations and look forward too to coming home when they are over. We can go out with others during these vacations. We seldom have any serious affairs, but we don't object to that either—it eventually wears off. For example, once I got lonesome for my summer love and Donna suggested I go where I might see this woman. I did, and that was all there was to it. Donna and I feel that these vacations and experiences make us appreciate each other more.

___ Strongly agree/approve
___ Agree/approve
___ Disagree/disapprove
___ Strongly disagree/disapprove

4. Mary and Todd are married and have been having problems for some time but are not sure they want to divorce. They have not had sexual relations with one another for many months. One of them is off on a business trip or goes to visit friends/relatives and meets someone very attractive. Without planning to, he or she winds up having a brief affair. The husband or wife does not find out and it never happens again.

___ Strongly agree/approve
___ Agree/approve
___ Disagree/disapprove
___ Strongly disagree/disapprove

5. My husband and I both work. Not that we have to but we like it this way. Many of our friends drop hints that it is time Jack and I have children. We talked it over and agreed we don't want kids. We can make a contribution in other ways. It annoys me that people assume reproduction is a moral obligation.

___ Strongly agree/approve
___ Agree/approve
___ Disagree/disapprove
___ Strongly disagree/disapprove

Behaviors

Survey questions can ask about your actual past behaviors or intended future behaviors.

1. How many children do you plan to have? __0 __1 __2 __3 __4+

2. Have you ever had sexual intercourse? ___Yes ___No (*If no, skip to question 3*)

    2.1   Have you ever had *premarital* intercourse? ___Yes ___No

    2.2   What age were you the very first time you had intercourse? ___ years

    2.3   How many different individuals (including spouses) have you ever had sexual relations with? *please fill in:* ___

    2.4   In the past year, your frequency of intercourse was closest to how many times?
       ___ daily   __ weekly   __ monthly   __ rarely   __ abstinence

    2.5   In the past year, your frequency of ANY type of sexual activity was closest to:

       ___ daily   __ weekly   __ monthly   __ rarely   __ abstinence

    2.6   Have you ever had any sexually transmitted diseases? ___Yes __No

    2.7   Cohabitation is defined as two unmarried adults living together, sharing household responsibilities and having a sexual relationship. Have you ever cohabited? ___Yes ___ No

3. Would you ever cohabit?   ___Yes ___ No

4. How likely is it that you would use a written cohabitation agreement if you decided to live with someone outside of marriage?

Definitely yes	Maybe yes	Undecided	Probably not	Definitely not
1	2	3	4	5

5. Have you ever been in a situation where you felt you were being pressured by a dating partner to engage in sexual behavior? ___Yes ___ No

    5.1   If yes, in your overall dating experience, how often has this happened?

       ___rarely ___regularly ___frequently

6. Have you ever been in a situation where you were the one pressuring a partner for sex? ___Yes ___No

The Janus Report Questionnaire—Sample Items (Janus and Janus 1993)

	Strongly Agree	Agree	No Opinion	Disagree	Strongly Disagree
Schools should teach sex education.	——	——	——	——	——
Divorce is too easy now.	——		——	——	——
Family is still a major source of personal fulfillment.	——	——	——	——	——
In the past few years I have become more cautious about sex.	——	——	——	——	——
There is still a double standard in sex regarding men and women.	——	——	——	——	——
Extramarital affairs do not seriously affect marriages.	——	——	——	——	——
I prefer experiencing a large variety of sexual techniques.	——	——	——	——	——
Family is the most important institution in society.	——	——	——	——	——

Demographic Variables

Surveys typically obtain background information on social characteristics that often influence attitudes and behaviors.

1. Sex: ___Male ___Female

2. Age: _____

3. Current Marital Status:

   ___Married ___Widowed ___Divorced ___Separated ___Never Married

4. Have you ever spent time as a parent or child in a single-parent family?

   __ as a child __ as a parent __ both __ neither

5. Ever spent time as a member of a stepfamily?

   __ as a child __ as a parent __ both __ neither

Open-Ended Questions

Open-ended questions permit respondents to answer as they choose, without using designated categories.

1. How did you meet the last person you dated?

2. Please briefly describe what you consider to be your "worst" experience with sexual pressure in a marriage or dating relationship.

3. Make a short list below for each question.

   a. What do you wish men knew about sex?

   b. What do you wish women knew about sex?

4. There are probably good and bad ways to communicate with a partner about sex. What is your best advice?

   a. How to talk to a partner about sex:

   b. How *not* to talk to a partner about sex:

Miscellaneous

1. I learned about sex from: *(check all that apply)*

   ___parents ___siblings ___other relatives
   ___school ___church ___friends ___books ____TV/movies
   ___personal experience ("trial and error")
   ___other, *please specify:* _____

2. Mostly, I learned about sex from _____. *(fill in)*

3. Right now, how attractive to you is single life as compared to married life?

   __much better __ better __ about the same __ worse __ much worse

4. Marriage plans:
   __ already married
   __ will marry soon
   __ will marry eventually
   __ probably will not marry

5. How religious would you describe yourself to be?

    ___ very ___ moderately ___ somewhat ___ not at all

6. My preferred sexual partner would be someone:

    __ opposite sex __ same sex __ either

Self Study and Diagnostic Questions

Self-study and diagnostic purposes are also served by questionnaires. In answering particular items, respondents can learn more about themselves, their partners, and relationships.

1. I view my parents' marriage as a happy one.

    ___ Strongly agree
    ___ Agree
    ___ Slightly agree
    ___ Slightly disagree
    ___ Disagree
    ___ Strongly disagree

2. There are household chores specifically suited for men and others for women.

    ___ Strongly agree
    ___ Agree
    ___ Slightly agree
    ___ Slightly disagree
    ___ Disagree
    ___ Strongly disagree

3. Husbands should still be the head of the household.

    ___ Strongly agree
    ___ Agree
    ___ Slightly agree
    ___ Slightly disagree
    ___ Disagree
    ___ Strongly disagree

4. For me, divorce is unacceptable.

    ___ Strongly agree
    ___ Agree
    ___ Slightly agree
    ___ Slightly disagree
    ___ Disagree
    ___ Strongly disagree

5. I have the necessary skills to be a good parent.

___ Strongly agree
___ Agree
___ Slightly agree
___ Slightly disagree
___ Disagree
___ Strongly disagree

6. Only one parent should work, so the other can raise the child.

___ Strongly agree
___ Agree
___ Slightly agree
___ Slightly disagree
___ Disagree
___ Strongly disagree

7. I would seek professional counseling if I thought my marriage was in trouble.

___ Strongly agree
___ Agree
___ Slightly agree
___ Slightly disagree
___ Disagree
___ Strongly disagree

8. Problems in a marriage should stay between the couple, not be discussed with outside family or friends.

___ Strongly agree
___ Agree
___ Lightly agree
___ Slightly disagree
___ Disagree
___ Strongly disagree

9. Marriage is a lifetime relationship that should never be ended except under extreme circumstances.

___ Strongly agree
___ Agree
___ Slightly agree
___ Slightly disagree
___ Disagree
___ Strongly disagree

10. In marriage, the partners must have freedom to also do what they want
individually.

___ Strongly agree
___ Agree
___ Slightly agree
___ Slightly disagree
    Disagree
___ Strongly disagree

Suggested Question

Finally, suggest a question you would like to see asked:

References

Introduction

Allport, Gordon W. 1968. "The historical background of modern social psychology." Pp. 1-80 in G. Lindzey and E. Aronson (Ed.), *The Handbook of Social Psychology*, Second Edition. Reading, MA: Addison-Wesley.

Bellah, Robert N., Richard Madsen, William M. Sullivan, Ann Swidler, and Steven M. Tipton. 1985. *Habits of the Heart: Individualism and Commitment in American Life*. New York: Harper and Row.

Charon, Joel M. 1995. *Ten Questions: A Sociological Perspective*. Belmont, CA: Wadsworth.

Coontz, Stephanie. 1992. *The Way We Never Were: American Families and the Nostalgia Trap*. New York: Basic Books.

DeLora, Jack R. and Joann S. DeLora. 1972. *Intimate Life Styles: Marriage and Its Alternatives*. Pacific Palisades, CA: Goodyear Publishing.

Ford, Clellan S. and Frank A. Beach. 1951. *Patterns of Sexual Behavior*. New York: Harper and Row.

Geertz, Clifford. 1968. "The impact of the concept of culture on the concept of man." Pp.16-29 in Y.A. Cohen (Ed.), *Man and Adaptation: The Cultural Present*. Chicago: Aldine.

Giddens, Anthony. 1982. *Sociology: A Brief But Critical Introduction*. New York: Harcourt Brace Jovanovich.

Harlow, Harry F. and Margaret K. Harlow. 1962. "Social deprivation in monkeys." *Scientific American* 207(5): 137-147.

Kinsey, Alfred C., Wardell B. Pomeroy, and Clyde E. Martin. 1948. *Sexual Behavior in the Human Male*. Philadelphia: W.B. Saunders.

Kinsey, Alfred C., Wardell B. Pomeroy, Clyde E. Martin, and Paul H. Gebhard. 1953. *Sexual Behavior in the Human Female*. Philadelphia, W.B. Saunders.

Kluckhohn, Clyde. 1948. "As an anthropologist views it." Pp. 88-104 in Albert Deutch (Ed.), *Sex Habits of American Men*. New York: Prentice-Hall.

Lauer, Robert H. and Jeannette C. Lauer. 1991. *Marriage and Family: The Quest for Intimacy*. Dubuque, IA: Wm. C. Brown.

Mace, David R. 1985. "Contemporary issues in marriage." Pp. 5-10 in L. Cargan (Ed.), *Marriage and Family: Coping with Change*. Belmont, CA: Wadsworth.

Mills, C. Wright. 1959. *The Sociological Imagination*. New York: Oxford University Press.

Reiss, Ira L. 1988. *Family Systems in America*, Fourth Edition. New York: Holt, Rinehart and Winston.

Robertson, Ian. 1987. "Sexuality and society," pp. 225-249 in *Sociology,* Third Edition. New York: Worth Publishers.
Tiefer, Lenore. 1995. *Sex Is Not a Natural Act and Other Essays.* Boulder, CO: Westview Press.

Chapter 1

Babbi, Earl. 1995. *The Practice of Social Research,* Seventh Edition. Belmont, CA: Wadsworth.
Bartell, Gilbert D. 1970. "Group sex among the mid-Americans." *Journal of Sex Research* 6(2): 113-130.
Benjamin, Lois. 1991. *The Black Elite.* Chicago: Nelson-Hall.
Berardo, Felix M. 1991. "Family research in the 1980s: Recent trends and future directions." Pp.1-11 in A. Booth (Ed.), *Contemporary Families: Looking Forward, Looking Back.* Minneapolis, MN: National Council on Family Relations.
Bogdan, Robert. 1974. *Being Different: The Autobiography of Jane Fry.* New York: John Wiley and Sons.
Charon, Joel M. 1995. *Ten Questions: A Sociological Perspective.* Belmont, CA: Wadsworth.
Day, Randal D., Kathleen R. Gilbert, Barbara H. Settles, and Wesley R. Burr. 1995. *Research and Theory in Family Science.* Pacific Grove, CA: Brooks/Cole.
Etaugh, Claire and Joann Malstrom. 1981. "The effect of marital status on person perception." *Journal of Marriage and the Family* 43(4): 801-805.
Foster, Lawrence. 1991. *Women, Family and Utopia: Communal Experiments of the Shakers, the Oneida Community and the Mormons.* Syracuse, NY: Syracuse University Press.
Glenn, Norval D. 1991. "Quantitative research on marital quality in the 1980s: A critical review." Pp. 28-41 in A. Booth (Ed.), *Contemporary Families: Looking Forward, Looking Back.* Minneapolis, MN: National Council on Family Relations.
Glenn, Norval D. 1997. "Closed hearts, closed minds: The textbook story of marriage." New York: Institute for American Values.
Henry, Jules. 1973. *Pathways to Madness.* New York: Random House.
Humpreys, Laud. 1975. *Tearoom Trade: Impersonal Sex in Public Places,* Second Edition. Chicago: Aldine.
Janus, Samuel S. and Cynthia L. Janus. 1993. *The Janus Report on Sexual Behavior.* New York: John Wiley and Sons.
Kennedy, Robert E. Jr. 1986. *Life Choices: Applying Sociology.* New York: Holt, Rinehart and Winston.
Kephart, William M. and William W. Zellner. 1994. *Extraordinary Groups: An Examination of Unconventional Lifestyles.* New York: St. Martin's.
Kersten, Karen Kayser and Lawrence K. Kersten. 1988. *Marriage and the Family: Studying Close Relationships.* New York: Harper and Row.

Kinsey, Alfred C., Wardell B. Pomeroy, and Clyde E. Martin. 1948. *Sexual Behavior In the Human Male*. Philadelphia: W.B. Saunders

Kinsey, Alfred C., Wardell B. Pomeroy, Clyde E. Martin, and Paul H. Gebhard. 1953. *Sexual Behavior in the Human Female*. Philadelphia: W.B. Saunders.

Kirby, Douglas. 1981. "Methods and methodological problems of sex research." Appendix, pp. 563-592, in J. S. DeLora, C. A. B. Warren, and C. R. Ellison (Eds.). *Understanding Sexual Interaction*, Second Edition. Boston: Houghton Mifflin.

Laing, R. D. and Aaron Esterson. 1970. *Sanity, Madness and the Family*. Baltimore, MD: Penguin Books.

LaRossa, Ralph (Ed.). 1984. *Family Case Studies: A Sociological Perspective*. New York: Macmillan.

Masters, William H. and Virginia E. Johnson. 1966. *Human Sexual Response*. Boston: Little, Brown.

Masters, William H. and Virginia E. Johnson. 1970. *Human Sexual Inadequacy*. Boston: Little, Brown.

Miller, Brent C., J. Kelly McCoy, Terrance D. Olson, and Christopher M. Wallace. 1986. "Parental discipline and control attempts in relation to adolescent sexual attitudes and behavior." *Journal of Marriage and the Family* 48(3): 503-512.

Palson, Charles and Rebecca Palson. 1972. "Swinging in wedlock." *Society* 9(4): 28-37.

Straus, Murray A. and Richard J. Gelles. 1990. *Physical Violence in American Families*. New Brunswick, NJ: Transaction.

Strong, Bryan and Christine DeVault. 1989. *The Marriage and Family Experience*, Fourth Edition. St. Paul, MN: West.

Strong, Bryan and Christine DeVault. 1995. *The Marriage and Family Experience*, Sixth Edition. St. Paul, MN: West.

Weinberg, Martin and Colin Williams. 1974. *Male Homosexuals: Their Problems and Adaptations*. New York: Oxford University Press.

Willie, Charles Vert. 1988. *A New Look at Black Families*, Third Edition. Dix Hills, NY: General Hall.

Chapter 2

Ahlburg, Dennis A. and Carol J. DeVita. 1992. *New Realities of the American Family*, Population Bulletin (vol. 47, no. 2). Washington, DC: Population Reference Bureau.

Ahuvia, Aaron C. and Mara B. Adelman. 1992. "Formal intermediaries in the marriage market: A typology and review." *Journal of Marriage and the Family* 54(2): 452-463.

Aldous, Joan. 1990. "Family development and the life course: Two perspectives on family change." *Journal of Marriage and the Family* 52(3): 571-583.

Allon, Natalie and Diane Fishel. 1981. "Singles bars as examples of urban courting patterns." Pp.115-120 in P. Stein (Ed.), *Single Life: Unmarried Adults in Social Context*. New York: St. Martin's Press.

Bernstein, Barton E. 1985. "So put it in writing." Pp.134-138 in L. Cargan (Ed.), *Marriage and Family: Coping with Change.* Belmont, CA: Wadsworth.

Boss, Pauline G., William J. Doherty, Ralph LaRossa, Walter R. Schumm, and Suzanne K. Steinmetz (Eds.). 1993. *Sourcebook of Family Theories and Methods.* New York: Plenum.

Brown, Susan L. and Alan Booth. 1996. "Cohabitation versus marriage: A comparison of relationship quality." *Journal of Marriage and the Family* 58 (August): 668-678.

Bumpass, Larry. 1990. "What's happening to the family? Interactions between demographic and institutional change." *Demography* 27(4): 483-498.

Bumpass, Larry L., James A. Sweet, and Andrew Cherlin. 1991. "The role of cohabitation in declining rates of marriage." *Journal of Marriage and the Family* 53 (November): 913-927.

Cate, Rodney M., Ted L. Huston, and John R. Nesselroade. 1986. "Premarital relationships: Toward the identification of alternative pathways to marriage." *Journal of Social and Clinical Psychology* 4: 3-22.

Clayton, Richard R. 1979. *The Family, Marriage, and Social Change,* Second Edition. Lexington, MA: D.C. Heath.

Day, Randal D., Kathleen R. Gilbert, Barbara H. Settles, and Wesley R. Burr (Eds.). 1995. *Research and Theory in Family Science.* Pacific Grove, CA: Brooks/Cole.

DeLora, Jack R. and Joann S. DeLora. 1975. "Dating and mate selection." Pp.1-4 in J.R. DeLora and J.S. DeLora (Eds.), *Intimate Lifestyles: Marriage and Its Alternatives.* Pacific Palisades, CA: Goodyear.

Duff, J. and G.G. Truit. 1991. *The Spousal Equivalent Handbook.* Houston, TX: Sunny Beach Publications.

Garrison, M.E. Betsy, Lydia B. Blalock, John J. Zarski, and Penny B. Merritt. 1997. "Delayed parenthood: An exploratory study of family functioning." *Family Relations* 46(3): 281-290.

Glenn, Norval. 1997. *Closed Hearts, Closed Minds: The Textbook Story of Marriage.* New York: Institute for American Values.

Glick, Paul C. and Arthur J. Norton. 1979. "Marrying, divorcing and living together in the U.S. today," *Population Bulletin* vol. 32, no. 5. Washington, DC: Population Reference Bureau.

Glick, Paul C. and Graham Spanier. 1980. "Married and unmarried cohabitation in the United States." *Journal of Marriage and the Family* 42(1): 19-30.

Glick, Paul C. and Graham Spanier. 1981. "Cohabitation in the United States." Pp. 194-209 in P.J. Stein (Ed.), *Single Life: Unmarried Adults in Social Context.* New York: St. Martin's Press.

Hendrick, Clyde and Susan S. Hendrick. 1992. *Liking, Loving and Relating,* Second Edition. Pacific Grove, CA: Brooks/Cole.

Jedlicka, Davor. 1985. "Formal mate selection networks in the United States." Pp. 102-107 in L. Cargan (Ed.), *Marriage and Family: Coping with Change.* Belmont, CA: Wadsworth.

Jentz, Gaylord. 1992. *Texas Family Law,* Seventh Edition. Austin, TX: University of Texas.

Jillson, Joyce. 1984. *The Fine Art of Flirting.* New York: Simon and Schuster.

Kennedy, Robert E. Jr. 1986. *Life Choices: Applying Sociology.* New York: Holt, Rinehart and Winston.

Kerckhoff, Alan C. and Keith E. Davis. 1962. "Value consensus and need complementarity in mate selection." *American Sociological Review* 27(3): 295-303.

Keyes, Ralph. 1975. "Singled out." Pp. 328-337 in J.R. DeLora and J.S. DeLora (Eds.), *Intimate Lifestyles: Marriage and Its Alternatives.* Pacific Palisades, CA: Goodyear.

Klein, David M. and James M. White. 1996. *Family Theories: An Introduction.* Thousand Oaks, CA: Sage.

Knox, David and Kenneth Wilson. 1981. "Dating behaviors of university students." *Family Relations* 30(2): 255-258.

Macklin, Eleanor D. 1975. "Heterosexual cohabitation among unmarried college students." Pp. 291-302 in J.R. DeLora and J.S. DeLora (Eds.), *Intimate Lifestyles: Marriage and Its Alternatives.* Pacific Palisades, CA: Goodyear.

Makepeace, James M. 1997. "Courtship violence as a process: A developmental theory." Pp. 29-47 in A.P. Cardarelli (Ed.), *Violence Between Intimate Partners: Patterns, Causes and Effects.* Needham Heights, MA: Allyn and Bacon.

Murstein, Bernard I. 1970. "Stimulus-value-role: A theory of marital choice." *Journal of Marriage and the Family* 32(3): 465-481.

National Film Board of Canada. 1961. *Courtship.* Montreal: National Film Board.

Population Today. 1995. "Report from PAA: Demographers ponder benefits of marriage, and more." Pp. 3-5 in *Population Today,* vol. 23(6): 3-5.

Rindfuss, Ronald and Audrey VandenHeuvel. 1990. "Cohabitation: A precursor to marriage or an alternative to being single?" *Population and Development Review* 16(4): 703-726.

Rossi, Alice. 1977. "Transition to parenthood." Pp. 219-235 in P.J. Stein, J. Richman, and N. Hannon (Eds.), *The Family: Functions, Conflicts and Symbols.* Reading, MA: Addison-Wesley.

Schoen, Robert and Robin M. Weinick. 1993. "Partner choice in marriages and cohabitations." *Journal of Marriage and the Family* 55(May): 408-414.

Seff, Monica. 1995. "Cohabitation and the law." *Marriage and Family Review* 21 (3-4): 141-168.

Shulman, Alix Kates. 1977. "The war in the back seat." Pp. 150-157 in P.J. Stein, J. Richman, and N. Hannon (Eds.), *The Family: Functions, Conflicts and Symbols.* Reading, MA: Addison-Wesley.

Speer, Ocie. 1961. *Speer's Marital Rights in Texas,* Fourth Edition by Edwin Stacey Oakes. Rochester, NY: Lawyer's Cooperative Publishing.

Sprecher, Susan and Rachita Chandak. 1992. "Attitudes about arranged marriages and dating among men and women from India." *Free Inquiry in Creative Sociology* 20(1): 59-69.

Stein, Peter J. 1977. "Singlehood: An alternative to marriage." Pp. 382-396 in P.J. Stein, J. Richman, and N. Hannon (Eds.), *The Family: Functions, Conflicts and Symbols.* Reading, MA: Addison-Wesley.

Stein, Peter J. 1981. *Single Life: Unmarried Adults in Social Context.* New York: St. Martin's.

Stein, Peter J. 1985. "Major tasks faced by single adults." Pp.116-125 in L. Cargan (Ed.), *Marriage and Family: Coping with Change.* Belmont, CA:Wadsworth.

Surra, Catherine A. 1991. "Research and theory on mate selection and premarital relationships in the 1980s." Pp. 54-75 in A. Booth (Ed.), *Contemporary Families: Looking Forward, Looking Back.* Minneapolis, MN: The National Council on Family Relations.

Texas Family Code. 1996. St. Paul, MN: West.

Thornton, Arland and Deborah Freedman. 1982. "Changing attitudes toward marriage and single life." *Family Planning Perspectives* 14(6): 297-303.

U.S. Bureau of the Census. 1994. "Marital status and living arrangements: March 1994." Current Population Reports, Series P20-484. Washington, DC: Department of Commerce, Bureau of Census.

U.S. Bureau of the Census. 1996. *Statistical abstract of the United States:1996* (116th edition). Washington, DC: Department of Commerce, Bureau of the Census.

Weiss, Robert S. 1981. "The study of loneliness." Pp. 152-163 in P.J. Stein (Ed.), *Single Life: Unmarried Adults in Social Context.* New York: St. Martin's.

Whyte, Martin King. 1990. *Dating, Mating and Marriage.* New York: Aldine de Gruyter.

Whyte, Martin King. 1992. "Choosing mates—the American way." *Society* 29(3): 71-77.

Winton, Chester A. 1995. *Frameworks for Studying Families.* Guilford, CT: Dushkin.

Chapter 3

ASHA. 1991. *STD (VD).* Research Triangle Park, NC: American Social Health Association.

Benford, Robert D. 1992. "Social movements." Pp. 1880-1887 in E.F. Borgotta and M.L. Borgotta (Eds.), *Encyclopedia of Sociology* (volume 4). New York: Macmillan.

Boston Women's Health Book Collective. 1971. *Our Bodies, Ourselves: A Course by and for Women.* Boston: New England Free Press.

CDC Centers for Disease Control. 1990. *Annual Report.* Division of STD/HIV Prevention. Atlanta.

CDC Centers for Disease Control. 1995. *HIV/AIDS Surveillance Report* 6(2). Atlanta.

Charon, Joel M. 1995. *Ten Questions: A Sociological Perspective.* Belmont, CA: Wadsworth.

Cowan, Connell and Melvyn Kinder. 1985. *Smart Women/Foolish Choices.* New York: New American Library.

Cuber, John. 1975. "How new ideas about sex are changing our lives." Pp. 80-86 in J.R. DeLora and J.S. DeLora (Eds.), *Intimate Life Styles: Marriage and Its Alternatives,* Second Edition. Pacific Palisades, CA: Goodyear.

Davis, James A. and Tom W. Smith. 1986. *General Social Surveys, 1972-1986: Cumulative Codebook.* Chicago: National Opinion Research Center.

Davis, James A. and Tom W. Smith. 1994. *General Social Surveys, 1972-1994: Cumulative Codebook.* Chicago: National Opinion Research Center.

Davis, James A. and Tom W. Smith, and C. Bruce Stephenson. 1981. *General Social Survey Cumulative File 1972-1980.* Chicago: National Opinion Reserach Center.

Day, Randal D., Kathleen R. Gilbert, Barbara H. Settles, and Wesley R. Burr. 1995. *Research and Theory in Family Science.* Pacific Grove, CA: Brooks/Cole.

Drinnin, B. 1993. *Human Sexuality in a World of Diversity,* Instructor's Annotated Edition. Boston: Allyn and Bacon.

Durkheim, Emile. 1938. *The Rules of Sociological Method.* New York: Free Press.

Francoeur, Robert T. 1991. *Becoming a Sexual Person,* Second Edition. New York: Macmillan.

Freudberg, Frank and E. Stephen Emanuel. 1982. *Herpes: A Complete Guide.* Philadelphia: Running Press.

Galvin, Kathleen M. and Bernard J. Brommel. 1991. *Family Communication: Cohesion and Change,* Third Edition. New York: Harper Collins.

Goodman, Ellen. 1992. "Female condom isn't sign of empowerment." News column distributed by the Washington Post Writers Group.

Grieco, A. 1987. "Cutting the risks for STDs." *Medical Aspects of Human Sexuality* 21(March): 70.

Gwartney-Gibbs, Patricia A., J. Stockard, and S. Bohmer. 1987. "Learning courtship aggression: The influence of parents, peers and personal experiences. *Family Relations* 36(3): 276-282.

Janus, Samuel S. and Cynthia L. Janus. 1993. *The Janus Report on Sexual Behavior.* New York: John Wiley and Sons.

Kaats, Gilbert R. and Keith E. Davis. 1975. "The dynamics of sexual behavior among college students." Pp. 32-45 in J.R. DeLora and J.S. DeLora (Eds.), *Intimate Lifestyles,* Second Edition. Pacific Palisades, CA: Goodyear.

Kanin, Eugene J. 1985. "Date rapists: Differential sexual socialization and relative deprivation." *Archives of Sexual Behavior* 14(3): 219-231.

Kersten, Karen Kayser and Lawrence K. Kersten. 1988. *Marriage and the Family: Studying Close Relationships.* New York: Harper and Row.

Kirkpatrick, Clifford and Eugene Kanin. 1957. "Male sexual aggression on a university campus." *American Sociological Review* 22(1): 52-58.

Knox, David and Caroline Schacht. 1991. *Choices in Relationships: An Introduction to Marriage and the Family.* St. Paul, MN: West.

Koss, Mary P. 1988. "Afterword." Pp. 189-210 in Robin Warshaw, *I Never Called It Rape.* New York: Harper and Row.

Koss, Mary P. 1992. "Commentary." *Journal of Interpersonal Violence* 7(1):122-126.

Koss, Mary P., Christine A. Gidycz, and Nadine Wisniewski. 1987. "The scope of rape: Incidence and prevalence of sexual aggression and victimization in a national sample of higher education students." *Journal of Consulting and Clinical Psychology* 55(2): 162-170.

Ku, Leighton, Freya L. Sonenstein, and Joseph H. Pleck. 1995. "When we use condoms and why we stop." *Population Today* 23(3).

Lloyd, Sally A. 1991. "The darkside of Courtship: Violence and sexual exploitation." *Family Relations* 40(1): 14-20.

Malamuth, Neil. 1982. "Rape proclivity among males." *Journal of Social Issues* 37(4): 138-157.

Nass, Gilbert D., Roger W. Libby, and Mary Pat Fisher. 1984. *Sexual Choices: An Introduction to Human Sexuality*. Monterey, CA: Wadsworth Health Sciences.

Nevid, Jeffrey S. 1998. *Choices: Sex in the Age of STDs,* Second Edition. Needham Heights, MA: Allyn and Bacon.

Pirog-Good, Maureen A. and Jan E. Stets. 1989. *Violence in Dating Relationships.* New York: Praeger.

Powell, Elizabeth. 1991. *Talking Back to Sexual Pressure.* Minneapolis: CompCare.

Reiss, Ira L. and Gary R. Lee. 1988. *Family Systems in America,* Fourth Edition. New York: Holt, Rinehart and Winston.

Robinson, Ira E., Karl King, and Jack O. Balswick. 1975. "The Premarital Sexual Revolution Among College Females." Pp. 46-52 in J.R. DeLora and J.S. DeLora (Eds.), *Intimate Lifestyles,* Second Edition. Pacific Palisades, CA: Goodyear.

Rouse, Linda P., Richard Breen, and Marilyn Howell. 1988. "Intimate abuse: A comparison of married and dating students." *Journal of Interpersonal Violence* 3(4): 414-429.

Sadeghin, Peggysue. 1989. "Religion and Reproductive Roulette." Master's thesis, University of Texas at Arlington.

Shelton, Deborah. 1996. "STDs: A hidden epidemic." *American Medical News* 39(46): 23, 24. American Medical Association.

Staggenborg, Suzanne. 1996. "The pro-choice movement: Confrontation and direct action." Pp. 398-407 in G. Massey (Ed.), *Readings for Sociology.* New York: W.W. Norton.

Voydanoff, Patricia and Brenda W. Donnelly. 1990. *Adolescent Sexuality and Pregnancy.* Newbury Park, CA: Sage.

Warshaw, Robin. 1988. *I Never Called It Rape: Recognizing, Fighting and Surviving Date and Acquaintance Rape.* New York: Harper and Row.

Wright, Derek. 1975. "The New Tyranny of Sexual 'Liberation.'" Pp. 87-89 in J.R. DeLora and J.S. DeLora (Eds.), *Intimate Lifestyles,* Second Edition, Pacific Palisades, CA: Goodyear.

Chapter 4

Adams, Bert N. 1980. *The Family: A Sociological Interpretation,* Third Edition. San Diego, CA: Harcourt Brace Jovanovich.

Albrecht, Stan L. and Phillip R. Kunz. 1980. "The decision to divorce: A social exchange perspective," *Journal of Divorce* 3(4): 319-337.

Blumstein, Philip and Pepper Schwartz. 1983. *American Couples: Money, Work and Sex.* New York: William Morrow.

Bohannon, Paul. 1985. "The six stations of divorce." Pp. 310, 311 in L. Cargan (Ed.), *Marriage and Family: Coping with Change.* Belmont, CA: Wadsworth.

Breedlove, William and Jerrye Breedlove. 1964. *Swap Clubs.* Los Angeles: Sherbourne.

Byers, E. Sangra and Larry Heinlein. 1989. "Predicting initiations and refusals of sexual activities in married and cohabiting heterosexual couples." *Journal of Sex Research* 26(2): 210-231.

Call, Vaughn, Susan Sprecher, and Pepper Schwartz. 1995. "The incidence and frequency of marital sex in a national sample." *Journal of Marriage and the Family* 57(August): 639-652.

Charny, Israel W. and Sivan Parnass. 1995. *Journal of Sex and Marital Therapy* 21(2): 100-115.

Davis, James A. and Tom W. Smith. 1994. *General Social Surveys, 1972-1994: Cumulative Codebook.* Chicago: National Opinion Research Center.

Denfeld, Duane. 1974. "Dropouts from swinging." *Family Coordinator* 23(1): 45-59.

Denfeld, Duane and Michael Gordon. 1975. "The sociology of mate swapping." Pp. 279-290 in J.R. DeLora and J.S. DeLora (Eds.), *Intimate Life Styles: Marriage and Its Alternatives.* Pacific Palisades, CA: Goodyear.

Donnelly, Denise A. 1993. "Sexually inactive marriages." *Journal of Sex Research* 30(2): 171-179.

Edwards, John and Alan Booth. 1976. "Sexual behavior in and out of marriage." *Journal of Marriage and the Family* 38(1):73-81.

Gebhard, Paul H. 1975. "Factors in marital orgasm." Pp. 96-102 in J.R. DeLora and J.S. DeLora (Eds.), *Intimate Lifestyles: Marriage and Its Alternatives.* Pacific Palisades, CA: Goodyear.

Glass, Shirley P. and Thomas L. Wright. 1992. "Justifications for extramarital relationships: The association between attitudes, behaviors and gender." *Journal of Sex Research* 29: 361-387.

Hite, Shere. 1976. *The Hite Report: A Nationwide Study of Female Sexuality.* New York: Macmillan.

Hite, Shere. 1981. *The Hite Report on Male Sexuality.* New York: Ballantine.

Hunt, Morton. 1974. *Sexual Behavior in the 1970s.* Chicago: Playboy Press.

Janus, Samuel S. and Cynthia L. Janus. 1993. *The Janus Report on Sexual Behavior.* New York: John Wiley and Sons.

Knox, David and Caroline Schacht. 1991. *Choices in Relationships: An Introduction to Marriage and the Family,* Third Edition. St. Paul, MN: West.

Masters, William H., Virginia E. Johnson, and Robert C. Kolodny. 1985. *Human Sexuality,* Second Edition. Boston: Little, Brown.

Oggins, Jean, Douglas Leber, and Joseph Veroff. 1993. "Race and gender differences in black and white newlyweds' perceptions of sexual and marital relations." *Journal of Sex Research* 30(2): 152-160.

O'Neill, Nena and George O'Neill. 1972. *Open Marriage.* New York: M. Evans.

O'Neill, Nena and George O'Neill. 1975. "Open marriage: A synergic model." Pp. 150-158 in Jack R. and Joann S. DeLora (Eds.) *Intimate Lifestyles: Marriage and Its Alternatives.* Pacific Palisades, CA: Goodyear.

Patterson, James and Peter Kim. 1991. *The Day America Told the Truth.* New York: Prentice-Hall.

*Population Today.*1995. "Report from PAA: Demographers ponder benefits of marriage, . . . and more." (June): 23(6) 3-5.

Ross, Catherine E. 1995. "Reconceptualizing marital status as a continuum of social attachment." *Journal of Marriage and the Family* 57(February): 129-140.

Snyder, Douglas and Phyllis Berg. 1983. "Determinants of sexual dissatisfaction in sexually distressed couples." *Archives of Sexual Behavior* 12(3): 237-247.

Tannen, Deborah. 1990. *You Just Don't Understand: Women and Men in Conversation.* New York: Ballantine Books.

Texas Family Code. 1996. St. Paul, MN: West.

Thompson, Anthony P. 1984. "Emotional and sexual components of extramarital relations." *Journal of Marriage and the Family* 46(1): 35-42.

Wadsworth-Denny, Nancy, Jeffrey K. Field, and David Quadagno. 1984. "Sex differences in sexual needs and desires." *Archives of Sexual Behavior* 13(3): 233-247.

Weiss, David L. 1983. "The emergence of nonexclusive models of the marital relationship." Pp. 199-209 in E.D. Macklin and R.H. Rubins (Eds.), *Contemporary Families and Alternate Lifestyles.* Beverly Hills, CA: Sage.

Wheaton, Blair. 1990. "Life transitions, role histories and mental health." *American Sociological Review* 55(2): 209-223.

Whitehurst, Robert N. 1977. "Open marriage: Problems and prospects." Pp. 342-352 in P.J. Stein, J. Richman, and N. Hannon (Eds.), *The Family: Functions, Conflicts and Symbols.* Reading, MA: Addison-Wesley.

Woestendieck, John. 1998. "Swinging in Dallas." *Star-Telegram,* Fort Worth, TX, March 1.

Wolf, Robin. 1996. *Marriages and Families in a Diverse Society.* New York: Harper Collins.

Chapter 5

Al Anon. 1976. *Alcoholics Anonymous.* New York: Alcoholics Anonymous World Services.

American Psychiatric Association. (1994). *Diagnostic and Statistical Manual of Mental Disorders*, Fourth Edition. Washington, DC: The American Psychiatric Association.

Bryant, Clifton D. (Ed.). 1977. *Sexual Deviancy in Social Context*. New York: New Viewpoints/Franklin Watts.

Bryant, Clifton D. 1982. *Sexual Deviancy and Social Proscription*. New York: Human Sciences.

Carnes, Patrick. 1990. *Don't Call It Love*. Bantam Books.

Carnes, Patrick. 1992. "Learning from sexual addiction: Healthy sexuality." *Recovery* (April): 15, 20.

Cozic, Charles P. 1995. *Sexual Values: Opposing Viewpoints*. San Diego, CA: Greenhaven.

Dietz, Paula (Ed.). 1985. *Texas Criminal Laws*. Austin, TX: Department of Public Safety.

Francoeur, Robert T. 1991. *Becoming a Sexual Person*, Second Edition, New York: Macmillan.

Gagnon, John H. and William Simon. 1967. *Sexual Deviance*. New York: Harper and Row.

Gagnon, John H. and William Simon. 1973. *Sexual Conduct*. Chicago: Aldine.

Giddens, Anthony. 1996. *Introduction to Sociology*, Second Edition. New York: W.W. Norton.

Greenberg, Jerrold S., Clint E. Bruess, and Debra W. Haffner. 2000. *Exploring the Dimensions of Human Sexuality*. Sudbury, MA: Jones and Bartlett.

Harrison, Marvel and Terry Kellogg. 1992. "Sexual addiction." *Recovery* (April): 9,18.

Holland, Michael. 1985. "Sexual hang-ups." Student presentation, University of Texas at Arlington.

Hoshii, Iwao. 1987. *Sex in Ethics and Law*. Woodchurch, England: Paul Norbury.

Janus, Samuel S. and Cynthia L. Janus. 1993. *The Janus Report on Sexual Behavior*. New York: John Wiley and Sons.

Kaplan, Helen Singer. 1979. *Disorders of Sexual Desire*. New York: Brunner/Mazel.

Kaplan, Helen Singer. 1995. *The Sexual Desire Disorders: Dysfunctional Regulation of Sexual Motivation*. New York: Brunner/Mazel.

King, Bruce M., Cameron J. Camp, and Ann M. Downey. 1991. *Human Sexuality Today*. Englewood Cliffs, NJ: Prentice-Hall.

Kinsey, Alfred C., Wardell B. Pomeroy, and Clyde E. Martin. 1948. *Sexual Behavior in the Human Male*. Philadelphia: W.B. Saunders.

Kinsey, Alfred C., Wardell B. Pomeroy, Clyde E. Martin, and Paul H. Gebhard. 1953. *Sexual Behavior in the Human Female*. Philadelphia: W.B. Saunders.

Landers, Ann. 1989. Column, *Dallas Morning News*, November 5.

Masters, William H., Virginia E. Johnson, and Robert C. Kolodny. 1992. *Human Sexuality*, Fourth Edition. New York: Harper Collins.

Matousek, Mark. 1993. *Common Boundary,* March/April.

Matousek, Mark. 1995. "Sexual addiction is a serious problem." Pp.176-183 in B. Stalcup (Ed.), *Human Sexuality: Opposing Viewpoints.* San Diego: Greenhaven Press.

McWhorter, William. 1977. "Flashing and dashing: Notes and comments on the etiology of exhibitionism." Pp. 101-108 in C. D. Bryant (Ed.), *Sexual Deviancy in Social Context.* New York: New Viewpoints/Franklin Watts.

Parmelee, Maurice. 1966. *The Play Function of Sex.* New York: Vantage Press.

Rice, F. Philip. 1989. *Human Sexuality.* Dubuque, IA: Wm. C. Brown.

Roberson, Cliff. 1996. *Texas Criminal Law.* Thousand Oaks, CA: Sage.

Rosellini, Lynn. 1995. "Many Americans are unsatisfied with their sex lives." Pp. 203-211 in B. Stalcup (Ed.), *Human Sexuality: Opposing Viewpoints.* San Diego: Greenhaven Press.

Rubin, Lilian Breslow. 1976. *Worlds of Pain: Life in the Working Class Family.* New York: Basic Books.

Stoller, Robert J. 1977. "Sexual deviations." Pp. 204-205 in F. A. Beach (Ed.), *Human Sexuality in Four Perspectives.* Baltimore, MD: Johns Hopkins University Press.

Strean, Herbert S. 1983. *The Sexual Dimension.* New York: Free Press.

Strong, Bryan, Christine DeVault, and Barbara Werner Sayad. 1999. *Human Sexuality: Diversity in Contemporary America,* Third Edition. Mountain View, CA: Mayfield.

Templeman, T. and R. Stinnett. 1991. "Patterns of sexual arousal and history in a 'normal' sample of young men." *Archives of Sexual Behavior* 20(2): 137-150.

Tiefer, Leonore. 1995. *Sex Is Not a Natural Act and Other Essays.* Boulder, CO: Westview.

Wood, Frederic C. Jr. 1968. *Sex and the New Morality.* New York: Newman Press.

Chapter 6

Allen, Catherine R. and David H. Demo. 1995. "The families of lesbians and gay men: A new frontier of family research." *Journal of Marriage and the Family* 57(1): 111-127.

Bieber, Irving. 1962. *Homosexuality: A Psychoanalytic Study.* New York: Basic Books.

Bigner, Jerry J. and R. Brooke Jacobsen. 1989. "The value of children to gay and heterosexual fathers." Pp. 163-172 in F.W. Bozett (Ed.), *Homosexuality and the Family.* Binghamton, NY: Harrington Park Press.

Blumenfeld, Warren J. and Diane Raymond. 1993. *Looking at Gay and Lesbian Life,* Second Edition. Boston: Beacon Press.

Blumstein, Philip and Pepper Schwartz. 1983. *American Couples: Work, Money, Sex.* New York: Morrow.

Bono, Chastity and Billie Fitzpatrick. 1998. *Family Outing.* Boston: Little, Brown.

Bozett, Frederick W. 1987. *Gay and Lesbian Parents.* New York: Praeger.

Bozett, Frederick W. (Ed.) 1989. *Homosexuality and the Family*. Binghamton, NY: Harrington Park Press. See also special issue of the *Journal of Homosexuality*, 1989, 18 (1/2).

Cooley, Charles Horton. 1983. *Human Nature and the Social Order*. New Brunswick, NJ: Transaction.

Cornett, Carlton. 1995. "Homosexuality is normal behavior." Pp. 139-145 in B. Stalcup (Ed.), *Human Sexuality: Opposing Viewpoints*. San Diego, CA: Greenhaven Press.

D' Augelli, Anthony and Charlotte J. Patterson (Eds.). 1995. *Lesbian, Gay, and Bisexual Identities over the Lifespan*. New York: Oxford University Press.

Davis, James A. and Tom W. Smith. 1986. *General Social Surveys, 1972-1986: Cumulative Codebook*. Chicago: National Opinion Research Center.

Davis, James A. and Tom W. Smith. 1994. *General Social Surveys, 1972-1994: Cumulative Codebook*. Chicago: National Opinion Research Center.

Fassinger, Ruth E. 1991. "The hidden minority: Issues and challenges in working with lesbians and gay men." *Counseling Psychologist* 19(2): 157-176.

Ford, Clellan S. and Frank A. Beach. 1951. "Human sexual behavior in perspective." Pp. 250-267 in *Patterns of Sexual Behavior*. New York: Harper and Row. Reprinted, pp. 155-171, in Arlene S. Skolnick and Jerome H. Skolnick (Eds.). 1971. *Family in Transition*. Boston: Little, Brown.

Gagnon, John and Bruce Henderson. 1977. "The social psychology of sexual development." Pp. 116-121 in A. Skolnick and J. H. Skolnick (Eds.), *Family in Transition*, Second Edition. Boston: Little, Brown.

Gilbert, Lucia Albino. 1993. *Two Careers/One Family*. Newbury Park, CA: Sage.

Gould, Stephen Jay. 1986. "Of wasps and WASPS: Farewell to pigeonroles." *Networker* (January-February): 13-17.

Hare, Jan. 1994. "Concerns and issues faced by families headed by a lesbian couple." *Families in Society: The Journal of Contemporary Human Services* 75(1): 27-35.

Harry, Joseph. 1983. "Gay male and lesbian relationships." Pp. 216-234 in E. D. Macklin and R. H. Rubin (Eds.), *Contemporary Families and Alternative Life Styles*. Beverly Hills, CA: Sage.

Harvard Law Review (Eds.). 1990. *Sexual Orientation and the Law*. Cambridge, MA: Harvard University Press.

Herdt, Gilbert (Ed.). 1992. *Gay Culture in America: Essays from the Field*. Boston: Beacon.

Hunter, Ski, Coleen Shannon, Jo Knox, and James I. Martin. 1998. *Lesbian, Gay and Bisexual Youths and Adults*. Thousand Oaks, CA: Sage.

Janus, Samuel S. and Cynthia L. Janus. 1993. *The Janus Report on Sexual Behavior*. New York: John Wiley and Sons.

Kinsey, Alfred, Wardell B. Pomeroy, and Clyde E. Martin.1948. *Sexual Behavior in the Human Male*. Philadelphia: W. B. Saunders.

Kinsey, Alfred, Wardell B. Pomeroy, Clyde E. Martin, and Paul H. Gebhard. 1953. *Sexual Behavior in the Human Female*. Philadelphia: W.B. Saunders.

Kreston, Jo-Ann and Claudia S. Bepko. 1980. "The problem of fusion in the lesbian relationship." *Family Process* 19(3): 277-289.

Kurdek, Lawrence A. 1991. "Sexuality in homosexual and heterosexual couples." Pp. 177-191 in K. McKinney and S. Sprecher (Eds.), *Sexuality in Close Relationships.* Hillsdale, NJ: Lawrence Erlbaum.

Laird, J. 1993. "Lesbian and gay families." Pp. 282-328 in F. Walsh (Ed.), *Normal Family Processes,* Second Edition. New York: Guilford.

Laumann, Edward O., John H. Gagnon, Robert T. Michael, and Stuart Michaels. 1994. *The Social Organization of Sexuality: Sexual Practices in the United States.* Chicago: University of Chicago Press.

Mackey, Richard A., Bernard A. O'Brien, and Eileen F. Mackey. 1997. *Gay and Lesbian Couples.* Westport, CT: Praeger.

Marmor, Judd (Ed.). 1980. *Homosexual Behavior: A Modern Reappraisal.* New York: Basic Books.

Masters, William H. and Virginia E. Johnson. 1979. *Homosexuality in Perspective.* Boston: Little, Brown.

McWhirter, David P. and Andrew M. Mattison. 1984. *The Male Couple.* Englewood Cliffs, NJ: Prentice-Hall.

Nass, Gilbert, Roger W. Libby, and Mary Pat Fisher. 1984. *Sexual Choices: An Introduction to Human Sexuality.* Monterey, CA: Wadsworth.

National Association of Social Workers. 1984. "What non-gay therapists need to know to work with gay and lesbian clients." *Practice Digest* 7(1): 28-31.

National Association of Social Workers. 1996. *The NASW Code of Ethics.* Washington, DC: NASW.

Ortiz, Elizabeth T. and Patrick R. Scott. 1994. "Gay husbands and fathers: Reasons for marriage among homosexual men." *Journal of Gay and Lesbian Social Services* 1(1): 59-71.

Patterson, Charlotte J. 1992. "Children of lesbian and gay parents." *Child Development* 63(5): 1025-1042.

Patterson, C.J. 1994. "Lesbian and gay families." *Current Directions in Psychological Science* 3(2): 62-64.

Peplau, Letitia A. 1981. "What homosexuals want in relationships." *Psychology Today* 15(3): 28-38.

Robertson, Ian. 1981. "Sexuality and society" in *Sociology.* New York: Worth.

Robertson, Ian. 1987. "Sexuality and society." Pp. 223-249 in *Sociology.* New York: Worth.

Slater, Suzanne and Julie Mencher. 1991. "The lesbian family lifecycle: A contextual approach." *American Journal of Orthopsychiatry* 61(3): 372-382.

Socarides, Charles W. 1994. *Washington Times,* July 5.

Stalcup, Brenda (Ed.). 1995. *Human Sexuality: Opposing Viewpoints.* San Diego, CA: Greenhaven Press.

Sutcliffe, Lynn. 1995. *There Must Be Fifty Ways to Tell Your Mother.* London: Cassell.

Tafoya, Terry. 1995. "Society should celebrate all forms of sexuality." Pp. 86-92 in B. Stalcup (Ed.), *Human Sexuality: Opposing Viewpoints.* San Diego, CA: Greenhaven Press.

Tully, Carol T. 1994. "To boldly go where no one has gone before: The legalization of lesbian and gay marriages." *Journal of Gay and Lesbian Social Services* 1(1): 73-87.

Wiggins, James A., Beverly B. Wiggins, and James Vander Zanden. 1994. *Social Psychology,* Fifth Edition. New York: McGraw-Hill.

Chapter 7

Ahlburg, Dennis A. and Carol J. DeVita. 1992. "New realities of the American family." *Population Bulletin,* 47(2).

Anderson, Margaret L. 1993. *Thinking About Women: Sociological Perspectives on Sex and Gender.* New York: Macmillan.

Barnett, Rosalind C., Nancy L. Marshall, and Judith D. Singer. 1992. "Job experiences over time, multiple roles and women's mental health: A longitudinal study." *Journal of Personality and Social Psychology* 62(4): 634-644.

Beck, Joan. 1985. "Working moms face backlash." *Fort Worth Star-Telegram.* March 24, 1985. Chicago: Chicago Tribune Media Services.

Booth, Alan and John N. Edwards. 1992. "Starting over: Why remarriages are more unstable." *Journal of Family Issues* 13(2): 179-194.

Bray, James H. and Sandra H. Berger. 1990. "Non-custodial father and paternal grandparent relationships in stepfamilies." *Family Relations* 39(4): 414-419.

Brazelton, T. Berry. 1992. *Touchpoints: Your Child's Emotional and Behavioral Development.* Reading, MA: Perscus Books.

Cherlin, Andrew. 1978. "Remarriage as an incomplete institution." *American Journal of Sociology* 84(3): 634-650.

Coontz, Stephanie. 1992. *The Way We Never Were.* New York: Basic Books.

Coontz, Stephanie. 1997. *The Way We Really Are.* New York: Basic Books.

Fine, Mark A., Brenda W. Donnelly, and Patricia Voydanoff. 1991. "The relation between adolescents' perceptions of their family lives and their adjustment in stepfather families." *Journal of Adolescent Research* 6(4): 423-436.

Furstenberg, Frank F. Jr. 1979. "Recycling the family: Perspectives on a neglected family form." *Marriage and Family Review* 2(3): 12-22.

Ganong, Lawrence H. and Marilyn Coleman. 1984. "The effects of remarriage on children: A review of the empirical literature." *Family Relations* 33(3): 389-406.

Ganong, Lawrence H. and Marilyn Coleman. 1992. "Gender differences in expectations of self and future partner." *Journal of Family Issues* 13(1): 55-64.

Gilbert, Lucia A. 1993. *Two Careers/One Family.* Newbury Park, CA: Sage.

Gilbert, Lucia A., Suzanne Dancer, Karen M. Rossman, and Brian L. Thorn. 1991. "Assessing perceptions of occupational-family integration." *Sex Roles* 24(1/2): 107-119.

Hobart, Charles. 1990. "Relationships between the formerly married." *Journal of Divorce and Remarriage* 14(2): 1-23.

Hobart, Charles. 1991. "Conflict in remarriages." *Journal of Divorce and Remarriage* 15(3/4): 69-86.

Hochschild, Arlie. 1989. *The Second Shift: Working Parents and the Revolution at Home.* New York: Viking Penguin.

Kimmel, Michael. 1996. *Manhood in America: A Cultural History.* New York: Free Press.

Kimmel, Michael S. and Michael A. Messner. 1998. *Men's Lives,* Fourth Edition, Boston: Allyn and Bacon.

Knaub, Patricia Kain, Deanna Baxtor Eversoll, and Jacqueline Holm Voss. 1983. "Is parenthood a desirable role?: An assessment of attitudes held by contemporary women." *Sex Roles* 9(3): 355-362.

Kohen, Janet, Carol A. Brown, and Roslyn Feldberg. 1981. "Divorced mothers: The costs and benefits of female family control." Pp. 288-305 in P.J. Stein (Ed.), *Single Life: Unmarried Adults in Social Context.* New York: St. Martin's Press.

Kurdek, Lawrence A. 1990. "Effects of child age on the marital quality and psychological distress of newly married mothers and stepfathers." *Journal of Marriage and the Family* 52(1): 81-85.

Mainardi, Pat. 1975. "The politics of housework." Pp. 237-241 in J. R. DeLora and J.S. DeLora (Eds.), *Intimate Lifestyles: Marriage and Its Alternatives.* Pacific Palisades, CA: Goodyear.

Mead, Margaret. 1935/1969. *Sex and Temperment in Three Primitive Societies.* New York: Dell.

NBC. 1986. *How Divorce Is Changing America.* Documentary. National Broadcasting Corp.

Olson, Myrna and Judith Haynes. 1993. "Successful single parents." *Journal of Contemporary Human Services*: 74(5):259-287.

Pasley, Kay and Marilyn Ihinger-Tallman. 1994. *Stepparenting: Issues in Theory, Research and Practice.* Westport, CN: Praeger.

Pleck, Joseph. 1975. "Work and family roles: From sex-patterned segregation to integration." Paper presented at the annual meeting of the American Sociological Association, San Francisco, CA.

Pleck, Joseph H. 1992. "Work-family policies in the United States." Pp. 248-275 in H. Kahne and J. Giele (Eds.), *Women's Lives and Women's Work: Parallels and Contrasts in Modernizing and Industrial Countries.* Boulder, CO: Westview.

Pleck, Joseph H. 1994. "Are family-supportive employer policies relevant to men?" Pp. 217-237 in Jane C. Hood (Ed.), *Men, Work, and Family.* Newbury Park, CA: Sage.

Rapoport, Rhona and Robert N. Rapoport. 1969. "The dual career family." *Human Relations* 22(1): 3-30.

Rossi, Alice. 1977. "Transition to parenthood." *Journal of Marriage and the Family* 30(1): 26-39.

Schroeder, Pat. 1998. *24 Years of House Work and the Place Is Still a Mess: My Life in Politics.* Kansas City: Andrews McMeel Publishing.

Spock, Benjamin and Steven Parker. 1998. *Baby and Child Care,* Seventh Edition. New York: Penguin Putnam.

Staples, Robert. 1977. "Public policy and the changing status of black families." Pp. 111-117 in P.J. Stein, J. Richmon and N. Hannon (Eds.), *The Family: Functions, Conflicts and Symbols.* Reading, MA: Addison-Wesley.

Stein, Peter J. (Ed.) 1981. *Single Life: Unmarried Adults in Social Context.* New York: St. Martin's.

Stewart, D. L. 1986. "Busy parent misses joys of fatherhood." *McNaught Syndicate.* Chicago: Chicago Tribune Media Services.

Tennyson, Alfred Lord. 1902. *In Memoriam, The Princess and Maud.* London: Methuen.

Turnbull, James M. and Sharon K. Turnbull. 1986. "To dream the impossible dream: An agenda for discussion with step-parents." Pp. 143-145 in O. Pocs and R.H. Walsh (Eds.), *Marriage and Family Annual Editions 85/86.* Guilford, CT: Dushkin Publishing.

U.S. Bureau of the Census. 1999. Press release.

U.S. Department of Labor, Women's Bureau. 1989. *Employers and Child Care: Benefiting Work and Family.* Washington, DC: Government Printing Office.

U.S. Department of Labor, Women's Bureau. 1991. *Facts on Working Women.* Washington, DC: Government Printing Office.

Vuchinich, Samuel, E. Mavis Hetherington, Regina A.Vuchinich, and W. Glenn Clingempeel. 1991. "Parent-child interaction and gender differences in early adolescents' adaptation to stepfamilies." *Developmental Psychology* 27(4): 618-626.

Wallerstein, Judith S. and Susan Blakeslee. 1989. *Second Chances: Men, Women and Children a Decade After Divorce.* New York: Ticknor and Fields.

Weitzman, Lenore J. 1977. "To love, honor and obey?: Traditional legal marriage and alternative family forms." Pp. 118-135 in P.J. Stein, J. Richman, and N. Hannon (Eds.), *The Family: Functions, Conflicts and Symbols.* Reading, MA: Addison-Wesley.

Weitzman, Lenore J. 1985. *The Divorce Revolution: The Unexpected Social and Economic Consequences for Women and Children in America.* New York: Free Press.

Williams, John E. and Deborah L. Best. 1990. *Measuring Sex Stereotypes: A Multination Study.* Newbury Park, CA: Sage.

Chapter 8

Aiken, Lewis R. 1982. *Later Life,* Second Edition. New York: Holt, Rinehart and Winston.

Bowen, Gary L. and Jack M. Richman. 1991. "The willingness of spouses to seek marriage and family counseling services." *Journal of Primary Prevention* 11(4): 277-293.

Braito, Rita and Donna Anderson. 1980. "Singles and aging: Implications for needed research." Pp. 327-334 in P.J. Stein (Ed.), *Single Life: Unmarried Adults in Social Context*. New York: St. Martin's.

Brehm, Sharon S. 1985. "Therapeutic interventions." Pp. 363-386 in *Intimate Relationships*. New York: Random House.

Bringle, Robert C. and Diane Byers. 1997. "Intentions to seek marriage counseling." *Family Relations* 46(3): 299-304.

Bulcroft, Kris A. and Richard A. Bulcroft. 1991. "The nature and functions of dating in later life." *Research on Aging* 13(2): 244-260.

Campbell, James L. and Mark E. Johnson. 1991. "Marital status and gender similarity in marital therapy." *Journal of Counseling and Development* 69(4): 363-366.

Cargan, Leonard (Ed.). 1985. *Marriage and Family: Coping with Change*. Belmont, CA: Wadsworth.

Carter, Betty and Monica McGoldrick (Eds.). 1999. *The Expanded Family Lifecycle: Individual, Family and Social Perspectives*. Boston: Allyn and Bacon.

Chevan, Albert. 1996. "As cheaply as one: Cohabitation in the older population." *Journal of Marriage and the Family* 58(August): 656-667.

Cicirelli, Victor. 1995. *Sibling Relations Across the Life Span*. New York: Plenum.

Family Therapy News. 1990. "Healthy families featured in Washington conference." (July/August): 8.

Gubrium, Jaber. 1975. "Being single in old age." *International Journal of Aging and Human Development* 6(1): 29-41.

Hallstrom, Tore and Sverker Samuelsson. 1990. "Changes in women's sexual desire in middle life." *Archives of Sexual Behavior* 9(3): 259-267.

Hillig, Chuck. 1985. "Your beliefs can sabotage your relationships." Pp. 182-184 in L. Cargan (Ed.), *Marriage and Family: Coping with Change*. Belmont, CA: Wadsworth.

Kaslow, Florence W. and Helga Hammerschmidt. 1992. "Long term 'good' marriages: The seemingly essential ingredients." *Journal of Couples Therapy* 3(2/3): 15-38.

Kellett, J.M. 1991. "Sexuality of the elderly." *Sexual and Marital Therapy* 6(2): 147-155.

Kinsey, Alfred C., Wardell B. Pomeroy, and Clyde W. Martin. 1948. *Sexual Behavior in the Human Male*. Philadelphia: W. B. Saunders.

Larson, Jeffry H. and Thomas B. Holman. 1994. "Premarital predictors of marital quality and stability." *Family Relations* 43(2): 228-237.

Larson, Jeffry H., Thomas B. Holman, David M. Klein, and Dean M. Busby. 1995. "A review of comprehensive questionnaires used in premarital education and counseling." *Family Relations* 44(3): 245-252.

Lauer, Robert H. and Jeanette C. Lauer. 1986. "Factors in long-term marriages." *Journal of Family Issues* 7(4): 382-390.

Lazarus, Arnold A. 1995. "Adjusting the carburetor: Pivotal clinical interventions in marital and sex therapy." Pp. 81-85 in R.C. Rosen and S.R. Leiblum (Eds.), *Case Studies in Sex Therapy.* New York: Guilford.

Levine, Stephan B. 1995. "The vagaries of sexual desire." Pp. 96-109 in R.C. Rosen and S.R. Leiblum (Eds.), *Case Studies in Sex Therapy.* New York: Guilford.

Litwin, H. 1996. *The social networks of older people,* Greenwood, CT: Praeger.

Mackey, Richard E. and Bernard A. O'Brien. 1995. *Lasting Marriages: Men and Women Growing Together.* Westport, CT: Praeger.

Maltin, Lawrence and Joan D. Atwood. 1992. "The tasks and traps of relationships." *Journal of Couples Therapy* 3(4): 111-131.

Masters, William H. and Virginia E. Johnson. 1966. *Human Sexual Response.* Boston: Little, Brown.

Masters, William H. and Virginia E. Johnson. 1970. *Human Sexual Inadequacy.* Boston: Little, Brown.

Masters, William H., Virginia E. Johnson, and Robert C. Kolodny. 1982. *Human Sexuality.* Boston: Little, Brown.

Masters, William H., Virginia E. Johnson, and Robert C. Kolodny. 1992. *Human Sexuality,* Fourth Edition. New York: Harper Collins.

Matthews, Sarah. 1994. "Men's ties to siblings in old age." Pp. 178-196 in Thompson (Ed.), *Older Men's Lives.* Thousand Oaks, CA: Sage.

Newsweek. 1983. "A great emptiness." November 7, 120-126. Reprinted pp.152-155, in O. Pocs and R.H. Walsh (Eds.), *Annual Editions: Marriage and Family 85/86.* Guilford, CT: Dushkin.

Olson, David H. 1991. *Building a Strong Marriage.* Minneapolis: Prepare/Enrich.

Olson, David H. and Dale R. Hawley. 1992. *Self-training counselor's manual: Prepare-Enrich.* Minneapolis: Prepare/Enrich.

Palmore, Erdman. 1981. *Social Patterns in Normal Aging: Findings from the Duke Longitudinal Study.* Durham, NC: Duke University Press.

Porcino, Jane. 1985. "The need for intimacy." Pp. 152-155 in O. Pocs and R. H. Walsh (Eds.), *Annual Editions: Marriage and Family 85/86.* Guilford, CT: Dushkin.

Rosen, Raymond C. and Sandra R. Leiblum. 1995. *Case Studies in Sex Therapy.* New York: Guilford.

Rubin, Isadore. 1968. "The 'sexless older years': A socially harmful stereotype." *The Annals of the American Academy of Political and Social Sciences* 376 (March): 86-95.

Sex Over Forty. 1982. Saul H. Rosenthal, editor. Chapel Hill, NC: PHE, Inc.

Stein, Peter J. 1981. *Single Life: Unmarried Adults in Social Context.* New York: St. Martin's.

Stinnett, Nick. 1985. "In search of strong families." Pp.172-176 in L. Cargan (Ed.), *Marriage and Family: Coping with Change*. Belmont, CA: Wadsworth.

Strong, Bryan, Christine DeVault, and Barbara Sayad. 1998. *The Marriage and Family Experience*, Seventh Edition. Belmont, CA: Wadsworth.

Thompson, Edward H. Jr. (Ed.) 1994. *Older Men's Lives*. Thousand Oaks, CA: Sage.

Ubell, Earl. 1984. "How to think clearly." *Parade Magazine*, October 7. 12,14,15.

Walker, Bonnie. 1997. *Sexuality and the Elderly: A Research Guide*. Westport, CT: Greenwood.

Wallerstein, Judith S. and Sandra Blakeslee. 1995. *The Good Marriage*. New York: Warner Books.

Walsh, Froma. 1999. "Families in later life: Challenges and opportunities." Pp. 307-326 in B. Carter and M. McGoldrick (Eds.), *The Expanded Family Life Cycle: Individual, Family and Social Perspectives*. Boston: Allyn and Bacon.

Wiggins, James A., Beverly B. Wiggins, and James Vander Zanden. 1994. *Social Psychology*, Fifth Edition. New York: McGraw-Hill.

Chapter 9

Axinn, Wiliam G. and Jennifer S. Barber. 1997. "Living arrangements and family formation attitudes in early adulthood." *Journal of Marriage and the Family* 59(3): 595-611.

Britton, Thomas F. 1990. "How shall we end the century? Behavior and sexually transmitted disease." *Our Sexuality Update: Newsletter for Human Sexuality Instruction*. Redwood City, CA: Benjamin/Cummings.

Bumpass, Larry, James Sweet, and Andrew Cherlin. 1991. "The role of cohabitation in declining rates of marriage." *Journal of Marriage and the Family* 53(4): 913-927.

Demo, David H., Katherine R. Allen, and Mark A. Fine (Eds.). 2000. *Handbook of Family Diversity*. New York: Oxford University Press.

Depner, Charlene E. and James A. Bray (Eds.). 1993. *Nonresidential Parenting: New Vistas in Family Living*. Newbury Park, CA: Sage.

Eshleman, J. Ross. 1997. *The Family*, Eighth Edition. Needham Heights, MA: Allyn and Bacon.

Goldstein, Abraham S. and Joseph Goldstein (Eds.) 1971. *Crime, Law, and Society*. New York: Free Press.

Herold, Edward S., Kathryn E. Kopf, and Maria DeCarlo. 1974. "Family life education: Student perspectives." *Canadian Journal of Public Health* 65(September/October): 365-368.

Janus, Samuel S. and Cynthia L. Janus. 1993. *The Janus Report on Sexual Behavior*. New York: John Wiley and Sons.

Josselson, Ruthellen. 1996. *Revising Herself*. New York: Oxford University Press.

Kissman, Kris and Jo Ann Allen. 1993. *Single-Parent Families*. Newbury Park, CA: Sage.

Kohler, Julie K. and Shirley L. Zimmerman. 2000. "Policy issues and families over the life course." Pp. 230-241 in S.J. Price, P.C. McKenry and M.J. Murphy (Eds.), *Families Across Time: A Life Course Perspective*. Los Angeles: Roxbury.

Lazarus, Arnold A. 1995. "Adjusting the carburetor: Pivotal clinical interventions in marital and sex therapy." Pp. 81-95 in R. C. Rosen and S. R. Leiblum, *Case Studies in Sex Therapy*. New York: Guilford.

Leigh, Geoffrey K. 2000. "Cohabiting and never-married families across the life course." Pp. 79-89 in S.J. Price, P.C. McKenry and M.J. Murphy, *Families Across Time: A Life Course Perspective*. Los Angeles: Roxbury.

Lerner, Richard M., Elizabeth E. Sparks, and Laurie D. McCubbin. 2000. "Family diversity and family policy." Pp. 380-401 in D.H. Demo, K.R. Allen, and M.A. Fine (Eds.). *Handbook of Family Diversity*. New York: Oxford University Press.

Mackey, Richard E. and Bernard A. O'Brien. 1995. *Lasting Marriages: Men and Women Growing Together*. Westport, CT: Praeger.

Macklin, Eleanor D. 1987. "Nontraditional family forms." Pp. 317-351 in M. B. Sussman and S.K. Steinmetz (Eds.), *Handbook of Marriage and the Family*. New York: Plenum.

Manning, Wendy D. and Daniel T. Lichter. 1996. "Parental cohabitation and children's economic well-being." *Journal of Marriage and the Family* 58(4): 998-1010.

Marks, Stephen R. and Leigh A. Leslie. 2000. "Family diversity and intersecting categories: Towards a richer approach to multiple roles." Pp. 402-423 in D.H. Demo, K.R. Allen, and M.A. Fine (Eds.). *Handbook of Family Diversity*. New York: Oxford University Press.

Mason, Richard L. 1985. "Fourteen days to a richer marriage: A do-it-yourself marriage enrichment program." Pp. 176-181 in L. Cargan (Ed.), *Marriage and Family: Coping with Change*. Belmont, CA: Wadsworth.

Muehlenhard, Charlene L. and Hollabaugh, Lisa C. 1988. "Do women sometimes say no when they mean yes? The prevalence and correlates of women's token resistance to sex." *Journal of Personality and Social Psychology* 54(5): 872-879.

Myers-Walls, Judith A. 2000. "Family diversity and family life education." Pp. 359-379 in D.H. Demo, K.R. Allen, and M.A. Fine (Eds.). *Handbook of Family Diversity*. New York: Oxford University Press.

Nock, Stephen P. 1998. *Marriage in Men's Lives*. New York: Oxford University Press.

Prinz, C. 1995. *Cohabiting, Married, or Single*. Brookfield, VT: Avebury.

Rosenfeld, Isadore. 2000. "New treatments, renewed hope." *Parade Magazine* (July 23): 4-6.

Seltzer, Judith A. 1991. "Relationships between fathers and children who live apart: The father's role after separation." *Journal of Marriage and the Family* 53(1): 79-101.

Staples, Robert. 1977. "Public policy and the changing status of black families." Pp. 111-117 in P.J. Stein, J. Richmon, and N. Hannon (Eds.), *The Family: Functions, Conflicts and Symbols*. Reading, MA: Addison-Wesley.

Sweet, James A. and Larry L. Bumpass. 1992. "Young adult's views of marriage, cohabitation and family." Pp.143-170 in S. J. South and S. E. Tolnay (Eds.), *The Changing American Family: Sociological and Demographic Perspectives*. Boulder, CO: Westview.

Tolson, Jay. 2000. "No wedding? No ring? No problem." *U.S. News and World Report* (March 13): 48.

Treas, Judith. 1995. "U.S. aging: 'Golden oldies' remain vulnerable." *Population Today* 23(5): 1,2.

United Nations. 1995. *Demographic Yearbook, 1993*. New York: United Nations.

Waite, Linda J. 1995. "Does marriage matter?" *Demography* 32: 483-505.

Waite, Linda J. (Ed.). 2000. *The Ties That Bind: Perspectives on Marriage and Cohabitation*. Hawthorne, NY: Aldine de Gruyter.

Walsh, Froma. 1999. "Families in later life: Challenges and opportunities." Pp. 307-326 in B. Carter and M. McGoldrick (Eds.), *The Expanded Family Life Cycle: Individual, Family and Social Perspectives*, Third Edition. Boston: Allyn and Bacon.

Willie, Charles Vert. 1988. *A New Look at Black Families*, Third Edition. Dix Hills, NY: General Hall.

Whyte, Martin King. 1992. "Choosing mates—The American way." *Society* 29(3) 71-77.

Zimmerman, Shirley L. 1995. *Understanding Family Policy: Theories and Applications*, Second Edition. Thousand Oaks, CA: Sage.

Appendix

Cuber, John. 1975. "How new ideas about sex are changing our lives." Pp. 80-86 in *Intimate Lifestyles: Marriage and its Alternatives*, Second Edition. Pacific Palisades, CA: Goodyear.

Davis, James A. and Tom W. Smith. 1994. *General Social Surveys, 1972-1994: Cumulative Codebook*. Chicago: NORC.

Janus, Samuel S. and Cynthia L. Janus. 1993. *The Janus Report on Sexual Behavior*. NY: John Wiley and Sons.

Index

Page numbers followed by the letter "f" indicate figures; those followed by the letter "t" indicate tables.

Afterplay, 135, 136
Alternate lifestyles
   arise when, 3, 16, 53, 185, 267
   defined, 3
   difficulty studying, 10, 127, 177
   overcoming strains, 224
   role ambiguity in, 208
   and social change, 169
   and traditional family, 3, 281
   unplanned, 281

Baby boomers. *See* Cohorts
Birth control. *See also* Contraception
   abortion, 150
   changing technology, 3, 4, 85, 279
   unplanned pregnancy, 13, 92, 93,
      96, 104
   use of, 88, 97, 111

Census data. *See also* Household
      composition
   and secondary data analysis, 37
   U.S. Bureau of the Census, 26, 27,
      69, 70, 233
children. *See also* Family size
   and cohabiting couples, 267
   contemporary issues, 278-279
   custody and child support, 221-222
   desire for, 6, 74, 149, 215-216
   and divorce, 121, 122, 220,
      222-223, 224, 229
   in dysfunctional families, 32, 33,
      162, 164
   latchkey kids, 219, 220

children *(continued)*
   and marital relationship, 23, 67, 256,
      257, 258
   preparation for parenting, 216
   in various family types, 6, 68,
      194-196, 199, 228-229
   work and family, 216-220
Church
   in the Middle Ages, 12
   and sexual morality, 105, 149-151
Cohabitation
   by age and marital status, 69-70
   defined, 69
   duration of, 73, 266
   facts and figures, 267
   increase in, 70t, 71, 264, 266
   in later life, 240
   legal aspects, 77-83
   in other countries, 266
   reasons for, 73-74, 76, 91, 240
   significance of, 74-77, 83
   strains, 77
Cohorts (age or birth)
   baby boomers, 47-48, 73, 233, 279
   defined, 46
   effects, 49
Communication
   about sex, 94-98, 102-103, 114,
      141-142, 269
   before marriage, 242
   and conflict, 242-243, 248, 251,
      253-254
   in effective relationships, 254, 284
   gender differences, 128, 253
   regarding STDs, 111-114
Comparison level and comparison level
      for alternatives, 255
Conjugal and romantic love, 257-258

319

Contraception
  abstinence, 104, 105
  need for, 104, 110
  and religion, 105, 149
  reproductive roulette, 105
  steps in, 104
Counseling
  bibliotherapy, 285
  causal attributions, 249
  children, after divorce, 222-223
  cognitive distortion, 249, 250
  conjoint, 242
  in contemporary marriages, 5,
      143-144, 283, 284
  couples counseling, 242
  defense mechanisms, 247
  directional, 242
  and family of origin, 243
  and homosexuality, 178-180
  inhibited sexual desire, 163-164
  marital enrichment, 283, 284
  power struggles, 242-243
  reluctance to seek, 236, 244-245,
      259
  sensate focus, 260
  sex therapy, 259-262
  sexual addiction, 161-162
  sexually distressed couples, 133-135
  and stepfamily issues, 229-231
  theoretical perspectives, 246-251
  transference, 246
  unfinished emotional business, 243
Cross-cultural
  arranged marriages, 52, 53
  cohabitation research, 266
  comparative research method, 38
  family studies, 272
  findings about sexuality, 11-12, 273
  research on sex roles, 201, 202
  study of homosexuality, 38-39,
      173-174, 181

Date rape, 98-103, 114, 269
Dating, 52-60, 62-67, 283
Definition of the situation, 115
Demography, 26-27
Deviance
  defined, 10, 147, 155

Deviance *(continued)*
  normal and abnormal, 155-156,
      170-171
  and social sanctions, 97, 129, 147
Diversity
  coping with, 281-282
  intersecting categories, 272
  of lifestyles, 197-198, 272-273,
      277-278
  in a pluralistic society, 166
  race, ethnicity, and social class, 272,
      277
  sexual, 166, 170-171
  and social policy, 276-277
  within groups, 272
Divorce
  acceptance of, 6, 49
  alimony, 221
  career assets, 221
  effects on children, 121, 122,
      220-231
  effects on men and women, 119,
      205, 221
  and infidelity, 122, 124
  insupportability as grounds, 120
  mediation, 283
  reasons for, 122-124, 125
  as a safety valve, 119-120
  six stations of, 120-121
Divorce rate
  after first marriage, 48, 228
  increase in, 3, 16, 48
  as related to marriage, 2, 142, 242
  and societal values, 2
  stabilization of, 264-265
  as a structural issue, 1, 119-120,
      264, 270
Double standard, 2, 3, 12, 63, 89-90,
      269
Dual-career couples, 207-210, 211-212

Egalitarian. *See* Marital interaction
Empowerment, 102, 112
Ethics, 150, 151, 166, 171
Ethnocentrism, 22, 272
Expectations
  of aging, 279-280
  changing gender roles, 204-205
  in dating, 66, 102

Expectations *(continued)*
    of marriage, 6, 48, 124, 140, 143,
        149, 249
    of parenthood, 215-216
    relationship myths, 251
    of sex by gender, 97, 135-136, 139,
        143
    of sexual fulfillment, 14, 17, 91,
        134-135, 142-144, 149, 163
    shaped by social roles, 199, 208
    in stepfamilies, 227
    in traditional marriage, 2, 215, 211
    work and family, 207
Explained and unexplained variance,
        124, 125, 134
Extramarital sex
    attitudes toward, 87t, 122, 123t, 126,
        127, 150
    impact on marriages, 143
    and marital strain, 124, 127
    participation in, 125-127
    women and men compared, 126

Facts and values, 20-22, 146, 198,
        270-271
Family life cycle, 241
Family life education, 263, 282
Family of affinity, 239
Familism, 8, 258
Family of origin, 243, 246
Family size, 2, 4, 6, 215-216
Female orgasm, 136-139, 143
Foreplay, 11, 135-136, 137-138, 166
Frequency of intercourse, 11, 124,
        133-135, 136, 139-141,
        143, 144, 234, 257
Friendship, 51, 57, 62, 65, 121, 128,
        240, 282

Gender and gender roles
    androgynous, 203-204
    and cohabitation, 73
    and content analysis, 37
    cross-culturally, 201, 202
    in dating, 56, 57, 62-63
    defined, 37, 56, 199-200

Gender and gender roles *(continued)*
    effects on individuals, 200-203,
        212-213
    gender identity, 203-204, 246
    and housework, 207-208
    and marriage, 199, 200, 210
    masculinity and femininity,
        201-203, 204
    Mead, Margaret, 201
    parenting, 278
    patriarchy, 200, 212, 215, 264
    same-sex couples, 192
    and self-concept, 213
    sex role and trait stereotyping,
        201-203
    sex role differentiation, 201
    in sexual encounters, 89, 90t, 91,
        96-98, 99, 102-103, 113, 238
General Social Survey (GSS)
    description of, 30
    findings, 48, 86, 87t, 88, 122, 180
    sample items, 287
Generalizability of findings, 25-29, 32,
        36, 271
Good girl-bad girl dichotomy, 3, 164
Growing older, 233-241, 279, 280

Homosexuality
    attitudes toward, 87t, 175, 180t,
        180-182, 197
    bisexuality, 175, 177, 184
    causes, 174-177
    coming out, 174, 186-191, 192, 193
    cross-culturally, 38-39, 173-174
    defined, 173
    exclusivity, 193
    gay or lesbian parents, 194-196
    gender differences, 192-193
    heterosexism, 173
    Humphreys' research, 36-37
    laws, 181
    and mental health perspectives,
        178-180
    participation in, 177, 182-184
    same-sex couples, 191-194,
        197-198, 268
Household composition
    married couple households, 7f, 48
    percent single vs. married, 46, 46t

Household composition *(continued)*
    traditional families, 16
    variety in, 4, 7, 7f

Individualism
    and cohabitation, 76
    in dating and mate selection, 52, 61,
        94
    and divorce rate, 264
    expressive and instrumental, 8, 16
    and help-seeking, 246
    and open marriage, 127
    right to pursue happiness, 24, 281
    and sexual expression, 171
Infidelity. *See* Extramarital sex
Inhibited sexual desire, 155, 163-164

The Janus Report
    description, 31
    extramarital sex, 123, 123t, 124,
        125, 126t
    frequency, 139, 140t
    homosexuality, 183-184
    sample items, 291
    sex and singles, 92, 93t,
Jealousy, 66, 69, 103, 129, 130, 193,
        230, 245, 252

Kinsey et al., 8-9, 16, 40-42, 125,
        175-176, 177, 180, 182

Later life
    dating in, 56, 57
    marriage chances, 48, 49
    sex in, 233-238
Laws
    asset allocation, 221
    and cohabitation, 77-83
    coverture, 200
    custody and child support, 221-222,
        224
    felonies and misdemeanors, 151
    grounds for divorce, 120
    and homosexuality, 181

Laws *(continued)*
    prohibiting sex acts, 12, 152
    scientific, 22
    and sexual morality, 147, 148, 150,
        151-154, 169-170, 273-274
Lifestyles. *See also* Alternate lifestyles
    defined, 1
    diversity, 272-273, 277-278
    single vs. married, 45-52
Loneliness, 38, 45, 50-51, 74, 129, 239,
        240, 255, 267
Longevity, 17, 233, 241, 279, 280, 282
Looking glass self, 197

Marital conflicts
    cognitive distortion, 251
    communication, 253, 254
    conflict defined, 253
    effective conflict resolution,
        253-254, 256, 257, 283
    gender issues, 204
    relationship myths, 251-252
    stepfamilies, 229
    unconscious motivation, 246-247,
        252
    unrewarding exchanges, 247
Marital enrichment programs, 283-284
Marital interaction
    decision-making, 204, 253
    division of labor, 204, 206, 207,
        215, 256
    dominant-subordinate power
        relations, 5, 203, 204, 210,
        242-243, 271
    egalitarian/equal partnership, 5,
        210-215
    and gender identity, 203-205
    perceived fairness in, 214, 215
    the politics of housework, 206-207,
        213
    segregated spheres of influence, 5,
        204, 212, 219-220
    as social exchange, 247-248, 255
    traditional, 5, 203
Marital satisfaction
    and children, 23, 256, 258
    contributing factors, 243-244,
        253-254, 255-259
    in dual-career couples, 208-209, 214

Marital satisfaction *(continued)*
    long-term, 258, 282, 285
    and marital stability, 255
    maximum joint profit, 255
    measurement of, 24-25, 118
    and relationship quality, 117, 118f
    and role congruence, 205, 215
    and sex, 133-141, 143-144, 164,
        257, 262
    in stepfamilies, 229, 230
Marital stability
    and companionate marriage, 5
    and role congruence, 205
    second marriages, 49
    sex contributing to, 136
    versus marital happiness, 255
Marriage
    age at first marriage, 3, 4, 16, 46-47
    arranged, in India, 52-53
    benefits, 117, 140, 266
    career assets, 221
    changes in the U.S. since the 1950s,
        2, 4, 5, 143
    changing picture of, 4, 5, 120, 282
    and children, 6, 121, 199, 256, 257,
        258
    and cohabitation, 76, 77-79, 83,
        266
    cohesion vs. coercion, 5, 285
    common law, 78
    coverture, 200
    and dating, 66
    defined, by Westermarck, 4
    and divorce, 1, 2, 120, 142
    and frequency of intercourse,
        139-140, 143
    goal of, 4, 5, 14
    good marriages, 5, 255-259, 284
    marital status, 48
    open marriage, 127-133, 143
    pressures to marry, 4, 240
    role sharing, 209, 214
    sex in, 123, 124, 133-144, 237
    and women's identities, 2, 200, 206
Marriageability, 243-244
Masters and Johnson
    on communication, 141-142
    on homosexuality, 176, 178
    laboratory observation, 42-43
    sex therapy, 44, 260-261

Mate selection
    and dating opportunities, 63, 65
    and divorce, 55, 242
    theories of, 60-62
Mate swapping. *See* Swinging
Methods of data collection. *See*
        Research methods
Monogamous nuclear family, 2

Normative integration, 147-148, 151,
        153, 171
Norms. *See also* Sexual morality
    anomie, 15, 208
    and child support, 222
    defined, 10
    of reciprocity, 255
    regarding sexual conduct, 12, 111,
        145-148, 281
    and sexual socialization, 9, 164
    subjective norms, 245

Objectives
    of clinical practice, 262
    of dating, 52, 54-55, 58, 65-66
    of family policy, 274
    of marriage, 4, 5, 6
    of open marriage, 128, 129, 130
    of social science, 1, 19, 21, 22-23,
        24, 146, 178, 198
    of text, 1, 263, 285
    and value judgments, 273
Occupational cohesion, 219
Open marriage, 124, 127-133

Paraphilias, 156-160, 170-171
Parental influence
    and authority, 2
    on coming out, 186-191
    effects of divorce, 222, 278-279
    and gender roles, 278
    in mate selection, 53, 58, 62
    noncustodial parenting, 278
    on sexual aggression, 100, 101, 102
    in stepfamilies, 228-229
    and teenage sex, 23, 67
    work and family, 199, 219

Paths
  in relationships, 68, 185, 277-278,
    281
  sexual, 175, 198, 278, 281
Pluralism, 166, 282
Pluralistic ignorance, 168, 273
Premarital sex
  attitudes and behaviors, 85-90, 268
  and dating, 56
  teenage participation, 23, 67, 91-94
  as studied scientifically, 21
  women and men compared, 85,
    88-89
Preventive intervention, 222, 283, 285
Primate behavior
  Harlow's experiment, 10
  homosexuality, 174
Probabilistic prediction, 22, 23, 24
Pushes and pulls
  defined, 49
  single parents, 224
  single versus married, 50-52, 62

Relationships
  myths about, 251-253
  open and closed, 128f, 129
  and psychological distress, 118
  quality of, 117, 118f, 119, 122, 283
  same sex couples, 191-194, 197-198
  sexual adjustment, 144, 262
  starting new, 52, 62-65, 192
  successful, 244, 253, 255-259, 283
Religion. *See* Church
Remarriage. *See also* Stepfamilies
  divorce rate, 48
  in later life, 238-239
  likelihood, 6, 48, 49, 120
  remarried family, defined, 227
  and prior cohabitation, 70
  single parents, 224
Research
  defined, 19
  empirical, 19, 21, 40
  evaluating social policies, 276
  journals, 20, 262
  longitudinal and cross-sectional,
    234, 235
  marginals, 139

Research *(continued)*
  multiple causes, 23, 124, 139, 266,
    270
  open-ended and closed questions,
    57, 291
  refusals, 29, 41
  reliability, 42
  sample survey items, 287-295
  sampling and representativeness,
    27-29, 39, 40-41
  social desirability effect, 30, 89
  vignettes, 288
Research methods
  clinical studies, 31-33
  comparative studies, 38-39
  content analysis, 37
  experiments, 10, 34-35
  National Opinion Research Center,
    30, 86, 180, 287
  naturalistic (direct) observation,
    35-37
  nonclinical case studies, 33-34
  secondary data analysis, 37
  surveys, 29-31, 85-86, 90, 168, 234
Rules and exceptions, 22-24

Second shift, 206, 220
Self-fulfilling prophesy, 233-234
Sex education, 20, 21, 96, 112, 164,
    225, 226, 269-270
Sex ratio, 56, 272
Sexism, 203
Sexual addiction, 161-162
Sexual attitudes and behaviors
  age at first intercourse, 92, 93t, 268
  among older persons, 234-238
  attitudes vs. actual practice, 9, 12,
    16, 85, 125, 126-127, 147-148
  extramarital sex, 122-137
  The Janus Report 31, 92-93,
    123-126, 139-140, 183-184
  liberalization in behaviors and
    attitudes, 3, 4, 16, 85, 163
  masturbation, 165-166
  number of partners, 90t, 92, 93t,
    154, 162
  premarital sex, 85-90
  and religion, 149-150

Sexual attitudes and behaviors
(continued)
  restrictive vs. permissive, 12, 88, 89,
    125, 145, 164, 169
  sexually open marriages, 127-133
  women and men compared, 85,
    88-89, 134, 135-136, 143,
    160, 164, 192-193, 234-238
Sexual hang-ups
  defined, 146
  and deviance, 147, 154, 169, 170,
    171
  inhibited sexual desire, 155,
    163-164
  normal and abnormal, 155-156, 167,
    170-171
  the paraphilias, 156-160, 170-171
  sexual addiction, 160-163
Sexual morality
  abortion, 150
  changing standards of, 12, 13, 16,
    149, 169-171
  defined, 145
  ethics, 150, 151, 166, 171
  good sex, 13-14, 94, 102, 114, 136,
    162-163, 257, 269
  and law, 147, 148, 151-154, 164,
    167, 169-170
  and mental health professions,
    154-156, 169, 170-171
  and religion, 149-151, 169
  and social policy, 273-274
  value conflicts, 171
Sexual practices, terminology
  addictive sex, 162
  adultery, 150
  autoerotic asphyxiation, 158, 161
  bestiality, 153, 158
  bondage, 167, 168
  censorship, 171
  cunnilingus, 166
  domination, 167
  erotica, 167
  exhibitionism, 156
  felatio, 166
  fetishism, 154, 156
  frottage, 160
  gymnophobia, 150
  incest, 151
  kinky, 167

Sexual practices, terminology
(continued)
  klismaphilia, 159
  masturbation, 165, 235
  necrophilia, 153
  nymphomania, 166-167
  obscenity, 153, 157, 167
  oral-genital sex, 166
  paraphilia, 156-160
  pedophilia, 157
  pornography, 167
  procreative, 149
  sadism-masochism, 157-159, 167
  satyriasis, 166
  transvestism, 158
  voyeurism, 158
  zoophilia, 158
Sexuality. *See also* Homosexuality
  and aging, 233-239, 279
  biology and culture, 9-10, 16, 174, 176
  cross-cultural conduct, worldwide,
    10, 11-12
  Freud, Sigmund, 8, 178
  importance of, 9, 14, 171, 236
  oral-genital contact, 12, 166
  penile intromission, 137, 138-139
  philosophical approaches, 166
  sex guilt, 105, 144, 146, 149, 156,
    160, 165, 269
  sex therapy, 259-262
  sexual dysfunctions, 260-261
  sexual positions, 11, 166, 236, 238
  sexual scripts, 94, 112, 145, 175,
    234, 238
  societal ambivalence, 95-96, 147,
    153, 171, 237, 270
  what is "natural," 10, 16, 146, 171,
    177, 181
Sexually transmitted diseases, 13, 91,
    105-114, 268-269
Single parents
  after divorce, 221, 224
  benefits, 225t
  dating, 69, 224
  increase in, 3, 6, 16, 223
  role and task overload, 224
  and sex, 91
  and social policies, 225, 226, 273
  successful family functioning, 226
  types of, 224

Singles. *See also* Dating
    being single, 45-52
    contributing factors, 49
    and dating, 66
    in later life, 240
    as percent of households, 45, 46t
    pros and cons, 49-52
    and sex, 85-115
Social attachment, 117-118, 122, 241,
        282, 283
Social change. *See also* Trends
    and birth cohorts, 46
    in developmental theories, 67-68,
        266
    effects of, 6, 15, 90-94
    in gender roles, 204-205, 215
    and the individual, 114-115, 169
    sexual morality, 12, 163, 165, 169
    and social movements, 48, 85, 115,
        174, 178, 200
    U.S. in the 60s, 70s and 80s, 3-4, 12,
        16, 45, 85-86, 178
    and working wives, 205-207, 278
Social comparison, 15, 91, 100, 127,
        168, 197
Social facts, 97, 200, 270
Social policy
    defined, 274
    and diversity, 276-277
    and the elderly, 240, 280
    examples of, 274-275
    family policy objectives, 274
    participatory evaluation, 276
    research and program evaluation,
        276
    and sexual morality, 273-274
    and single parents, 225, 226, 273
    unintended effects, 274, 276
Social roles. *See also* Gender roles
    defined, 199
    in later life, 241
    as learned in dating, 54
    role ambiguity, 67, 208, 216, 227
    role and task overload, 224
    role congruence, 61, 204-205
    role reversal, 201, 204
    role sharing, 209, 214
    sex roles, 199-203, 212
    stepfamily roles, 227

Social roles *(continued)*
    traditional husband-wife, 2, 53, 199,
        211, 219
Social sanctions, 147-148, 151, 154,
        167, 204
Social scripting
    and aging, 233-234
    defined, 94
    and homosexuality, 175, 177, 195
    masculinity, 203
    men and women sexually, 97, 112,
        269
    reframing, 116
    and social change, 114, 198, 215
Social structure
    and divorce, 119-120, 264, 270
    and family, 2, 17, 67, 120, 143, 200,
        272
    functions and dysfunctions, 54, 55
    and gender, 200-201
    and the individual, 169, 178, 200,
        234, 273
    and power relations, 200
    promoting or inhibiting lifestyles,
        45, 185, 194, 212, 215, 217
    as recurring patterns, 2, 22, 54, 199
    social systems, 53, 55, 56, 67, 120
Socialization
    by dating, 54
    in family of origin, 243, 246
    and gender, 204
    how paraphilias arise, 158-159
    and men's identities, 216-217
    for parenting, 216
    and relationship myths, 252
    sexual, 9, 95-97, 105, 113, 152, 164,
        165, 177
    and social change, 114
    and social facts, 200
    and worldview, 22
Sociological imagination, 1, 16, 102,
        142, 200, 282
Sociology
    defined, 1
    goals, 1, 2, 16, 26, 39, 146, 168,
        270-272
    individual and society, 16-17, 114,
        142, 145, 169, 199-203,
        212-213, 276

Sociology *(continued)*
perspective on sexuality, 9, 10, 147, 168, 171-172, 176, 198
and social research, 19, 22, 23, 198, 270, 276
Socratic method, 22
Stages
of dating, 58-59
of development, 67-69
Statistics
how to interpret, 70-72, 134, 138, 264, 271
importance of, 6-7
median defined, 46
Stepfamilies
advice for, 230, 231
complexity of, 227, 230
counseling issues, 229-231
divorce rate, 228, 230
increase in, 3, 6, 16, 226, 228
research studies, 228-229
role ambiguity, 227, 228
Swinging, 36, 130-133

Technology. *See also* Birth control
computer-assisted communication, 65, 127, 279
reproductive, 194, 279
sexual interventions, 261, 279
Theories
Behavioral, 247-248
Cognitive, 249-251
Developmental, 67-69
of the life course, 198, 241, 279, 282
of mate selection, 60-62
Psychodynamic, 246-247
Social Exchange, 62, 247-248, 255, 267
and social policy, 276
sociological, defined, 60
Structure-Functional analysis of dating, 53-56
Traditional family
and alternate lifestyles, 3, 16, 281
critique, 3
idealized structure, roles and values, 2, 6, 206, 211, 219, 277
marriage in, 199, 200, 203, 204
and moral majority, 149

Traditional family *(continued)*
as percent of households, 16
in television sitcoms, 3
Transsexual 33
Trends
aging, 233, 279, 280
changing picture of marriage, 4, 5, 120
cohabitation 73-74, 240
concerning singles, 46, 49, 85, 240
diversity, 197, 273
in household composition, 6
influencing parenting, 216
interrelated, 264
lifestyle diversity, 277
participation in premarital sex, 4, 16, 85, 86f
as tracked by surveys 30, 85
work and family, 219-220
working wives, 205-206

Validity of measurement, 24-25, 242, 271
Values
and child rearing, 217-218
conflict in, 1, 15, 171, 185, 204-205
defined, 8, 21
ethics, 151
individualism and familism, 8, 16
respect for diversity, 273
and sex role stereotyping, 202-213
traditional, sex before marriage, 2
unintended consequences, 225
versus facts, 20-22, 198, 270-271
Virginity, 3, 56, 105

Widows and widowers, 46, 69, 234, 238-240
Women in the paid labor force
in dual-career marriages, 207-210, 214
extent of, 205, 216
and family finances, 205-206, 217
historically, 212, 214, 219-220
increase in, 3, 16, 17
results of, 6, 45, 206, 210, 215, 216, 264, 278
the second shift, 206
Work and family, 210, 212, 213, 214, 215, 216-220, 240

Order Your Own Copy of
This Important Book for Your Personal Library!

MARITAL AND SEXUAL LIFESTYLES IN THE UNITED STATES
Attitudes, Behaviors, and Relationships

_____in hardbound at $59.95 (ISBN: 0-7890-1070-4)

_____in softbound at $34.95 (ISBN: 0-7890-1071-2)

COST OF BOOKS_____

OUTSIDE USA/CANADA/
MEXICO: ADD 20%____

POSTAGE & HANDLING_____
(US: $4.00 for first book & $1.50
for each additional book)
Outside US: $5.00 for first book
& $2.00 for each additional book)

SUBTOTAL_____

in Canada: add 7% GST____

STATE TAX____
(NY, OH & MIN residents, please
add appropriate local sales tax)

FINAL TOTAL____
(If paying in Canadian funds,
convert using the current
exchange rate, UNESCO
coupons welcome.)

❑ **BILL ME LATER:** ($5 service charge will be added)
(Bill-me option is good on US/Canada/Mexico orders only;
not good to jobbers, wholesalers, or subscription agencies.)

❑ Check here if billing address is different from
shipping address and attach purchase order and
billing address information.

Signature_____

❑ **PAYMENT ENCLOSED: $_____**

❑ **PLEASE CHARGE TO MY CREDIT CARD.**

❑ Visa ❑ MasterCard ❑ AmEx ❑ Discover
❑ Diner's Club ❑ Eurocard ❑ JCB

Account # _____

Exp. Date_____

Signature_____

Prices in US dollars and subject to change without notice.

NAME_____

INSTITUTION_____

ADDRESS_____

CITY_____

STATE/ZIP_____

COUNTRY_____ COUNTY (NY residents only)_____

TEL_____ FAX_____

E-MAIL_____

May we use your e-mail address for confirmations and other types of information? ❑ Yes ❑ No
We appreciate receiving your e-mail address and fax number. Haworth would like to e-mail or fax special
discount offers to you, as a preferred customer. **We will never share, rent, or exchange your e-mail address
or fax number.** We regard such actions as an invasion of your privacy.

Order From Your Local Bookstore or Directly From
The Haworth Press, Inc.
10 Alice Street, Binghamton, New York 13904-1580 • USA
TELEPHONE: 1-800-HAWORTH (1-800-429-6784) / Outside US/Canada: (607) 722-5857
FAX: 1-800-895-0582 / Outside US/Canada: (607) 722-6362
E-mail: getinfo@haworthpressinc.com
PLEASE PHOTOCOPY THIS FORM FOR YOUR PERSONAL USE.
www.HaworthPress.com

BOF00